FRANCIS GALTON

The Life and Work
of a Victorian Genius

FRANCIS GALTON

The Life and Work
of a Victorian Genius

D. W. FORREST

TAPLINGER PUBLISHING CO., INC.
NEW YORK

78-680

FIRST PUBLISHED IN THE UNITED STATES IN 1974 BY
TAPLINGER PUBLISHING CO., INC.
NEW YORK, NEW YORK

© PAUL ELEK (SCIENTIFIC BOOKS) LTD., 1974
ALL RIGHTS RESERVED
PRINTED IN GREAT BRITAIN

Library of Congress Catalog Card Number: 74-5819

ISBN 0-8008-2682-5

Contents

List of Plates

TO
MY MOTHER AND FATHER

Preface

The name, Francis Galton, will be familiar to many, but few are likely to appreciate the breadth of his interests. He first attracted the notice of Victorian scientific circles with an account of his exploration of South West Africa, and it was as geographer and meteorologist that his first enquiries bore fruit. It was not until his forties that his interest turned to heredity, which became the dominant theme underlying most of his subsequent research. The ramifications from that theme were many and led him to undertake psychological investigations of great originality, to establish an anthropometric laboratory from which data were collected which enabled him to devise new statistical methods and to publish a definitive work on fingerprints. Towards the end of his life his main efforts were directed towards furthering the progress of eugenics, in which he believed with a religious fervour.

In many ways Galton was ahead of his time and some of his ideas have still not been assimilated today. Few of his books are available in modern reprints and his numerous papers are lost in nineteenth-century periodicals. Among the possible factors contributing to the comparative neglect of this polymath, one is outstandingly obvious. Since his friend and pupil, Karl Pearson, wrote his biography in the early years of this century, no more recent writer has attempted the task. The deterrent effect of Pearson's mammoth 2000 page biography is considerable. It was written as a monument to the man whom Pearson admired above all others, but its sheer bulk resulted in the burial of the man beneath the monument. When Galton as a person emerges from those pages it is as a paragon, a scientific father-figure without blemish. The difficulty in achieving a more balanced assessment of Galton's personality lies in the scarcity of the relevant material; Galton was always extremely reticent about his personal affairs. For example, even what appears to be a minor quarrel between his two brothers, the details of which he kept long after their deaths, is recorded in an indecipherable code. However, an objective account of what material there is seemed to be a practical proposition : hence the present biography.

Without Pearson's compilation it would have required many more years to complete this book. I must therefore express my great debt to his work before thanking those who have aided me in other ways. Miss Edmiston of the Eugenics Laboratory, University of London, provided me with useful information about Galton's publications, and Dr J. C. Kenna kindly allowed me to use his bibliography of Galton's work as the main source for the bibliography published here. Mrs Perceval and her assistants in the Library of University College, London, were of great assistance, as was Miss Walters, Librarian of the Eugenics Society. I am indebted to Mrs Middleton, the authority on Victorian geography, for a valuable discussion about the Galton-Butler connection. Mrs Kelly, Archivist of the Royal Geographical Society, helped me through the correspondence and Minute Books of the Society. Among colleagues at Trinity College, Dublin, I have received valuable help from Professor Davies, Professor Furlong, Dr Fuller, Dr Scaife, Dr Smith and Mr Stevens. Mrs Carol Ervine was responsible for much of the library search and she and Miss Caroline Stewart helped to compile the list of Galton's writings. Mr Holohan and Mr Bolger drew the maps and diagrams, while Mrs Beatrix Pope did more than type the manuscript, her comments and questions led to much clarification. Miss Maureen Cardiff helped in the final stages of manuscript preparation and devised the index. Finally, my wife was of inestimable help and support during the four years that I have been engaged on this task.

Acknowledgements

I wish to express my gratitude to the following individuals and organisations for permission to reproduce material:

Professor Egon Pearson on behalf of the *Biometrika* trustees for extracts from Karl Pearson's *Life, Letters and Labours of Francis Galton* (C.U.P., 1914–30).

The Director of the Royal Geographical Society for material from the archives of the Society.

Methuen and Co. Ltd. for the quotations from Galton's autobiography, *Memories of My Life* (1908).

J. M. Dent and Sons Ltd. for extracts from Galton's *Inquiries into Human Faculty; its Origins and Development* (Everyman, 1951).

David and Charles Ltd. for extracts from *Francis Galton's Art of Travel* (1971).

Frank Cass and Co. Ltd. for extracts from Galton's *English Men of Science: their Nature and Nurture* (1970).

Da Capo Press for extracts from Galton's *Finger Prints* (1965).

William Collins and Sons Ltd. for Tables 7.1 and 7.2 and other extracts taken from Galton's *Hereditary Genius* (Fontana, 1962).

Hurst and Blackett Ltd for Plate IV from C. J. Andersson's *The Okavango River* (1889).

I

The Early Years

Francis Galton was a Victorian. His life spanned the whole of Victoria's reign : a schoolboy of 15 when she came to the throne, he was to outlive her by 10 years. That he was also a genius should become apparent during the course of this book.

A prolific writer with over 300 publications to his credit, Galton achieved most renown with his *Hereditary Genius* in which he argued that talent was inherited. Such a viewpoint was almost inescapable for a man with his predecessors and we in turn cannot avoid some examination of their lives. Through them the genetic stage was set for a performance of exceptional virtuosity.

His mother was a Darwin : the eldest daughter of Erasmus Darwin by his second marriage, she was reared in an unusual house. Erasmus Darwin (1731–1802) combined the busy life of a popular and highly-skilled general practitioner with a penchant for speculative science and mechanical invention.[1] After his first marriage to a young Lichfield girl, Mary Howard, Darwin worked hard to establish a medical reputation second to none in England. Patients came to him from all over the country and although King George III wanted him as a personal physician Darwin refused to live in London. His wife was a sickly woman, weakened further 'by the frequency of her maternal situation' and suffering from spasmodic abdominal pains which according to her husband were of hysterical origin.[2] Her habit of drinking spirits to assuage her pain may have exacerbated a liver disease from which she died at the age of 31.

Erasmus did not marry again for eleven years, but during that period he fathered two illegitimate daughters whom he brought up with his own three surviving children. Then, in his late forties, he fell in love with Elizabeth Pole (née Collier), a woman of wit and beauty, who was the illegitimate daughter of 'Beau' Colyear, the second Earl of Portmore. Erasmus wooed her in passionate verse but their relationship otherwise remained on a formal basis until the death of her husband who was 30 years her senior. Within six months of his death they were married. To the five children Erasmus already had, his marriage to Elizabeth was to add another seven. They needed and bought a large house in Derby with a garden sloping down to the river beyond which was an orchard reached by a mechanical ferry, one of Erasmus' most successful inventions. (Others included a canal lift, a speaking machine, a completely automated lavatory, windmills and steam engines.)

It was at this house in Derby that Erasmus wrote his major scientific works. Much of his scientific writing was clothed in poetic language, notably *The Loves of the Plants* (1789) in which a description of the reproductive processes in plants was elaborated in 2000 lines of verse. The book was immensely popular until Canning, then Foreign Under Secretary in Pitt's government, parodied the poem in *The Loves of the Triangles* and effectively killed Darwin's poetical reputation.

Darwin's more solid scientific contributions were contained in the two volumes of *Zoonomia* (1796) in which he propounded his Theory of Generation. This early attempt at an evolutionary theory, although popular enough to go to three editions in seven years, had too little factual support to command general acceptance by the scientific community of the time. Darwin's speculations certainly influenced later theorists, such as Lamarck, and there are striking parallels between *Zoonomia* and *The Origin of Species* (1859). Yet Charles Darwin refused to acknowledge any intellectual debt to his grandfather although he had been much impressed by *Zoonomia* when he read it in his youth. But Charles' virtue, sadly lacking in Erasmus, was a passion for facts and it was the overwhelming mass of evidence which finally compelled acceptance of evolutionary theory. Nevertheless, it can be argued that the evolutionary honours have been unevenly distributed and that Erasmus deserves more credit for his influential speculations than he at present receives.

Longevity was not a characteristic of the Darwin family, Erasmus himself died at 69, and it appears to have been the Collier genes that were responsible for the long lives of the descendants of the union of Erasmus and Elizabeth. Elizabeth lived until she was 85, while her daughter, Violetta, Galton's mother, lived to 91. Most of Violetta's own children lived to their nineties or near nineties and Francis Galton's retention of considerable intellectual and physical powers until the age of 89 was not exceptional in the family context.

Francis Galton describes his mother as 'a joyous and unconventional girl'[3] (See Plate I). Possessing little of the Quaker temperament herself she married into that sect and her children by Samuel Tertius Galton possessed a fascinating amalgam of sobriety and high spirits. Samuel Tertius (See Plate II) was the second son of Samuel Galton (1753–1832) who had acquired a large fortune mainly from gun manufacture, an unusual enterprise for a man with Quaker principles. He was indeed formally disowned by the Quakers but refused to abandon his business and continued to attend Quaker meetings. In 1804 he began the Galton bank in Birmingham in which he was partnered by Samuel Tertius.

Samuel Galton's spare time was devoted to a scientific self-education. His regular purchases of scientific apparatus include a microscope, a reflecting telescope, a camera obscura and a variety of small optical equipment. He published little on the research he carried out with this apparatus but his early work on colour vision is worthy of note. An account appeared in the *Monthly Magazine* for 1799 antedating Thomas Young's trichromatic theory by several years. On the strength of his scientific interests he was elected a Fellow of the Royal Society, numbering among his proposers his friends Joseph Priestly and Josiah Wedgewood.

Other scientific contacts were made through the locally famous Lunar Society, so named from its rule that club dinners should be held at the time of the full moon.[4] Galton must have known James Watt, John Baskerville (the printer, who although an atheist achieved renown through his beautiful bibles), James Keir (the founder of the modern chemical industry), William Murdock (the inventor of gas-lighting), and Withering (the botanist), all of whom were members. Erasmus Darwin was a founder member of the Society and was retained by Galton as the family physician.*

Samuel Galton's marriage to Lucy Barclay in 1777 produced ten children; the eldest boy died in infancy leaving Samuel Tertius Galton to continue the business. Samuel Tertius (1783–1844) did not possess his father's drive although he retained his scientific interests. As a person he was, according to his son,

> 'one of the most honourable and kindly of men and eminently statistical by nature. He wrote a small book on currency, with tables, which testifies to his taste. He had a scientific bent, having about his house the simple gear appropriate to those days, of solar microscope, orrery, telescopes, mountain barometers without which he never travelled, and so forth. A sliding rule adapted to various uses was his constant companion. He was devoted to Shakespeare and revelled in *Hudibras*; he read *Tom Jones* through every year, and was gifted with an abundance of humour. Nevertheless he became a careful man of business, on whose shoulders the work of the Bank chiefly rested in troublous times. Its duties had cramped much of the joy and aspirations of his early youth and manhood, and narrowed the opportunity he always eagerly desired, of abundant leisure for systematic study. As one result of this drawback to his own development,

---

* Darwin's fees were by no means modest: there survive records of bills for 40 and 100 gns, the latter for attendance on the eldest child who had a fever.

he was earnestly desirous of giving me every opportunity of being educated that seemed feasible and right.'[5]

His eldest daughter has this to say about him.

'When we children quarrelled and went to my Father or Mother to complain, he used to send one into one corner of the room, and the other into the opposite corner, and at a word of command, each had to rush into the other's arms. This made us laugh and ended the dispute. My father was a *true peace-maker*, he always turned the matter off playfully.'[6]

His peace-making qualities were certainly widely appreciated: he served as High Bailiff of Birmingham and, after his retirement, as magistrate and deputy lieutenant in Leamington.

His marriage to Violetta Darwin took place in 1807 when they were both aged 24. Children followed in quick sucession at a rate of about one a year until 1816, after which there was a gap of six years until the birth of their last child, Francis. Of their nine children, seven survived past infancy, four girls and three boys. After the death of their child in 1817 Violetta persuaded her husband to accept baptism into the Church of England. This was the final break with the Quaker sect and the children in turn were never to return to that faith.

Violetta's sketch and plan of the family house to which they moved shortly before Francis was born show it to be a three-storey Georgian building with two large wings. It stood in spacious gardens and took its name, The Larches, from two large specimens of that tree which grew on either side of the house and which were reputed to have been among the first ever brought to England. The Larches was situated in the Sparkbrook district of Birmingham about a mile from the Galton bank and at the time of Francis' birth surrounded by fields.

Another house with which Francis and the other children were familiar was that of their grandfather, Samuel Galton. Duddeston appears from a sketch by Francis' sister, Emma, to have been even grander than The Larches. The freehold was bought in 1820 for £8000 by Francis' father; he never lived there but remained at The Larches until he retired from the bank and left Birmingham for Leamington in 1831. He did however have a summer residence, Claverdon, an estate about 6 miles from Warwick, which he purchased in 1824 and which became the family centre.

The eldest children in the family were Francis' four sisters, Elizabeth, Lucy, Adèle and Emma. Elizabeth, the eldest and prettiest of them, was an especial favourite of her father: she accompanied him on walks and practised archery with him. Lucy, the next in age, suffered from rheumatic fever and does not figure much in her father's diary, except as his opponent in chess which she invariably won.[7] Adèle too was not able to enjoy a normal life but was confined to a couch with what was loosely diagnosed as 'spinal weakness'. That there may have been a strong hysterical component to the complaint is evident from her general personality characteristics. Emma was the plain one and her father took her on his rougher walking expeditions.

Darwin, the eldest son, was eight years older than Francis and by no means his father's favourite. He had no interest in science or literature but enjoyed country pursuits and was a popular boy among his contemporaries. Erasmus, one year younger, was a quieter boy who was little at home. He joined the Navy at the age of 12 and later saw service in the militia. Neither brother played much part in Francis' development, although Darwin used him as a fag and taught him a few smart tricks. On the other hand, three of his sisters were to play an important role in his life.

As the baby of the family, Francis was much indulged. His sister, Elizabeth, recalls his earliest years :

'On the 16th February [1822] my youngest brother Francis was born, he was 6 years younger than the youngest of us and never was a baby more welcomed. He was the pet of us all, and my mother was obliged to hang up her watch, that each sister might nurse the child for a quarter of an hour and then give him to the next. He was a great amusement to Adèle and as soon as he could sit up, at five or six months old, he always preferred sitting on her couch to be amused by her.'[8]

From a childhood memory, Galton himself draws an interesting comparison of Elizabeth and Adèle :

'It is curious how unchangeable characters are : my eldest sister was just, my youngest was merciful. When my bread was buttered for me as a child, the former picked out the butter that filled the big holes, the latter did not. Consequently, I respected the former and loved the latter.'

He continues :

'But I must not stop at this period of my reminiscences to speak of other sisters than Adèle, with whom my heart was then so intimately associated. I am enormously indebted to the influence of her pious, serene, and resolute disposition.'[9]

Adèle, who was 12 at the time of his birth, requested that she might have the sole care and instruction of Francis until he was of an age to go to school. Francis' cot was placed in her room and she began his education by teaching him his letters in play; he could point to them all before he could speak and used to cry if they were removed from sight. By the age of 2½ he could read a little book, *Cobwebs to Catch Flies*, and a few months later he could sign his name. A small exercise book survives from his fourth year :

> 'The Lord is gracious and full of compassion, slow to anger and of great mercy. The Lord is good to all and his tender mercies are over all his works. Papa why do you call my books dirty, that one came from the Ware-House, I think they are very clean.'

It was at this age that Francis was observed to be hoarding any pennies that he was given. When asked why, he replied that he was saving up to buy honours at university.

At the end of his fourth year some indication of his educational progress can be obtained from this letter to his sister :

> 'My dear Adèle,
>   I am four years old and can read any English book. I can say all the Latin Substantives and adjectives and active verbs besides 52 lines of Latin poetry. I can cast up any sum in addition and multiply by
>
> 2, 3, 4, 5, 6, 7, 8, (9), 10, (11)
>
> I can also say the pence table, I read French a little and I know the Clock.
>
> Francis Galton
> February-15-1827'

The only misspelling is in the date which Francis corrected. The numerals 9 and 11 have been obliterated, 9 by means of a penknife and 11 by a pasted piece of paper. As Karl Pearson remarks,[10] it would seem that Francis realised after writing the letter that he had claimed too much, tried to erase the 9 with the penknife but tore the paper and profiting from the experience used paste on the 11 !

When he was five Adèle thought it advisable to send him to the local dame school so that he could mix with boys of his own age. Mrs French's school was not far from The Larches and Francis walked there and back each day. He thought at first that his mother would not let him stay at the school as the boys were so vulgar they had never heard of Marmion or the Iliad, but he remained there for three years, having been made head boy on his arrival. Poor Mrs French did not know what to make of the young gentleman who was 'always to be found studying the abstruse sciences.'[11] But she arranged for him to have extra tuition in Latin from a master at King Edward's School where he was later to be further educated.

By the time he left Mrs French's school at the age of eight and a half he had, according to his mother, read and learnt the following books: Eton Latin Grammar, *Delectus*, Eutropius, Phaedrus' *Fables*, Ovid's *Metamorphoses* (to where the Medusa turns the men into stones) and three quarters through Ovid's *Epistles*. His father confirms in his diary that he came across Francis in bed one morning studying Ovid with great interest.

Although Adèle had gone to immense pains to learn Latin and some Greek in order to keep ahead of Francis, she did not restrict him solely to the classics. She showed him how to collect and classify insects and taught him a little geology. His father records the following conversation in a diary entry for 4th April 1830:

'I read him an extract about locusts in Peru and Violetta said she'd seen lots at Ramsgate. Francis: "Oh, those were cockchafers." "Well," said Violetta, "they are the same things." Francis: "Oh no, they're quite different, for the cockchafer belongs to the order Coleoptera but the locust belongs to the order Neuroptera." '

Shortly after the publication of the first volume of Karl Pearson's biography which contained several instances of Galton's precocity, Lewis Terman, the American psychologist perhaps best known for his standardisation of the Binet Intelligence test, wrote a paper in which he attempted an estimate of Galton's I.Q.[12] Many of the young Galton's dated achievements have been standardised by psychologists on unselected children of different ages. For example, whereas Francis could tell the time and knew his pence and multiplication table at the age of four, the average age at which these skills are attained is between eight and nine. Thus, Francis' mental age was double his chronological age and according to the Binet system of calculation ($IQ = \frac{MA}{CA} \times 100$) his I.Q. was therefore 200.*

Although I.Q.'s today are not linked to the concept of a mental age but are expressed in terms of deviations from a mean score of 100, nevertheless there is little difficulty in accepting Terman's comment that Galton's performance was so exceptional as to be termed that of a genius. Indeed, Terman estimated that an I.Q. of 200 was 'not equalled by more than one child in 50 000 of the generality.'[13]

At the age of eight Francis was sent as a boarder to a school at Boulogne. The purpose behind this move was apparently to teach him to speak fluent French, although instead he was forced to speak under penalty of a fine what turned out to be a limited patois.

---

* Terman was misled by Francis' letter to Adèle which begins, 'I am four years old.' The date shows that it was only one day short of his fifth birthday. The calculations should therefore be amended to give an I.Q. of about 160.

In his autobiography he recalls the following incidents :

'We were daily marched off in a long row of pairs, usually for a walk round the ramparts, sometimes to Napoleon's Column, then in process of building, and in the summer, not infrequently, to bathe by rocks near the old fort. We prepared ourselves for the latter grateful occasions by saving bread from breakfast; then, after having gathered mussels, we spread their delicious contents on it to eat. An opportunity was then afforded of inspecting with awe the marks of recent birchings, which were reckoned as glorious scars. The birchings were frequent and performed in a long room parallel to, and separated from, the schoolroom by large ill-fitting doors, through which each squeal of the victim was heard with hushed breaths. In that room was a wardrobe full of schoolbooks ready for issue. It is some measure of the then naiveté of my mind that I wondered for long how the books could have been kept so fresh and clean for nearly two thousand years, thinking that the copies of Caesar's Commentaries were contemporary with Caesar himself.'[14]

With his father's retirement from the bank and the removal of the family from The Larches to Leamington, it was decided, much to Francis' relief, to bring him home from Boulogne. He was now sent to a small private school at Kenilworth kept by the Rev. Atwood, who without great academic ability but with much sympathy for boyish aspirations encouraged Francis to develop freely. The tuition offered must have been heavily spiced with theology to judge from a letter from Francis to his father :

December 30, 1832

'My dearest Papa,

It is now my pleasure to disclose the most ardent wishes of my heart which are to extract out of my boundless wealth in compound, [left by his grandfather who had recently died] money sufficient to make this addition to my unequalled Library.

The Hebrew Commonwealth by John	9	
A Pastor advice	2	
Hornne's Commentaries on the Psalms	4	6
Paley's evidence on Christianity	2	
Jones' Biblical Cyclopoedia	10	
	27	6

All books much approved of.'

When Francis reached 14, it was time to send him to a bigger school and his father's Quaker repugnance for the usual type of Public school

led to his choice of King Edward's School, Birming'
the Free School) to which Dr Jeune, later Master of ~~ ~~
Cambridge and Bishop of Peterborough, had recently been appointed
as Head Master. Dr Jeune was a scholar of great ability and educational
zeal, but it is quite clear from Galton's autobiography that he was not
happy there:

'. . . the character of the education was altogether uncongenial to
my temperament. I learnt nothing, and chafed at my limitations. I
had craved for what was denied, namely, an abundance of good
English reading, well-taught mathematics, and solid science.
Grammar and the dry rudiments of Latin and Greek were abhorrent
to me, for there seemed so little sense in them.'[15]

In another publication and in more general terms he castigated his
schooling as:

'that unhappy system of education that has hitherto prevailed, by
which boys acquired a very imperfect knowledge of the structure of
two dead languages, and none at all of the structure of the living
world.'[16]

Dr Jeune, on the other hand, was more than happy to have Francis
at his school. In writing to request £50 as fees for Francis' first six months'
tuition he comments:

'Francis has great powers; if he should apply them he must hold
a very distinguished position both in his school and in the world hereafter . . . He possesses a mind of no vulgar order.'[17]

During his second term at the Free School, Francis wrote to ask his
father to remove him. Nothing happened in immediate response to his
letter but by the end of the year he received the glad news that he had
been accepted as an indoor pupil at Birmingham General Hospital and
would be leaving school early in 1838 at the age of 16.

Plans for a medical education had been laid before Francis went to
Dr Jeune's. The practice of medicine was a family tradition on his
mother's side and she very much wanted her youngest and ablest son to
carry on that tradition. His father fully concurred with her desire and
began to take an active interest in Francis' studies. As he wrote in the
first of his excellent letters of advice to Francis:

'You must be careful to avoid low company and not be led astray
by any pupils that may not be equally well disposed, but I have great
confidence in your wish to do what is right, and when we meet at
your approaching holidays, we will talk over your plans and arrange-

ments in good earnest and particularly in reference to your masters and studies whilst at the Hospital.'[18]

The holiday between leaving school and beginning hospital work was a memorable one. Queen Victoria's coronation took place in June and the various members of the Galton family were disposed along the route, Elizabeth having a place in the Abbey, Emma being at the Reform Club, and Francis having a seat in Pall Mall which cost him 30 shillings. His reactions on this occasion are not recorded, but must have been favourable in view of his life-long fascination with such public spectacles which he attended whenever he could.

The remaining two months of the holiday were devoted to a summer tour arranged by his father. In the company of two newly-qualified doctors young Francis was to combine an inspection of continental hospitals with a holiday abroad. One of his companions, William Bowman, later became eminent as an authority on diseases of the eye, and it was he who led the party.

They left London for Antwerp, travelled through Belgium and down the Rhine, then to Heidelberg, Munich and Vienna, returning on the more northerly route via Prague, Dresden, Berlin and Hamburg back to Hull.

The many long letters written to his father contain little reference to continental hospital practice: they witnessed but one minor operation. Instead Francis fills his letters with amusing details of their encounters with other nationalities. One example must suffice, his first letter from Vienna which describes their encounter with the Austrian customs:

'Out popped an Austrian officer with mustachios like sweep's brushes looking thunder and lightning. "Kein Tabac" growled or rather roared the officer in interrogation. Three "Kein Tabacs" followed each other uttered in a most submissive tone of voice from us, like the echoes of Oberwessel. The officer's eyes flared. He pointed to the luggage, down in the twinkling of an eye it came and was opened. He looked awful at my green bags with black strings, in which two or three dirty shirts were esconced, and terrible at the other luggage; he made signs that everything must come out, when in a moment 3 Zwanzigers (a coin about 10d.) touched his hand—a galvanic shock seemed to thrill his whole system. The sour of his disposition, like the acid in Volta's pole seemed only to increase the change. The flare of his eye changed in an instant to a twinkle, the baggage was shut up and the officer fell into a "paroxysm of bows" and away we drove.'[19]

It is noticeable that from the time he left school nearly all Francis' letters are addressed to his father and very few are sent to his mother.

His sister, Elizabeth, appears to take over his mother's role and Francis appeals to her for advice on social custom, diet and health. Adèle, whose influence also begins to lessen at this time, typically receives short notes about his current intellectual preoccupation, while with Emma he discusses anything he has seen of artistic and architectural merit.

The steamer from Hamburg took four days to reach Hull, and Francis reports that he was dreadfully sea-sick. He went almost at once to Birmingham and began his medical training in earnest.

At first he was confined to the dispensary. It is a tribute to his scientific curiosity if not to his prudence that his pharmacological studies induced him to sample for himself the effects of different medicines. Thus he began working through the pharmacopoeia taking small doses of the different drugs beginning with the letter A. He did not get further than C being stopped by the effects of two drops of Croton oil which had a marked purgative and emetic effect!

He was then gradually introduced to the wards, accompanying the surgeons on their rounds and being present at operations and post mortems. Chloroform anaesthesia had not then been discovered and major operations had to be carried out on conscious patients.

'The cries of the poor fellows who were operated on were characteristic; in fact, each class of operation seemed to evoke some peculiar form of them. All this was terrible, but only at first. It seemed after a while as though the cries were somehow disconnected with the operation, upon which the whole attention became fixed.'[20]

As a clinical clerk, he enjoyed neat bandaging, setting broken limbs and even reducing dislocations.

'The mechanism of the body began to appear very simple in its elementary features. At one time no less than sixteen fractures, dislocations, or other injuries to the arms, or parts of them, were practically under my sole care all at the same time.'[21]

In spite of being supervised in his work it is obvious that considerable responsibility was his. In a letter to his father dated 10th November 1838 he gives us an idea of what he has to do in the hospital :

'I will give you a sort of diary of the evening of the day before yesterday. $\frac{1}{2}$ past 5 p.m. went round all the wards (No joke I assure you)—made up about 15 prescriptions. Awful headache etc. Entered in the Hospital Books records etc. of patients; writing in my case book etc., hard work till 9. Supper. Went round several of the wards again. Accident came in—broken leg, had to assist setting it. $\frac{1}{2}$ past 11, had to read medicine etc. 12, very sleepy indeed, lighted my candle to go to bed. A ring at the Accident Bell; found that it was a tremendous fracture. Was not finished till $\frac{1}{2}$ past 1. Went to bed and in the arms of Porpus. 3 a.m. in the morning : a tremendous knocking at the door; awful compound fracture, kept me up till 5. Went to Bed—up again at 7 o'clock. Rather tiring work on the whole, but very entertaining. Attended a post mortem and dissection 2 days ago—Horror-Horror-Horror ! I do not know when I shall get over the impression. It was a woman whose wounds I had assisted to dress. I made her medicine and prescribed once or twice for her. My first regular patient died also, yesterday morning. However, as it was a burn, my mind is perfectly easy. Don't tell this it won't sound well. I shall set up a case of instruments soon. I can write prescriptions splendidly, and moreover begin to understand all the humbug of medicine, which is not a little. I am very sorry that you have got the gout, if I were at home I would prescribe for you with great pleasure. Tell Bessy that I have some valuable receipts— such as splendid Tooth-Powder—Glorious Perfumes—Beautiful Varnishes. Also Lucy's Biscuit Pie Crust answers very well.

'I expect to cut Gil Blas quite out. I can hardly refrain from sending you a splendid receipt for cure of the Gibberish . . . Please blow up Adèle for sending that parcel [of books] here after I told her what to do with it. Please send me my Delphin Horace, and Ainsworth's Dictionary, and Schrevelius' Lexicon.'

Of course it is probable that this was an exceptional day, but Francis does seem to have been worked very hard and we must remember that he was only 16 years old. Yet a few weeks later he is telling his father that he is having lessons in mathematics and German besides reading Horace and Homer when his headache permits ! No break occurred in this intensive routine until the following summer when his father, deciding his son needed a rest, took him on a Scottish holiday.

To obtain better theoretical instruction he was now sent to King's College, London, where his professors were eminent men. Chemistry lectures were given by Daniell who had invented one form of the galvanic cell. Francis studied physiology under Professor Todd, who was at that time collaborating with Bowman in writing their well-known *Encyclopaedia of Physiology*. Most of his time was spent in the dissecting room where his friend Bowman was his immediate chief. The Professor of Anatomy was Richard Partridge, and Francis with one or two other students lodged at his house. He was fortunate in this respect as he was invited to Partridge's dinner parties and listened to, even if he did not participate in, the brilliant talk. Partridge had been friendly with Charles Lamb, his brother was a well-known artist, he had a wide circle of acquaintances and Francis must have profited greatly from the extension to an otherwise narrow medical education.*

An interesting change in his routine from that followed in Birmingham was the time now allotted to physical exercise and social activities:

'I am as well as possible, getting thorough exercising twice a week at Angelo's either at Carte and Tierce, or else in pitching into a huge Life Guardsman, six feet and a half high in his slippers, or rather in his pitching into me with single stick. I have no headaches or anything of the sort and dissecting increases the appetite wonderfully.'[22]

This happy state of affairs was not to last long. Less than two months later he was writing to his sister:

'Dear Bessy. Thanks for your letter and missal forthcoming. But don't please put any advice in the middle (even though it's an ancestor's) for I am sure I have had enough. It's quite as eternal and does me no more good than Dr Sangrado's Warm Water.

'O Bessy, Bessy, I have another boil exactly by the side of the former which has partially reappeared. The new one is mountainous, but alas! not snow-capped like Ben Nevis, but more like Ben Lomond covered with scarlet heather. I shall have a complete Snowdonia of them soon and my mouth is rather sore. Paws rather improved . . .

'Diet. Breakfast.   1 largish cup of tea.
                1 round dry toast.
        Luncheon, not always, Bread and Cheese.
        Dinner, 1 or 2 times of meat, vegetables, melted butter. 3 glasses wine. Pudding or Tart. 1 glass of water.
        Tea, several small cups, bread and butter.

'This is my full diet. Please Emma tell me what sort of low diet will do. I have fearful indigestion, sleepiness, variable appetite etc. etc. etc.'[23]

The diet appears quite inadequate. He was spending one shilling a week on luncheon whereas his tailor's bills were in excess of £27. A fastidiousness about dress and a wish not to appear in any way conspicuous were two characteristics of lifelong duration. The fear of transgressing social convention was at its height during his London stay. Sister Elizabeth was his mentor in the social proprieties. Thus the above note to her concludes:

'(1) When a note of invite is sent unpaid by the twopenny post, may I answer it by ditto or how?

---

* It is perhaps significant that Wheatstone, the inventor of the electric telegraph, was a regular visitor to Partridge's house. Galton's first publication was to be the invention of a form of printing telegraph.

'(2) Ought I to call at St James Square [his great aunt's] before these boils go away and take the chance of more not coming, or not? . . . '(3) When the Horners invite with a note beginning with "My dear Francis" how am I to answer it?'

The replies of his father and sister have not been preserved, but Francis seems to have enjoyed an increasing social round. He continued with his social calls and heavy work load until Christmas which he spent with his family in Leamington. On his return to London in the 'Coventry and Leamington Omnibus' he met a Captain Sayers who had travelled much in Africa and who regaled Francis with tales of that continent and showed him how to make a turban out of his plaid. Another ten years were to elapse before Galton was to undertake his own exploration, but his choice of Africa may have been determined by this chance meeting.

The work routine continued until April 1840 when the Spring examinations took place. A few days before they began he took a break to watch the Oxford and Cambridge boat race and nearly lost his life. He describes the episode in detail in a letter to Elizabeth from which the long first sentence that follows is taken:

'My dear Bessy,
    Yesterday at 17 minutes and 45 seconds to 5 (I know the time because my watch was stopped), just when you were puzzling yourself over some cross-stitch pattern and whilst Delly was trying to find out a type in the Old Testament for the fact that St Paul left his cloak behind at Ephesus—well, as you were both amusing yourselves at that said time—I, your humble servant, Lord Torment and Tease, clothes and boots on, was floundering under the wheels of a Steam Packet, the paddles of which were bumping upon my head with a 15-horse power, and some time afterwards I found myself kicking about some 8 or 10 feet deep, rising to the top, which instead of reaching, I merely knocked my head against a huge piece of wood and sank down again, at the same time gulping in water like a fish and bubbling out air like a blacksmith's bellows, my life worth "a little less than nothing at all", as the sailors say.'[24]

The paddle steamer had collided with Battersea Bridge and the paddle-box split open throwing Francis head first among the paddle wheels. He was then trapped by his clothing on projecting nails under the boat but finally freed himself and dived clear. The first boatmen who appeared on the scene demanded a sovereign before they would take him on board, so he remained floating on part of the wreckage until another boat arrived.

His examination technique was none the worse for the experience as he reports in an exuberant little note to Adèle:

'Dear Delly,

Hurrah! Hurrah!! I am 2nd Prizeman in Anatomy and Chemistry. I had only expected a certificate of honour. Hurrah! Go it, ye cripples*!!!'[25]

He now dropped anatomy to concentrate on forensic medicine and botany with chemical manipulation and surgical operations as subsidiaries, a strangely haphazard combination of subjects. In the July examination in forensic medicine he was again second out of a class of 60 to 70, but there was only a first prize and he had to be content with a certificate. In his autobiography he wrongly recalls winning the first prize in this subject which was his favourite.

'It had a sort of Sherlock Holmes fascination for me, while the instances given as cautions, showing where the value of too confident medical assertions had been rudely upset by the shrewd cross-questioning of lawyers, confirmed what I was beginning vaguely to perceive, that doctors had the fault, equally with parsons, of being much too positive.'[26]

Francis, as well as his two elder brothers, was required to furnish detailed weekly accounts of his expenditure to his father, who with a banker's precision corrected and annotated them. During his stay in Birmingham and the first few months in London many letters to his father contain apologies for the inadequacy of his accountancy. But by 1840 it is a different story :

'My dear Father,

Thanks for your unanswered letters . . . Everything gets on capitally, especially accounts. When I want to know if I have any coppers in my pocket to give to a begging crossing sweeper I do not condescend to feel but pull out my pocket-book add up and the result is sure to be correct . . .

Accounts.   Tuesday 17th–29th

	£	s	d
Boots	1	15	6
Dinner with Bowman twice		6	1
Books	2	3	6
Grubs (very numerous)		9	6
3 Washing bills		10	2
Shaving soap and brush		3	6
Larks (I blush—Taglioni has just left town)		19	6

* Not a very tactful exclamation addressed to a crippled sister.

'So much for business. Went to the Opera last night, Taglioni, last appearance—am quite hoarse with bellowing out bravo! . . . I went to see Courvoisier hung, and was close to the gallows, poor fellow. I went professionally for death by hanging is a medico-legal subject of some importance.

'Tell Delly that I have not seen a scrap of her handwriting for ages and that she must send me a letter . . . If she divides her attention between two sets of objects—to both of which she is attached—school and farm—her health will be wonderfully improved, Frampton's pills of health discarded and steel mixtures thrown down the sink.'*[27]

Francis' time in London was nearly up. A scheme for interrupting his medical education so that he might take a Cambridge degree in mathematics had been tentatively discussed before he had left Birmingham. The desirability of such a plan was now confirmed in conversation with Bowman and Charles Darwin, Francis' cousin. It was never intended that he should give up medicine completely although there was an obvious risk that he might become diverted from that goal. Francis took some pains to reassure his father of his good intentions and to convince him that mathematics would profit him in his later career as a doctor.

'Bowman . . . says that every high mathematical MD that he knows got on well . . . Charles Darwin recommends next October and to read Mathematics like a house on fire . . . He said very truly that the faculty of observation rather than that of abstract reasoning tends to constitute a good Physician. The higher parts of Mathematics which are exceedingly interwoven with Chemical and Medical Phenomena (Electricity, Light, Heat etc., etc.) all exist and exist only on experience and observation ∴ don't stop halfway. Make the most of the opportunity and read them. I quite agree with all he said.'[28]

Charles Darwin had recently married and Francis was a frequent visitor to his house in Gower Street. Darwin had published his *Journal of the Voyage of the Beagle* the previous year and his travels must have figured largely in their conversation. One result was the dissatisfaction Francis began to feel for his static life in London.

'In the spring of 1840 a passion for travel seized me as if I had been a migratory bird. While attending the lectures at King's

* This last paragraph suggests that Francis was by now aware, probably through his medical experience with hysterical patients, that Adèle's spinal complaint was an attention-seeking device which would be ameliorated if she could devote herself to a variety of occupations. Accompanying his recognition of the true nature of her complaint a certain lack of sympathy was becoming evident.

College I could see the sails of the lighters moving in sunshine on the Thames, and it required all my efforts to disregard the associations of travel which they aroused.'[29]

Fortunately, he was able to indulge his inclinations almost at once. A fellow student, William Miller, had arranged to spend the summer in the German town of Giessen where the organic chemist, Liebig, had his laboratory which was attracting students from all over Europe. He asked Francis if he would like to accompany him. Francis wrote immediately to his father presenting many cogent reasons for the additional training and asking for his consent and for funds. By return of post his father agreed and enclosed a draft on Barclay's bank for £100.

The intention was to remain at Liebig's laboratory over the summer and to return in time for the beginning of the Michaelmas term at Cambridge. Francis' letters had, in this respect also, been successful and convinced by his son's arguments Samuel Tertius had entered him at Trinity College. But there is little doubt that as far the Giessen trip was concerned Francis had not the serious intent that motivated his colleague, Miller, who was to specialise in chemistry in later life.* Thus one can detect some relief in Francis' first letter from Giessen in which he explains that Liebig's method of instruction is not adapted to his needs as it presupposes an efficiency in manipulating apparatus which is the very thing he wishes to acquire. Instead, he proposes to devote his whole time to improving his German. Certainly he took at least one German lesson, as he was able to describe the Professor with his 17 pipes. He also practised the language with the chemistry students who dined together every evening and who adopted various German student customs :

'If one student calls out to another "Sie sind Doktor", it is a challenge to drink 2 glasses of wine; if "Sie sind Professor", then 4 and so on.'[30]

But as he complains in this second letter to his father there is nothing for him to do during the day and if it is a question of learning German then he is sure that he will learn more on a trip to Athens and Constantinople!

Before his father had a chance to disagree and five days after his arrival in Giessen he had left by coach for Passau on the Danube. At Passau he found that the Danube steamer was under repair and so took a small boat with one oarsman and lending a hand himself rowed downstream to Vienna. Then he caught the steamer to Budapest where he wrote a long letter home illustrated by several excellent sketches.

'I never fully understood what a hot day was till I came here—in truth sightseeing opens the mind and the perspiratory pores also

* He held the Chair of Chemistry in King's College, London for many years.

. . . I must really invest in a parasol to-day, the heat at midday is absolutely awful . . . The nights are bitterly cold. Yesterday to economise I tried the 2nd place [class], but I find that it really wont do in the lower part of the river. There are no berths and we stay on board at least 8 nights—fellow passengers are beastly, spitting ad infinitum and very much crowded. . . In the first place, on the quarter deck, (as in all steamers) very few *beastly* snobs are present.* The difference is £4 between the 2 places so I shall take my place on the quarter deck . . . As it is very hot and I have had a splendid dinner with very fair wine for 1s. 4d. I cant stir out and so will copy a scetch [*sic*] . . . In 11 days more I am in Istanboul, hurrah! I remember a bit of advice of Darwin's when I was climbing up a ladder to the cistern in the yard at the Larches. Not to look down but only upwards and see what is left to be climbed (not "clomb"). Just so with my present tour. I fancy myself not much farther than Belgium, quite at home and only calculate what I have to do.'[31]

One further letter was sent from Istanbul where he spent a happy week.

'Here I am at Constantinople—among Turks, Armenians, Greeks, Jews and Franks in a good Lodging House, as well as possible and happier and happier every day. The Golden Horn is just in front of me, crammed full of mosques and minarets, Seraglios and Towers . . . The seraglios are splendid, ditto palaces, such a great deal of trellis work about them, and then there are cypresses, and the veiled ladies just looking out between folds of gauze and very pretty eyes they have too . . . I saw the women's slave-market today—if I had 50 pounds at my disposal I could have invested in an excessively beautiful one, a Georgian . . . Most of the black ones were fettered, but they seemed very happy dancing and singing and looking on complacently whilst a couple of Turks were wrangling about their prices. I took a Turkish bath today, such a shampooing and lathering and steaming. Now about getting home. These plaguy quarantines have been extended though there is no plague now in Turkey (a great bore for I wanted to see some cases) and that at Syra with that at Trieste will be, I fear 24 days. I therefore shall scarcely be able to see you before going to Cambridge.'[32]

* 'Snob' should, of course, be understood in its Victorian sense where it was typically applied to a shopkeeper attempting to pass himself off for a gentleman. The distinction between a gentleman and a snob must have held some significance for Galton, as among his papers in the Galton Archives is a newspaper cutting, heavily underlined, which attempts to clarify the difference.

The journey home cannot now be traced exactly as his diary is very incomplete. He must have sailed to Smyrna where he records walking across the aqueduct (500 yd long and only from 3 to 5 ft wide),

'A feat which my valet de place had told me had been once accomplished at great peril by an adventurous Englishman.'[33]

Another boat took him to Syra where he had to remain in quarantine for 10 days, then on to Athens and Trieste. At Trieste he was able to shorten the period of his quarantine by 'making Spoglio'. After inspection by a doctor he lined up with others on a quay. On a second quay, separated from the first by a 20ft strip of sea-water, the old-clothes men displayed their wares. Francis concluded a shouted bargain with one of them, stripped off his own clothes, and plunged in to emerge naked on the opposite quay. His money and papers were fumigated and passed over to allow him to pay for the inferior garments which were to be his. This curious process was based on the belief that the apparently healthy human body when washed would be less liable to carry any infection than the clothes worn during previous exposure to it.

Two of the days of quarantine thus saved were spent in a visit to the Adelsberg caverns where Francis bought two of the amphibia known as *proteus*. He then took a steamer to Venice and a diligence via Milan to Boulogne. On the week's journey from Milan to Boulogne he sat day and night in the diligence nursing the *proteus* in a bottle (under his coat when crossing the Alps to prevent the water freezing). They were the first living examples of *proteus anguinus* to be brought to England and Francis presented them most appropriately to his own London college.

In October 1840 Francis and his father took the stagecoach to Cambridge. Samuel Tertius had himself been in residence at Trinity College at the age of 16 but had left without matriculating to pursue a commercial career. The 40 years between father and son had seen little change in the tuition available : undergraduates still had to read either for the mathematical or for the classical tripos as no other subjects were available to them. Dr Jeune's tuition had killed Francis' childhood interest in the classics, and the professional advantages of having a mathematical training accorded well with his own preferences.

He appears to have settled down from the beginning to intensive study. One of his first letters to his father, dated 3rd November 1840, describes his 'Gumption-Reviver machine'—a device for continuously wetting the head with cold water during the difficult period of study from 10 p.m. to 2 a.m. An unusual discipline for a first year undergraduate ! But then his programme of study was as hard as ever :

'Distribution of Time. Up at Chapel at 7; ditto to $7\frac{1}{2}$. Reading and breakfast to 9. Lectures to 11. Reading by myself and with

O'Brien [his tutor] to 2, walk to 4—a 4 mile walk—Hall to 4.20. Read to 10.30 including tea. Lectures 2 hours a day, reading (full tide) $10\frac{1}{2}$ hours. I shall cut this down to 6, as it is Really too much. Tell Bessy that there is the most extraordinary possible change in my complexion, the tan having quite disappeared. Breadth of phiz on the wane.'

Some time during 1840 he sat for his first portrait (Plate III). The painting by Oakley shows him to have been slim with fair hair, a high brow and large pale blue eyes. The mouth cannot have been portrayed accurately; a little later in life it was wide with thin lips, the upper protruding slightly over the lower. His dress in the portrait is typical of the undergraduate of the period :

'A not too new black coat (frock or cutaway), trousers of some substantial stuff, grey or plaid, and a stout waistcoat, frequently of the same pattern as the trousers . . . The only showy part of the attire is the cravat, which is apt to be blue or some other decided colour, and fastened in front with a large gold-headed pin.'[34]

With his unusual background Francis had met few prospective Cambridge men prior to his arrival. During the whole of his first year he led a very quiet social life, visiting his cousin Theodore for *eau sucrée* which they drank while smoking Francis' German or Turkish pipes, calling on Mathew Boulton, an old friend from Mr Atwood's School, for tea and talk, but playing no games, taking part in no societies and making little impact on Cambridge life.

After less than a month at college he was taken ill, not, he explains to his father, on account of over-reading but with an attack of rheumatism. Whatever the truth of the matter he was confined to bed for two weeks and stopped work until the following term.

The Christmas vacation was partly spent with his brother, Erasmus, who was now farming on his estate at Loxton in Somerset. Sister Adèle was also there, as Francis describes in a letter to his father :

'I gigged it to Loxton . . . Somersetshire is really the most beautiful country I have ever seen, north of the Alps (for Bessy), and of all dull pig-headed stupid bipeds the Somersetshire clown stands preeminent. Arrived at Loxton, the manor house commodious but not gaudy. Eras : girth visibly increased, Delly all smiles and lawn collar, the last mentioned article being as whitewash to a sepulchre or as charity covering a multitude of deficiencies . . . In the evening whilst Delly writes letters for 4 hours and reads others for 1 quarter, Rassy pulls Track (the dog) by his tail and ears alternately, causing him to

1 Violetta Galton

II Samuel Tertius Galton

growl ferociously, for one hour, then sleeps $3\frac{1}{4}$; and after that both adjourn to the dinner room to edify 3 maid servants and a small boy with a learned commentary on the psalms.'[35]

The three month interruption to his studies was probably responsible for his third class in the May examinations, but the inclusion of some classics may have contributed. His tutor was convinced of his ability and suggested that next year he should work under William Hopkins, a more eminent mathematician. Meanwhile there was the summer vacation, which Francis spent at Keswick with a reading party.

It proved to be a very active and convivial holiday. He did an immense amount of walking and danced and drank with the locals. Francis was joined by his father and sister Emma in August, but only after he had been able to reassure his father that their visit would be welcome. During his stay at Keswick Samuel Tertius caught a chill when out riding which proved the precursor of a serious illness. He never fully recovered his health, arthritis and asthma proving particularly troublesome until the end.

Francis entered his second year at Cambridge in an exuberant mood. Hopkins, his new tutor, was a change for the better. Francis explains in a letter that Hopkins enters into the metaphysics of mathematics in a most entertaining way with the result that his tutorials are the most enjoyable experience Francis has ever had.[36] Hopkins in turn gave Francis much encouragement and even complimented him on his mechanics. He could not, however, do better than a second class at the 'Little Go' examination in March, whereas several of Hopkins' other pupils obtained firsts.

Hopkins believed in working his pupils very hard; three of them could not stand the pace and had to leave his class, and Francis was obviously finding it hard to keep up in 14 different mathematical subjects.

'On thinking over about the approaching Scholarship Examination, I so plainly see that I have no chance whatever of getting one this year that I really think it quite useless to compete . . . My head is already rather bad from having overworked myself in attempting to get up these subjects as well as doing what Hopkins has set us for this vacation.'[37]

He appears to have stayed up for the Easter vacation, but in June he joined a reading party, led by the Senior Wrangler, Arthur Cayley, which travelled up to Aberfeldy in Perthshire. Although there appears to have been the usual round of amusements, including a highland wedding where they danced from three in the afternoon until four next morning, Francis' letters to his father are curiously lifeless in comparison with the energetic writing of his letters from Keswick during the previous summer. He found the countryside monotonous and did comparatively little walking. He could read little as a headache and dizziness occurred whenever he began work.

On his return to Cambridge at the beginning of his third year the evidence that he was heading for a breakdown becomes more obvious and he prepared his father for a subsequent abandonment of honours by pointing out the prevalence of the practice.

'My head is very uncertain so that I can scarcely read at all, however, I find that I am not at all solitary in that respect. Of the year above me the *first 3 men* in their College examinations are all going out in the poll,* the first 2 from bad health and the third, Boulton, from finding that he could not continue reading as he used to do without risking it. Fowell Buxton is quite knocked up and goes out in the poll, so does Bristed, one of the first classics in our year, in fact the whole of Trinity is crank.'[38]

Four weeks later he details his symptoms :

'I am quite ashamed at not having written oftener but my head generally is not as well as might be at the orthodox letter writing time, namely about 7 a.m. I find myself quite unable to do anything in reading for by really deep attention to Maths I can bring on my usual dizziness etc. almost immediately though generally I feel much better than I used to. Palpitations of the heart have lately come on when I read more than I ought to do which I am rather glad of than otherwise, as it saves my head.'[39]

In his autobiography he recalls that soon after this letter he broke down entirely and had to go home. He likens his illness to a mill working inside his head so that he could not banish obsessive thoughts. It became painful even to look at a printed page, and as a brief interval of complete mental rest did some good he thought it likely that a longer period might lead to a complete cure.

Ascribing the breakdown to overwork meant that he was able with a good conscience and without unduly disappointing his father to give up working for honours and to content himself with a poll degree. The remainder of his time at Cambridge was to be spent mainly in social and literary activities but he did attend a few medical lectures to obtain the quota necessary for a medical qualification.

It was certainly true of Galton that he succeeded in making many acquaintances at university who were to be of great use to him in later

* 'To go out in the poll' was to take a pass degree;

life. His autobiography is full of the names of fellow undergraduates who later achieved eminence. Many of these able men he met through two close friendships he made in his second year with F. Campbell and H. F. Hallam. Campbell was the son of Lord Campbell, then Lord Justice of Appeal, while Harry Hallam was the son of the historian, Henry Hallam, and brother to Arthur Hallam, the subject of Tennyson's *In Memoriam*.

Harry Hallam was one of the earliest members of the Historical Society founded in opposition to the Union by Galton and Brixton, a fellow mathematician manqué. Union debates had become disorderly and their subject matter uncongenial to Galton. He spoke there only occasionally, although he had stood for the Presidency and been defeated. The objective of the Historical Society was to preserve the decorum of philosophical debate, which was achieved by a careful selection of the first members. The presidency rotated among the nine original members and the club met quietly in the current president's rooms where they were entertained with wine. Soon numbers appear to have grown to as many as sixty and Galton presided over these more public meetings at the Black Bear.

Galton also founded an English Epigram Society of a dozen members who wrote short and generally amusing poems on given subjects. He himself wrote further and more serious poems at this time of his life, but probably realising his lack of talent did not continue the practice after leaving Cambridge.

Besides his poetical attempts Galton's creativity during his Cambridge years was manifest in his invention of mechanical contrivances in which field he was certainly more gifted. Details of a new type of oil lamp, a lock, a balance and a rotating vane steam engine are preserved in letters he wrote from Cambridge to his father. Several of these early inventions received serious consideration from experts although none was ever patented or manufactured. His later inventions include a great variety of machines and equipment, the last dating from 1906 when he was 84 years old.*

With medical experience and travel in Eastern Europe to his credit, Galton must have been able to bring novelty to the many social functions he attended towards the end of his Cambridge career. He attracted additional notoriety from the feat of entering a lion's den when a travelling circus visited Cambridge. He was only the fourth person ever to have dared to do so.[40]

In spite of his physical courage there is no evidence that he continued with his fencing after the regular London sessions ceased nor did he take any other regular physical exercise but was content with an occasional row on the river and an even rarer game of hockey. His companions were

---

* In order to retain continuity, detailed consideration of Galton's inventions has been reserved for Appendix I.

drawn more from the intellectual and literary sets than from the ranks of the sportsmen. With them he seems to have led a gay and fairly self-indulgent existence. An allowance of £300 per annum from his father, who had released him from the requirement that he should provide details of his expenditure, meant that he could entertain liberally and dress well.

His social activities did not exclude the opposite sex, as he makes quite clear in his letters home. For example,

'I am much obliged to Bessy for the melancholy news about Miss H. I was however aware of my misfortune the same week that the engagement took place, but had not been informed who Mr Edward was, there is one thing that acts as a poultice to my wounded feelings which is that that small chimpanzee Mr Saville is not the happy man. Time has done wonders for me, in soothing etc. but, oh Bessy!! Miss D. has done much more, she is without exception the most beautiful etc. etc. etc. I have ever seen. I was at a hop at her Ma's house the other night (I know most of the families in Cambridge now) I was dancing with her (the daughter not the Mamma) in a quadrille with one of my Little-Go examiners for a vis-a-vis. Today as the sun was shining beautifully I decked myself out in resplendent summer apparell [*sic*], light trousers, light waistcoats, (those that I had last year) to make a call upon this fair creature, but as I was just finishing my toilette and was 'throwing a perfume over the violet' in the way of re-arranging my cravat ties, the wind blew and the rain fell horribly and the streets were one mass of mud. Of course I was in despair, but reflecting that if Leander swam the Hellespont for Hero, *I* was in duty bound to *wade* as far as the Fitzwilliam for Miss D., off I set. When however I arrived at their door, I wisely reflected on the splashed state of my trousers before I knocked and then retreated crest-fallen.'[41]

One of the advantages of Harry Hallam's friendship was that he had a sister, Julia, with whom Francis' sister, Emma, became friendly. During the last long vacation at Cambridge Harry and Julia joined Francis and Emma on a continental holiday. It appears that the Hallams travelled separately and met the Galtons in Dresden. They again separated and met for ten days in Munich. But only an outline of the trip survives in Emma's sketchy diary and in one uninformative letter home.

It is possible that Francis was keen on Julia Hallam although the only evidence is an insubstantial hint in a letter to his father written a few months after their return. He mentions there that he has visited the Hallam house and continues directly:

'Dear Emma, *She* is sweeter than ever. F.G.'[42]

Julia was, however, to marry a Captain Cator (later Sir John Farnaby Lennard) who was a widower. Francis was not in England at the time and his reaction to the news of the marriage is unrecorded. His friendship with Julia's brother, Harry, was to continue very close for the next few years.

Back at Cambridge Galton found that he needed to stay until June 1844 to complete his medical studies. He began 'working ferociously', as he put it, to complete his degree work and to regain the medical knowledge that he had by now forgotten. He took his B.A. in January 1844 and continued to work hard at medicine, but the family, and Bessy in particular, were not convinced that he would persist. His father writes to him on the 4th of February 1844 :

> 'As Bessy has no doubt given you much salutary advice as to exclusive attention to medicine, I forbear repeating to you all that Horner said to me on the importance of it to success in London practice.'

In his reply written at the beginning of March Francis claims that he is getting more and more fond of medicine every day. He tells his father that he is trying out a method of recording the severity of a patient's symptoms by means of a bar graph for each symptom, daily checks and comparisons to be made to chart the course of the illness.[43]

Pleased with his son's apparent determination his father wrote in one of his last letters :

> 'My dear Francis,
> Your letter has given me much pleasure, both because it assures me that you are going on satisfactorily with your studies, and also because the sight of your handwriting is always welcome to me . . .
> 'I am extremely glad that you take so fondly to your profession upon every account, as an occupation useful to yourself and to others, and as a source of pecuniary independence, which, after all, it is among the number of our duties to promote.'[44]

Francis' own letters to his father were now full of medical advice delivered in a light-hearted manner and accompanied by amusing banter and riddles. He advises his father that he will make a perfect recovery to full health if a little hospital discipline is enforced.

> 'My prescriptions are :
> 1st that the Hospital Patient do on no occasion feel his pulse.
> 2nd that the H.P. do never look in the glass to see whether his eyes are red.
> 3rd that the H.P. do never examine his own health with a view to self-doctoring.

4th that the H.P. do make improvements at Claverdon, and commit prisoners at Leamington when so inclined, but that he never attend canal-meetings, nor put himself to inconvenience or anxiety.

5th that the H.P. do henceforth enjoy an "otium cum dignitate" and leave hard work to younger heads for whom it is a duty.

And now my dear Father I have finished doctoring for the present, but shall go on writing doctor's letters until I hear that you obey my rules.'[45]

Even in his evident anxiety over his father's health, Francis was an irregular correspondent. A letter from Elizabeth is quite explicit:

'Do write soon and regularly. It as a duty, dear Francis, you owe to your parents, and one of the few you are amiss in. My father is far from well, being extremely feeble and his spirits low . . . Every day he regrets not hearing from you, and wishes you to write, so do, dearest Francis, write *immediately* a nice *steady* letter telling him what you are studying and talk of your profession with pleasure, it would do him more good than anything, and make a point of writing at least once a fortnight.'[46]

In September 1844, in the hope that a change of air would be beneficial, Francis accompanied his father in the dual role of companion and physician to St Leonards-on-Sea. But by October his father's health had further deteriorated and his mother, Bessy and Emma were summoned to join them. A fortnight later, on 23rd October, Tertius Galton died at the age of 61 and his son accompanied his father's coffin back to Leamington and to Claverdon where he was buried.

With his father's death we reach a critical point in Francis Galton's career when he appears to lose for a time all sense of vocation and scientific purpose.

2

Egypt and Syria

The death of Samuel Tertius Galton in 1844 led to the complete breakup of the family. His two elder sons were already leading separate lives. Darwin had contracted the first of three marriages and was living at Edstone, his mother-in-law's country house, near Stratford-upon-Avon. Erasmus continued to live on his Somerset estate and was to remain a bachelor.

Of the four daughters only Lucy had left home. She had married James Moilliet in 1832 and had three children by this time. She was in very poor health and was to live but three years longer. Elizabeth and Adèle both married within a year of their father's death, Elizabeth to Edward Wheler by whom she was to have two children, and Adèle to the Rev. Robert Bunbury. Adèle's husband died the following year leaving her with a daughter. Emma, more restless than the others, began a series of continental tours which lasted two years before she settled down with her mother at Claverdon. Emma was to play a more important role in Francis' life in the future than she had done in the past as it was she who continued the main bulk of the correspondence with him over the next 50 years. Francis also wrote to his mother but his letters were very different from those to his father. He appeared to assume, probably rightly, that his mother would not be interested in his ideas and impressions, while in the letters which his father so carefully preserved it is obvious that a warm supportive relationship existed in which his father was vicariously living the life of the scholar to which he was suited, rather than the life of the banker to which he had been committed. And yet his father had been pushing him towards a profession with which Francis was becoming steadily disillusioned. Although Francis was careful never to reveal the fact in his filial correspondence it later emerged that he hated the idea of practising medicine on account of all the humbug necessary to be a successful G.P.[1] He had inherited sufficient wealth to be independent of any profession and it was with some relief that he relinquished his almost completed medical studies.

How he spent the year after his father's death is unknown. He returned to London and took rooms at 105 Park Street where two Cambridge acquaintances were lodging, one of whom was W. F. Gibbs, later tutor to the Prince of Wales. Legal business over his father's estate must have required his presence in England, because as soon as he possibly could he left for the Middle East.

A letter from Harry Hallam indicates that Galton had asked him to come with him on a shooting trip up the Nile.

> 'I have been deliberating since I received your letter on the desirability of joining you and though finally overcome by the prospect of minor and highly conventional difficulties relating to degrees and other matters equally contemptible, I envy you exceedingly. The pleasure of shooting at so large a mark as a hippopotamus of respectable size is peculiarly attractive to the mind of the infant sportsman, who like myself has been vainly endeavouring to rid creation of an orthodox number of partridges during the last month.'[2]

Galton left London alone in mid-October 1845, and travelled through France and on to Malta. On the steamer from Malta to Alexandria he met two Cambridge friends, Montagu Boulton and Hedwith Barclay, who had been travelling together in Greece and who now intended to go up the Nile. Galton was invited to join them and their two servants, who were to act as butler and cook to the party. When they reached Cairo Galton made his contribution to their comfort by engaging a dragoman, Ali. An Arab boy aged 10, who went by the name of Bob and who acted as coffee bearer and general help, completed the entourage.

Hiring a lateen rigged Nile sailing boat they lived a life of some luxury as they made their way slowly upstream. (See Map I.)

> 'The mornings were delightful. We rolled out of our beds half awake and tumbled ourselves into the river, climbing back very wide awake indeed into the boat by help of the big rudder, to the exquisite enjoyment of the first cup of coffee and a pipe. We chattered with Bob, the captain, sailors, and others, and soon smattered in Arabic.'[3]

Barclay had had an audience with Mehemet Ali, then ruler of Egypt, and had received a firman entitling the party to enrol men from the river bank to help pull the boat against the current where it was very strong. But a little beyond the first cataract, near Korosko,* when they needed this help the men were giving precedence to a dirty-looking Egyptian boat which they claimed had a Bey on board. After a contre-

---

* Galton's spelling of place names and the names of native peoples has been retained throughout.

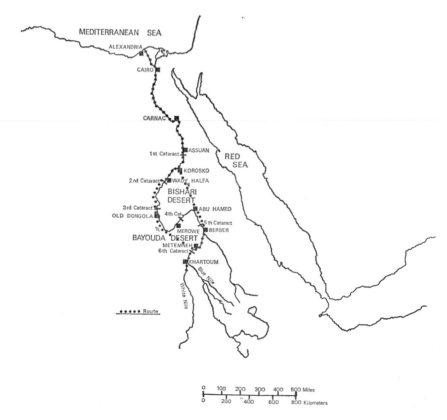

MAP I. Galton's Nile journey

temps, they invited the Bey to dinner and discovered he was Arnand
Bey, a well-known St Simonian exile in the service of Mehemet Ali. During the course of the meal the Bey suggested that they should do something a little more enterprising than the usual tourists who turned back
at Wady Halfa. Why not leave the boat and travel by camel across the
Bishari desert to Khartoum? The local sheikh, who could guide them, was
at that moment in Korosko; he was summoned to the boat.

'I shall never forget his entrance. The cabin reeked with the smells
of the recent carouse, when the door opened and there stood the tall
Sheikh, marked with sand on his forehead that indicated recent
prostration in prayer. The pure moonlight flooded the Bacchanalian
cabin, and the clear cool desert air poured in. I felt swinish in the
presence of his Moslem purity and imposing mien.'[4]

Nevertheless they came to a bargain and, leaving the boat in charge of
Bob who was to take it to Wady Halfa, they set out on camels. The first

day's journey was the customary short one in case their animals and gear were not in perfect condition and they needed to return. The following seven days were spent in the arid desert with its extremes of heat and cold. Galton awoke one cold dawn to find that Ali had removed his own coat during the night to wrap it around his shivering master. Their caravan was joined by various picturesque travellers as they slowly made their way along the old caravan trail. One mild looking Egyptian possessing little more than a sword was on his way to join a slave raiding expedition on the Abyssinian border.

> 'It was a moot question with him on each occasion when a man had been captured, whether to mutilate him at once or not. If so, the man was apt to die, and would certainly require costly attention for a long time; on the other hand, if he recovered, his market value was greatly increased.'[5]

The slave dealer consented to price Galton as if he were a light coloured African and estimated his worth, in view of the prevailing high price of the market, to be about £20.

After a journey of eight days they reached the Nile at Abu Hamed, having cut across a large bend, and continued along its banks to Berber where they were civilly received by the Governor with sherbet and the gift of a monkey. The Governor lodged them in a mud house and gave them permission to hire a boat to take them to Khartoum. The local people proved troublesome and tried to detain the boat, but Barclay took charge and cast off the boat and with one or two of the crew managed to set the sail. The remainder of the crew ran along the bank and swam out to join them. The boat was small with a 4 ft high cabin abounding with cockroaches but it sufficed to take them first to Meroue where Galton visited the mud pyramids. His name can still be seen carved in one of the temples of the forecourt.[6]

They reached Khartoum without incident and took possession of a mud hut facing the Nile. At that time Khartoum consisted of a mere group of such huts surrounding a hall where the audiences of the Pasha were held. Hearing that an extraordinary Englishman had recently arrived in Khartoum they went to call on him.

> 'We came into the presence of a white man nearly naked, as agile as a panther, with head shorn except for the Moslem tuft, reeking with butter, and with a leopard skin thrown over his shoulder.'[7]

Mansfield Parkyns was a former Trinity student who had had to leave college after some undisclosed incident and who had since lived in Abyssinia.[8] He willingly acted as their guide to Khartoum.

'The saying was that when a man was such a reprobate that he could not live in Europe, he went to Constantinople; if too bad to be tolerated in Constantinople, he went to Cairo, and thenceforward under similar compulsion to Khartoum. Half a dozen or so of these trebly refined villains resided there as slave-dealers; they were pallid, haggard, fever-stricken, profane, and obscene. Mansfield Parkyns complacently tolerated and mastered them all . . . With all their villainy there was something of interest in their talk, but I had soon quite enough of it. Still, the experience was acceptable, for one wants to know the very worst of everything as well as the very best.'[9]

In Parkyns' company they now sailed a little farther up the White Nile. The river was slow and marshy and abounding in hippopotamus. Galton was unsuccessful in his efforts to shoot one from the boat in spite of blazing away at more than forty in a single day. Boulton and Parkyns even spent a night ashore in an endeavour to shoot one, but succeeded only in killing a cow that had come down to the river to drink. Fearful of the clamour that would succeed its discovery the next day, they persuaded the crew to set sail before daybreak and returned to Khartoum.

Leaving Parkyns at Khartoum they sailed on to Metemneh where they discharged the boat and hired camels with the object of riding across the Bayouda Desert to Dongola.

They found the going very easy with plentiful water :

'We had become by that time used to camel-riding, we were well mounted and travelled even as much as eighteen hours out of the twenty-four, on more than one day. The Polar Star and the pointers of the Great Bear served as the hands of a huge sidereal clock to tell the weary time.'[10]

Galton was now in native dress, a simple white robe that left the arm and shoulder bare. The result was that he was badly sunburned. His agony was increased when he severely cut his feet trying to climb Jebel Barkal barefooted out of bravado. A vase with a representation of the God Bess on it was purchased here and another monkey from the local Pasha was added to Galton's camel load. (Unlike the *proteus* of Galton's previous journey, the monkeys did not survive longer than their first night in London, being found next morning frozen to death in one anothers' arms. The vase was given to the British Museum.)

From Dongola they rode along the left bank of the Nile to Wady Halfa, passing the beautiful little temple of Semneh where the river was so narrow that they tried to throw stones across, Galton's efforts being lamentable failures. At Wady Halfa they found their boat waiting for them in perfect order with Bob very much in command. He had actually ordered the crew to flog their captain for some offence and the men had complied. Galton comments:

> 'Such a difference between Berbers and Egyptians, you can not strike a Berber but may flog as many Egyptians and beat them with sticks as much as you like, they are thoroughly slavish.'[11]

Their voyage downstream was uneventful if unpleasant owing to the Khamseen which had begun to blow. At Cairo they hired a house and lived there a week conforming as far as possible to native custom. They then separated: Barclay returned home to Scotland, Boulton went farther east to continue his study of Arabic, and Galton accompanied by his dragoman and two pet monkeys took a steamer to Beyrout.

The first sight of the shores of the Holy Land seems to have made a deep impression on Galton; forty years later he records it as a still-living picture in his memory.[12] But the people he found to be disagreeably go-ahead and much less appealing than the more sedate Egyptians.

The countryside was attractive and he immediately began exploring from his base at Beyrout. As it was difficult to hire good riding horses he travelled inland to buy a pair for himself and Ali. He camped in style with a large tent, canteen, coffee and pipe equipment, but chose an unfortunate site intersected by ditches of stagnant water. Here he caught a sharp intermittent fever and had temporarily to forego any plans for extensive travel.

Instead he made his way to Damascus where he settled at the house of the English doctor. He took elementary lessons in Hebrew and witnessed many Jewish domestic ceremonies. It was here that Ali contracted violent dysentery and after a short illness died. Galton seems to have been much affected by his loss. Ali had been a thoughtful and faithful servant and travelling companion. His death was shortly to make Galton's return to England more precipitous than it might otherwise have been.

When the heat of summer made Damascus unpleasant, Galton took a house in Salahieh and lived in oriental style, becoming fluent in common Arabic although never mastering the script. Salahieh was a pleasant environment with public coffee-houses and gardens through which the clear river water was diverted.

In the comparative coolness of the autumn he began to tour again. He first visited Aden on the Lebanon, not far from the cedar groves, and then proceeded to Tripoli. Riding back to Beyrout he crossed tracks with Boulton who was on his way to Damascus and Bagdad. After a short and joyful reunion they parted and never met again. Boulton was killed by a chance shot during the British siege of Multan in the Punjab.

Galton had to remain at Beyrout for a few weeks as he fell ill again either with a recurrence of the earlier fever or from some other cause. There are discrepancies in the two accounts provided by Galton in (i) the unpublished account of his travels in Egypt and Syria written in 1885, and in (ii) the published account contained in his autobiography of 1908.

The autobiographical account does not seem to have been derived from the earlier document although it agrees with it on the details of his journey on the Nile. The inconsistencies occur when he reaches this period of time in Syria. According to the earlier version he caught the fever at Tripoli in the Lebanon before the meeting with Boulton in the autumn of 1846, and although it recurred over the next few years it ceased altogether with his S.W. African journey of 1851. In the later version he caught the fever soon after his first arrival in Beyrout in the Spring of 1848 and it continued to recur occasionally up to the date of writing his autobiography. Both versions agree that he contracted the illness by sleeping on low lying ground.

A letter from Montagu Boulton throws further light on the matter. His letter, in reply to one of Galton's, is dated 30 September 1846, and is addressed to Bianci's Hotel, Beyrout. Boulton's letter is curiously phrased if it is intended to refer to an unpleasant night's camping :

'What an unfortunate fellow you are, to get laid up in such a serious manner for, as you say, a few moments' enjoyment.'

The letter continues :

'I have been in treaty for the purchase of a slave, and have had several Abyssinians brought for shew, but none as yet sufficiently pretty . . . The Han Houris are looking lovelier than ever, the divorced one has been critically examined and pronounced a virgin.'[13]

Although it would be foolhardy to place any reliance on such an insubstantiality we are forced from the negligible information at our disposal to explore the possibility hinted at in Boulton's letter.

There does appear to have been a change in Galton's attitude to women after his Syrian experiences which could owe its origin to an unfortunate encounter in Beyrout. In his Cambridge letters home he refers to several occasions on which he has met attractive women. There is no trace of heterosexual interest after 1846, apart from his marriage in 1853, and for the remainder of his life his attitude to women is one of polite indifference—so much so that Darlington has referred to him as a 'natural celibate.'[14]

It would be usual to place more reliance on the earlier account of events, but the illness cannot have occurred *before* he met Boulton as Boulton obviously knew nothing of it until he received Galton's letter.

The present tentative interpretation assumes that he had two illnesses which merged in his memory into one. He actually fell ill with fever in the spring when procuring horses for his subsequent travels. The later infection of unknown origin was picked up in Beyrout in the autumn.

Being unfit, therefore, to ride to Jerusalem which he now intended to visit, he found his way to Jaffa on board an empty but dirty collier. Preferring the greater comfort of a camel he chose this unusual method of conveyance to take him to Jerusalem. His exultation at the sight of its walls was too great to be more than momentary and the city itself appeared drab and noisy.

It was while he was in Jerusalem that he planned a small expedition, the aim of which was to follow the valley of the Jordan from Tiberius to the Dead Sea. Surprisingly enough no Christian had followed the course of the Jordan since Crusader times, not on account of any great difficulties in the terrain but owing to the wars of the various tribes whose territory one would have to cross. As the tribes were momentarily at peace, Galton's plan to float down the river on a raft, accompanied by the remainder of his party riding along the bank, seemed feasible.

The raft of water skins was put together where the Jordan runs out of the Lake of Tiberius (Sea of Galilee), and he set off with an escort of horsemen who had orders to ride along the bank and to render assistance when required. He capsized almost at once to the huge amusement of his followers; a second capsize was followed by a more serious misadventure when the river swirled under overhanging boughs which knocked him off. It did not seem to be a practicable proposition at that time of the year and he was forced to relinquish his plan and to take to his horse again.

'I had to ride in Arab head dress with a fillet and my men with their clump of long spears with ostrich feathers at the top looked very well indeed. After a while we came to a great Arab encampment, that of the Emir Ruabah . . . He was civil but wary and punctilious, and wherever I went I was watched.'[15]

The omission of a Moslem ceremony, that of slitting the throat of a desert partridge he had shot but failed to kill outright, made his presence even less acceptable to the Bedouin and he was glad to be allowed to depart.

On the way back to Jerusalem Galton began to elaborate plans to have a boat brought from Jaffa to the Dead Sea which he then proposed to circumnavigate. The feat had been attempted by Captain Costigan only a few years previously but had ended with his death from sunstroke. On his arrival in Jerusalem Galton found letters awaiting him that made it advisable for him to drop the scheme.

Ali's death had brought complications. Galton believed that he had discharged his obligations in this matter by tracing Ali's wife and sending her late husband's outstanding wages and a small gift. But his charity had aroused the greed of all those who could claim the remotest kinship with the deceased and he was inundated with requests for money which became more urgent until finally an official letter arrived threatening a law suit. Galton's banker advised him to leave the country to avoid involvement in what might turn out to be a long and costly legal action.

There was another reason for leaving : his sister Adèle had written to ask his assistance in legal matters arising from the sudden death of her husband. Believing he would soon return to Syria, he set sail for Marseilles, where he spent ten days in quarantine, and then proceeded via Paris to London which he reached in November, 1846.

Although Galton had had no scientific purpose in travelling to the Near East his experiences were to prove valuable in the major exploration which he was shortly to undertake. He had acquired many of the practical skills necessary to the traveller; he had learnt how to organise a camp, how to handle unfamiliar animals, how to maintain direction by sun and stars, and how to cope with extreme temperatures. He had necessarily learned self-reliance and he had gained some experience in engaging servants and guides. Above all, he had been exposed to peoples of very different customs and beliefs.

He seems to have been from the first sympathetic towards the Arabs and their religion; it is likely that Mohammedanism appealed to Galton quite as much as Christianity had ever done. But there is no evidence that his orthodox Christian beliefs were modified by his experiences in the Near East, although a comparative attitude towards the benefits of religion may have been induced. Indeed, he appears to have contemplated a religious vocation at this time, but it may have been no more than a passing whim which followed his final decision to drop medicine. There is a reference to the matter at the end of a long letter from Harry Hallam which followed him home and from which the following extract is taken :

'My dear Galton, . . . your letter is a great work of art, worthy to be ranked with the most ingenious productions of modern times; of course I don't believe it, and am inclined to think you have been all the time in 105 Park St. concealed, and examining the map of Africa. If I really could put my faith in what you tell me I should look upon you as the real Carlylese hero, the 'coming man' of whom Tooke used to talk at the Union . . . As it is, I waver in thinking you either destined to be the greatest man of your age, or as having been the perpetrator of a gigantic hoax . . .

'Your giving up mediculeizing is a great blow : who is henceforth to tell me pleasant stories about lupus, and purpuristic elephantiasis

of the pia mater; you had much better not become a parson, but come
with me to Maimachtin in 3 or 4 years.

Ever most sincerely yours, H. F. Hallam.'[16]

The year following his return to England Galton spent at Claverdon
with his mother and Emma. He explains in his autobiography, which is
our sole source of information, that as he was inexperienced in shooting
and totally ignorant of hunting he decided to remedy these deficiencies.
His brother Darwin took over the paternal role for a time and initiated
Francis into the world of the English country gentleman. He bought a
hunter and a hack and began to hunt regularly in Warwickshire.

The following year he established himself at Leamington where he
belonged to a small and select Hunt Club.

'A more or less unfortunate fate befell most of my other companions at the Hunt Club. Many of the small party who habitually
dined there were social favourites, and two at least of them were of
more than average social rank. Five of these men contrived to ruin
themselves by betting and gambling, and to end unhappily. For all
that, they were bright companions in the heyday of their fortunes.
They lived in good style and as a rule not very prodigally, though
all had fits of recklessness. One of the most valuable qualities in a
man of moderately independent means who has to live in a society of
this kind is a carelessness to the attraction of gambling.'[17]

In the company of this fairly wild set, which included Jack Mytton
who wasted a fortune in spite of great ability and power over others,
Galton became a proficient rider and huntsman. Skill in shooting was
acquired on a Leamington friend's moor in the Highlands. At the end
of the season he made his way to John O'Groats' House, sailed over to
the Orkneys and settled in Kirkwall for the winter of 1848–9.

The next year he started before the grouse season began and spent the
whole summer in the Shetlands, boating, seal-shooting and bird-nesting.
Most of the population were expert rock climbers and Galton was taught
how to descend a cliff with a rope to rob the nests of sea birds.

'It is nervous work going over the edge of a cliff for the first time;
however, the sensation does *not* include giddiness. Once in the air,
and when confidence is acquired, the occupation is very exhilarating.
The power of locomotion is marvellous: a slight push with the
foot, or a thrust with a stick, will swing the climber twenty feet to
a side.'[18]

He finally left Shetland in the autumn of 1849 taking with him a crate
packed with an assortment of seabirds for his brother Darwin's estate.

Three quarters of the birds died of cold on the railway journey south, but the remainder throve for a while on the large freshwater lake at Edstone.

For four years these pleasant undirected activities had continued. His sporting trips had been interspersed with visits to London where he seems to have spent much time walking and riding in the company of Harry Hallam. One attempt was made at ballooning; Galton experienced some embarrassment in his compulsory descent on to the lawns of a stately mansion to surprise its owner with an unexpected and inconvenient visit.

'It will be thought . . . that I was leading a very idle life, but it was not so. I read a good deal all the time, and digested what I read by much thinking about it. It has always been my unwholesome way of work to brood much at irregular times.'[19]

The main problem over which he was brooding concerned his own future and his lack of any goals. In an attempt to obtain an objective assessment of his virtues and failings he visited the London Phrenological Institute where he had his 'bumps read' and was furnished with a report by the chief phrenologist, Donovan :

'Head : 22 inches. Temperament : Sanguine.

'Men of this class are likely to spend the earlier years of manhood in the enjoyment of what are called the lower pleasures, and particularly of those which the followers of Mahomet believe to form the chief rewards of virtue in the realms above . . . Self-will, self-regard and no small share of obstinacy form leading features in this character . . . There is much enduring power in such a mind as this— such that qualifies a man for "roughing it" in colonising . . . He is not calculated to gain good will on a brief acquaintance . . . As regards the learned professions I do not think this gentleman is fond enough of the midnight lamp to like them, or to work hard if engaged in one of them.'[20]

It can be seen that Donovan believed in committing himself, and Galton was much impressed. Throughout his life he retained a belief in the high intelligence of those, like himself, with large heads, although he came to doubt the view that specific abilities were related to skull shape.[21]

One phrase in Donovan's account stuck in Galton's mind. He had already observed in himself the physical and mental endurance necessary for rough travel. He was very soon to find the occasion on which he would be able to put this characteristic to greater use.

3

South West Africa

Little was known about Africa in 1849. The whole southern interior was a complete blank on the map and the courses of the great rivers were uncharted. The attractions of the country for those who wished to combine exploration with big game hunting were immense, and among such people Galton numbered himself. But he had never forgotten Arnand Bey's injunction to go further than the ordinary tourist and he sought a worthier object for his next expedition than the mere amusement it might provide.

He mentioned his desire to visit South Africa to a cousin, Captain Douglas Galton, who was a Fellow of the Royal Geographical Society and who arranged to introduce him to the leading members of that body. In discussions with them his vague plans were rendered more precise, and by the March of 1850 he was able to submit to the Society a detailed plan of the journey he proposed to make from Cape Town to Lake Ngami and from thence along the river said to flow out of that lake. Lake Ngami had recently been reached from the Cape by Livingstone, Oswell and Murray; Galton sought to take advantage of this new approach and to open up the country to the north towards the boundary with Portuguese Angola. Unknown to Galton and the Royal Geographical Society, Livingstone was actually at work to the north of the lake and it was well that Galton did not persevere in his original project. As it was, external events forced him to abandon Livingstone's route to Ngami and from that change other possibilities emerged.

As a second-in-command, a young Swede, Charles Andersson, was recommended to him by a shooting friend, Sir Hyde Parker. Andersson was an amateur naturalist whose main motive in accompanying Galton was to retrieve representative specimens of the flora and fauna of the area. Physically tough and energetic, he was responsible for extending Galton's explorations in future years and for achieving the two goals which Galton set himself but never reached (See Plate IV).

Articles of exchange and presents for the native people were bought before leaving. Besides guns, knives, and 1 cwt of Cavendish tobacco in 1 oz sticks—he was to wish he had taken 5 cwt—Galton stocked up with a large miscellany of the usual beads, chains, ornamental belts, bright uniforms, Jew's harps and, from Drury Lane, a fine theatrical crown,

> 'which I vowed to place on the head of the greatest or most distant potentate I should meet with in Africa.'[1]

His selection of articles was made in ignorance of their relative value in the eyes of the peoples whose lands he was to traverse, and he acquired much that was to prove useless as barter.

On 5th April 1850 Galton and Andersson set sail from Southampton aboard the *Dalhousie*, an old teak-built East Indiaman, which was incapable of beating against a head wind and which took 86 days to reach Cape Town having been swept as far west as the South American coast. Galton spent his time in reading, in learning the Bechuana language at the rate of 20 words per day, and in practising with a sextant. He had studied the theory of navigation and surveying before leaving and it was with what practice he could get on board that he hoped to achieve sufficient proficiency to record the positions of hitherto unknown landmarks.

The Royal Geographical Society had provided him with introductions to various influential people in Cape Colony, including the Governor, Sir Harry Smith, after whose wife Ladysmith was named. Sir Harry was in possession of recent news which destroyed Galton's hopes of reaching Lake Ngami overland. The Boers had broken out in open revolt and had annexed the whole breadth of habitable country north of the Orange River; they were effectively astride the main route from the Cape to Lake Ngami and were determined not to allow the passage of strangers. Possible alternative land routes ran up either coast; that to the east crossed fever stricken country which it would have been foolhardy to enter, while that to the west ran over desolate country on the edge of the Kalahari desert and would entail a four month journey by oxcart.

Another possibility was to take a boat up the east coast to Mozambique and to cut inland, but they would then have had to rely on native porters for transport and Andersson needed wagons to carry his specimens.

A boat up the west coast was a more practical proposition. Several missionary stations were established inland from Walfisch Bay along the Swakop river on the borders of Damaraland. (See Map II.) It would be necessary to cover about 550 miles to reach Lake Ngami from Walfisch Bay if Galton still wished to pursue his original objective. But Damaraland itself had never been penetrated by Europeans. The missionaries had contemplated an expedition northward through that country towards the

Cunene river which bordered Portuguese Angola. If Galton explored Damaraland he could count on every assistance from the missionaries.

Adopting this line of approach and postponing any definite decision about his route until he could obtain firsthand information from the missionaries there, Galton chartered a schooner to sail to Walfisch Bay. His basic equipment consisted of two wagons and light cart. Besides horses as mounts for himself and Andersson, and mules to pull the cart, at least

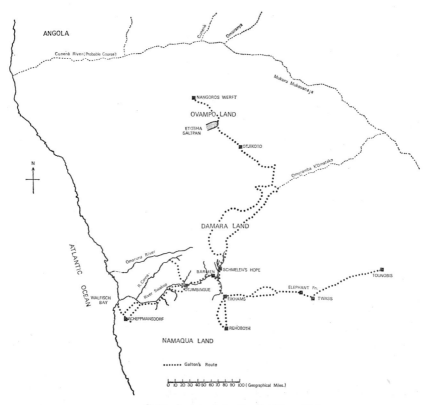

MAP II.   Galton's travels in South West Africa

60 oxen would be needed for the wagons and it was hoped to buy these latter animals from the native Namaquas, several days' journey from Walfisch Bay. Seven servants were engaged in Cape Town and after a month of preparation the party sailed to Walfisch Bay arriving in a week.

The Bay was a wide indentation on a desolate and barren piece of coast. The shore was dancing with mirage and it was only with difficulty that they could make out the one building there, a wooden shanty which served as a storehouse. A few natives appeared and a runner was dispatched the 20 miles to the nearest missionary station at Schepmannsdorf. Meanwhile, everything was landed by instalments in a dinghy. The animals swam ashore and were taken to the nearest source of water a few miles distant at Sand Fountain.

'My imagination had pictured, from its name a bubbling streamlet; but in reality it was a hole, six inches across, of green stagnant water.'[2]

The missionary and his helper arrived next day and arranged for Galton's party to stay at Schepmannsdorf. It took them three weeks to assemble the wagons and cart and with the help of the missionaries' oxen to shift all their equipment there.

The helper, Stewartson, was willing to guide the party to the next missionary station at Otjimbinguè. Stewartson had had a chequered career as a tailor, dissenting minister, and failed cattle trader. Although Galton is careful to avoid any direct criticism of the man it is obvious from his account of their journey that he did not look upon Stewartson's services as a series of unalloyed blessings.

For the journey to Otjimbinguè Galton took the mule cart and horses, while Stewartson rode on an ox and the others walked. Neither men nor animals were fit for the arduous journey across the semidesert and after a few days' journey, during which Stewartson lost his way for a time, it became imperative to rest the mules as soon as they could reach the pasture land beside the Swakop river. But the river banks turned out to be unsuitable for a camp and with some misgivings Galton took Stewartson's advice that, as no wild animal tracks had been seen, the horses and mules would be quite safe beside the river while they camped a couple of miles away. Next morning he found his misgivings justified when no animals were at first to be found and when later search revealed the remains of the larger horse and a mule.

Lions had certainly been at work and as it was thought likely that they would return Galton and Andersson decided to sit up that night with their rifles on a ledge in a cliff too steep it was thought for a lion to climb. They cut some meat off the dead animals for their own consumption and stored it temporarily on the ledge. When they returned towards nightfall Galton left his gun at the bottom of the rock and clambered up to bring down the meat which his men were to carry back to camp. A sudden cry from Stewartson warned Galton that he was in danger; the lions had returned earlier than expected and one had climbed to a position a few feet above his head and was now crouched like a cat over a mousehole.

'I *did* feel queer, but I did not drop the joint. I walked steadily down the rock, looking very frequently over my shoulder; but it was not till I came to where the men stood that I could see the round head and pricked ears of my enemy peering over the ledge under which I had been at work.'[3]

Galton had one further unpleasant experience of coming to close quarters with a lion when insufficiently armed, but again the animal did not spring. Lions were numerous in the region but were not generally troublesome to the expedition and caused little damage.

Fortunately the remaining mules had escaped the attentions of the lions and were found next day, but it was a depleted caravan that continued the journey with Galton and Andersson sharing the one remaining horse. Stewartson seemed to be unnerved by the incident and insisted that they should travel in the middle of the day and in the centre of the dried-up river bed in order to avoid marauding lions. His foolish insistence almost led to Andersson's death. Andersson was on foot in pursuit of some interesting animals and somewhat separated from the main party when he began to feel giddy. He realised that he was suffering from sunstroke and was fortunate in being able to attract Galton's attention before collapsing. The heat was certainly intense, 157° F in the sun at midday.

'This appeared quite incredible to me, but I have compared 7 thermometers of 5 different makers and they all agree, so there can be no doubt about it.'[4]

The mules soon became exhausted and incapable of more than three hours' travel a day. They finally broke down not far from Otjimbinguè and oxen were brought from the missionary station to haul the cart over the final stretch.

Otjimbinguè was beautifully situated where the Swakop river ran through a broad plain, and grass and water were in abundance. The missionary received Galton kindly but had some startling news. The nearby mission at Schmelen's Hope had recently been attacked by Namaquan Hottentots who had mutilated and murdered the local Damara tribe and had frightened the missionary into leaving. Schmelen's Hope was the *ultima Thule* of the missionaries and Galton had intended it as the starting point for his exploration proper, whether to the north or to the east. In spite of the news Galton decided to press on at least to the intermediate station at Barmen where he could obtain the latest intelligence on the movements of the Hottentots.

Before leaving Otjimbinguè, another man was recruited. He was Hans Larsen, a former sailor, who had lived for several years in the country bordering the Swakop river and who had been largely responsible for shooting off most of the game.

'I found him in the neatest of encampments, with an old sail stretched in a sailorlike way to keep the sun off, and in an enclosure of thick reeds that were cut and hedged all round. The floor was covered with sheepskin mats : shooting things, knick-knacks, and wooden vessels were hung on the forked branches of the sticks that propped up the whole . . . The style of the man was exactly what I desired, for he was quiet, sedate, but vigorous and powerfully framed, showing in all his remarks the shrewdest common sense, and evidently, from the order around him, an excellent disciplinarian.'[5]

Larsen agreed to accompany Galton as his headman and with Stewartson as a third and leaving the bulk of the safari behind they rode on to Barmen. They were mounted on oxen, Galton's first experience at riding this animal for any distance. He comments,

'I think I can sit more hours on oxback than on horseback, supposing in both cases the animals to walk. An ox's jogtrot is not very endurable, but anything faster abominable. His character is very different from that of a horse, and very curious to observe; he is infinitely the more sagacious of the two but never free from vice.'[6]

In two days they reached Barmen where the missionary from Schmelen's Hope had fled for refuge. It was difficult to estimate how many persons had been killed in the attack as the natives had scattered and dead bodies were soon devoured by hyaenas. But Galton had firsthand proof of the mutilations :

'I saw two poor women, one with both legs cut off at her ankle joints, and the other at one. They had crawled the whole way on that eventful night from Schelen's Hope to Barmen, some twenty miles. The Hottentots had cut them off after their usual habit, in order to slip off the solid iron anklets that they wear. These wretched creatures showed me how they had stopped the blood by poking the wounded stumps into the sand, . . . One of Jonker's sons, a hopeful youth, came to a child that had been dropped on the ground, and who lay screaming there, and he gouged out its eyes with a small stick.'[7]

Jonker, the most powerful of the Namaquan tribal leaders, had led the raid on Schmelen's Hope. In common with many of his senior men he was an 'Oerlam', that is, of mixed Dutch-Namaquan parentage, and was legally British having been born in Cape Colony. As a minor chief in the Orange River region he had taken his small tribe northwards to make common cause with the Namaqua in their raids on Damaraland. Now, after many successes, a large group of Namaqua under his leadership were well provided with guns and horses, obtained at the Cape in exchange for stolen Damara cattle. The Damara themselves, although living in fear of the better armed Namaqua, were not averse to retaliatory action and to fighting among themselves. Thus the whole country ahead was in turmoil and it was impossible for Galton to proceed without coming to some sort of *modus vivendi* with the various factions.

Galton's first attempt at a settlement took the form of a polite but vaguely worded letter to Jonker in which he pointed out that the Governor of the Cape had instructed Galton to express the goodwill of the government towards the native peoples and to warn the Namaqua that if they persisted in their attacks they would incur the same displeasure as had the emigrant Boers at Orange River. The concluding sentence of Galton's letter is worth quoting :

> 'I wish strongly to urge you on the behalf of common humanity and honour to make what amends you can for your late shameless proceedings. Your past crimes may profitably be atoned for by a course of upright wise and pacific policy, but if the claims of neither humanity, civilisation or honour have any weight with you perhaps a little reflection will point out some danger to your personal security.'[8]

This letter was sent by messenger to Jonker's village which was situated at the foot of a range of hills visible from Barmen.

While awaiting a reply Galton spent his time at Otjimbinguè where there was much to be done. The remaining horse and most of the mules soon died of distemper and they were now limited to oxen for transport. Luckily, Larsen was willing to sell 50 oxen and Galton bought them with some sheep and goats. Most of the party now returned to Schepmannsdorf to collect the wagons and Stewartson took the opportunity of leaving the expedition at this point.

Galton passed a month at Otjimbinguè learning the Damara language and practising with his sextant but no reply came from Jonker. Finally, in some desperation, Galton set off once more to Barmen to await developments. The reply when it came was couched in even vaguer terms than the original and agreed to nothing specific. Fearing that his whole expedition might be jeopardised by the whim of this man, Galton wrote a much more strongly worded letter in which he made clear his determination to proceed with his journey and to use force if Jonker attempted to oppose him. Another letter was dispatched to all the Damara chiefs, telling them that Galton came from a great white chief who wished them no harm but who desired to trade iron for their cattle, and asking them to permit him to cross their land.

The mission station at Barmen was a large one; besides the missionary and his family and servants, there were several Hottentot interpreters and their wives. One wife was a veritable Hottentot Venus and she was the subject of one of Galton's more unusual enquiries :

'I profess to be a scientific man, and was exceedingly anxious to obtain accurate measurements of her shape; but there was a difficulty in doing this. I did not know a word of Hottentot, and could never therefore have explained to the lady what the object of my footrule could be; and I really dared not ask my worthy missionary host to interpret for me. The object of my admiration stood under a tree, and was turning herself about to all points of the compass, as ladies who wish to be admired usually do. Of a sudden my eye fell upon my sextant; the bright thought struck me, and I took a series of observations upon her figure in every direction, up and down, crossways, diagonally, and so forth, and I registered them carefully upon an outline drawing for fear of any mistake : this being done, I boldly pulled out my measuring tape, and measured the distance from where I was to the place where she stood, and having thus obtained both base and angles, I worked out the results by trigonometry and logarithms.'[9]

Galton questioned many of the Damara who called at the station about the country to the north and east. Most of them were completely ignorant of everything outside a radius of two days' journey, until one man reported that he had been ten days' journey to the north and had seen a lake named Omanbondè.

'The name was pretty; the idea of a lake in this dusty sun-dried land was most refreshing, and, according to my temperament, I became immediately sanguine and determined to visit it.'[10]

Moreover, a highly civilised agricultural people, the Ovampo, were said to live in the same direction and this information gave an added spice to Galton's curiosity. But he remained a little sceptical about his informant's accuracy in view of the further claim that another race of men in that neighbourhood were without elbow and knee joints and, being unable to lift anything to their own mouths, had to dine in pairs, each feeding the other!

About six weeks after their departure for Schmelen's Hope Andersson and the rest of the party returned with the wagons and partially broken-in oxen. No reply had yet been received from Jonker although some of the Damara chiefs had replied in a friendly fashion to Galton's circular letter. However, no Damara would agree to accompany Galton as a guide and there was growing fear among his own men that Jonker would mount an attack if they moved on any further.

Galton now made a rapid and courageous decision. Taking Larsen and a couple of men he rode off to call at Jonker's headquarters at Eikhams (the present site of the capital, Windhoek). In order to maximise the surprise effect he wore his red hunting coat and cap, jackboots and cords, a costume unknown in those parts. After a week's ride they came to Jonker's village and urging his ox to a trot Galton charged towards the huts : a small stream was taken at a jump and he rode straight up to the largest hut and pushed the ox's head as far into the doorway as possible.

Jonker was enjoying an evening pipe and was completely overcome by Galton's sudden appearance in all his finery. With severe mien Galton began to berate him soundly in English and after a while condescended to use an interpreter. Jonker never dared to look him in the face but rapidly mumbled his assent to Galton's demands. The main requirement was for him to arrange a meeting there and then with the other Namaquan chiefs; meanwhile, Galton would commandeer a hut and wait until they were assembled.

Several meetings took place and Galton spoke to the chiefs to such good effect that they were unanimous in their desire that he should draw up a system of law to help control the common situations of cattle robbery and murder. Galton's law code, which has survived in manuscript, made the theft of oxen, when proven, punishable by 40 lashes and a fine of double the number of oxen taken. It forbade the disfigurement of women and all punishment of innocent persons. Murderers were to be put to death.

Simple as it was, this code brought peace to the area for a full year. News of Jonker's submission spread rapidly among the Damara and the way lay open for Galton to proceed towards the unknown lands of the north.*

It was not until March 1851, that Galton was ready to leave Schmelen's Hope on his way towards Lake Omanbondè. The party now numbered 28 and included native wives and children. The wives were useful additions to the expedition as they carried their husbands' baggage, constructed the sleeping huts and made their meals, leaving the men free to drive and care for the oxen.

Galton took 75 oxen, most of them being needed to pull the two wagons although 20 were destined for slaughter as were similar numbers of cows and sheep. That was meat enough for ten weeks, exclusive of game. Very

* It is arguable that in the long term Galton's peace treaty did more harm than good. As Heinrich Kleinschmidt, the missionary at Reheboth, noted in translating the treaty into Dutch:

'At present Jonker is afraid of the Englishman but how long will it last—what will remain if he has no force behind him. Tricks of this kind only do harm.'[11]

Jonker broke loose as soon as Galton had left the country and made good the time he had lost by falling on the Damara with renewed force.

little remained of their original stores; the vegetables and biscuits had all been eaten but there was still ample coffee and tea.

An early difficulty arose over the differences in eating habits among the various tribal members. Some eschewed cattle of a certain colour or sheep spotted in a particular way, and none would eat the flesh of goats. These taboos began to weaken as food became scarce and options were eliminated, and were of no consequence in the later stages of the journey. The general attitude of the Damara towards meat was another source of friction; they were not accustomed to eat it regularly but treated it as an occasion for a feast to which all were invited. As the expedition's two daily meals were composed solely of meat a radical adjustment in their attitude was necessary. When strangers in the vicinity of the camp were invited to share it, Galton's wrath was aroused as it jeopardised the future survival of the party. Superstitions about milk were also rife. Although available in abundance and the staple food of some tribes, it was almost impossible to buy it except at an exorbitant rate of exchange, such as one zebra for one gallon.

Galton appears to have had little interest in these taboos or in the reasons for their maintenance, but treats them purely as hindrances to the expedition's main purpose. Indeed, nothing about the Damara people aroused his curiosity and he was able to dismiss them in these words:

'There is hardly a particle of romance, or affection, or poetry, in their character or creed; but they are a greedy, heartless, silly set of savages.'[12]

Discipline was maintained among them by methods that must have reminded Galton of his schooldays with Dr Jeune:

'I had to hold a little court of justice on most days usually followed by corporal punishment, deftly administered. At a signal from me the culprit's legs were seized from behind, he was thrown face forward on the ground and held, while Hans applied the awarded number of whip strokes. This rough-and-ready justice became popular. Women, as usual, were the most common causes of quarrel.'[13]

Apart from the problems that arose from within the caravan, the terrain they had to cross presented its own peculiar difficulties. From the very beginning their route ran up along a ridge of jagged rock with a precipitous fall down to the Swakop river on their left. The surface was atrocious and the oxen still semi-wild. The plan of travel was to move steadily on for three hours and after that time to stop whenever they came across water; in this way they could conserve the strength of the oxen for the long haul which sooner or later they would have to undertake. The route continued to climb until they were travelling over a plateau of 6000 ft. Here they decided to make a detour to avoid an unsympathetic Damara chief who was likely to bar their passage. The detour led them over barren country covered in thick thorn bushes which forced them to travel along dried-up water courses which led in the general direction of Lake Omanbondè. It was difficult to reconcile the conflicting reports they were receiving from wandering Damara and bushmen about the size of the lake. Part of this difficulty arose over the lack of a word for 'lake' in the Damara language. It was either perfectly dry or it was 'as broad as the heavens' but at least all agreed that it contained hippopotamus.

Their own guides were exasperating as they appeared to have little notion of time or distance. Although Galton was not inclined to place much credence on his earlier informant's tale that he had made the journey to the lake in ten days, it seemed a more reasonable estimate than that of another Damara who told him that he would be an old man by the time he returned. The guides themselves seemed to predict a journey of between five days and six weeks, which was not very helpful. Part of the difficulty arose from their inability to use any numeral greater than three.

> 'When they wish to express four, they take to their fingers, which are to them as formidable instruments of calculation as a sliding-rule is to an English schoolboy. They puzzle very much after five; because no spare hand remains to grasp and secure the fingers that are required for 'units'. Yet they seldom lose oxen: the way in which they discover the loss of one, is not by the number of the herd being diminished, but by the absence of a face they know.'[14]

In this connection Galton noted that their language was very rich in descriptive terms for cattle, with every imaginable variation in colour patterns being nameable. In fact there were more than 1000 words to describe the different colours and markings of animals. He adds:

> 'It is not strong in the cardinal virtues; the language possessing no word at all for gratitude; but on looking hastily over my dictionary I find fifteen that express different forms of villainous deceit.'[15]

After one month's travel they finally reached a hilltop below which Omanbondè was said to lie. In great excitement they pressed forward and were struggling through a large field of dry reeds when they realised that the guides were loitering behind and seemed to be looking about for something. In one of the driest years known, the lake, which was a long reach of the broad Omoramba river, had completely dried up and their present field of reeds was where the lake should have been located.

The men had been promised a fortnight's rest beside the lake with shooting and fishing. Galton was able to suppress an incipient revolt with gifts of assegais and calico for new shirts; these were sufficient to keep the men with him as he made ready to leave the land of the Damara and to enter that of the Ovampo.

Not all the party were able to visit that fertile country. As they reached the northernmost limit of Damaraland one of the wagons came to a halt with a broken axle. They were forced to make camp on the spot; fortunately, they were near water, trees, and a tribe of friendly Damara. Timber was found to make a new axle but as the wood had to be seasoned there was no question of that wagon proceeding farther at that time. Larsen undertook to remain behind in charge of the main party and to see to the repair work while Andersson and three men accompanied Galton on ride-oxen towards Ovampoland.

A little after they started they met a caravan of 24 Ovampo on their way to buy cattle from the Damara. Galton was struck by their appearance:

'They were ugly, bony men, with strongly marked features, and dressed with a very funny scantiness of attire. Their heads were shaved, and one front tooth was chipped out. They carried little light bows three and a half feet long, and a small and well made assegai in one hand. On their backs were quivers, each holding from ten to twenty well-barbed and poisoned arrows, and they carried a dagger-knife in a neat sheath, which was either fixed to a girdle round the waist, or else to a band that encircled the left arm above the elbow. Their necks were laden with necklaces for sale, and every man carried a long narrow smoothed pole over his shoulder, from either end of which hung a quantity of packages. These were chiefly little baskets holding iron articles of exchange, packets of corn for their own eating, and water bags.'[16]

Although polite the Ovampo insisted that Galton's small party should wait until they had finished their bartering and that they would then guide them back to Ovampoland. It took two weeks of travel over an uninhabited country of barren plains and thorn bushes before they reached the southern limit of the Ovampo people. En route they passed a remarkable small lake, Otchikoto. There were various superstitions about this deep bucket-shaped hole which was supposed to be bottomless and bewitched so that no living thing could survive immersion in its waters. In order to dispel the first of these illusions Galton used a plumb line and sounded the depth from overhanging cliffs. His measurement of 180 ft has been confirmed on several occasions since. Strangely enough, his judgment of the width of the lake (400 ft) appears to have been a gross underestimate.[17] To test the efficacy of the magic he and Andersson

stripped and swam all about the lake to the astonishment and suspicion
of the Ovampo who had never seen a person swim. They emerged
refreshed and still alive, Galton having inscribed his name on the rock
a little above the surface level : it was reported still to be legible in 1908.[18]

Their journey now took them past the Etosha salt pan, one of the
largest in the world and then quite unknown to geographers. The
boundary of Ovampoland was unmistakable : suddenly the thick thorn
bushes ceased and they emerged into large fields of yellow corn surrounded
by dense timber trees and high palms. The narrow roads wound through
the stubble and it was as well that they were mounted on oxen as there
would have been no room for the wagons. Homesteads were scattered
about with about three to every square mile and there were no villages.
The land was most uniform in appearance and Galton realised that he
would never find his way back without guides.

After a day's travel the Ovampo ordered them to camp near a fine
clump of trees a quarter of a mile from the king's palisade. After a great
deal of trouble the oxen were allowed down to the wells but there was
no place for them to feed. Everyone ignored them and Galton had suspicions that the Ovampo policy was to keep his oxen in low condition
so that he might be less independent.

After several days the king emerged from the palisade and waddled
down to meet them surrounded by courtiers.

> 'I hardly knew what to do or what to say for he took no notice
> of an elegant bow that I made to him, so I sat down and continued
> writing my journal till the royal mind was satisfied. After five or six
> minutes Nangoro walked up, gave a grunt of approbation, and
> poked his sceptre into my ribs in a friendly sort of manner, and then
> sat down . . . Nangoro had quite a miniature court about him;
> three particularly insinuating and well-dressed Ovampo were his
> attendants in waiting; they were always at his elbow and laughed
> immoderately whenever he said anything funny, and looked grave
> and respectful whenever he uttered anything wise, all in the easiest
> and most natural manner.'[19]

The Ovampo now became more friendly and Galton obtained the
impression of a kindhearted, cheerful and domestic people. However, his
relationship with Nangoro remained distant as he made one social gaffe
after another. Although the king was moderately pleased with his gift of
an ox, he requested a cow as well. The other presents were quite inappropriate :

> 'It would look as *outré* for an Ovampo to wear any peculiar orna-
> ment as it would for an Englishman to do so. The sway of fashion

is quite as strong among the negroes as among the whites; and my
position was that of a traveller in Europe, who had nothing to pay
his hotel bill with but a box full of cowries and Damara sandals.'[20]

When invited to a meal Galton refused to take part in a cleansing
ritual in which the host gargled water and ejected it over the guest's
face. As this technique had been devised by Nangoro himself as a counter-
charm against witchcraft, Galton's unclean presence at the table led to
some constraint.

The travellers were invited to the nightly dance held by Nangoro for
the élite of Ovampoland. In his account of the proceedings Andersson
claims that they took no part in the dancing but spent their time gazing
at the Ovampo women.[21] Galton, on the other hand, describes stamping
around the courtyard to the beat of a tomtom and suggests, by omission,
that he was impervious to the charms of the women :

'[The women] hummed sentimental airs all day long, swaying
themselves about to the tune, and completely ruined the peace of
mind of my too susceptible attendants.'[22]

Galton's sexual unsusceptibility was the cause of his greatest offence
to Nangoro who hospitably presented him with the Princess Chipanga
as a temporary wife.

'I found her installed in my tent in negress finery, raddled with
red ochre and butter, and as capable of leaving a mark on anything
she touched as a well-inked printer's roller. I was dressed in my one
well-preserved suit of white linen, so I had her ejected with scant
ceremony.'[23]

Matters were slightly improved when Galton produced the Drury Lane
crown which he solemnly placed on Nangoro's head while discoursing on
the importance of the ceremony in white tribal circles. Nangoro, while
pleased with the effect in Galton's looking-glass, could not believe in the
existence of any country inhabited solely by whites whom he considered
comparable to rare migratory animals. Neither was he satisfied that they
were white all over and one of Galton's men had to strip repeatedly to
convince the many doubters.

Nevertheless the Ovampo were much more sophisticated than the
Damara. They used beautifully worked cooking utensils and weapons.
They could count to the hundreds and had more consistent ideas of
distance than those Galton had encountered earlier. It was clear from
their talk that a great river lay within four days' journey to the north.
Galton was right in his assumption that the Ovampo were describing the
Cunene river over which they carried on a little local trade with the

natives in Portuguese territory. The possible commercial importance of the river was great, if it were navigable, as it would give direct access to Ovampoland, and enable traders as well as missionaries and other agents of European civilisation to penetrate to the centre of Africa. (A hope that was never realised as the river proved unnavigable.)

The short journey to the river over easy terrain would have been well within their normal compass but the position of his party was becoming increasingly precarious. After a week's camp with no proper foodstuffs and little water the oxen were very weak. Their own food supply was dwindling and their articles of exchange were reduced to a few handfuls of beads. Galton approached Nangoro for permission to leave but could obtain no direct answer for several days. He then received an order that he was to make his farewell to the king and to leave the following day but only on condition that he followed the route by which he had entered the country from the south. Sensibly he decided to yield to the king's demand, and with regret at relinquishing a worthwhile objective coupled with relief at escaping the king's restraint Galton allowed his party to be guided through the rich lands of the Ovampo, across the barren border country, back to the place where they had left the broken wagon.

The place was quite deserted and they had to travel on for five anxious days, before they met Larsen and found nothing amiss. He had moved camp to avoid thieving bushmen in the vicinty; the wagon had been mended, sheep had been bought and the oxen were thriving.

In good spirits they travelled south by the more direct route avoiding their earlier detour as they had heard that the hostile chief was now in a distant part of his territory. Game was now abundant and they fed well. No incident occurred to slow them down over the last stretch of their journey. Galton calculated the return distance to be 462 miles which they covered in 49 days arriving at Schmelen's Hope five months after leaving.

It was now a year since Galton had left Cape Town and 16 months since he had left England. In that time he had received little news of the outside world. One English newspaper had been brought to Walfisch Bay by a settler and had been passed along the chain of missionary stations. But no letters had come from home nor were any to be expected for another four months when the next boat from the Cape arrived at Walfisch Bay. Galton decided that he would leave on that boat and occupy the interval in exploring the country to the east towards Lake Ngami.

Galton claimed to be indifferent about reaching the lake itself as he had heard that the country was unhealthy and the people hostile.* Besides, it was now two years since its discovery and it had been well explored

* Andersson comments that he was amazed to read this statement of Galton's; as far as he was concerned the lake had always been the main goal of the expedition.[24]

III   Francis Galton at Cambridge

iv   Charles Andersson

from the south. But it was not known whether it could be reached from Schmelen's Hope. A guide was willing to take them as far as Elephant Fountain which was the furthermost point east reached in the past by missionaries and traders, although no wagon had gone that way for years. Beyond Elephant Fountain there was said to be impassable desert.

Again Larsen remained behind; he took one wagon down to Walfisch Bay to bring back articles of exchange left in store there. Galton, Andersson and a small party of eight men took the other wagon.

Conditions were much as they had been on the trip to the north with a scarcity of water and uncertainty over the way, but they had become more confident and efficient in dealing with the usual run of emergencies. They arrived at Elephant Fountain in twelve days. The place had acquired its name from the enormous number of elephant tusks that had been found there, enough it was said to fill two wagons. One of the Namaquan Hottentot leaders, Amiral, was camped there with forty of his men and the two parties joined up for a shooting expedition.

Although Galton had triangulated the country to within a short distance of Elephant Fountain there were now no landmarks to be seen and he had to be content with lunar observations made with a large sextant for which he had contrived a stand. The same problem had arisen on his northward journey where the triangulations had ceased before leaving Damaraland.

Galton left his wagon at Elephant Fountain in the care of some of his men and taking to ride-oxen, he, Andersson and Amiral rode on to Twas which was the farthest point east known to Amiral. Ahead of them lay an arid plain which took them 20 hours to cross before they emerged suddenly into ideal big game country. Crowds of bushmen were encamped around a watering place, known as Tounobis, and Galton's party joined them. The soft ground was covered with a great variety of animal tracks and they soon began to enjoy excellent shooting, especially of the large white rhinoceros (now almost extinct).

They remained a week at Tounobis enjoying the bushmen's stories of the animals, real and fabulous, that lived around Lake Ngami. Two of the animals described in detail in these stories certainly resembled the unicorn and the cockatrice. The former had the spoor of a zebra and the horn of a gemsbok but mounted centrally on its forehead; it was almost certainly an inaccurate description of an oryx. The latter was some kind of tree snake with the comb of a guinea fowl and a cry like the clucking of a hen, but without the legendary wings.

It was only a few days' travel to the lake but they were warned that it would be a very severe ordeal as the year was so dry. Their informants were correct, as Andersson confirmed in his later travels. There would have been no water until they had travelled at least $3\frac{1}{2}$ days from Tounobis,

c

and such a journey would have been difficult even for fresh oxen. Galton decided that they could not survive any worsening of the conditions, and, as Amiral also wished to return, the whole party left Tounobis to travel back the way they had come.

The journey back through Schmelen's Hope to Barmen, a total distance of 311 miles, was uneventful and they found Larsen waiting there for them. It remained for Galton to divide up his possessions between Andersson and Larsen, both of whom were remaining in the country, and to make his way to Walfisch Bay, there to await the Cape Town schooner. It arrived in early January and he reached England in April 1852, two years to the day from leaving it.

A short account of his journey and a sketch map of his route from Walfisch Bay to the interior had been sent from Africa to the Royal Geographical Society. It reached London two months before he did; thus the geographers were able to assess the merits of his work before he appeared in person before them.

4

Marriage. 'The Art of Travel'

Galton arrived home to find his family in good health and eager to welcome him. But there was bad news to limit his enjoyment: Harry Hallam had died in Italy soon after Galton had left for Africa. Galton took an early opportunity to visit the church at Clevedon where several members of that unfortunate family were buried and kneeling in front of a commemorative tablet he broke down and wept without restraint for the greater part of an hour.[1]

He had also to forsake Julia Hallam's companionship. She had married barely two months previous to his arrival in England.

Saddened by the double loss and not in the best of health, Galton soon sought a respite from the round of social engagements that had greeted his return. He was glad to accept an invitation from his friend, Sir Hyde Parker, to sail and fish in Norway during the summer of 1852, but he was still not fit on his return and after watching in cold weather the funeral of the Duke of Wellington he found that he was hardly able to stand. He returned to Claverdon to be nursed by his mother and Emma. By Christmas he was much improved, and the three Galtons went to Dover to see the winter through.

It was at a Twelfth Night party in Dover that Galton first met Louisa Butler, the eldest daughter of the Rev George Butler and a member of an academically distinguished family. Her father had been Senior Wrangler at Cambridge and Head Master of Harrow before his present position as Dean of Peterborough. Her youngest brother, Montagu, was Senior Classic at Cambridge and after succeeding his father at Harrow was to become Dean of Gloucester and Master of Trinity College, Cambridge. Her three other brothers all took first class degrees; George and Arthur then followed the family tradition and became headmasters of public schools, while Spencer became a barrister. (The family has retained its distinction to the present day, the Master of Trinity, Lord Butler, being the grandson of Spencer.)

A few jottings in a diary of 1853 reveal that he was invited to four more parties at the Butlers', who were staying next door, followed on 12th February by a small dinner party at a Mr Winthrop's which included Louisa and himself with two other guests. That he was being paired with Louisa after only a month's acquaintance speaks for a rapid courtship. The diary restricts itself to laconic if frequent entries: 'Walked with Miss Butler.'[2]

On 22nd March Galton left for London; during his stay in Dover he had completed the first part of the manuscript of a full-length book of his travels and it was time to see John Murray, the publisher. A few weeks later Louisa passed through London on her return to Peterborough and Galton took her on an outing to see the Crystal Palace, where they became engaged.

Galton now wrote formally to Louisa's father to request her hand and heard in the affirmative on 23rd April. In the following week the second part of his book was completed and in high spirits he set off for Peterborough arriving on Saturday evening, 30th April: to find that the Dean had suddenly died earlier in the day and that the wedding would have to be postponed.

In the meantime the Royal Geographical Society had decided that Galton's journey merited one of their two annual gold medals.

In the words of the citation it was awarded

'for having at his own cost and in furtherance of the expressed desire of the Society, fitted out an expedition to explore the centre of South Africa, and for having so successfully conducted it through the countries of the Namaquas, the Damaras, and the Ovampo (a journey of about 1700 miles), as to enable this Society to publish a valuable memoir and map in the last volume of the Journal, relating to a country hitherto unknown; the astronomical observations determining the latitude and longitude of places having been most accurately made by himself.'[3]

In presenting Galton with the medal Sir Roderick Murchison, the R.G.S. President, commented:

'So long as Britain produces travellers of such spirit, resolution, conduct and accomplishments as you possess, we may be assured that she will lead the way in advancing the bounds of geographical knowledge.'[4]

This recognition of the geographical merit of Galton's travels gave him an established position in the scientific world as well as within the Royal Geographical Society. His election to the Council of that body in 1854 was followed by election to the Athenaeum Club on the grounds of scientific distinction. The French Geographical Society now awarded him their Silver Medal and he was made a Fellow of the Royal Society in 1856.

The full account of Galton's journey appeared in the early summer of 1853 with the title, *Tropical South Africa*.[5] The book contains a lively account of the expedition omitting the more technical details suitable for the earlier paper communicated to the R.G.S. There are, as we have seen, some small discrepancies with Andersson's account of their journey, but it is obvious from both books that a warm relationship existed between the two men, similar to that between Speke and Grant on their later more significant travels.

Galton's book is lacking in any description of the flora and fauna of the country, although his observations of the behaviour of his pack and ride oxen were to form the basis of a later paper on the nature of gregariousness. There is also no evidence of the type of detailed anthropological interest shown by Richard Burton. Galton was at this time very much the budding geographer fascinated by instrumental observation. Considered as an explorer's journal written in the traditional manner it was a useful addition to contemporary knowledge of South West Africa. A second edition was not called for until 1889 when it appeared in the Minerva Library of Famous Books. No modern reprint is currently available.

Of the various congratulatory letters he received upon the book's first publication he prized most the response from Charles Darwin.

> 'I last night finished your volume with such lively interest, that I cannot resist the temptation of expressing my admiration at your expedition, and at the capital account you have published of it . . . What labours and dangers you have gone through : I can hardly fancy how you can have survived them, for you did not formerly look very strong, but you must be as tough as one of your own African waggons ! . . . I live at a village called Down near Farnborough in Kent, and employ myself in Zoology; but the objects of my study are very small fry, and to a man accustomed to rhinoceroses and lions, would appear infinitely insignificant.'[6]

With the book finished and three months having elapsed since the Dean's death, Frank and Loui, as they called each other, were free to marry. Although their courtship had been brief Galton had given much thought to the step he was about to take. His attachment to Louisa does not appear to have been a romantic or sexual one. She was evidently plain and although some facial resemblance can be detected between the couple he was more handsome as a man than she beautiful as a woman. (See Plate V.) She was certainly intellectually gifted and was to follow with interest much of her future husband's research. But perhaps of equal importance to the personal qualities of Louisa herself was the intellectual ambience that surrounded her. In the early 1850s Galton had few intellectuals as close friends. Certainly the situation was soon to be remedied by the consequences of the accolade of the Royal Geographical Society, but in the meantime the Butler family served to supply the deficiencies of his own, and they and their friends began to enlarge Galton's intellectual circle. His ties with his wife's relatives, cemented more closely by the untimely death of the Dean, were to remain strong over many years and were to lead to much interchange of visits.

Galton was undoubtedly thinking back to his own situation when in his old age he wrote :

'I protest against the opinions of those sentimenal people who think that marriage concerns only the two principals; it has in reality the wider effect of an alliance between each of them and a new family.'[7]

On 1st August Francis and Louisa were married and left immediately for the continent. Their honeymoon tour took them first to Switzerland which was to remain their favourite choice for subsequent holidays. They moved on to Florence and Rome, mainly in order to satisfy Louisa's artistic curiosity, and wintered there. In the spring of 1854 they returned via Paris to temporary lodgings in London. Galton's diary lists 14 possible addresses with rents ranging from 3 to 8 gns a week. The final choice was a Mrs Hilton's at 11 Portugal Street, off Kingsway, where for 6 gns a week they could enjoy the services of a cook, housemaid, landlady and boy to run errands. They took it for three months but then found more suitable longterm accommodation at 55 Victoria Street, S.W.1.

Servant trouble, which was to dog Louisa all her life, now began. Galton notes : 'Harrison goes. Mrs Joyce comes,' and two days later : 'Mrs Joyce goes.' He drafts out an advertisement to meet their requirements :

'Man as cook and general house servant and to go out with carriage; woman to attend to housework and wait on lady. Can she dress hair?'[8]

It is not known whether their requirements were met immediately; probably not, as they left for a seven month holiday within a few weeks of taking the Victoria Street house.

Before going Galton wrote a short piece for the 1854 volume of the R.G.S. *Journal*, which on this occasion was entirely devoted to the needs of travellers.[9] His contribution was merely to list and to describe the uses of various scientific and mapping instruments which it would be most valuable to pack for a journey into unknown country. Under the title

Hints for Travellers it was to become the Society's most successful publication; with its contents expanding from edition to edition, it is still in print today. Galton was to write for and jointly edit the next two editions and to edit alone the fourth edition of 1880, described by Clements Markham, then R.G.S. Secretary, as a 'very handy little square book of 104 pages [which] had a rapid and extensive sale.'[10]

For their holiday the Galtons toured in France in some style without any attempt at economy. A stay in Chambord cost Galton £104 and included riding lessons, fishing tackle and expensive cigars. They moved on to Blois, Nantes and Avranches where they were joined by Charles Andersson.

Andersson had remained a further year in Africa principally in order to investigate the natural history of the countries Galton had explored. He had succeeded in extending Galton's route as far as Lake Ngami and had since returned to London in search of a publisher for his own book which comprised a parallel account of the journey with Galton supplemented by details of his subsequent solitary expedition. He had reached London with a small amount of capital which he was in process of exhausting. Andersson asked Galton for several loans of money during this period, but Galton steadfastly refused. As Galton wrote in reply to one of these requests :

'I for my part cannot help you in the way you wish. I have nothing like fortune sufficient to do so. If you had struggled hard with a scrupulous economy, and if as Sir James Brooke did, you had even worked your passage home like a common sailor, if you had lived thriftily and frugally determining to keep as much as possible of what you had so well earned in order to win more, the world would have respected you the more highly. The example you would have set the world would have been a noble one, but a fatal pride has made you take another course and placed you, as I am sure you must acknowledge in a very false position. We all of us make our mistakes in life. The true plan is to use faults as lessons to make us wiser.'[11]

Galton did, however, help Andersson to receive recognition from the Royal Geographical Society and he was presented with a box of scientific instruments in 1855 which he took with him on his subsequent explorations in South West Africa.[12]

Galton had an ulterior motive in inviting Andersson to Avranches which perhaps explains his *largesse* in sending Andersson £35 to cover the cost of the journey. He had begun to make notes for a book for travellers which was to go far beyond the short technical contributions he had made to the R.G.S. publication. The idea for the book had occurred to him during his African journey when he had suffered from a dearth of the kind of information he now began to compile. Andersson and he were able to recapitulate their African experiences together and to recall much of the bushcraft taught them by Hans Larsen. The book began to take shape and various provisional titles scribbled in a diary indicate what he had in mind: *Hints for Australian Emigrants; Bushcraft; The Science of Travel; Hints on Rough Travel.*[13]

On his return to London he began intensive work on the book, studying the 15 volumes of *Pinkerton's Travels,* writing and talking to as many travellers as he could, and using the facilities of the Royal Geographical Society to the greatest advantage. John Murray agreed to publish the book and the first edition appeared within the year under the title, *The Art of Travel; or, Shifts and Contrivances Available in Wild Countries.*

> 'If you have health, a great craving for adventure, at least a moderate fortune, and can set your heart on a definite object, which old travellers do not think impracticable, then—travel by all means.'

With these words Galton begins his little book which was to reach five editions, each more crammed with information than its predecessors. No additions occurred after the fifth edition of 1872, although three further editions were issued. All quotations are from the fifth edition which is the most easily procurable in an excellent modern reprint.[14] It is an impossible book to summarise as the information is so tightly packed and ranges from methods of bivouacing to the layout of log books, from seeing under water to medical remedies. There are notable deficiencies in its anthropological and biological coverage, and in its later editions the mathematical excesses must have worried a few non-numerate travellers who lost their way and who had to understand eight closely reasoned pages before they could begin to search for the best path. Nevertheless, the practicality of the book is enormous, as the following sample of extracts may illustrate.

A condition for success in travel

'Interest yourself chiefly in the progress of your journey, and do not look forward to its end with eagerness. It is better to think of a return to civilisation, not as an end to hardship and a haven from ill, but as a close to an adventurous and pleasant life.'

Medicine

Doctors: 'The traveller who is sick, away from help, may console himself with the proverb, that "though there is a great difference between a good physician and a bad one, there is very little between a good one and none at all." '

Emetics: 'For want of proper physic, drink a charge of gunpowder in a tumblerful of warm water or soap suds, and tickle the throat.'
Blistered feet: 'To prevent the feet from blistering, it is a good plan to soap the inside of the stocking before setting out, making a thick lather all over it. A raw egg broken into a boot, before putting it on, greatly softens the leather . . . After some hours on the road, when the feet are beginning to be chafed, take off the shoes, and change the stockings; putting what was the right stocking on the left foot, and the left stocking on the right foot.'
Wasp stings: 'The oil scraped out of a tobacco pipe is a good application.'

Measurement

Rate of walking: 'Observe the number of paces (n) taken in 5·7 seconds: let i be the number of inches (to be subsequently determined at leisure) in a single pace; then $\frac{ni}{100}$ is the rate (in statute miles per hour).'
Angles: 'I find that a capital substitute for a very rude sextant is afforded by the outstretched hand and arm. The span between the middle finger and the thumb subtends an angle of about 15°, and that between the forefinger and the thumb an angle of $11\frac{1}{4}°$, or one point of the compass . . . The sun travels through 15° in each hour; and therefore, by "spanning" along its course, as estimated, from the place where it would stand at noon (aided in this by the compass), the hours before or after noon, and similarly after sunrise or before sunset, can be instantly reckoned.'

Rivers

Swimming with a horse: 'Lead him along a steep bank, and push him sideways, suddenly into the water: having fairly started him, jump in yourself, seize his tail, and let him tow you across. If he turns his head with the intention of changing his course, splash water in his face with your right or left hand, as the case may be, holding the tail with one hand and splashing with the other; and you will, in this way, direct him just as you like.'
Fording: 'In fording a swift stream, carry heavy stones in your hand, for you require weight to resist the force of the current . . . Rivers cannot be forded if their depth exceeds 3 feet for men or 4 feet for horses . . . Fords should be tried for where the river is broad rather than where it is narrow, and especially at those places where there are bends in its course . . . By entering the stream at one promontory, with the intention of leaving it at another, you ensure that at all events the beginning and end of your course shall be in shallow water.'

Clothing

To carry a coat : 'There are two ways. The first is to fold it small and strap it to the belt (so that it lies in the small of the back). The second is the contrivance of a friend of mine, an eminent scholar and divine, who always employs it in his vacation rambles. It is to pass an ordinary strap, once round the middle of the coat and a second time round both the coat and the left arm just above the elbow, and then to buckle it . . . A coat carried in this way will be found to attract no attention from passers by.'

Shirt sleeves : 'When you have occasion to tuck up your shirt sleeves, recollect that the way of doing so is, not to begin by turning the cuffs inside out, but outside in—the sleeves must be rolled up inwards, towards the arm, and not the reverse way. In the one case, the sleeves will remain tucked up for hours without being touched; in the other, they become loose every five minutes.'

Wet clothes at sea : 'Captain Bligh, who was turned adrift in an open boat after the mutiny of the "Bounty", writes thus about his experience : "With respect to the preservation of our health, during a course of 16 days of heavy and almost continual rain, I would recommend to every one in a similar situation the method we practised, which is to dip their clothes in the salt water and to ring them out as often as they become filled with rain . . . it felt more like a change of dry clothes than could well be imagined." '

Keeping clothes dry in rain : Galton follows Mansfield Parkyns in suggesting the simple solution of taking off all one's clothes and sitting on them.

Fire

Flints : 'If we may rely on a well known passage in Virgil, concerning Aeneas and his comrades, fire was sometimes made in ancient days by striking together two flints, but I confess myself wholly unable to light tinder with flints alone, and I am equally at a loss to understand what were the "dry leaves" that they are said in the same passage to have used for tinder.'

Lighting a match : 'In a steady downfall of rain, you may light a match for a pipe under your horse's belly. If you have paper to spare, it is a good plan to twist it into a hollow cone; to turn the cone with its apex to the wind; and immediately after rubbing the match, to hold it inside the cone. The paper will become quickly heated by the struggling flame and will burst into a miniature conflagration, too strong to be puffed out by a single blast of air.'

Fuel : 'There is a knack in finding firewood. It should be looked for under bushes; the stump of a tree that is rotted nearly to the ground has often a magnificent root, fit to blaze throughout the night.'

Food

Pemmican: 'Pemmican is a mixture of about five-ninths of pounded dry meat to four-ninths of melted or boiled grease; it is put into a skin bag or tin can whilst warm and soft . . . Wild berries are sometimes added.'*

Bones: 'Contain a great deal of nourishment, which is got at by boiling them, pounding their ends between two stones, and sucking them. There is a revolting account in French history, of a besieged garrison of Sancerre . . . digging up the graveyards for bones as sustenance.'

Flesh from live animals: 'The truth of Bruce's well known tale of the Abyssinians and others occasionally slicing out a piece of a live ox for food is sufficiently confirmed . . . When I travelled in South-West Africa, at one part of my journey a plague of bush-ticks attacked the roots of my oxen's tails. Their bites made festering sores, which ended in some of the tails dropping bodily off . . . The animals did not travel the worse for it. Now oxtail soup is proverbially nutritious.'

Tea: 'To prepare tea for a very early breakfast, make it over night, and pour it away from the tea leaves, into another vessel . . . In the morning, simply warm it up. Tea is drunk at a temperature of 140°, or 90° above an average night temperature of 50°. It is more than twice as easy to raise the temperature up to 140° than to 212°, letting alone the trouble of tea making.'

To filter muddy water: 'Suck the water through your handkerchief by putting it over the mouth of your mug.'

To find honey when bees are seen: 'Dredge as many bees as you can, with flour from a pepperbox; or else catch one of them, tie a feather or a straw to his leg, which can easily be done (natives thrust it up into his body), throw him into the air, and follow him as he flies slowly to his hive.'

Hiding objects

Hiding small things: 'It is easy to make a small *cache* by bending down a young tree, tying your bundle to the top, and letting it spring up again.'

---

* As a domestic equivalent of pemmican Galton recommends a picnic lunch of two slices of bread half an inch thick, an equally thick slice of cheese and a handful of raisins.[15]

Secreting jewels: 'Before going to a rich but imperfectly civilised country, travellers sometimes buy jewels and bury them in their flesh. They make a gash, put the jewels in, and allow the flesh to grow over them as it would over a bullet . . . A traveller who was thus provided would always have a small capital to fall back upon, though robbed of everything he wore.'

Animals

The rush of an enraged animal: 'Unthinking persons talk of the fearful rapidity of a lion or tiger's spring . . . But the speed of a springing animal is undeniably the same as that of a ball, thrown so as to make a flight of equal length and height in the air . . . If charged, you must keep cool and watchful, and your chance of escape is far greater than non-sportsmen would imagine.'

Dogs kept at bay: 'A watchdog usually desists from flying at a stranger when he seats himself quietly on the ground, like Ulysses.'

Management of savages*

General remarks: 'A frank, joking but determined manner joined with an air of showing more confidence in the good faith of the natives than you really feel, is the best.'

Feast days: 'Interrupt the monotony of travel, by marked days, on which you give extra tobacco and sugar to the servants . . . Recollect that a savage cannot endure the steady labour that we Anglo-Saxons have been bred to support. His nature is adapted to alternations of laziness and of severe exertion. Promote merriment, singing, fiddling, and so forth, with all your power.'

Women

Kindliness: 'Wherever you go, you will find kind-heartedness amongst women. Mungo Park is fond of recording his experiences of this; but I must add, that he seems to have been an especial favourite with the sex.'

Strength: 'It is the nature of women to be fond of carrying weights; you may see them in omnibuses and carriages, always preferring to hold their baskets or their babies on their knees, to setting them down on the seats by their sides. A woman whose modern dress

---

* The diary in which some of the ideas for *The Art of Travel* were first drafted contains a more punitive approach to the African servant problem:

'1. Stop tobacco; 2. Stop food; 3. Flog . . . Do not hit at a nigger's head. If wrestling, press at his spine if taken by the throat . . . Boiling water, hot sand on their naked bodies . . . Don't take counsel of the men or confide your thoughts to them. The discipline of shipboard is a good general guide for that of an expedition.'[16]

includes, I know not how many cubic feet of space, has hardly ever pockets of sufficient size to carry small articles; for she prefers to load her hands with a bag or other weighty object.'

On concluding the journey

'When your journey draws near its close, resist restless feelings; make every effort before it is too late to supplement deficiencies in your various collections; take stock of what you have gathered together, and think how the things will serve in England to illustrate your journey or your book . . . Make presents of all your travelling gear and old guns to your native attendants, for they will be mere litter in England, costly to house and attractive to moth and rust; while in the country where you have been travelling, they are of acknowledged value, and would be additionally acceptable as keepsakes.'

While some of the book is obviously of only quaint and historical interest, as a whole it is still a useful compendium which has not been effectively superseded. Armed with the practical knowledge contained in the book—and justice has not here been done to the exhaustive treatment Galton gives to such important topics as shelter, bedding, conveyances, navigation, hunting and fishing—prospective travellers could contemplate with realism tempered with optimism a journey into unexplored territory.

One immediate practical use for many of Galton's suggestions lay in their application to the life of the soldier on campaign. The outbreak of the Crimean War in 1855 had revealed the helplessness of the British soldier in the face of primitive conditions. Galton offered to help combat their ignorance by giving lectures on techniques of survival. But his letters to the War Office were ignored until he ventured to write to the Prime Minister, Lord Palmerston, who obtained immediate action.

Two huts were placed at Galton's disposal at the newly founded camp at Aldershot; one hut was turned into a museum stocked with models and drawings of contrivances, the other served as a workshop. In July 1855, Galton took a house, Oriel Cottage, about two miles away from the camp and walked there and back each day. For three months he lectured three times a week, combining the lectures with practical demonstrations of such skills as hole digging with a stick, fire making, soap and candle making and so on. He then took a break and, reunited with Louisa and accompanied by his sister Emma, went to Paris until Christmas. He returned to complete a further three months of lectures at the camp.

Unfortunately, the inertness shown at the highest military level was accompanied by a similar lack of interest among the lower officer ranks : on no occasion did attendance at his lectures exceed 15 and it was often reduced to 3, a number which invariably included his faithful brother, Erasmus, who was then serving as a Captain in a Warwickshire regiment.

Galton was never at his best on the lecture platform; he seems to have been incapable of that empathic identification with an audience necessary to catch and hold their interest. And his practical demonstrations were probably regarded with some amusement by officers untried in the field.

He returned to London gloomy and disillusioned. A cabinet of the models he had used to illustrate the art of camp life finally found its way to the Royal Geographical Society where it was preserved in the museum, a quaint reminder of Galton's shortlived interest in military matters.

5

The Royal Geographical Society

For a few years after his marriage Galton remained unsettled. He contemplated permanent emigration to a British colony but nothing came of his plans. Possibly Louisa objected; she certainly would not have been happy in a less civilised setting. Galton was also tempted to follow up Sir Roderick Murchison's proposal that he should undertake another exploration : the persistent rumours of the existence of a great lake in Central Africa which might provide the source of the Nile were beginning to excite the interest of the geographers. But Galton felt insufficiently confident of his health and general fitness to leave Britain in the immediate future and decided instead to make a permanent home in London. In 1857 he purchased for £2500 a house in South Kensington about a quarter of a mile from the Science Museum. From photographs, the house at 42 Rutland Gate appears to have been a fairly modest two storey Victorian town house built in the Georgian style with imposing balustraded first floor windows. (At the time of writing, houses in the same road are priced at about £60 000. Galton's house still stands, having narrowly escaped destruction during the bombing of London in the Second World War, but it has been modified by subsequent owners and is recognisable only by its identifying plaque.)

Galton's financial state was extremely sound and was to improve over the next few years. The sale of the family houses brought him £12 700 and with canal shares and legacies he was soon to have a capital of £26 000. His sister Emma's diary characteristically details the family's finances at this time and reveals that Francis as the youngest was also the least wealthy of the sons, Erasmus having £30 000 and Darwin £36 000.[1]

The house was taken partly furnished and a diary of Galton's indicates the trouble he took in the design and arrangement of the additional furniture. There are pages of sketches and measurements of tables, chairs and cupboards. His interest in the arrangement of the household was a reflection of his practicality and not of his aestheticism; the strange jumble of

furniture was an interior designer's nightmare. An instance of his practicality could be seen in the Rutland Gate lavatory which was situated at
the top of a flight of stairs leading up from the ground floor. Galton had
one of the wooden panels of the door replaced by frosted glass and fixed a
vertical rod to the bolt. When the lavatory was occupied and the bolt
across, this rod could be clearly seen from the bottom of the stairs. Thus
a futile climb was obviated and the occupant could remain undisturbed.

The interior of Rutland Gate has been described by Karl Pearson as
he remembered it in Galton's old age :

> 'The light and airy, white enamelled drawing-room with its furni-
> ture of many periods and styles; the long dining-room with its book-
> case at the back, Galton's working table in the front window, and on
> the walls the prints of Galton's friends—Darwin, Grove, Hooker,
> Broderick, Spencer, Spottiswoode, etc.; the dark back room with its
> shelves loaded with pamphlet cases filled with letters and manuscripts,
> the boxes of models, and the notes of a long lifetime of collection,
> mostly indexed by Galton himself, all those will be familiar memories
> to his friends, and formed a singularly unique environment, very
> characteristic of the man.'[2]

One unusual aspect of the rooms at that time was the spartan seating
and the parquet flooring without carpets. It is probably safe to ascribe
the lack of upholstered easy chairs to Galton's own preference and not, as
Hesketh Pearson has suggested, to Louisa's lack of interest in her husband's
welfare.[3] In later life Galton suffered, as had his father, from severe
asthma, attacks occurring in thickly carpeted rooms. He mentions
having to avoid the reading room of the Athenaeum for this reason, and
the carpets were therefore removed from Rutland Gate during the later
years of his residence.

Apart from one trip to Egypt Galton never again travelled outside
the confines of Western Europe, but he and Louisa always escaped the
rigours of winter by taking long vacations abroad, and many months of
each year were spent away from Rutland Gate, visiting friends, touring
on the continent and visiting spas.

There was much to keep him busy in London. The beginning of his
active involvement in the affairs of the Royal Geographical Society was
marked by great enthusiasm on Galton's part. He had Murchison's full
confidence and served on many of the Society's subcommittees, namely
those concerned with publications, finances, expeditions and the library.
He became a member of the Geographical Club and dined with a select
group after every Monday meeting. There he met, among others, Admirals
Murray and Fitzroy (the former Captain of Charles Darwin's ship, *The
Beagle*), Clements Markham (later President of the Geographical Society),

Laurence Oliphant, Mansfield Parkyns and Richard Burton. In his auto-biography Galton recalls his amusement at being present at the introduc-tion of Burton to Bishop Wilberforce, both men trying their hardest to appear inoffensive to the other.[4]

Markham, who was an acute judge of men, has described the impression Galton made on him at this time :

> 'He had intelligent rather eager blue eyes and heavy brows, a long straight mouth, bald head. He was very clever and perfectly straight in all his dealings with a strong sense of duty. Without an atom of vanity he held to his own opinions and aims tenaciously. His mind was mathematical and statistical with little or no imagination. He was essentially a doctrinaire not endowed with much sympathy. He was not adapted to lead or influence men. He could make no allowance for the failings of others and had no tact.'[5]

This latter failing of Galton's was to lead to a bitter quarrel with Dr Norton Shaw. Shaw's energetic efforts as the salaried Executive Secretary since 1849 had been largely responsible for the now flourishing state of the Society and he was highly regarded by the body of the Fellows and indeed by Murchison. But, according to Markham, Shaw had too little knowledge of geography and was excessively vain.[6] He certainly seems to have taken upon himself the most important executive role and soon began to resent what he considered to be Galton's unjustifiable interference in his sphere of duties.

Soon after his election to Council Galton had begun to agitate for a change in the Society's publication policy. The *Journal*, which at that time appeared annually, had been much criticised for its dullness and lack of immediacy. Galton proposed its supplementation by a more frequent periodical in which an account could be given of papers read to the Society soon after they were delivered : any discussion and correspondence that ensued could also find a place in this new venture. His proposals saw fruit and in 1855 the *R.G.S. Proceedings* began to appear under Shaw's editorship.

At least that was the formal decision that had been reached. Galton naturally took a fatherly interest in his brainchild and began to act as co-editor from the very beginning. Thus in 1856 we find him writing to Shaw :

> 'Do you still want me to undertake the chief share in editing *Proceedings* for next session? I do not in any way covet the task, neither do I suppose it would prosper better under my charge than anyone else's, but I am very anxious for their success and my engage-ments leave me time.'[7]

Many letters exist in the R.G.S. Archives from Galton to Shaw with regard to the contents of the *Proceedings*. Galton's concern for detail is very evident as he suggests different formats for the publication and urges Shaw to make it of greater interest to its readers.

The correspondence between the two men between 1855 and 1862 reflects the increasing strain they both felt. Galton's early letters are addressed to 'My dear Dr Shaw' and are written in a friendly and informal style, but the correspondence closes with formal and hardly civil communications headed with a curt 'Dear Sir'.

Galton's very active role on Council led to his nomination for one of the two joint Honorary Secretaryships of the Society and he assumed that office in 1857, his colleague being Dr Hodgkin, a Quaker, dressing in strict Quaker fashion.

The clash with Norton Shaw now began to assume larger proportions as Galton interpreted his own function to be more than nominal. In an attempt to clarify the respective roles of the Honorary and Executive Secretaries he wrote to Shaw :

> 'Send me reference to the laws by which the duties and title of your office are defined, especially in reference to that held by myself.'[8]

Whatever information Galton received in reply he now began to adopt a more authoritarian approach to Shaw. In a curt letter of 1858 he requests a list of all papers printed in the *Journal* and in the *Proceedings* to be sent to him so as to arrive the following morning. Galton was in process of compiling a library catalogue but the urgency of his request appears to have been unnecessary as it was another month before the catalogue was ready for the printer.

Last minute requests of this sort and the detailed instructions about proofs and orthography must have made Shaw despair of carrying out any of his other secretarial duties. By 1861 he had had enough and relinquished the editorship of the *Proceedings* to leave Galton in sole control. But, as Markham put it,

> 'Two men so diametrically opposite in every point of their character could not work harmoniously.'[10]

And there was still much work they had to do in common in running the Society under its aged President. Sir Roderick Murchison, now in his 71st year, was serving his third term of office and disinclined to bother himself with the minutiae of administration. Dr Hodgkin attempted to preserve the peace but finally gave up the struggle and resigned the other Honorary Secretaryship in 1862 in favour of William Spottiswoode.

Spottiswoode was a close friend of Galton's; they had planned a visit together to the Sinai Pininsula a few years previously but Galton had had to call the trip off as he had fallen ill with an abcess of the tongue.[11] Spottiswoode now threw himself into the fray and backed Galton in all his proposals for reform of the structure of the Society's secretariat. But Norton Shaw was busy spreading his version of the controversy among the Fellows and Galton's popularity began to wane. In spite of Spottiswoode's reinforcement there were ominous signs that Galton was beginning to crack. For instance, he wrote to Shaw in April 1862 scolding him for omitting to read out a particular letter at the last Council meeting and telling him to enter it in the letter book and to read it on the next occasion. Shaw has pencilled his comments on Galton's letter to the effect that not only was the letter entered and read out at the meeting but that the reader was Galton himself![12]

No details of the final quarrel exist but it was probably insignificant in itself and merely represented the end point beyond which the parties felt they could not proceed. Markham has provided a general account of events:

'In March 1863 Sir Roderick sent for me to talk over the situation. He said he had the resignations of both the Honorary Secretarys and the Assistant Secretary* in his pocket. Sitting in his library at 16 Belgrave Square he confided his opinion of the crisis to me and asked what I thought. Norton Shaw was in the wrong but the Society owed much to him and he was very popular. He must be treated liberally. Galton's resignation must be accepted but Spottiswoode must be persuaded to remain at least for another year. Sir Roderick then asked me to accept the post of Honorary Secretary second to Spottiswoode.'[13]

And so it was. Galton was replaced by Markham while Spottiswoode agreed to continue in office for another year for the sake of appearances. Although they continued to work without financial remuneration the term 'Honorary' was dropped from their titles and they were expected to carry the bulk of the executive function. Norton Shaw was retired with a golden handshake of a year's salary and a new Assistant Secretary was appointed whose duties were limited to editorship of the Society's publications and who received a salary of £300 p.a.

The quarrel had unfortunate consequences for Galton as many felt he should also resign his seat on Council and play no further part in the administration of Society affairs. There was talk of opposing his election to Council and a General Meeting had to be called to clarify the situation. Murchison effectively mastered the dissentients and nothing was done.[14] But it was several years before Galton was able to regain his popularity and to bring about a further change in Society policy. His seat on Council

* An error for 'Executive Secretary'.

was, however, never again seriously threatened and he was able to retain his seat almost without interruption until 1894 when the Society was split over a more important issue.

It would be wrong to assume that Galton's difficulties with Shaw overcast all his work for the R.G.S. in this early period. Relationships with colleagues on the various subcommittees appear to have been genial and much useful work was done. He was a new member of the Expeditions Committee when the Burton–Speke expedition of 1856 was given its instructions to explore the lake regions in Central Africa, and, on that occasion, he appears to have played only a minor part.

The story of the expedition has been told many times.[15] Burton's unfortunate illness on reaching Lake Tanganyika, their first discovery, meant that Speke alone penetrated to Lake Victoria Nyanza which he intuitively guessed to be the source of the Nile. Speke returned to England before Burton and, breaking an agreement not to speak, naturally acquired most of the credit, but at the cost of a final breach between them. Neither had ever found the other congenial; Galton describes Speke as 'a thorough Briton, conventional, solid and resolute,' and Burton as 'a man of eccentric genius and tastes, orientalised in character and thoroughly Bohemian.'[16]

In spite of his earlier friendship with Burton, Galton undoubtedly felt more sympathy for the younger Speke. His partiality was evident when he helped to decide which of the two men the Society should back in their next attempt. Only two other members of the Expeditions Committee were present at the meeting of 1859 when Speke and Burton presented their plans. The Committee recommended to Council that funds should be sought to support Speke; on Council, Murchison's voice prevailed and at that time he was a strong advocate of Speke's merits.[17]

Instructions for Speke, who was to be accompanied by Grant, were drafted by Galton and Findlay in May 1860.[18] Later in the same year Galton, with Oliphant and Arrowsmith, drew up suggestions for Baker who hoped to meet Speke and Grant on their return down the Nile.[19]

Galton has described the scene when Speke and Grant took their farewell:

'They were fine manly fellows, and I can see them now in my mind's eye, as they came to take a final leave, when I knocked two nails into the side of a cupboard as they stood side by side with their backs to it, to mark their respective heights and as a memento of them when away.'[20]

The success of their expedition is well known : they followed the Nile, not however without a break, from Victoria Nyanza into Egypt meeting Baker at Gondokoro. For the discovery of Victoria Nyanza and for his general exploratory zeal, Speke was proposed by Galton as a worthy candidate for an R.G.S. award, and he received the Founders' Medal in April 1861.[21] By this date the Nile problem was virtually solved. Yet the break in the journey, plus Speke's hypothetical location of the Mountains of the Moon, gave Burton ammunition for attack. The controversy dragged on until 1864 when a decisive encounter was arranged on the occasion of the British Association meeting at Bath.

Galton was a member of the Committee of the Geographical Section which was in preliminary session before Speke was due to give his paper, when the news arrived that Speke had shot himself a few hours previously. It was widely believed, although apparently mistakenly,[22] that his death was suicidal and not accidental. Burton certainly subscribed to this view, and although Galton was only peripherally concerned in the affair he was deeply upset. He seems to have considered that the long continued controversy was too much for Speke and that if his own powers as a mediator had been more skilfully exercised the tragedy might have been averted.

It was at the joint instigation of Galton and Murchison that subscriptions were now sought for a public memorial to Speke. It was decided to erect an obelisk in Kensington Gardens, but difficulties arose over a suitable inscription as many still maintained with Burton that Speke had not discovered the true source of the Nile. The final choice of words was noncommittal: the legend ran 'Victoria Nyanza and the Nile 1864.' On two subsequent occasions, the deaths of Burton and Grant, Galton made attempts to have a second memorial erected near the Speke obelisk to commemorate these and other British explorers of Africa. But representatives of Speke opposed the move and nothing came of it.[23]

Besides his R.G.S. work Galton had other allied committee duties which are worth brief mention. A friendship with Sir Edward Sabine, whom he met at the Royal Society, led to his nomination in 1858 to the Managing Committee of Kew observatory of which Sabine was chairman. The Observatory had a high reputation for its standardisation of astronomical instruments. Galton's participation resulted in the extension of its services to the testing of thermometers, watches, compasses and sextants, work he found peculiarly satisfying.

His membership of the Kew Committee led to an invitation to visit Spain in the company of a group of astronomers to view the total eclipse of the sun in July 1860. He was instructed by Sir John Herschel in the use of an actinometer, which Herschel had invented to measure delicate variations in temperature such as those radiated by the sun's corona during the eclipse. The party sailed in H.M.S. *Himalaya* to Bilbao and then travelled inland to Logroño near which they were to set up their instruments. On unpacking the equipment the actinometer was found to have been broken in transit, and instead of spending the precious minutes watching the instrument Galton was free to observe the full glory of the eclipse. His scientific conscience was salved by directing his observations towards changes in the appearance of colours on a chart of his own devising and in sketching the corona.

'The corona very rapidly formed itself into all its perfectness. It did not appear to me to *grow*, but to stand out ready formed as the brilliant edge of the sun became masked. I do not know to what I can justly compare it, on account of the peculiar whiteness of its light, and of the definition of its shape as combined with a remarkable tenderness of outline. There was firmness but not hardness. In its general form, it was well balanced, not larger on one side than the other. It reminded me of some brilliant decoration or order, made of diamonds and exquisitely designed.'[24]

His sketch showed some of the rays of the Corona to be curved, a fact which had not been noted by the other observers and which many astronomers doubted at the time, but which subsequent work confirmed.[25]

Galton's account of his Spanish trip is noteworthy for its descriptions of the Basque peasantry and for his comments on the behaviour of the Spanish people which are acute and amusing. In the mornings the streets of Logroño were busy with churchgoers and Galton attended a service:

'I was vastly interested in the movements of the ladies' fans at church. All the world knows that Spanish fans are in perpetual motion, and betray each feeling, real or assumed, that passes through the mind of its bearer. I felt convinced I could guess the nature of the service at any particular moment by the way in which the fans were waving. The difference between a litany and a thanksgiving was unmistakable; and I believe that far minuter shades of devotion were also discernible.'[26]

In the afternoons a military band played in the square and Galton was much amused by the behaviour of the nursemaids who flocked to listen:

'The instant the music began, every nurse elevated her charge sitting on her hand, at half-arm's length into the air, and they all kept time to the music by tossing the babies in unison, and slowly rotating them, in azimuth (to speak astronomically), at each successive toss. The babies looked passive and rather bored, but the energy and enthusiasm of the nurses were glorious. At each great bang of the drummers a vast flight of babies was simultaneously projected to the utmost arms' length. It was ludicrous beyond expression.'[27]

He travelled by diligence from Spain to Bordeaux where he met Louisa and together they began a tour in the Pyrenees. Galton had had a little previous climbing experience in 1857 when a major part of his Swiss holiday had been spent at Courmayeur and he had climbed the Col du Géant with Leslie Stephen.[28] But now he became bitten with the mania. Leaving Louisa at convenient hotels he made many expeditions, notably the ascent of the Pic de Néthou, in the company of Charles Packe, the botanist and climber, who was extremely knowledgeable about the region.

Galton was especially intrigued by the sheepskin sleeping bags carried by the French soldiers who patrolled the mountain passes for smugglers. He borrowed one and took it 1000 ft up a mountain above Luchon where he and Louisa were staying in a comfortable hotel. A night spent on the bare mountain in a thunderstorm tested the bag's efficiency to Galton's satisfaction and he was able to give an account of it in the next edition of the *Art of Travel*.[29] Sleeping bags were not in general use by climbers or travellers at the time, except in the Arctic, and Galton's strong advocacy of them led to his being toasted at a dinner of the Alpine Club as 'the greatest bagman in Europe.'*

On his return from Spain Galton was approached by the publisher, Alexander Macmillan, with a plan to produce an annual volume of travellers' accounts of their vacation journeys. A similar enterprise had been started by John Ball, the first President of the Alpine Club, who had persuade William Longman to publish *Peaks, Passes and Glaciers* in the previous year.[31] The first volume of that series had been marvellously successful and it is likely that Macmillan was seeking to emulate his rival with his own scheme. Galton readily agreed to edit the Macmillan series and the first volume appeared in 1860 under the clumsy title, *Vacation Tourists and Notes of Travel*.[32]

His own account of his visit to Spain was included in the first volume, as was Charles Packe's description of their tour in the Pyrenees. But, although nine of the contributors to the three volumes that appeared were members of the Alpine Club, the scope was much wider than accounts of mountaineering holidays. As editor, Galton received many articles for his consideration and his main duty was to prime and discard rather than to gather contributions.† A high standard resulted and some of the essays have acquired an additional historical value today; for example, included is an eyewitness account of the Garibaldi uprising. But the series did no more than pay its way and was discontinued after the third volume.

Soon after the Macmillan venture failed, Galton's first publisher, Murray, asked him to compile a guide to Switzerland on a smaller scale

---

* His later recommendation of a sleeping bag made of mackintosh instead of one of sheepskin came in for heavy criticism by Edward Whymper of Matterhorn fame: 'They are very uncomfortable: hot and close in warm weather or rain, and during cold, exceedingly cold.'[30]

† For example, thirteen separate descriptions of seasickness were submitted to one volume![33]

than his own large handbook and intended for the walker rather than the climber. Galton was able to draw upon his experiences of Switzerland derived from the half a dozen holidays he had spent there with Louisa. He supplemented his knowledge by making a special excursion on his own during August 1863 and the *Knapsack Guide to Switzerland* was ready by the end of the year.[34]

This book was omitted from Galton's own list of his publications contained in his autobiography. The reason for the omission is not hard to seek: the book received a very poor review in the *Alpine Journal*.

'Independently of mere verbal errors and misspellings of proper names, which might pass uncriticised but for the usual accuracy of Mr Murray's handbooks in such matters, defects of a more important kind are sufficiently numerous to mar the usefulness of the knapsack guide under the very circumstances for which it was specially intended.'[35]

The anonymous reviewer castigates Galton for the inaccuracy in the times given for various tours, the omission of any list of trustworthy guides, and the lack of any allusion to certain passes coupled with detailed information about others of equal or lesser importance. He concludes that only if the guide were revised by more experienced travellers would it be rendered worthy of inclusion in the Murray series.

Murray paid Galton £150 for the copyright with £50 for his travelling expenses. He now offered him £100 for a revision of his existing *Handbook of South Germany*, but Galton refused on the grounds that he could not spare the time although it may have been the critical review of his Swiss guide that deterred him.

Galton had joined the Alpine Club in 1861 and was to remain a member for ten years. The Alpine Club register of members in the first years of its existence reads like a *Who's Who*. Apart from Leslie Stephen and Charles Packe, Galton climbed mainly with Professor John Tyndall, the physicist, and Vaughan Hawkins, a barrister who had been Senior Classic at Cambridge. Louisa's brother, Montagu, was also a member of the club and preceded Galton on the Monte Rosa climb.

Galton made one contribution to the club's journal, not however an account of one of his climbs but details of an unusual route to the foot of a ravine from which one could view in complete safety, or so he assured his readers, the avalanches dashing down the face of the Jungfrau.

'The entire fall of the avalanche is nearly 5000 feet of perpendicular descent. The finest effect was at the very foot of the ravine. I stood at one time so near to it that, had I been equipped as a fisherman, I could have thrown a fly over the avalanche. I waited for the third

and finest avalanche under one of the overhanging slabs of rock
. . . but though I persuaded myself of the absolute safety of my
position, I freely acknowledge that the advent of the avalanche
alarmed me. It gave notice of its coming by a prodigious roar,
and the appearance of an exceedingly menacing cloud of snow-dust,
that was shot out far above my head. I knew not what was coming,
and I ran away as fast as I could, till I was reassured that all was
right by the appearance of the ice cataract in its wonted channel;
when I hurried back again to its side, to rejoice in the storm and
uproar.'[36]

A literary and editorial commitment at this time was in connection
with a weekly journal, *The Reader*. Galton was responsible for the geographical coverage and wrote several reviews of exploratory work.[37] The
prime object of the journal was to serve as an organ of communication
among scientists and between them and the general public. Established
in 1863, *The Reader* was purchased towards the end of 1864 by a small
company, each member of which subscribed £100.[38] Besides Galton,
there were Herbert Spencer to cover philosophy, Tyndall to cover the
physical sciences, Huxley to cover physiology, and a dozen others. Tom
Hughes (the author of *Tom Brown's Schooldays*) lent his rooms to the
enterprise and with the powerful backing of many of the great names of
Victorian science and literature the project seemed set for success.

There were several reasons why it survived no longer than 1866.
Herbert Spencer was not an ideal co-editor, a role he shared with Lockyer
and Galton. He wasted the time of the Committee with constant dilations
on first principles.[39] The subeditor employed what the committee considered to be underhand methods in obtaining advertisements. The many
distinguished reviewers were difficult to hold to any publication schedule.
Above all, the journal was dull to read, the layout serving to bemuse the
reader. Three years after it ceased publication its function was replaced
by *Nature* under the sole editorship of Lockyer. Galton was a frequent
contributor to *Nature* from its inception until 1910, the year before his
death.

In addition to his writings of this general kind Galton made several
contributions to the more technical literature, especially in the field of
meteorology where he was able to demonstrate his aptitude for original
scientific enquiry.

6

Meteorological Research

Galton wrote several papers on geographical topics. None of them was of great moment nor requires extended discussion here. In his first paper he described ways in which geography needed to be developed in the Britain of the mid-nineteenth century.[1] The acceptance of geography as a serious subject at school and at university was the prime necessity in order to produce scholars of some geographical sophistication. At that time it was still regarded as impossible to set problems in the subject that would exercise the intellect of the student as mathematics and classics were supposed to do. As we shall see, Galton was subsequently to invoke the aid of the R.G.S. in instituting a system of prizes for outstanding scholastic performance in geography. He was also to be instrumental in having the subject introduced at Oxford University.

A second plea in this paper was for an improvement in map making. Travellers should receive instruction in the use of instruments and in the drawing of maps before they left on journeys to unknown lands. Their maps could later be radically improved by artistic map makers who had access to their sketches and surveys.

> 'The strictly accurate, but meagre information that is afforded to the student by ordinary maps is more tantalising than satisfactory. A blind man fingering a model could learn as much from his sense of touch alone, as they convey to our eyes. They are little more than an abstraction, or a ghost of the vivid recollection with which the memory of the traveller is stored.'[2]

Ideally, Galton wanted maps to be pictorial, giving a bird's-eye view of the countryside in all its colour and relief. Ten years were to elapse before he could provide a partial answer to the problem in the form of a stereo-scopic map.[3] By photographing models of mountainous country with a stereoscopic camera and viewing the resultant pairs of pictures with a simple pocket stereoscope an extremely realistic aerial view was obtained. His efforts appear to have remained a curiosity and apart from a limited use in aerial reconnaisance the method has not been generally developed, although atlas maps especially of mountainous countries could gain much from stereoscopic presentation. (Galton fell out with a cousin, Douglas Galton, over this stereoscopic work. Douglas claimed that Francis had wrongly taken credit for the idea which was really that of another cousin, Cameron Galton. Cameron had actually only helped Francis with the photography of the models and Francis kept the correspondence to prove the facts.)[4]

To his own journal, the R.G.S. *Proceedings*, Galton contributed a paper entitled, *The exploration of arid countries*.[5] In it Galton dealt with the problems arising in the determination of the optimal amount of supplies needed for exploratory and supporting parties in an expedition over arid terrain. The idea was a simple one and yet no one had yet adopted it.

After the whole expedition had reached a certain distance from the base camp, and one section of the supporting party had exhausted their loads by furnishing meals and caches to the entire expedition, it would return home. This process was to be repeated until the explorers were left alone with their supplies intact and a series of caches available all along the route back to base.

If Galton's scheme could have been applied to Australian exploratory endeavour, his next paper, *Recent discoveries in Australia*, might have made less depressing reading. It was written for the *Cornhill* and described various journeys into the interior including Burke's fatal attempt.[6]

Another paper was written in response to a request from the Church Missionary Society for information about Zanzibar, where they were thinking of establishing a missionary station. They had originally approached Richard Burton who had refused to undertake the task, although he now generously lent Galton his notes taken during his stay there in 1856. As in all Burton's work the notes were extremely detailed and enabled Galton to discuss effectively and apparently at firsthand the main physical features of the island, its climate and its native peoples. Galton's conclusion was certainly not favourable to any Christian missionary enterprise.

'What we find in Zanzibar is a far-reaching and far-influencing but not a strong power; anxious to do well, seeking to consolidate itself, amenable to a good English influence, but above all things, the *sine qua non* of its existence is that it should be Moslem.'[7]

The Missionary Society took the hint and did not intrude.

Two years after his paper on Zanzibar, which had included details of the climate of that island, he published a paper devoted entirely to climate, that of Lake Nyanza.[8] The observations on which the paper was based had been made by Speke and Grant on their journey to the source of the Nile; Galton collated their figures and drew up tables showing the rainfall, maximum, minimum and average temperatures for nearly every week in the year.[9]

The representation of this kind of information on a map so as to show the variations from place to place was Galton's ultimate concern. He was not the first to think of doing this; the French astronomer, Le Verrier, was already issuing daily charts of the weather in the Atlantic but his efforts were generally agreed to be unsatisfactory as the observations were derived from such few and scattered sources.

Galton's first attempts were restricted to the British Isles for which he had data from some 50 weather stations. These early trials are interesting as they show Galton grappling with the difficulties that confront anyone attempting to combine several pieces of information in a readily intelligible symbolic form. The problem was to represent such variables as temperature, pressure, wind direction and force, and the condition of the sky in a single rectangle or circle which could then be printed on the map at the position of the appropriate weather station so that a simultaneous display of the weather conditions in the British Isles at a particular time could be achieved.

One early attempt used stamps which were stuck on to the map and the whole then photographed. Barometric movement was indicated by the shape of the stamp, hexagonal representing falling, circular representing stationary, and a composite of the two representing rising; wind force was shown by the number of arrows and its direction by their direction, and the condition of the sky by the amount of shading on the stamp.

Although the finished map looked attractive Galton soon discarded this method, which had led to the omission of temperature and pressure figures, and adopted small rectangular symbols in which these data were included. The map with the rectangular symbols was printed in three colours and was included with a circular he sent out to induce other meteorologists to collaborate in a meteorological map of Northern Europe. The circular, printed in three languages, specified that observations were to be taken thrice daily during the month of December 1861.

Response to the circular was a little disappointing as few returns came from France or Italy and none at all from Sweden and Denmark. The bulk of the returns originated from Holland (where Buys Ballot gladly cooperated), Belgium, Austria and Germany. However, the data were sufficient for Galton to proceed with his weather map of a large area. He was particularly fortunate in his choice of month as the prevailing weather conditions were such that he was able to make a significant discovery.

It was surmised at the time that in ordinary weather the direction of the wind was governed by a similar system of pressure as obtained in the tropical whirlwind. Such 'cyclones' were known to consist of a centre of low pressure around which in the northern hemisphere winds blew in an anticlockwise direction, the direction of rotation being ascribed to the rotation of the earth. When Galton began to plot his data for the beginning of the month it became evident that general cyclonic conditions were prevailing over Europe. At about the middle of the month the black shading that he was using to indicate low pressure gave way to red shading for high pressure. Accompanying the change, the anticlockwise winds were replaced by clockwise winds flowing out from the high-pressure core; in other words, a reversal of cyclonic conditions had occurred, to which Galton gave the now familiar name of 'anticyclone.' He communicated his findings in a paper to the Royal Society[10] and in more detail in a book, *Meteorographica* (1863).[11] The latter publication presented in a long series of maps all the weather data he had accumulated from his European colleagues.

The maps were not really adequate for their purpose. The whole of the Atlantic was a blank and Galton notes that the areas of high and low pressure were typically very large and in no case completely circumscribed by the extent of the map. He also points out that these pressure areas did not move with regularity nor keep their shape for long. Thus, accurate prediction as distinct from description of the weather would remain an impossibility until information could be gathered from even wider areas than the continent of Europe. Such an extension was certainly the first necessity, although it is ironic to note that the major advance in understanding the role of warm and cold fronts in depressions was brought about by the isolation of Vilhelm Bjerknes and colleagues in Norway during the First World War.[12]

Within Britain the little that had been done in the way of weather reporting before the 1860s had been due to the almost solitary efforts of Admiral Fitzroy who issued storm warnings from his Meteorological Office. (Fitzroy's 'cone' is still the standard gale warning.) Fitzroy's suicide in 1865 left Britain without any vestige of a weather service and Galton was asked to sit on a Board of Trade Committee with Lord Farrer and Sir Frederick Evans to investigate the possibilities. The Committee recommended the formation of a Meteorological Committee (later to be called the Meteorological Council). The Committee was to have as its main functions the provision of storm warnings for sea ports and the establishment of selfrecording weather stations in the British Isles.

Galton was elected to the Committee when it came into being in 1868 and served until 1901. In the first few years of his membership he was very active in designing instruments for the weather stations and for weather mapping. But once these devices were working satisfactorily there were few challenges to his ingenuity and the work of the Committee became 'the usual routine,' as he later expressed it.[13]

Besides the theoretical advance Galton had made in the identification of the anticyclonic system, a practical and familiar result was to emerge from his research work: the newspaper weather map. It was some years before the data from the various weather stations could be assembled and the technical printing difficulties overcome. Galton's first weather map appeared in *The Times* on 1st April 1875. A comparison of that map with a current version shows but slight differences, with the inclusion of isobars and fronts and the omission of sea conditions characterising the modern map.

Several papers which deal with particular problems associated with ocean travel in sailing ships can be conveniently mentioned here. Galton was surprised to discover that few nautical men knew the sailing qualities of their own vessels along various compass courses supposing the wind to be constant in one direction. 'Wind charts', which showed the relative time over which the wind blew from each of the main compass points, were readily available through the initiative of Admiral Fitzroy and were issued from the Meteorological Office. Such wind charts could be converted into 'passage charts' if information could be obtained about the sailing efficiency of a particular ship at different angles to the wind. Galton's first paper on the topic showed how the conversion could be made, the result showing in diagrammatic form the efficiency of a ship on a particular course.[14]

By 1872 the meteorologists were in a position to supply information on the direction and strength of both wind and current for $1°$ segments of the principal oceans. In Galton's next paper he was concerned with a method of including all this information in his passage charts so that the sailing efficiency of a ship could be even more accurately estimated.[15] His results were expressed in terms of 'isochrones' which were closed curves plotted in such a way that the distance from a central point represented the distance that a standard ship would cover in a time of 8 hours. He suggested that isochrones should be drawn for various classes of ship and should be issued to cover the main sea areas in a $2°$ network. A curious development of the isochrone idea was its application to the individual traveller. The fifth edition of *Hints to Travellers* has as its frontispiece a map of the world with isochronic zones indicating the time required to reach all parts of the world from London. Galton constructed this map, his last contribution to geography, in 1881 from the timetables of railway and steamship companies. It required a unit of time of 10 days!

Galton's scheme had obvious advantages: it would have led to a reduction in the length of voyages with a resultant financial gain to the shippers. But much greater advantages were accruing from the general replacement of sail by steam, which process was accelerating greatly by the second half of the nineteenth century and with ships no longer dependent on favourable winds Galton's proposals came to nothing.

7

'Hereditary Genius'

Besides his membership of the Royal Geographical Society and the Kew Observatory Committee Galton became a regular attender at British Association meetings. Soon after his marriage he began the routine of interrupting his summer vacation in order to return to England to take in the annual meeting of the B.A. He read his first paper to the Association in 1858 and was acquainted with the members of the Committee who at that time included Murchison, Sabine and William Hopkins, his Cambridge mathematics tutor. Murchison's regret over Galton's enforced resignation from his R.G.S. post after the quarrel with Norton Shaw was probably instrumental in causing Galton to be offered the Secretaryship of the Association. William Hopkins wrote describing the post:

'The office is a very pleasant and gentlemanly one, requiring of course attention and courtesy without much time or trouble.'[1]

Galton accepted the post and joined Hopkins, the other General Secretary, in 1863. He served actively for three years and nominally for 1866–7.

Although, as Hopkins had implied, it was not a very onerous duty, it did mean that he had to help organise the annual meetings. When it is remembered that in addition to his various committee duties he was also a member of the Athenaeum, Royal Society, Geographical and Alpine Clubs it will be evident that he was not much in Louisa's company. Her complaints about his absences from home find expression in her *Annual Record* and intermingled with an overconcern with her own health make some of the entries in the *Record* depressing to read.

The *Record* was Louisa's attempt to summarise the year's events in a few paragraphs.[2] It was begun at the time of their marriage, the years back to 1830 being entered in parallel columns headed *Frank's Life* and *Louisa's Life*. Thus, we learn that Louisa caught typhus fever in 1831 when she was nine years old, her sister Marianne dying from the infection. In 1840 she 'came out' and a little later was enjoying riding and singing lessons. But she was never a strong child; she had been baptised at home soon after her birth in view of her sickly condition. However, the first three years of her married life contain no references to ill-health. Then in 1856 she had fever and some infection of the mouth which led to the extraction of all her teeth in the following year.

The entry for 1860 runs:

'Went to Leamington and Claverdon early in January. Let our house from May 1st for two months. Took lodgings at Richmond. Constant bad weather. Home sick to a painful degree and Frank almost always away in London or at Kew Observatory. Frank went to the British Association at Oxford end of June and I to Harrow and staid over the Speeches . . .'

The B.A. meeting at Oxford was the occasion for the notorious Huxley–Wilberforce debate on Darwin's work. There is no report of Galton's reaction to the occasion although we may be sure where his sympathies lay. In his autobiography he describes the impact *The Origin of Species* had on his own thinking.

'The publication in 1859 of the *Origin of Species* by Charles Darwin made a marked epoch in my own mental development, as it did in that of human thought generally. Its effect was to demolish a multitude of dogmatic barriers by a single stroke, and to arouse a spirit of rebellion against all ancient authorities whose positive and unauthenticated statements were contradicted by modern science.'[3]

Galton's religious belief did not survive the experience. He describes the book as driving away 'the constraint of my old superstition as if it had been a nightmare.'[4] In this respect it is interesting to note the deletion of the reference to Adam and Eve in his section on the origin of fire making in the 1867 edition of *The Art of Travel*.[5] His subsequent writings on the religious temperament and his denial of the efficacy of prayer involved him in some acrimonious debate, while the effect on his relationship with Louisa, who remained a practising Christian until her death, can only be guessed at.

Louisa's main problem was to find something with which to occupy her time in London. A visit to an art gallery with Emma Galton where they occupied themselves with copying paintings, a series of music lessons from Schachner—these odd amusements were sufficiently unusual to merit inclusion in the annual record. Hating domesticity she took no interest in the everyday running of their small household. And it was rapidly becoming apparent by the 1860s that she was not going to bear any children.

Galton himself considered the interval of 13 years between his marriage

v   Francis and Louisa Galton at the time of their marriage

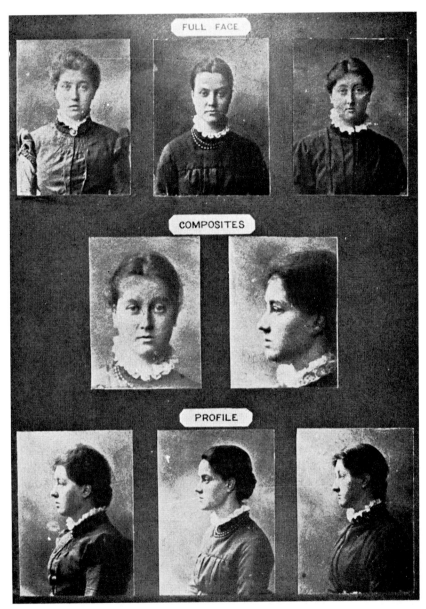

vi Composite portrait of three sisters

and the year 1866 as a crucial period in his own life for two reasons: because during this time his interest in geography began to wane to be replaced with a fascination with heredity, and because the period in question was marked by a succession of 'maladies prejudicial to mental effort,' which culminated in a breakdown in 1866.[6]

His growing interest in heredity dates from about the time when it was evident that his marriage was likely to prove infertile. There is no reason to suppose that the marriage was not consummated. It is more likely that the infertility was genetic: neither of his brothers had children and none of Louisa's sisters. He claims that it was at Cambridge that he first noticed that academic talent appeared to run in the families of his contemporaries. His own and particularly Louisa's family were now instances before his very eyes and it is not unlikely that his speculations over the possible fruits of their union, frustrated by the lack of direct confirmation, were diverted into a wider context.

In 1864 he began work on a long paper entitled *Hereditary Talent* which appeared in two parts in *Macmillan's Magazine* the following year.[7] The factual material he had obtained to support his claims that talent was inherited and that improvements in the human race were best to be obtained by selective breeding was to be supplemented over the next few years and to form the basis for his first important book, *Hereditary Genius*.[8] This later statement of his views appeared in 1869; to avoid repetition, discussion of Galton's argument will be postponed until that book is considered in detail.

Not only may Galton's interest in heredity have sprung from the sterility of his own marriage, but his mental breakdown may also have one of its origins there. Another possible precipitating factor was the loss of his religious faith which left him with no compensatory philosophy until his programme for the eugenic improvement of mankind became a future article of faith. Galton's obsessional characteristics had been evident from childhood and were responsible for the anxious overwork which had led to the less serious breakdown at Cambridge. Now he was again under great pressure and began to suffer from attacks of giddiness which left him whenever he took outdoor exercise or travelled abroad.

'The warning I received in 1866 was more emphatic, and alarming than previously, and made a revision of my mode of life a matter of primary importance. Those who have not suffered from mental breakdown can hardly realise the incapacity it causes, or, when the worst is past, the closeness of the analogy between a sprained brain and a sprained joint. In both cases, after recovery seems to others to be complete, there remains for a long time an impossibility of performing certain minor actions without pain and serious mischief,

D

mental in the one and bodily in the other. This was a frequent experience with me respecting small problems, which successively obsessed me day and night, as I tried in vain to think them out. These affected mere twigs, so to speak, of the mental processes, but for all that most painfully.'[9]

The first serious symptoms arose just before his 44th birthday. Two letters of sympathy and practical advice arrived from his mother and sister Bessy.

His mother wrote in an unusually affectionate vein on 14th February:

'My dearest Francis,

I am quite unhappy about your health. Do take your mother's advice and give up all writing and all head work for a year. Remember you have not got a strong constitution and overworking your mind falls upon your bodily health. Do, my love, be persuaded to lay aside all ambition and give yourself a complete year's rest and perhaps it may be the saving of your life. Come to me whenever you like and you shall have perfect quiet. My mind is with you by day and by night. I long to have you with me.

With love to you and Louisa. Believe me ever,

Your affectionate mother.'[10]

Bessy's advice was similar:

'My very dearest Francis,

It makes me sad to hear you are so unwell. Your birthday is on Friday and it is a day for making good resolutions. Now do make and keep this one, that is, to take a good long holiday and you will fully reap the benefit in the autumn and be brisk and well for the British Association. Your heredity will also be better by returning to it with a fresh eye and refreshed head. Do ponder on this and make us all happy. It will do Louisa good also.

With my best love.

Ever dearest Frank, your very affectionate sister.'[11]

Louisa's *Record* reveals that Bessy's advice was heeded and that the Galtons went abroad to the Italian lakes until June, returning to the English Lake District for the remainder of the summer. Constant rain allowed little physical exercise and Galton was not well when the British Association met at Nottingham at the end of August.

He was due to read his paper on the conversion of wind charts into passage charts but the multifarious duties of General Secretary and what he describes as the 'sustained racket' of the proceedings were too much for him and he precipitously withdrew from the meeting after arranging to have his paper read for him.[12]

He sought refuge, interestingly enough, not at his mother's but with Adèle in Leamington, where he was attended by a Dr Jephson, becoming increasingly weak under the treatment. After a short spell at home, he and Louisa spent the next three months at Hastings where he rode constantly. They then went to Italy and toured through Switzerland and Germany not returning home until the October of 1867.

> '1868. The year began by Frank being too poorly to dine at Mr Crawfurd's. Winter at home, but dined out very little . . . Frank went to his family. Not well in July.'[13]

They went abroad again, this time remaining in Switzerland for two months and by the end of the year Galton was much improved. Nothing was published during this period of ill health, yet Galton continued to work at a variety of subjects. A habit of using his foreign tours to clarify his thinking began to evolve at this time. Many cheap foreign exercise books bear witness to his constant industry. Two curious unpublished papers concern calculations in regard to currency problems. In one he calculates the bulk of the gold in the world and concludes that it could all be contained in his own room. In the other, he proposes the adoption of a decimal currency in Britain through the introduction of two new coins, a 'groat' ($\frac{1}{100}$ th of a pound) and a 'quint' ($\frac{1}{5}$th of a penny). The sixpence, shilling and florin were to be retained as multiples of quints, i.e., 30, 60 and 120 quints respectively.[14]

Whenever in London he went on attending R.G.S. Council meetings and began to press for their greater involvement in geographical education. Galton first elicited the cooperation of W. F. Farrar, then a master at Harrow, where Louisa's brother Montagu was Headmaster. He then discussed the matter with another brother-in-law, George, who was headmaster of Liverpool College. The Headmasters of Eton, Dulwich and Rossall also expressed interest and with this backing Galton put his scheme before the R.G.S. Council. The Society agreed to conduct a system of examinations, open to over 60 public schools. Two gold medals were to be awarded annually for the best performance in Physical and in Political Geography. The scheme was put into operation in 1869 and although it had a life of 16 years it was not an unqualified success. By the end of that period more than half the medals had been won by two schools, Liverpool and Dulwich Colleges, where selected pupils had been especially coached for the examinations. Most schoolmasters remained apathetic, the available textbooks were inadequate and one disastrous consequence of the better pupils' concentration on geography was their neglect of the traditional bread-and-butter subjects which alone were available for study in the universities. The competition was finally discontinued after a forcible protest from the Headmaster of Clifton which the R.G.S. Council was unwilling to ignore.[15]

Galton's scheme had from the first encountered opposition from some of the Council members and he had only been able to force his proposals through owing to the apathy of Murchison and the absence of Markham, who was in Abyssinia. With Markham's return and the final resignation of Murchison, the Council was much less willing to tolerate the continuance of the innovation. Markham's attitude towards geographical education was continuously hostile. He describes the long speeches from Galton which accompanied the presentation of the medals as 'a tiresome interruption to the business of the Anniversary Meeting.'[16]

In spite of the opposition Galton continued his efforts to improve geographical education and turned his attention to the universities with, as we shall see, much greater success. But all this geographical committee work was of minor significance in comparison with his original contributions to the study of heredity. The years from 1866–9 when his obsessional difficulties were at their height were those in which he collected the bulk of the factual matter on which his most influential book was based.

The title of the book, *Hereditary Genius*, led to some misunderstanding and Galton was later to express the wish that he had used the word 'talent' instead of 'genius'.[17] As he employs the term it is a synonym for exceptionally high ability and it is the thesis of the book that such ability is genetically rather than environmentally determined.

The first step of his argument entails a consideration of the methods whereby one might select highly gifted people in order to study their families. Part One of the book is devoted to appropriate methods of classification and selection.

Galton begins by considering the possibility of selecting people by their public reputation :

> 'I look upon social and professional life as a continuous examination. All are candidates for the good opinions of others, and for success in their several professions, and they achieve success in proportion as the general estimate is large of their aggregate merits.'[18]

In order to estimate the proportion of the general population which has succeeded in passing its relevant 'examinations' and become eminent, Galton examines a biographical handbook, the obituary of the year 1868 published in *The Times*, as well as various earlier obituaries. His sources concur in giving him about 250 names per million of the general population over middle age, or 1 in 4000; this proportion is then employed as Galton's criterion of eminence. As an analogy, to stress the magnitude of a man's performance for him to achieve such a degree of eminence, Galton points out that there are never as many as 4000 stars visible on the clearest of nights and we would account it an extraordinary distinction for a star to be the most brilliant in the sky. Nobody mentioned in the lists of kinsmen which constitute the second section of the book is in his opinion less distinguished. The illustrious men who are the main subject of enquiry are, Galton maintains, even more rigorously selected, being as rare as one in a million or more.

We now come to the most original part of the book in which Galton develops a method for classifying ability. That people differ in their abilities and that such differences are innate is, Galton claims, quite apparent.

'I have no patience with the hypothesis occasionally expressed, and often implied, especially in tales written to teach children to be good, that babies are born pretty much alike, and that the sole agencies in creating differences between boy and boy, and man and man, are steady application and moral effort. It is in the most unqualified manner that I object to pretensions of natural equality. The experiences of the nursery, the school, the university, and of professional careers, are a chain of proofs to the contrary.'[19]

Just as anyone who has trained his body discovers the extent of his muscular powers, so every student comes to realise the limitations of his mental powers. And that these limits differ enormously from one man to another is readily apparent if, for example, examination marks are scrutinised. Galton takes the marks assigned to candidates in their final examination for mathematical honours at Cambridge. In the instance he quotes, the top scorer, or Senior Wrangler, obtained 7634 marks, while the Second Wrangler obtained 4123 and the lowest man in the list of honours 237 only. Although there were 100 men above the lowest man, he in turn was above 300 'poll' men and of course these men were hardly representative of the mathematical ability obtaining in the general population. In others words, a tremendous range in mathematical ability is evident.

Galton claims that in whatever way we test ability we will arrive at equally enormous differences among people. In the matter of rote memory, for example, Lord Macaulay was able to recall whole pages of works he had read but once, a performance which is quite out of the reach of the average man. And just as some individuals exceed the average some fall well below, namely imbeciles and idiots.

'There is a continuity of mental ability reaching from one knows not what height, and descending to one can hardly say what depth. I propose . . . to range men according to their natural abilities, putting them into classes separated by equal degrees of merit, and to show the relative number of individuals included in the several classes.'[20]

In order to do this Galton applies the 'law of deviation from an average', now more usually known as the Gaussian or normal curve, to the range of human abilities. The mathematical equation of the normal curve had been developed by De Moivre in 1733 and worked on by Gauss and La Place in the early part of the nineteenth century. At about that time it was discovered that the errors made by astronomers in taking observations were distributed in a manner approximating to the normal curve and it was the Belgian astronomer, Quetelet, who showed that the heights of French conscripts, the chest measurements of Scottish soldiers, and various other kinds of physical data were similarly distributed. It is characteristic of such data that when the range of measurements is plotted against the frequency with which each occurs a bell shaped curve results which is symmetrical about the high point at the average.

Galton argues that if this state of affairs holds for stature and chest size then it should also be true of other bodily characteristics, such as head circumference, brain weight, number of nerve fibres, etc., from which it seems probable that it should apply to mental capacities. He gives only one direct instance of the applicability of the normal curve to mental ability and that is to measures of academic achievement as seen in the marks obtained in an examination for admission to Sandhurst. From an inspection of the marks he concludes that their distribution accords fairly well with the expected distribution derived from the theoretical postulate.

At that date there was no means at Galton's disposal for testing the probability that his data fitted a normal distribution. When the Sandhurst marks are re-examined in the light of a modern statistic it appears that his conclusion was in fact unjustified : as in examinations generally, the examiners tended to avoid the more extreme categories and to bunch the marks in the medium range.[21] Thus, his one attempt to apply the normal curve to mental measurement was a failure. Too much should not be made of the failure; the assumption of a normal distribution of mental ability has subsequently proved to be of great heuristic value and Galton proceeds to utilise the assumption to describe the rarity of extreme ability.

He divides the range of ability above the average into eight classes from A to G, the classes being separated by supposedly equal amounts of ability. A further class, X, includes anybody above the high class, G. The eight classes below the average are labelled a to g (with x, including all below g).

Although the choice of 16 classes appears to have been fairly arbitrary it does mean that 248 people per million will fall into the top classes F,

G and X, and thus these classes will include all those defined as eminent by his earlier criterion of public reputation. Inclusion in the X category alone requires a rarity value of about 1 in a million which accords with his earlier definition of 'illustrious'.

It is characteristic of the normal distribution that the majority of scores clusters around the average and in the case of Galton's 16 classes the 4 centre classes, b, a, A, B, contain more than four fifths of the entire population. Thus, there is an abundance of mediocrity which he defines as,

> 'the standard of intellectual power found in most provincial gatherings, because the attractions of a more stirring life in the metropolis and elsewhere, are apt to draw away the abler classes of men, and the silly and the imbecile do not take a part in the gatherings.'[22]

He continues :

> 'The class C possesses abilities a trifle higher than those commonly possessed by the foreman of an ordinary jury. D includes the mass of men who obtain the ordinary prizes of life. E is a stage higher. Then we reach F, the lowest of those yet superior classes of intellect, with which this volume is chiefly concerned.
>
> 'On descending the scale, we find by the time we have reached f, that we are already among the idiots and imbeciles.'[23]

Unfortunately, Galton makes an error in arriving at his estimate of 280 true idiots and imbeciles to every million of the population, a ratio which conveniently coincides with the numerical requirements of classes f, g and x. Extant statistics give him the figure of 50 000 idiots and imbeciles out of the twenty million inhabitants of England and Wales. He misreads this ratio of 1 in 400 as 400 per million instead of 2500 per million. He then adopts an estimate of a French authority, Dr Seguin, that about thirty per cent are inappropriately designated as idiots, and thus reaches a final figure of seventy per cent of 400, i.e., 280 true mental defectives per million of the population. Using Seguin's correction and applying it to the actual figure of 2500 per million, a final figure of 1750 should have been arrived at, which is greater than that expected in classes f, g and x.[24] Thus, we cannot accept his conclusion that,

> 'Eminently gifted men are raised as much above mediocrity as idiots are depressed below it; a fact that is calculated to considerably enlarge our ideas of the enormous differences of intellectual gifts between man and man.
>
> 'I presume the class F of dogs and others of the more intelligent sort of animals, is nearly commensurate with the f of the human race, in respect to memory and powers of reason. Certainly the class G of such animals is far superior to the g of humankind.'[25]

Having obtained a method of classifying people by ability he now proceeds to compare this classification with his earlier selection of people by reputation in order to ascertain whether he is justified in employing reputation as his sole criterion of ability.

'By reputation I mean the opinion of contemporaries revised by posterity—the favourable result of a critical analysis of each man's character, by many biographers. I do not mean high social or official position, nor such as is implied by being the mere lion of a London season; but I speak of the reputation of a leader of opinion, of an originator, of a man to whom the world deliberately acknowledges itself largely indebted.

'By natural ability, I mean those qualities of intellect and disposition, which urge and qualify a man to perform acts that lead to reputation. I do not mean capacity without zeal, nor zeal without capacity, nor even a combination of both of them, without an adequate power of doing a great deal of very laborious work. But I mean a nature which, when left to itself, will, urged by an inherent stimulus, climb the path that leads to eminence, and has strength to reach the summit—one which, if hindered or thwarted, will fret and strive until the hindrance is overcome, and it is again free to follow its labour-loving instinct. It is almost a contradiction in terms, to doubt that such men will generally become eminent. On the other hand, there is plenty of evidence in this volume to show that few have won high reputations without possessing these peculiar gifts. It follows that men who achieve eminence, and those who are naturally capable, are, to a large extent, identical.'[26]

In order to show that the qualities of capacity, zeal and industry are inherited and that men of repute possess this triad to a high degree, Galton relies on three strands of argument.

Many men rise from humble origins and compete successfully with those more fortunate in their childhood. These men are not all prodigies of genius and may have no future claim to eminence. While the obstacles in the path of the mediocre men below class D may prevent their rise, most of those above are able to succeed. Thus, Galton did not accept the view that the obstacles provided by the social structure of Victorian England were effectual in preventing high ability from being expressed in achievement. If they were, and this is Galton's second line of argument, then there would have been more eminent men in America where barriers were fewer. Galton did not consider that America produced more first class literature, philosophy or art. Thirdly, he argues that social advantages as such do not give eminence to men who are of only moderate ability. This argument is developed in Part Two of the book where the practice of nepotism among ecclesiastics is shown not to lead to eminence in those so favoured.

Galton's scepticism of the value of a good education for those of high ability can be inferred from these views. Indeed, the person of G intellectual ability is thought to be almost independent of ordinary school education and best left alone to educate himself. Thus it follows that it is fallacious to ascribe one's failure in later life to the want of a better education in one's youth.

> 'People are too apt to complain of their imperfect education, insinuating that they would have done great things if they had been more fortunately circumstanced in youth. But if their power of learning is materially diminished by the time they have discovered their want of knowledge, it is very probable that their abilities are not of a very high description, and that, however well they might have been educated, they would have succeeded but little better.'[27]

Having demonstrated that reputation is a fair measure of ability, Galton proceeds in the second part of the book to provide the data to substantiate his view that ability is inherited. From various independent sources he assembles lists of men eminent in different fields and examines their family records. The most thoroughly researched chapter is the first which concerns the English judges since the Reformation. Galton analyses the kinship of judges and tabulates the incidence with which their relatives achieve eminence. The same procedure is then adopted with statesmen, military commanders, literary men, scientists, poets, musicians, painters, Protestant divines, Senior Classics of Cambridge, oarsmen and wrestlers.

The sections are very uneven and inevitably reflect Galton's own interests and limitations, in addition to the relative comprehensiveness of his sources. Thus, in the chapter devoted to judges (which is an expanded version of the earlier articles in *Macmillan's Magazine*) Galton has recourse to an extensive compilation by Foss (*Lives of the Judges*). As Galton points out, to the average reader the names of the men included in that work are likely to be for the most part meaningless and insignificant, but upon deeper acquaintance with their biographies Galton himself came to look upon them as an 'august Valhalla.'[28] His fascination with the personalities and careers of the judges is evident throughout the chapter. Consider his description of their characteristics :

> 'They are vigorous, shrewd, practical, helpful men; glorying in the rough-and-tumble of public life, tough in constitution and strong in digestion, valuing what money brings, aiming at position and influence, and desiring to found families.'[29]

The question now arises : are these qualities inherited? Galton seeks to answer this question by examining the incidence with which the close relatives of judges follow a judicial career. Of the 286 judges who constitute the material of the enquiry, about one in nine has been either father, son or brother to another judge. This very high proportion leads Galton to conclude that the abilities peculiar to a judge are frequently transmitted by descent.

But it is not only as judges that the relatives of judges achieve eminence. Galton supplies a long list of bishops, admirals, generals, novelists, poets and physicians who are related to judges. Although it seems unlikely that the psychological characteristics enumerated earlier are to be found in all these relations—and that is a weakness in Galton's argument—nevertheless he shows quite clearly that a near-kinsman of a judge is much more likely to be eminent than one who is more distantly related. The conclusion he draws from this fact is that the original triad of characteristics (capacity, zeal and ability to work) necessary to eminence in any sphere must be innately supplied.

'The statistics show that there is a regular average increase of ability in the generations that precede the culmination (of ability), and as regular a decrease in those that succeed it. In the first case the marriages have been consentient to its production, in the latter they have been incapable of preserving it.'[30]

The following table vividly illustrates his claim. But it is based on an assumption about the number of children possessed by many of the judges for whom data were not available. Galton assumes that on an average a judge has one son who lives to an age at which he might become distinguished. If, as seems likely, this figure is an underestimate, then a smaller proportion of the children reached eminence than Galton assumed. Double or treble the number of sons, and the estimate in the table of 36% who reach eminence would have to be reduced to 18% or 12%.

Although we cannot place much reliance on the actual percentages, Galton's point that the percentages are drastically reduced at each remove is still valid. In the first degree of kinship (father, brother and son) the average percentage is about 28; in the second (grandfather, grandson, uncle and nephew) it is about 7; in the third (great grandfather, great grandson, great uncle, great nephew and cousin) it is reduced to 1.5. A near kinsman is much more likely to achieve eminence than one more remote.

It follows that the practice of primogeniture, as it applies to titles and property, cannot logically be based on the supposed hereditary transmission of ability.

TABLE 7.1

Percentage of eminent men in each degree of kinship to the most gifted member of distinguished families. (From *Hereditary Genius*, p. 123.)

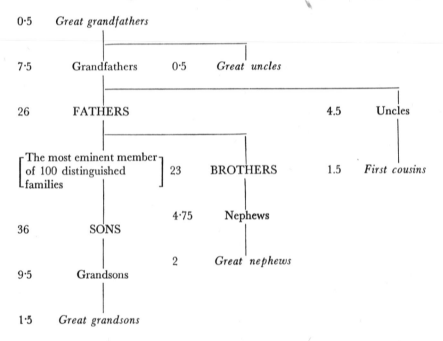

'A man who has no able ancestor nearer in blood to him than a great-grandparent, is inappreciably better off in the chance of being himself gifted with ability, than if he had been taken out of the general mass of men. An old peerage is a valueless title to natural gifts, except so far as it may have been furbished up by a succession of wise inter-marriages. When however, as is often the case, the direct line has become extinct and the title has passed to a distant relative, who has not been reared in the family traditions, the sentiment that is attached to its possession is utterly unreasonable. I cannot think of any claim to respect, put forward in modern days, that is so entirely an imposture, as that made by a peer on the ground of descent, who has neither been nobly educated, nor has any eminent kinsman, within three degrees.'[31]

A striking fact, particularly evident in the case of judges and statesmen who have been made peers, is that these eminent families tend to die out. Galton shows that the reason lies in their tendency to marry heiresses. The motives for such marriages are obvious : the heiress possesses a fortune but no title, while the peer has the title but seeks an increase in his possessions. These marriages are peculiarly unprolific because heiresses have been born of parents who are relatively infertile, an infertility which they themselves inherit.

The infertility of heiresses had been noted by Erasmus Darwin who had however ascribed it to the prevalence of hereditary diseases. Thus, he considered it hazardous to marry an heiress as she was likely to be the last of a diseased family. Such a possibility is not mentioned by Galton, although he had read *The Temple of Nature* in which his grandfather had written on the matter.[32] Galton's own view that fertility is genetically determined would be generally accepted today.[33]

In contrast to the full discussion of the judges, Galton's treatment of poets, musicians and painters is cursory, while the section devoted to the clergy is remarkable for its lack of sympathy with theological enquiry, a general sense of criticism pervading his whole account. As a group the clergy are but moderately prolific and do not emerge as the founders of influential families. Twenty six out of the divines whose lives Galton examines were certain invalids, and many suffered from poor health, 'a large part of religious biographies being given up to the occurrences of the sickroom.'[34]

Although their children appear frequently to follow their father's profession, from which fact Galton assumes that a pious disposition is inherited, there are some extreme exceptions to the rule, where the children turn out badly. Galton explains the exceptions by means of an ingenious hypothesis to the effect that religious people combine strong moral tendencies with instability of disposition, that is, with a liability to extremes. At one time they may appear sensual and selfish, at another ascetic and selfsacrificing.

'The amplitude of the moral oscillations of religious men is greater than that of others whose *average* moral position is the same.'[35]

The two characteristics of strong morality and instability are in no way correlated,* and the child of religious parents may inherit the instability without the piety.

In contrast to his treatment of the clergy the chapter on scientists is Galton at his most enthusiastic. The data provided in *Hereditary Genius* were shortly to be superseded by the more trustworthy facts included in his next major publication, *English Men of Science* (1874). We can note now an interesting similarity between the clergy and the scientists: both appear to be influenced by the attitudes of their mothers to a greater degree than men eminent in other spheres. Galton believes that whereas

---

* The first occasion on which Galton uses the term. He was not to discover a means of expressing correlation in a numerical sense for many years.

the clergyman needed a secure groundwork to his faith which was best laid by maternal conviction imparted during early childhood, the scientist required a mother who would show her child,

'by practice and teaching, that inquiry may be absolutely free without being irreverent, that reverence for truth is the parent of free inquiry, and that indifference or insincerity in the search after truth is one of the most degrading of sins.'[36]

This passage is the only one in the book in which Galton appears to accept the influence of early environment on attitudes held later in life. In *English Men of Science* he has more to say on the whole question of the interaction between hereditary endowment and environmental circumstance, and in his later twin studies he opens the way for a comparative evaluation of their respective influence.

Results from the various sections are brought together and discussed in Part III of the book. The following table, modified from *Hereditary Genius*, reveals the general uniformity in these results.

TABLE 7.2

Percentage of eminent men of various professional groups in each degree of kinship. (Table modified from *Hereditary Genius*, p. 375.)

Relationship	Percentage of eminent relatives found in the different groups								All groups together
	Judges	*Statesmen*	*Commanders*	*Literary men*	*Scientists*	*Poets*	*Painters and Musicians*	*Divines*	
Father	26	33	47	48	26	20	32	28	31
Brother	35	39	50	42	47	40	50	36	41
Son	36	49	31	51	60	45	89	40	48
Grandfather	15	28	16	24	14	5	7	20	17
Uncle	18	18	8	24	16	5	14	40	18
Nephew	19	18	35	24	23	50	18	4	22
Grandson	19	10	12	9	14	5	18	16	14
Great grandfather	2	8	8	3	0	0	0	4	3
Great uncle	4	5	8	6	5	5	7	4	5
First cousin	11	21	20	18	16	0	1	8	13
Great nephew	17	5	8	6	16	10	0	0	10
Great grandson	6	0	0	3	7	0	0	0	3
All more remote	14	37	44	15	23	5	18	16	31

The overall results are in very close agreement with those derived from the subgroup of judges. Eminent sons are again most frequent and sudden drops occur between 1st and 2nd grades of kinship and between 2nd and 3rd grades. Galton concludes:

'There cannot, therefore, remain a doubt as to the existence of a law of distribution of ability in families.'[37]

The exact nature of this 'law' escaped him at the time. Later, in *Natural Inheritance* (1889), he was to elaborate it in some detail and we shall consider it in that context.

Although Galton did not realise the importance of the social context in determining the extent to which inter-breeding is restricted, he was certainly aware of a mutually selective process in the marriages of his eminent men.

'Able men take pleasure in the society of intelligent women, and if they can find such as would in other respects be suitable, they will marry them in preference to mediocrities.'[38]

Thus, he assumes that the large number of eminent descendants found in his enquiry are the result of marriages of gifted partners, but lacking the wherewithal to estimate the ability of the wives he had to rest content with a less than complete picture.

From his main conclusions Galton proceeds to consider in a much more speculative vein their racial and national implications. Several pieces of evidence lead him to believe that negroes are two grades below the white races in their natural abilities. He argues that very few negroes have ever shown ability as high as our class F, which must therefore be regarded as equivalent to their class X. Secondly, white travellers invariably hold their own with the native chiefs with whom they come into contact. The chiefs are highly selected from among their own kind and maintain their place by their abilities; yet these abilities are inferior to those of the traveller who is not usually an outstanding individual in his own culture. Thirdly, the number of mentally deficient negroes is very large, a 'fact' which struck Galton during his own travels.

'The mistakes the negroes made in their own matters were so childish, stupid and simpleton-like, as frequently to make me ashamed of my own species.'[39]

It is unnecessary to submit his comments on racial differences to a detailed analysis in view of the mass of modern work by social anthropologists and psychologists in which the difficulties involved in making comparative assessments of ability between cultures are well documented.[40] Galton's complacent application of criteria of Victorian excellence to cultures so divergent from his own was commonplace among his contemporaries; such travellers as Burton and Baker adopt an equally derogatory tone whenever they refer to the African negro.

Galton's argument is even more suspect when his speculations take an historical turn. If, he claims, the negro is two grades below ourselves, the Athenian of 530–430 B.C. was as much above.

> 'This estimate, which may seem prodigious to some, is confirmed by the quick intelligence and high culture of the Athenian commonality, before whom literary works were recited, and works of art exhibited, of a far more severe character than could possibly be appreciated by the average of our race, the calibre of whose intellect is easily gauged by a glance at the contents of a railway bookstall.'[41]

Karl Pearson makes the telling point that Galton has completely ignored the existence of the 400 000 or so slaves who made up the labouring and artisan classes of ancient Athens, while he includes these categories of the population in his contemporary comparison.[42]

Galton appears to be on firmer ground when he examines the implications of his findings for the welfare of the nation. An enormous effect upon the average natural ability might be produced by a policy which encourages early marriage among the vigorous while retarding it among the weak. A very slight difference in fertility between two classes of the community will in a few centuries lead to an enormous change in the composition of that community. For example, if one class marries 11 years earlier than another equally large class, then in two centuries the mature descendants of the former will outnumber those of the latter in the ratio of 26 : 1.

The views of Malthus, which had increased enormously in popularity following the second edition of his book in 1803, were seen by Galton as menacing the survival of the more able.[43] According to Malthus, the most powerful check on population growth was to be provided by the 'moral restraint' of the people in postponing marriage. (He was completely opposed to the use of contraception within marriage.)[44] But, as Galton clearly saw, it would be the intelligent and thoughtful members of society who would be more likely to follow this course of action.

> 'I have no hesitation in saying that it is a most pernicious rule of conduct in its bearing upon race. Its effects would be such as to cause the races of the prudent to fall, after a few centuries, into an almost incredible inferiority of numbers to that of the imprudent, and it is therefore calculated to bring utter ruin upon the breed of any country where the doctrine prevailed. I protest against the abler races

being encouraged to withdraw in this way from the struggle for existence. It may seem monstrous that the weak should be crowded out by the strong, but it is still more monstrous that the races best fitted to play their part on the stage of life, should be crowded out by the incompetent, the ailing, and the desponding.'[45]

Even stronger condemnation is reserved for the part played by the Church in its selective influence on past breeding habits.

'Whenever a man or woman was possessed of a gentle nature that fitted him or her to deeds of charity, to meditation, to literature, or to art, the social condition of the time was such that they had no refuge elsewhere than in the bosom of the Church. But the Church chose to preach and exact celibacy. The consequence was that these gentle natures had no continuance, and thus, by a policy so singularly unwise and suicidal that I am hardly able to speak of it without impatience, the Church brutalised the breed of our forefathers.'[46]

In addition to extinguishing the gentle, the Church persecuted many intelligent freethinkers, who were imprisoned, executed, or forced to flee their countries.

'Those she reserved on these occasions, to breed the generations of the future, were the servile, the indifferent, and, again, the stupid . . . In consequence of this inbred imperfection of our natures, in respect to the conditions under which we have to live, we are, even now, almost as much harrassed by the sense of moral incapacity and sin, as were the early converts from barbarism, and we steep ourselves in half-unconscious self-deception and hypocrisy, as a partial refuge from its insistence. Our avowed creeds remain at variance with our real rules of conduct, and we lead a dual life of barren religious sentimentalism and gross materialistic habitudes.'[47]

Galton's concluding paragraph is worth quoting in its entirety, as it was his first clear statement of a programme for the future. He was to make many further appeals for race betterment in later years when his eugenic proposals had attracted the attention of a variety of enthusiasts.

'The best form of civilisation in respect to the improvement of the race, would be one in which society was not costly; where incomes were chiefly derived from professional sources, and not much through inheritance; where every lad had a chance of showing his abilities and, if highly gifted, was enabled to achieve a first-class education and entrance into professional life, by the liberal help of the exhibitions and scholarships which he had gained in his early youth; where marriage was held in as high honour as in ancient Jewish times;

where the pride of race was encouraged (of course I do not refer
to the nonsensical sentiment of the present day, that goes under that
name); where the weak could find a welcome and a refuge in celibate
monasteries or sisterhoods, and lastly, where the better sort of emigrants and refugees from other lands were invited and welcomed,
and their descendants naturalised.'[48]

In spite of its literary merits the nonscientific reviewers of *Hereditary
Genius* gave the book a poor reception, mainly on account of their distaste
for Galton's critical strictures on the Church and the clergy. The contemporary scientific reviewers were much more positive. Alfred Wallace,
reviewing it in the first volume of *Nature*, thought that the book would
'take rank as an important and valuable addition to the science of human
nature.'[49] But it was the response from Charles Darwin that gave Galton
the greatest delight :

'My dear Galton,
    I have only read about 50 pages of your book (to Judges), but
I must exhale myself, else something will go wrong in my inside.
I do not think I ever in all my life read anything more interesting
and original—and how well and clearly you put every point . . .
You have made a convert of an opponent in one sense, for I have
always maintained that excepting fools, men did not differ much
in intellect, only in zeal and hard work; and I still think this is an
eminently important difference. I congratulate you on producing
what I am convinced will prove a memorable work. I look forward
with intense interest to each reading, but it sets me thinking so
much that I find it very hard work; but that is wholly the fault of
my brain and not your beautifully clear style.
                              Yours most sincerely,
                                 Ch. Darwin'[50]

Darwin cannot have finished reading the book or he would surely have
commented on the final chapter which we have omitted from consideration here as it bears little relation to the rest of the book. In it, Galton
attempts to adapt Darwin's theory of inheritance to his own findings,
but in his exposition of that theory Galton shows, as we shall see, that
he was mistaken about its exact nature.

8

Heredity and Religion

In the mid-nineteenth century it was generally accepted that some substance derived from the parents went to form a mixture in the offspring who were thus intermediate in nature between the parents. Although Darwin accepted the view that inheritance was generally of this blending type he could see that it afforded a problem for his theory of natural selection as it would entail a reduction in variation from one generation to the next until complete uniformity would result.[1] Darwin's attempt to overcome this difficulty led him to postulate the theory of pangenesis. He supposed that each cell of the body contributed particles, or 'gemmules', which came together in the sperm or ova. Changes in the bodily organs would cause changes in the gemmules which would in turn cause new variations to arise. Thus, he thought environmental influences could lead to the acquisition of characters which could be transmitted to the offspring, essentially a Lamarckian standpoint.

Galton understood pangenesis to entail the circulation in the blood stream of the gemmules from the bodily cells. He presumed that the blood would normally be full of them and that they would live for a considerable time in the blood stream. It therefore seemed likely that the offspring of a pair of animals would be affected by any alteration in the blood of the parents which occurred not long before mating. He decided to begin a series of experiments with silver grey rabbits from which he intended to breed after transfusing them with blood from the common lop-eared rabbit.

According to Loiusa's *Record*, he joined the Zoological Society in 1870 and elicited the help of Dr Murie, the Prosector at the Zoological Gardens, who did the dexterous work.[2] Various techniques of transfusion were tried and the experiments lasted for two years. Towards the end of that time Murie and Galton had established a method of cross-circulation between the carotid arteries of the two varieties of rabbit in which as much as 50% of the total blood was sometimes interchanged. The animals were little affected by the operation and mated readily within minutes of its conclusion. Although at first excited by the appearance of white markings in the offspring of the transfused silver greys, Galton discovered on enquiry that such varieties were common. In fact, not a single instance of alteration in breed occurred out of a total of 88 young.

Galton concluded that the theory of pangenesis, as he had understood it, was incorrect.

'Let us consider what the alternatives were before us. It seems *a priori* that, if the reproductive elements do not depend on the body and blood together, they must reside either in the solid structure of the (reproductive) gland, whence they are set free by the ordinary process of growth, the blood merely affording nutriment to that growth, or else that they reside in the blood itself. My experiments show that they are not independent residents in the blood, in the way that Pangenesis asserts; but they prove nothing against the possibility of their being temporary inhabitants of it.'[3]

Thus the transfused gemmules may have perished, just like the blood corpuscles, before the animals had recovered from the operation. Galton suggests the possibility of further experiments in which rabbits might be mated immediately and at various times after the operation.

'It would be exceedingly instructive, supposing the experiments to give affirmative results, to notice the gradually waning powers of producing mongrel offspring.'[4]

It is clear that Galton was cautious in his partial rejection of Darwin's theory. The sharp riposte he now received from Darwin must have been totally unexpected in view of the fact that during the course of the experiments the two men had been in correspondence. Pearson has traced twelve letters from Galton to Darwin in which he requested technical advice and supplied full information about his provisional results.[5] It is difficult to understand how Darwin could have permitted Galton to continue in his belief that the work was relevant to the theory of pangenesis if he thought it was not. And yet he certainly expressed that opinion in a letter he wrote to *Nature* a month after Galton's paper appeared.

'In the chapter on Pangenesis in my "Variation of Animals and Plants under Domestication", I have not said one word about the blood, or about any fluid proper to any circulating system. It is, indeed, obvious that the presence of gemmules in the blood can form no necessary part of my hypothesis, for I refer in illustration of it to the lowest animals, such as the Protozoa, which do not possess blood or any vessels; and I refer to plants in which the fluid, when present in the vessels, cannot be considered as true blood. The fundamental laws of growth, reproduction, inheritance, etc. are so closely similar throughout the whole organic kingdom, that the means by which the gemmules (assuming for the moment their existence) are diffused through the body, would probably be the same in all beings; therefore the means can hardly be diffusion through the blood. Nevertheless, when I first heard of Mr Galton's experiments I did not sufficiently reflect on the subject, and saw not the difficulty of believing in the presence of gemmules in the blood. I have said . . . that "the gemmules in each organism must be thoroughly diffused; nor does this seem improbable, considering their minuteness, and the steady circulation of fluids throughout the body." But when I used these latter words and other similar ones, I presume that I was thinking of the diffusion of the gemmules through the tissues, or from cell to cell, independently of the presence of vessels. Nor can it be objected that the gemmules could not pass through tissues or cell walls, for the contents of each pollen grain have to pass through the coats, both of the pollen tube and embryonic sack.'[6]

Galton's reply appeared in the following week's edition of *Nature*. It is so characteristic of the man that although too long to reproduce in full I cannot refrain from quoting its concluding paragraph. Galton begins with a careful analysis of the words used by Darwin in his published account of his theory. Galton indicates the ambiguity contained in Darwin's statement that the gemmules must be 'thoroughly diffused' and that this it not improbable considering 'the steady circulation of fluids throughout the body,' a statement which apparently implicates blood flow. He suggests an alteration in Darwin's wording and concludes his letter with this pleasing simile :

'I do not much complain of having been sent on a false quest by ambiguous language, for I know how conscientious Mr Darwin is in all he writes, how difficult it is to put thoughts into accurate speech, and, again, how words have conveyed false impressions on the simplest matters from the earliest times. Nay, even in that idyllic scene which Mr Darwin has sketched of the first invention of language, awkward blunders must of necessity have often occurred. I refer to the passage in which he supposes some unusually wise ape-like animal to have first thought of imitating the growl of a beast of prey so as to indicate to his fellow monkeys the nature of expected danger. For my part, I feel as if I had just been assisting at such a scene. As if, having heard my trusted leader utter a cry, not particularly well-articulated, but to my ears more like that of a hyena than of any other animal, and seeing none of my companions stir a step, I had, like a loyal member of the flock, dashed down a path of which I had happily caught sight, into the plain below, followed by the approving nods and kindly grunts of my wise and most respected chief. And I now feel, after returning from my hard expedition, full of information that the suspected danger was a mistake, for there was no sign of a hyena anywhere in the neighbourhood. I am given to understand for the first time that my leader's cry had no reference to a hyena down in the plain, but to a leopard somewhere up in the trees; his throat had been a little out of order—that was all. Well, my labour has not been in vain; it is something to have established the fact that there are no hyenas in the plain, and I think I see my way to a good position for a look out for leopards among the branches of the trees. In the meantime, Viva Pangenesis!'[7]

Galton did not conclude his experiments with this recognition of his error but continued them on a less intensive scale for another two years with Darwin now taking a more active role. This increased interest on Darwin's part suggests that he must have considered the work to be of some relevance to his theory. But results continued to be negative and were never published. Darwin was, however, led to modify the wording in which he described the pangenesis theory in later editions of his book and to admit in a footnote that he would have expected to have found gemmules in the blood although their presence there was not necessary to his hypothesis.[8]

The progress of Galton's thinking about the hereditary mechanism during the 1870s can be traced in two papers written in 1872 and 1875 in which he achieved a partial rejection of pangenesis. That his rejection was not more complete can most probably be attributed to his great admiration for Darwin as a scientist.

Both papers were sent to Darwin for his comments but only in the case of the first was there time to incorporate his suggestions to make the text more intelligible. The argument in the second paper remains difficult to follow, complicated as it is by Galton's introduction of new and often undefined terms.

The first paper, entitled *On Blood Relationship*, has as its aim an elucidation of the word, 'kinship'.[9] Galton sets himself the task of describing the hereditary connections between an individual and his parents and more distant kinsfolk.

'From the well-known circumstance that an individual may transmit to his descendants ancestral qualities which he does not himself possess, we are assured that they could not have been altogether destroyed in him, but must have maintained their existence in a latent form. Therefore each individual may properly be conceived as consisting of two parts, one of which is latent and only known to us by its effects on his posterity, while the other is patent, and constitutes the person manifest to our senses.'[10]

Both patent and latent elements make their respective contributions to the heredity of the offspring, but the contribution of the latter far outweighs that of the former. Indeed, nearly all the characteristics of the organism have latent equivalents and it is rare for a purely patent characteristic to be transmitted.

The dichotomy between patent and latent elements was unfortunate. Galton appears to have been on the brink of asserting that only the latent elements were involved in hereditary transmission. If he could have taken this step and further have stated that the patent elements were always no more than an index to the latent elements he would have reached the theory of the continuity of the germ plasm.

However, an important point has been made in this paper. Galton expresses it in the following words :

'We cannot now fail to be impressed with the fallacy of reckoning inheritance in the usual way, from parents to offspring, using these words in their popular sense of visible personalities. The span of the true hereditary link connects, as I have already insisted upon, not the parent with the offspring, but the primary elements of the two, such as they existed in the newly impregnated ova, whence they were respectively developed.'[11]

Applying these principles to the inheritance of ability he concludes :

'It has been thought by some that the fact of children frequently showing marked individual variation in ability from that of their parents is a proof that intellectual and moral gifts are not strictly transmitted by inheritance. My arguments lead to exactly the opposite result. I show that their great individual variation is a necessity under present conditions : and I maintain that results derived from large averages are all that can be required, and all we could expect to obtain, to prove that intellectual and moral gifts are as strictly matters of inheritance as any purely physical qualities.'[12]

The second paper, *A Theory of Heredity*, represents a much more detailed approach to the hereditary mechanism coupled with a slight advance on the earlier argument.[13]

Galton begins by coining the word 'stirp' (from Latin *stirpes*, a root) to express the organised total of germs, or gemmules, in the newly fertilised ovum. Each stirp is held to contain a large variety of germs, some few of which develop into the individual, the larger remainder contributing to the stirp of the descendants. Those germs which develop into the somatic cells of the individual are still considered on occasion to give off gemmules which may find their way into the circulation and ultimately become lodged in the larger sexual part of the stirp. Thus Galton accepts the possibility that somatic alterations in the individual may be inherited by the offspring, but he considers it very rare. He cites numerous instances where the transmission of acquired characteristics has been claimed, but dismisses them all as a collection of coincidences without sufficient supporting evidence. It follows that the theory of pangenesis, if it is necessary to hold it at all, certainly cannot play more than a supplementary and subordinate role in any complete theory of heredity.

Concentrating his attention on the strip itself Galton considers the ways in which the germs within it must compete for survival. The necessity for competition results from the double parentage of a child, the stirp from which the child springs being only half the size of the combined stirps of the two parents; thus, one half of a child's parentage must be in some way suppressed. Although unable to understand the repulsions and affinities of the germs, Galton was able to draw an analogy :

> 'We may compare the stirp to a nation and those among its germs that achieve development, to the foremost men of that nation who succeed in becoming its representatives; lastly, we may compare the characteristics of the person whose bodily structure consists of the developed germs, to those of the house of representatives of the nation.'[14]

In animals of pure breed, whose stirp contains only one or a few varieties of each species of germ, the offspring will always resemble their parents and each other; the more mongrel the breed, the greater will be the variety of the offspring. Thus, it is no occasion for surprise that brothers and sisters are frequently dissimilar or that talented parents do not always produce talented children.

> 'The hypothesis of organic units enables us to specify with much clearness the curiously circuitous relation which connects the offspring with the parents. The idea of its being one of direct descent, in the common acceptance of that vague phrase, is wholly untenable, and is the chief cause why most persons seem perplexed at the appearance of capriciousness in hereditary transmission. The stirp of the child may be considered to have descended directly from a part of the stirps of each of its parents, but then the personal structure of the child is no more than an imperfect representation of each of their own stirps.'[15]

Galton was obviously very close to the discovery of the continuity of the germ plasm and to a complete rejection of pangenesis. It is curious too how close he was at this time to another discovery, that of Mendel's Principle of Segregation. In a letter to Darwin dated 19th December 1875, Galton discusses the production of a grey–coloured hybrid plant from the crossing of black and white varieties. The grey tint might be due to a mixture of black and white cells, or to the presence of grey cells. In the first case the structural unit would be identical with the organic unit, whereas in the second case the structural unit would not be an organic unit but an organic molecule due to the development of a group of gemmules in which the black and white species would be equally numerous.

'The larger the number of gemmules in each organic molecule the more *uniform* will the tint of greyish be in the different units of structure. It has been an old idea of mine, not yet discarded and not yet worked out, that the number of units in each molecule may admit of being discovered by noting the relative number of cases of each grade of deviation from the mean greyness. If there were 2 gemmules only, each of which might be white or black, then in a large number of cases one quarter would always be quite white, one quarter black, and one half would be grey. If there were 3 molecules, we should have 4 grades of colour (1 quite white, 3 light grey, 3 dark grey, 1 quite black and so on according to the successive lines of "Pascal's triangle"). This way of looking at the matter would perhaps show (a) whether the number in each given species of molecule was constant, and (b), if so, what those numbers were.'[16]

It is even stranger that, in an attempt to elucidate the hereditary mechanism, Galton now began to breed sweet peas. Mendel, unknown to the scientific world, had already conducted his crucial experiments with edible peas, the results of which form the basis of modern genetics. From his own experiments with peas Galton was to derive the regression line in a first attempt to obtain a measure of correlation between the characteristics of parents and offspring. But these beginnings of his statistical work can be more appropriately considered in a later chapter.

His domestic situation was much the same; Louisa was in indifferent health during the early 1870s and her usual difficulties with servants led to the loss of her personal maid and cook. Her husband had a better eye for a servant and engaged a Swiss, Albert Gifi, in 1870 who remained with him until the end. They saw little of Galton's brothers; Darwin had had an epileptic attack, and then lost his first wife. He remarried within three years, but his second wife was past the age of childbearing. Erasmus continued his solitary existence on his estate. Neither Adèle nor Bessy figures much in Galton's correspondence at this date. Emma who was still living with her mother at Leamington was the main source of family news. She had written a book in 1863 entitled *Guide to the Unprotected*, which had gone through four editions in three years. It was a handbook of advice to women on how to handle money, a matter in which Emma seems to have had great interest and competence.

In 1872 Louisa's mother died and Louisa made an unusually long entry in her *Record*.

'1872. A marked year in many ways and chiefly so by the death of my dearest mother on Feb 24 at Julian Hill after 6 days' illness from a chill by going into the cold drawing room. She had no strength to bear up against the attack. The week before we were at Southsea enjoying the Dockyard at Portsmouth and the sight of the great Ships of War. Capt. Hall took us about in his steam launch. We went over the Wellington, the Victory, the St. Vincent training ship, the Queen's yacht, the Enchantress and the Monarch and Devastation the great Ironclads, also the Trafalgar previous to its sailing next day. The Gassiots very kind to us. We were back home Feb 12 and had no uneasiness about dear Mother till Feb 23, the next day a Telegram summoned us hastily, but she was not conscious when we arrived. She was buried at Harrow on Feb 29, a solemn but striking day to us all, the arrangements beautifully made by Montagu. I had not seen her since Oct 17, as she had been feeble and had servants changing and was not able to have us.

'All the months after till Augt. we were often at Julian Hill. We went to Leamington for Easter on March 27. Mrs Galton well, left April 8. George and Josephine and sons came up in July. Family Meeting at Julian Hill July 6. The Gurneys returned from America May 8. Many pleasant meetings with them. Frank taken up with Spiritualism and attended meetings at Mr Crookes and Cox. We went to Brighton on Aug 8 for the Brit. Asstn, and Emma joined us on the 10th. Frank President of the Geographical Section : Stanley made himself most conspicuous and obnoxious. We left on the 24th and went home for a week and then to Tunbridge Wells having seen Dr de Mussey, on Sept 3. Very ill with cholera and F. with fever. Remained till Oct 14, when hurried home on account of dear Emma's operation for Ovarian Tumour on Oct 17. All went on well and she came to us the 13th of Decbr for a few days. We spent Xtmas with the Douglas Galtons at Hadzor [near Droitwich] very pleasantly. A remarkably wet year. Frank busy writing on Hereditary Subjects. A paper in Fraser. My sisters and Arthur went to Rome in December. Spencer to live at Julian Hill. Found the comfort of an extra servant this year. Missed the absence of E. Gurney and M. North very much. Arthur Smith died on Dec 26.'

Louisa's comment on her husband's fascination with spiritualism refers to a series of séances he attended at the houses of Mr Crookes and Sergeant Cox. He had first dabbled in spiritualism during the summer of 1853 soon after his engagement to Louisa. On that occasion he had been impressed by the medium's knowledge of the Damara language with which he tested her. As he was the only European with a knowledge of the language her messages from a deceased Damara chief could presumably only have been achieved by some form of telepathic communication from Galton. Results from the 1872 séances were also striking and Galton wrote enthusiastically to Charles Darwin :

'I can't write at length to describe more particularly the extra-ordinary things of my last séance on Monday. I had hold in one of my hands of *both* hands of Miss Fox's companion who also rested *both* her feet on my instep and Crookes had equally firm possession of Miss Fox. The other people present were his wife and her mother and all hands were joined. Yet paper went skimming in the dark about the room and after the word "Listen" was rapped out the pencil was heard (in the complete darkness) to be writing at a furious rate under the table, between Crookes and his wife and when that was over and we were told (rapped) to light up, the paper was written over—all the side of a bit of *marked* note paper . . . with very respectable platitudes—rather above the level of Martin Tupper's compositions and signed "Benjamin Franklin"! The absurdity on the one hand and the extraordinary character of the thing on the other, quite staggers me; wondering what I shall yet see and learn I remain at present quite passive with my eyes and ears open.'[17]

Séances with another medium, Home, were held in full gaslight and Galton was able to take a more active part, going under the table to hold the medium's feet while the table tilted.

'What surprises me, is the perfect apparent openness of Miss Fox and Home. They let you do whatever you like, within certain reason-able limits, their limits not interfering with adequate investigation. I really believe the truth of what they allege, that people who come as men of science are usually so disagreeable, opinionated and obstructive and have so little patience, that the seances rarely succeed with them . . . He and Miss Fox just want civil treatment and a show of interest. Of course, while one is civil and obliging, it is perfectly easy to be wary.'[18]

Galton tried to arrange for Charles Darwin and himself to be the only two present at the next séance, but Home did not reply to his invitation and left the country. A further attempt with another medium was inconclusive and Galton's attitude to spiritualistic phenomena now underwent a radical and unexplained change. He may have become aware of Robert Browning's poem, 'Mr Sludge, The Medium', in which Home had been exposed as a charlatan, or he may have read T. H. Huxley's critical analysis of a séance in which the manifestations were proved to be fraudulent.[19] At all events he did not attend any further séances and in a later letter to Pearson expressed an attitude of complete rejection.[20]

A strange omission from Louisa's *Record* is any reference to Galton's paper on prayer which appeared in the *Fortnightly Review*[21] and which led to an extended debate in the pages of *The Spectator*.[22]

In view of the publicity the paper received, she can hardly have remained in ignorance of its appearance, even if her husband had concealed its publication from her in order not to hurt her feelings. There is no record of her reaction at the time, although when the paper was reissued eleven years later there is indirect evidence of her distress on that occasion.

The substance of Galton's argument was assembled when he was working on the chapter in *Hereditary Genius* devoted to the clergy. He tried to publish it then but it was rejected by the *Fortnightly Review* on the grounds that the proprietors, although not the editor, were all Christians, and as the editor wrote,

'Your paper is too terribly conclusive and offensive not to raise a hornet's nest.'[23]

Two other rejections followed in the early 1870s until finally the new editor of the *Fortnightly Review*, John Morley, felt able to accept it.

Galton begins his paper by reference to a recent dictionary of the bible in which the scriptures are said to express the view that blessings, both spiritual and temporal, should be asked for in prayer. The question whether such temporal prayers are answered is amenable to statistical treatment. Two lines of enquiry are possible, either to deal with isolated instances, which may be open to bias on the part of the investigator, or to examine large classes of cases and to be guided by averages. In the latter case, examples need to be gathered from two groups of people, those of materialistic and those of prayerful persuasion. Thus we may take sick persons who pray and ask if they recover on the average more rapidly than those comparably sick who do not pray. Galton supplies no statistics in answer to this question but is content to cite the lack of medical support for the view that prayerful people have a better prognosis.

An enquiry of a somewhat similar nature concerns the longevity of prayerful people and that of persons whose lives are prayed for. Galton refers to a table of the mean age at death of males of various occupations compiled for the years from 1758 to 1843. The average for clergymen is

69·49 compared with the less prayerful professions of lawyer (68·14) and doctor (67·31). The small difference he attributes to the easy country life of the clergy favouring their health. When eminent members of these professions, whose names are to be found in a biographical dictionary, are compared, the averages are reduced and the trend reversed, clergymen living 66·42, lawyers 66·51 and doctors 67·04 years.

> 'Hence the prayers of the clergy for protection against the perils and dangers of the night, for protection during the day, and for recovery from sickness, appear to be futile in result.'[24]

The public prayer for the sovereign of the state is likewise shown to be completely ineffectual as sovereigns are the shortest lived of all those who have the advantage of affluence. Their average age of death is 64·04 years while the English aristocracy live until they are 67·31 and the English gentry until they are 70·22 years.

Missionaries, who pray much and are prayed for, often die in the tropical climates of the peoples they are sent out to convert shortly after their arrival there. Vessels on missionary enterprises do not appear to be favoured by success any more than those of traders embarked on purely profane activities. Commercial undertakings are not more secure when devout men are among the shareholders or when the funds of religious bodies are involved in their transactions. If prayerful habits had influence on temporal success it is very probable that insurance companies would make allowance for it. But no insurance company asks questions of its applicants about their private or family devotions. Nor do insurance companies take into account the relative risks run by ships and buildings owned by religious bodies. It was at one time considered to show mistrust in God to put lightning conductors on churches, but Arago's statistics showed that they were necessary. Many other items of ancient faith are now considered to be superstition: the laying on of hands by the sovereign, the burning of witches, the use of ordeals by fire, the miraculous power of relics have all been abandoned. Likewise, the civilised world must give up all belief in the efficacy of prayer. The evidence is consistently negative and the *onus probandi* rests with those who still believe in it.

But Galton does not deny the possible subjective efficacy of prayer. The mind may be relieved by the utterance of a prayer. Just as any mother who has lost her young may wander about moaning and looking for sympathy, so may those with more complex emotions put their pleas into prayerful form.

> 'A confident sense of communion with God must necessarily rejoice and strengthen the heart, and divert it from petty cares; and it is equally certain that similar benefits are not excluded from

those who on conscientious grounds are sceptical as to the reality of a power of communion. These can dwell on the undoubted fact, that there exists a solidarity between themselves and what surrounds them, through the endless reactions of physical laws, among which the hereditary influences are to be included. They know that they are descended from an endless past, that they have a brotherhood with all that is, and have each his own share of responsibility in the parentage of an endless future. The effort to familiarise the imagination with this great idea has much in common with the effort of communing with a God, and its reaction on the mind of the thinker is in many important respects the same. It may not equally rejoice the heart, but it is quite as powerful in ennobling the resolves, and it is found to give serenity during the trials of life and in the shadow of approaching death.'[25]

The publication of Galton's paper drew the fire of *The Spectator* and a controversy continued on fairly predictable lines. Galton, it was said, had ignored the distinction between the genuine earnest prayers of individuals and the merely formal petitions for the longevity of the monarch which barely deserved to be called prayers. He had also omitted consideration of prayers asking for guidance in coming to moral decisions. The upshot of the discussion was to identify Galton as an agnostic with a superficial knowledge of religious practice and to condemn him as a flippant opponent of Christianity. But such criticisms appear not to have disturbed him as he was by now safely ensconced in the milieu of militant scientific freethought with such men as Huxley and Tyndall as protagonists.

If Galton took the prayer controversy in his stride he was not so fortunate with regard to another debate which arose in the same year and which brought him somewhat reluctantly into the public arena.

9

The Stanley Affair

In order to understand Galton's involvement in what came to be called
'The Stanley Affair', it is necessary to trace the sequence of events that
preceded the arrival in England of H. M. Stanley, the newspaper correspondent, who brought with him the long awaited news of Britain's most
popular explorer, Dr Livingstone.

As far as the Royal Geographical Society was concerned the affair
can be said to have begun in November 1871 when they received news
from Dr Kirk, the British consul in Zanzibar, that Stanley had left for
the African interior. Kirk believed that Stanley had financed his own
expedition and that the possible discovery of Livingstone's whereabouts
was incidental to its main purpose which was to have an enjoyable shoot.

The Society itself had never expressed any fear about Livingstone's
safety although they had had no direct communication from him for two
and a half years. Livingstone had become very difficult and was extremely
suspicious of the motives of the 'insane geographers' whom he believed
to have one aim in view, the publication of his journal before he could
capitalise on it himself.[1] Even when the news came that Stanley's route
had been blocked by a hostile chief, Mirambo, who was determined to
control the route to Ujiji where Livingstone was thought to be, the Society
remained calm. Richard Burton's analysis of the situation made it clear
that Livingstone was too experienced a traveller to become involved in
a localised tribal uprising, however awkward that might be for a tyro such
as Stanley.

But the British public was not so sanguine : if Mirambo was blocking
the route to Ujiji how was Livingstone obtaining any supplies? Why had
the Geographical Society received no word from Livingstone for so long?
Criticism of the inactivity of the Society began to mount and rather against
his will the new President, Sir Henry Rawlinson, was pushed into action.
The Livingstone Search and Relief Committee was formed with Rawlinson
as President and Galton as Secretary. The first task of the Committee
was to open a fund to finance a British expedition to find and succour

Livingstone and possibly to relieve Stanley as well. Money poured in until £5000 was realised, of which the Society had contributed £500.

At this moment J. G. Bennett, the proprietor of the *New York Herald*, decided to publish the first of Stanley's dispatches. It fell like a bombshell on the R.G.S. Bennett was a notorious critic of British affairs and obviously could have no real interest in the welfare of the famous British explorer. Stanley's trip was nothing more than a newspaper stunt. Rawlinson could see but one course of action open to him : the British expedition must be rushed off with all speed so that it might reach Livingstone before Stanley could escape from Mirambo's blockade.

But by the time the expedition reached the East African coast Stanley had bypassed Mirambo, had found Livingstone at Ujiji, and was on his return to the coast. Advance runners informed the British expedition's leader, Lieutenant Dawson, to that effect and he promptly resigned his command. After some squabbling his colleagues, who included Livingstone's son, also decided that they should not proceed and the expedition broke up.

Sir Henry Rawlinson's reaction to the news that Livingstone was safe with Stanley was quite extraordinary. As he put it to the Society on 13th May :

> 'A belief seems to prevail that Mr Stanley has discovered and relieved Dr Livingstone; whereas, without any disparagement to Mr Stanley's energy, activity and loyalty, if there has been any discovery and relief it is Dr Livingstone who has discovered and relieved Mr Stanley.'[2]

Rawlinson repeated his theory on several further occasions until finally silenced by the appearance of Stanley's dispatch from Ujiji describing his meeting with Livingstone. Even now the geographers warned the public not to accept the report at its face value, but their chagrin was too evident and they were largely disregarded.

When, after an enthusiastic reception in Paris, Stanley reached England on 1st August he was ignored by the R.G.S. He read in *The Times* a letter from Rawlinson denying that there was anything of geographical interest in his dispatches and stating that there would be no special reception for him. As he was to write 30 years later :

> 'All the actions of my life, and I may say all my thoughts since 1872, have been strongly coloured by the storm of abuse and the wholly unjustifiable reports circulated about me then.'[3]

But nothing could dampen the public enthusiasm. Invitations poured in and he was feted everywhere. Nevertheless, Stanley still found it necessary to have Lord Granville, the Foreign Secretary, confirm the authenticity of official dispatches from Livingstone before all the doubters were convinced. Within a week Rawlinson capitulated : an official letter of congratulations was sent to Stanley with an invitation to address the British Association meeting at Brighton on 16th August.

Up to this time Galton had remained in the background; as an R.G.S. Council member and Secretary of the Relief Expedition Committee he had loyally supported his President. He now stepped into the limelight as 1872 was the year of his Presidency of the Geographical Section of the British Association.[4]

The large hall in Brighton held 3000 people and was filled to capacity half an hour before Stanley was scheduled to speak. The exiled Emperor Napoleon III with the Empress Eugénie were among the audience. Galton took the Chair ten minutes early and introduced the speaker. He was unable to make his introduction very long as he knew so little about Stanley. He hoped, he said, that Stanley would during the course of his talk clear up certain mysteries about himself and his nationality. Stanley had unwisely been insisting that he was an American and had been born in New York, but there was a persistent rumour that he was Welsh. He was in fact the illegitimate son of a Welsh farmer from Denbigh and had been christened John Rowland; he took his American benefactor's name upon adoption. Stanley's denial of his origin was probably partly motivated, as he later claimed, by a desire to protect his mother who had married and was still living in Denbigh.

The title of Stanley's lecture was suitably academic, 'Discoveries at the North End of Lake Tanganyika', but he decided on the spur of the moment to depart from his prepared script and began :

'I consider myself in the light of a troubadour, to relate to you the tale of an old man who is tramping onward to discover the source of the Nile.'[5]

And as he began he continued, talking at length of his many adventures and of the greatness of Livingstone. It was what most of the audience had come to hear and he had their attention and their applause. But for the geographers intent upon a scientific meeting it was calamitous. Finally, when Stanley concluded by turning on Galton and telling him that he was nothing more than a nosey-parker for his interest in Stanley's origins, Galton lost his temper. Already infuriated by the lack of positional observations and disregard for other geographical virtues, he burst out that this was all 'sensational geography'. What they needed were facts and they should now examine Stanley's stories to discover those facts. In that spirit he would ask the first question : 'Was the water of Lake Tanganyika sweet or brackish ?'

It was a combination of Galton's tone and Stanley's touchiness that

VII Composite portrait of Napoleon

VIII   Francis Galton, aged 66

led Stanley to think Galton's question was designed to make a fool of him. He replied that the water was delicious if not the best in the world, being particularly good for making tea. Any desire of Galton's to ask further questions was drowned in the applause that greeted Stanley's rejoinder, and he was forced to introduce the discussants. Among them were Dr Beke who maintained that Livingstone was mistaken in thinking the River Lualaba was the Nile; it was obviously the Congo. Sir Henry Rawlinson agreed with this contention. He added, with an attempt at heartiness, that he could express the sentiments of the R.G.S. in congratulating Stanley on his success.

Stanley had been quite unprepared for any discussion of his paper and took the criticisms of Livingstone's theories as personal insults to the man he most admired. He sprang to Livingstone's defence saying that the man on the spot should know a little more than Dr Beke living in London and he went on to castigate Rawlinson for drawing maps of Africa to suit his own convenience.

It was high time to close the meeting and Galton did so. But he could not resist reminding the audience that a man in London had access to many more facts than an explorer who might discover one or two more.

Although congratulated by his friends on his chairmanship, Galton's handling of the meeting could have been more adroit. His initial observation about Stanley's birth was quite unnecessary and his exclamation 'sensational geography' was seized upon by the newspapers. Stanley, they said, was guilty of telling 'sensational stories', the implication being that the reports of those travelling under R.G.S. auspices were more reliable.

A week after the B.A. meeting Stanley wrote to the papers:

'Let it be understood that I resent all manner of impertinence, brutal horse-laughs at the mention of Livingstone's name, or of his sufferings; . . . all statements that I am not what I claim to be—an American; all gratuitous remarks, such as "sensationalism", as directed at me by that sauve gentleman, Mr Francis Galton.'[6]

Stanley's dislike of Galton was more strongly expressed in a letter he now wrote to Clements Markham, who was still Secretary of the R.G.S.

'Let Francis Galton write to the newspapers and disclaim that word "sensational", let him apologise for doubting my nationality publicly since he made the affront public—and I shall immediately withdraw anything I may have said to wound the feelings of any member of that body and I shall be the first to let byegones be byegones. On the other hand if he does not—all I have to do is to retort upon him and the Society in the same vein, by pen, by speech in every way I can, and never to give it up until I shall have perfect satisfaction. A service you say was rendered to you—yet you resent

E

it having been done. You endeavour to injure the man who did the service to you—because he was not sent out by you. There is only one other way of silencing all these accusations against the Society, to show that they are all groundless—which I hope you have sufficient discernment to perceive. It is by far the most effectual, and requires no public retraction of any word or deed. If you did that there could be no more said, the very deed would show the confidence you had in me. But I leave it to you to suggest and to proffer.'[7]

Stanley appears to be suggesting to Markham that the award of the R.G.S. Medal would stop the allegations that the Society could not forgive Stanley for reaching Livingstone before their own expedition. Markham's response to Stanley's hint was never to write to him again. As Markham expressed it to Galton in sending him Stanley's letter: 'The blackguard took me in. What a gull I am!' By which he presumably meant that he had never suspected Stanley's ulterior motive. In a speech of thanks to the R.G.S. a few weeks later Stanley mentioned that he had been told by Livingstone that the Society would reward him in this manner. That fact perhaps excuses his opportunism.[8]

Galton never apologised and Stanley had to assuage his injured pride by unpleasant references to Galton. For instance, in a speech to the Savage Club:

'It was at the British Association where Mr Francis Galton, F.R.S., F.R.G.S. and God knows how many letters to his name, said "We don't want sensational speeches". That does stick in my throat. (Laughter.) I suppose that when I spoke of all the long names of which he had never heard before, I touched his technical heart. (Laughter.) He wanted facts. I gave him facts. (Cheers.) They required no gilding.'[9]

The dirt was not all thrown by Stanley. A series of letters were by now passing between Markham, Carpenter, Galton and other influential council members in which it was advocated that steps should be taken to ensure that the public, and in particular the Queen, should know the true facts about Stanley's birth. *The Caernarvon Herald* had published a true account of his origins some weeks earlier and the rumours had become more substantial as other newspapers repeated the story.

Queen Victoria had already (27th August) sent Stanley a fine gold snuff box with her compliments and thanks. On 8th September Carpenter wrote to Galton enclosing a copy of a letter that he had sent to Lord Granville from which the following extract is taken:

'As the marked notice which the Queen has taken of him will tend to *establish* him completely in the public mind, it seems to me necessary (I speak, of course, in entire submission to your better judgement) that the real state of the case should be made known, both to the Queen and to the world at large.'[10]

On 12th September he wrote again to Galton enclosing Lord Granville's reply. Lord Granville had advised no public action as the Queen had already received Stanley at Dunrobin, where he was staying at the personal invitation of the Duke of Sutherland.

'She recognised the great services which Stanley had rendered [and] she does not want to enter into the controversy over his birth and his private denial of the reports.'[11]

The Queen's reception of Stanley meant that he was now fully acceptable to all levels of society. All over the country banquets were given in his honour and the R.G.S. belatedly followed suit. Stanley even got his medal, Sir Henry Rawlinson presenting him with the Society's highest award, the Victoria Medal.

For the R.G.S., the Stanley affair did not end there: their ill-fated expedition was still coming under public scrutiny. Dawson's precipitate action in resigning his command had pleased nobody. It was unfortunate that his instructions contained no provision for his defeat in the race to Livingstone. It has been suggested that Rawlinson was personally responsible for Dawson's instructions but a draft exists in Galton's handwriting obviously intended for discussion at a meeting of the Livingstone Search and Relief Committee. All reference to Stanley is omitted, although various other eventualities are foreseen.[12] Dawson believed that an attempt had been made to use him as a catspaw to obtain Livingstone's diary and notebooks and that the R.G.S. had deliberately concealed from him Livingstone's hostility towards them. Having been misled by the R.G.S., he felt that the sole purpose of his mission must be to relieve Livingstone and that once he knew Livingstone was well he was justified in resigning.

Dawson was further aggrieved by the action of several members of the Livingstone Search and Relief Committee, including Rawlinson and Galton, in writing to the papers before he had returned to England and was in a position to make his case.

The geographers' viewpoint was well expressed by Galton in his letter to the *Daily News*:

'The Society is not a humane society, established to succour persons in distress, but for the promotion of geographical science. The 500 L voted for the expedition by the Council of the Royal Geographical Society would have been a malappropriation of the society's funds if there was no intention to utilise the expedition, as could perfectly be done, to obtain geographical facts. The public may be considered to have sent their subscriptions mainly, but not entirely, for the relief of a man personally dear to the nation, and the two objects of relief and geography admitted of being simultaneously fulfilled.'[13]

But it was the official report of the Committee that was most severe in its censure of Dawson.[14] One can see Galton's hand in the comment that the instruments entrusted to Dawson would have been particularly welcomed by Livingstone. It was Galton who had sent instructions for their use. And it was Galton who was publicly rebuked by Negretti and Zambra, the instrument makers, for his suggestion that Dawson should clean his barometers by poking an iron wire down them.[15]

Dawson made a spirited reply to the newspapers in the course of which he took a dig at Galton. Livingstone *had* been sent those instruments he said he needed, but

'Mr Galton's field-gun telescope, shipped at his request for a speculative observation of Jupiter's satellites, was shelved as useless lumber, cumbrous in transport and unavailable in survey.'[16]

The newspaper controversy over Dawson continued for many months and Stanley had left England before it closed. Galton's critical attitude towards Stanley never changed and in this respect he was not alone. The severity of Stanley's treatment of Africans, both those in his service and those whom he encountered en route, was thought by many other Fellows of the R.G.S. to merit a continuation of their early treatment of him. Thus, there were protests and resignations when Stanley was invited to speak to the Society six years later, after his return from his next great journey down the Congo.[17]

In an unsigned review of Stanley's dispatches Galton described that journey in the following words :

'With a larger military force than hitherto employed and making a determined use of it, Mr Stanley has conducted a geographical raid across the middle of Africa, which has led him into scenes of bloodshed and slaughter, beginning at the Victoria Nyanza, and not ending until he arrived in the neighbourhood of the Western Coast . . . The question will no doubt be hotly discussed how far a private individual, travelling as a newspaper correspondent, has a right to assume such a warlike attitude, and to force his way through native tribes regardless of their rights, whatever those may be.'[18]

Galton's last word on Stanley is to be found in his autobiography written in 1908 :

'Mr Stanley had other interests than geography. He was essentially a journalist aiming at producing sensational articles.'[19]

This dismissal of Stanley as a cheap journalist, however apparently appropriate in 1872, was certainly not an objective assessment of his later achievements. It is quite apparent that Galton was strongly prejudiced against Stanley from the very beginning. Being still identified with the affairs of the R.G.S., Galton possibly interpreted any slight to that body as a slight to himself, and when that slight originated from a bastard of the lowest social class he could not preserve an open mind.

Scientists and Twins

Galton's other activities had not submerged his intent to continue the type of work he had begun in writing *Hereditary Genius*. He had been collecting in a desultory way further data on men of high ability, but it was the appearance in 1872 of a book by the Swiss scientist, Alphonse de Candolle, that stimulated Galton into more directed activity. The book in question, *Histoire des Sciences et des Savants depuis deux Siècles*, was to some extent a response to *Hereditary Genius* which de Candolle believed overstated the case for the hereditary determination of ability.[1] De Candolle's approach was directed towards the study of environmental factors relevant to past scientific discoveries, and it became clear to Galton that he must extend his own future work to include the circumstances under which men are nurtured.

With advice from Herbert Spencer and Dr Farr of Somerset House, Galton compiled a lengthy questionnaire running to seven quarto pages which he distributed to 180 selected members of the Royal Society. The questionnaire covered a wide range of topics: family characteristics, physique, temperament and personality, special abilities, religious beliefs, details of upbringing and education, and the respondents' own views on the origin of their scientific interests.

'The size of my circular was alarming. Though naturally very shy, I do occasional acts, like other shy persons, of an unusually bold description, and this was one. After an uneasy night, I prepared myself on the following afternoon, and not for the first time before interviews that were likely to be unpleasant, by what is said to have been the usual practice of Buffon before writing anything exceptional, namely, by dressing myself in my best clothes.

'I can confidently recommend this plan to shy men as giving a sensible addition to their own self-respect, and as somewhat increasing the respect of others. In this attire I went to a meeting of the Royal

Society prepared to be howled at; but no! my victims, taken as a whole, tolerated the action, and some even approved of it.'[2]

As many of the eminent scientists of the day contributed answers to the enquiry, the data, which have been preserved in the Galton archives, provide a useful source for any historian of Victorian science. Darwin's answer may be of general interest.

'Special talents, none, except for business, as evinced by keeping accounts, being regular in correspondence, and investing money very well; very methodical in my habits. Steadiness; great curiosity about facts, and their meaning; some love of the new and marvellous.

'Somewhat nervous temperament, energy of body shown by much activity, and whilst I had health, power of resisting fatigue. An early riser in the morning. Energy of mind shown by vigorous and long-continued work on the same subject, as 20 years on the *Origin of Species* and 9 years on *Cirripedia*. Memory bad for dates or learning by rote; but good in retaining a general or vague recollection of many facts. Very studious, but not large acquirements. I think fairly independently, but I can give no instances. I gave up common religious belief almost independently from my own reflections. I suppose that I have shown originality in science, as I have made discoveries with regard to common objects. Liberal or radical in politics. Health good when young—bad for last 33 years.'

He adds in an accompanying letter :

'It is so impossible for anyone to judge about his own character that George [his brother] first wrote several of the answers about myself, but I have adopted only those which seem to me true.'[3]

Darwin's point about the impossibility of truthful self-assessment is, of course, a good one. Galton's questionnaire was an extremely crude instrument and many of his questions were biased. Thus, for example, he asked his subjects to discuss their independence of judgement, a request which was hardly likely to have produced admissions that they were lacking this quality. The data collected must have been partly reflections of what were regarded as socially desirable attributes.

Usable data were obtained from about 100 respondents and constituted the material for Galton's next book, *English Men of Science: their Nature and Nurture*, which was published in 1874.[4] Such a sample may appear too small to support any general conclusions, but Galton had reason to conclude that there were not more than 300 men of similar first class scientific ability in the whole of the British Isles.

The sample was drawn almost exclusively from the upper and middle classes, and from larger than average families despite the fact that the mothers were above average age when they gave birth to their first child. There were twice as many first than younger sons among the sample, a fact which Galton ascribes to their more favourable nurture.

'Elder sons are more likely to become possessed of independent means, and therefore able to follow the pursuits that have most attraction to their tastes; they are treated more as companions by their parents, and have earlier responsibility, both of which would develop independence of character; probably, also, the first-born child of families not well-to-do in the world would generally have more attention in his infancy, more breathing-space, and better nourishment, than his younger brothers and sisters in their several turns.'[5]

As details of the parents' physique, hair colour, and temperament were included in the questionnaire returns, Galton was able to draw up a series of tables giving the likelihood of contrast or harmony in these characteristics between the marital partners. This first attempt to examine the likelihood of assortative mating resulted in the conclusion that only in the case of physique was contrast as likely to occur as harmony, while in hair colour and temperament like tended to marry like.[6]

He now employs a similar argument to that elaborated in *Hereditary Genius* to estimate the influence of hereditary endowment upon scientific success. He takes certain relatives of the scientists, examines the incidence of distinction among them, and compares it with that among the general population. For example, there were about 660 men related to the sample, either as uncles or grandfathers. Thirteen men of these 660 were eminent in the sense that they were the subjects of numerous obituary notices. Previous work had established that not more than 50 men eminent by this criterion die annually in the United Kingdom. Thus, Galton concludes that,

'This small band of 660 individuals contains almost one-fourth as much eminence as is *annually* produced by the United Kingdom.'[7]

The incidence of eminence among the relatives of scientists can also be compared with more selected samples of the general population, namely those with a similar educational background of public school and university. Galton is content with very approximate estimates, but is probably correct in his conclusion that the families of scientists are more gifted than these comparison groups.

An estimate can also be made of the comparative success of relatives in different degrees of kinship to the scientists. Every 100 scientists are judged to have on the average 28 notable fathers, 36 brothers, 20 grandfathers and 40 uncles. The table is not extended to the remoter degrees of kinship considered in *Hereditary Genius* where the sample of scientists was smaller and more rigorously selected. Reference back to Table 7.2 will show that in the present case there is a less rapid fall off in the incidence of eminence as kinship becomes more remote. The criterion of eminence among the relatives is also more lax in the present enquiry.

The critic may easily put forward a similar objection to that made in relation to the earlier results : the occurrence of distinction in the families of established scientists does nothing to support the hereditarian viewpoint. Indeed, it could be argued that Galton's results support the notion that election to the Royal Society depends on the presence of distinguished relatives as well as on proven scientific work.

Galton now turns to an examination of the qualities of the men themselves. Taking the answers at face value, one of the most convincing attributes was the possession of great energy, 42 cases having energy much above the average and only 2 cases claiming less than average energy. Some examples follow :

> 'In 13 years I examined and named some 40,000 examples, described about 7,000 species, wrote some 6,000 pages of printed matter, carrying on at the same time a great deal of correspondence.'[8]

> 'At the age of 26, during 14 days, was only three hours per night in bed, and on two of the nights was up all night preparing certain scientific work.'[9]

> 'At the age of 60 made a tour, chiefly pedestrian, of four weeks in the Alps . . . walking sometimes 30 miles a day.'[10]

> 'Have dissected continually for three or four weeks eight or nine hours a day, devoting some sixteen hours to the work at critical times.'[11]

With regard to health most of the scientists reported excellent health.

> 'It is positively startling to observe in these returns the strong hereditary character of good and indifferent constitution.'[12]

It might have been expected, as was the case, that most of the respondents would be methodical, independent, and capable of great perseverance. Memory, on the other hand, was much more variable. About 30 men laid claim to an especially good memory, but 13 considered their memory poor. It is interesting to note that Galton adopts a classification of memory into verbal, numerical, memory for form and rote memory, which bears distinct resemblance to that currently employed.

Finally, mechanical aptitude was surprisingly prevalent, not only among physicists and engineers where it was to be expected, but also among other scientists, such as biologists and geologists, where it does not seem to have been such a necessary condition of their work.

Under the heading 'Religious Bias' Galton now turns to a consideration of the religious beliefs of his scientists. His questions on this topic leave much to be desired. In general terms he asks respondents to indicate whether or not they have a strong religious bias, their replies being interpreted in terms of the three elements which, so he understands, comprise religious belief. These are:

'(i) Great prevalence of the intuitive sentiments; so much so, that conflicting matters of observation are apt to be laid aside, out of sight and mind. The intuitive sense of a supreme God, who communes with our hearts and directs us.

'(ii) A sense of extreme sin and weakness . . .

'(iii) Revelation of a future life and of other matters variously interpreted by different sects, which more or less, satisfy the intuitive sentiments.'[13]

As very few of the scientists appeared to accept dogma and as, in view of their energy and health, few seemed to suffer from a general sense of unworthiness, it is only in the sense of the first category, the possession of an intuition about God allied with a philosophical frame of mind and a tendency to philanthropy, that he feels able to interpret the answers. In this sense, there were 18 instances of scientists who possessed a decided religious bias, the majority apparently being unbelievers although still claiming nominal allegiance to the established church.

The general question is followed by a more particular and leading question, 'Has the religion taught in your youth had any deterrent effect on the freedom of your researches?' For every person who answered this question in the affirmative, seven or eight answered 'No', but only where the bare answer was elaborated is it possible to deduce the meaning given by the respondent to the question.

Coupled with a general rejection of religious influence was a curiosity about facts and a hunger for truth, in some cases, notably Darwin's, carried so far as to lead to a repugnance for works of fiction.

The third chapter of the book is concerned with the origin of the taste for science. Galton is careful not to be too dogmatic about the results which are again based on the opinions expressed by the respondents. A little over one half of the sample considered that the taste was innate, only 11 asserted that it was not, while the remainder were doubtful. The question asked was, 'Can you trace the origin of your interest in science in general, and in your particular branch of it? How far do your scientific tastes appear innate?'

Some of the quoted replies reveal the unsatisfactory nature of the data:

'My tastes are entirely innate; they date from childhood.'[14]

'As far back as I remember, I loved Nature and desired to learn her secrets.'[15]

'Naturally fond of mechanics and of physical science.'[16]

'Thoroughly innate. My first taste for chemistry dates from the possession of a chemical box, when I was a little boy.'[17]

It is unnecessary to quote further. It can be seen that the evidence for an innate origin of scientific aptitude is quite misleading; the replies point to a childhood interest in science which has been generally misconstrued to merit the designation 'innate'. Indeed, if we examine the professions of the fathers, in no single case was there a scientist among them. For every father with scientific interests there were four without. From these facts Galton concludes that,

'Instinctive tastes for science are, generally speaking, not so strongly hereditary as the more elementary qualities of the body and mind.'[18]

But the conclusion that heredity plays any part in the origin of scientific interests is at variance with the facts and a reflection of Galton's belief in the prepotence of hereditary endowment.

Subsidiary factors leading to the adoption of a scientific career are briefly discussed. They include fortunate accidents, indirect opportunities, professional duties, encouragement at home, the influence of friends and teachers, and travel in distant parts.

Approximately one third of the scientists mention that their scientific interests were fostered by their parents, but it was the father's influence that was predominant (thrice as frequent as the mother's). This finding flatly contradicts the statement in *Hereditary Genius* that the mothers of scientific men play an important role in their choice of profession. Galton does not mention the discrepancy.

In a passage that reflects his own preferences, Galton states:

'In many respects the character of scientific men is strongly antifeminine; their mind is directed to facts and abstract theories, and not to persons or human interests. The man of science is deficient in the purely emotional element, and in the desire to influence the beliefs of others . . . In many respects they have little sympathy with female ways of thought.'[19]

Although only eight cases attribute their love of science to the results of travel Galton believes that travelling fellowships would be an appropriate method of furthering scientific research:

'Men are too apt to accept as an axiomatic law, not capable of further explanation, whatever they see recurring day after day without fail. So the dog in the backyard looks on the daily arrival of the postman, butcher, and baker, as so many elementary phenomena, not to be barked at or wondered about. Travel in distant countries, by unsettling these quasi-axiomatic ideas, restores to the educated man the freshness of childhood in observing new things and in seeking reasons for all he sees.'[20]

Besides these minor influences which urge men to pursue science, the *Zeitgeist* is also of importance :

'The natural condition most favourable to general efficiency is one of self-confidence, and eager belief in the existence of great works capable of accomplishment. The opposite attitude is indifferentism, founded on sheer uncertainty of what is best to do, or on despair of being strong enough to achieve useful results . . . A common effect of indifferentism is to dissipate the energy of the nation upon trifles; and this tendency seems to be a crying evil of the present day in our own country.'[21]

A comment on the supposed confidence of Victorian science that reads strangely a century later.

The book concludes with Galton's proposals for educational changes designed to foster the development of science. Sweeping reforms are advocated in the school curriculum, stress to be placed on mathematics, logic, observation, theory and experiment, accurate drawing and mechanical manipulation, all to be rigorously taught. The remaining time is to be spent on reading literature, poetry and history, besides sufficient language learning to enable the student to read 'ordinary books' in other languages. These recommendations are all based on the scientists' own views about the kind of education they would have preferred and from which they would have derived most profit. Galton's dislike of his own classical education was reinforced by the comments of many of his scientific colleagues and his curriculum has no place for either Greek or Latin.

Overteaching is to be carefully avoided, rather the educator should aim at awakening interests and encouraging his pupils to pursue them on their own.

'I am surprised at the mediocre degrees which the leading scientific men who were at the universities have usually taken, always excepting the mathematicians. Being original they are naturally less receptive, they prefer to fix of their own accord on certain subjects, and seem averse to learn what is put before them as a task. Their independence of spirit and coldness of disposition are not conducive to success in competition; they doggedly go their own way, and refuse to run races.'[22]

Galton's admiration was reserved for men of the originality of Darwin and Spencer and he always remained sceptical of the achievements of more orthodox academics. The suggestions made here for liberating education from the stronghold of the classics were not to be generally implemented until the turn of the century, and Galton's further advocacy of pupil-centred projects is of even more recent adoption.

Galton was well aware of the contemporary difficulties, stemming notably from the gigantic religious monopoly, that faced those who wished to see the development of the sciences. Yet, in addition, he foresaw the increased need in the universities, in industry and in the public health service for those with scientific qualifications, and he was able to look forward to the time when 'a sort of scientific priesthood' might be established whose broad function would be to increase the wellbeing of the nation and whose social position and rewards would be made commensurate with the importance of their role.

In this optimistic vein the book concludes, a book which, while lacking the brilliant originality of *Hereditary Genius*, is still of interest today when governmental anxieties over the supply of scientists have led to more sophisticated enquiries on similar lines to those initiated by Galton.[23]

The great nature/nurture controversy remained incapable of clarification by the methods Galton had thus far employed. On a slightly despairing note, he writes in the preliminaries to *English Men of Science*:

'The effects of education and circumstance are so interwoven with those of natural character in determining a man's position among his contemporaries, that I find it impossible to treat them wholly apart. Still less is it possible completely to separate the evidences relating to that portion of a man's nature which is due to heredity, from all the rest.'[24]

Galton advises the reader to make the required separation for himself, but, as we have seen, he finds it difficult to refrain from giving an occasional nudge in the hereditarian direction. Among other comments he draws the reader's attention to the similarity in body and mind of like-sex twins. It subsequently occurred to him that the whole topic of the supposed resemblance of twins deserved more elaborate treatment, for it seemed likely to provide him with a means of distinguishing the effects of heredity from those of environment.

Although there existed a large literature, mostly on the medical resemblances between twins, Galton could find nothing of direct relevance to his own problems. In view of the success of his questionnaire to scientists, he decided to adopt a similar approach and to circularise twins and the relatives of twins known to himself. They in turn were asked to supply the names of twins known to them and he repeated the procedure until he had returns from 94 sets of twins, which gave him sufficient material for two published papers.[25]

Of the 94 sets of twins the evidence of close similarity was strong in 35 pairs. Most of the reports from these 35 contain striking evidence of close physical resemblance. Mistakes by near relatives were common, particularly in early childhood when, for example, coloured ribbons had to be used to distinguish the members of some twin pairs. In spite of such precautions there were many instances when one twin was 'fed, physicked and whipped in mistake for the other.'[26] Even in adulthood amusing mistakes occurred, such as in five cases where a person engaged to a twin was never sure which was his future partner. Nine respondents were even misled by their reflection in a looking-glass, speaking to it in the mistaken belief that it was their twin.

Susceptibility to illness was very similar in these 35 pairs. For example, twins who at the age of 23 were each attacked by toothache had to have the same tooth extracted. In another case, one twin died of Wright's disease and his death was followed by that of his twin seven months later from the same disease. Another twin suffered from rheumatic ophthalmia while living in Paris; in a letter from Vienna his twin reported suffering from the same complaint at the same time.

'The steady and pitiless march of the hidden weaknesses in our constitutions, through illness to death, is painfully revealed by these histories of twins. We are too apt to look upon illness and death as capricious events, and there are some who ascribe them to the direct effect of supernatural influence, whereas the fact of the maladies of two twins being continually alike, shows that illness and death are necessary incidents in a regular sequence of constitutional changes, beginning at birth, upon which external circumstances have on the whole, very small effect . . . Necessitarians may derive new arguments from the life histories of twins.'[27]

In taste and disposition, 16 of the 35 pairs were closely similar; in the remaining 19 they were much alike, but showed differences in the intensity of a characteristic. For example, where one twin might be calm, the other would be more excitable; where one might be independent, the other would be more dependent. As Galton describes it, 'The difference was in the key-note, not in the melody.'[28]

Eleven cases testified to the similarity in the association of their ideas, shown by their tendency to make the same remarks on the same occasions. Such similarities are the probable source for the many stories of telepathic communication between twins. The most remarkable of Galton's examples concerned a twin, A, who while in a town in Scotland decided on the spur of the moment to buy a set of champagne glasses as a surprise for his brother, B. At the same time, B, who was in England, made a similar purchase as a surprise for A.

Strangely enough the one characteristic in which similarity was rare was in the handwriting. In all cases except one, the twins could always be distinguished from samples of their handwriting. In view of the noted psychological resemblances between twins, Galton seems to be in error in supposing that handwriting is 'a very delicate test of difference in organisation' and in recommending its use as a tool of psychological diagnosis.[29]

Anecdotal though much of this evidence was, Galton felt able to conclude that there were only two cases of strong bodily resemblance allied to psychological diversity and one case only of the converse kind.

The 35 pairs of similar twins had all had similar environments until early adulthood. Since then, the conditions of their lives had changed and it was with particular interest that Galton examined the data concerning their similarity in later life.

> 'In some cases the resemblance of body and mind had continued unaltered up to old age, notwithstanding very different conditions of life; and [the data] showed in the other cases that the parents ascribed such dissimilarity as there was wholly, or almost wholly, to some form of illness.'[30]

A concatenation of minor environmental events was sometimes invoked as partial explanations of later differences, but in no single instance were such differences said to result from the free choice of one twin.

Galton concludes that the positive evidence for close resemblance throughout life cannot be outweighed by any amount of negative evidence. In those cases where there is growing diversity it must be chiefly due to a lack of thorough similarity in the first place.

> 'Twins who closely resembled each other in childhood and early youth, and were reared under not very dissimilar conditions, either grow unlike through the development of natural characteristics which had laid dormant at first, or else they continue their lives, keeping time like two watches, hardly to be thrown out of accord except by some physical jar.'[31]

Galton was aware of the two separate causes of twin births; the 35 very similar cases examined in detail are examples of what we should now call identical twins. He has little to say about the remaining cases, which probably included some identicals but must have had a preponderance of fraternals. In 20 of these cases sharply contrasting characteristics of body and mind were mentioned by the respondents. For example, in the words of one parent:

> ' "I can answer most decidedly that the twins have been perfectly dissimilar in character, habits, and likeness from the moment of

their birth to the present time, though they were nursed by the same woman, went to school together, and were never separated until the age of fifteen." [32]

Not a single case occurred in which originally dissimilar personalities became alike through similarity of nurture.

Galton summarises his results in these words :

'The impression that all this evidence leaves on the mind is one of some wonder whether nurture can do anything at all, beyond giving instruction and professional training. It emphatically corroborates and goes far beyond the conclusions to which we had already been driven by the cases of similarity. In these, the causes of divergence began to act about the period of adult life, when the characters had become somewhat fixed; but here the causes conducive to assimilation began to act from the earliest moment of the existence of the twins, when the disposition was most pliant, and they were continuous until the period of adult life. There is no escape from the conclusion that nature prevails enormously over nurture when the differences of nurture do not exceed what is commonly to be found among persons of the same rank of society and in the same country.'[33]

As we can see from the concluding sentence, Galton was careful to ascribe a dominant role to heredity only within narrow environmental limits. Subsequent research has explored wider environmental divergencies and has placed more stress on the *interaction* of nature and nurture. But the importance of this first attempt to study twins for the light it might throw on the nature/nurture controversy should not be underestimated. In spite of the rudimentary treatment of his data and the possible selection of material to suit his argument, Galton's method of twin study has proved a powerful tool in the hands of later investigators.[34]

II

Psychology and Photography

The experiments on pangenesis, the hypotheses about the hereditary mechanism, the enquiries into the nature and nurture of scientists and twins, the involvement in geographical and religious debate, all these activities were compressed into the first half of the 1870s. Even so, the list is not exhaustive. During that same five-year period Galton began research of remarkable originality into the anthropological and psychological fields.

The first paper on a specifically psychological topic was written in 1871, the same year as the pangenesis paper.[1] Entitled 'Gregariousness in cattle and in men' the paper has as its main theme the survival value of gregarious behaviour. During his travels in South West Africa, Galton had been struck by the way in which his pack-oxen, although remaining self-absorbed in the midst of the herd and showing little liking for one another, would nevertheless exhibit signs of panic whenever separated from their fellows. This fear of isolation caused great difficulties to the explorers in their attempts to select oxen to lead a team; it was even more difficult to find oxen that would consent to be ridden apart from the herd.

Galton claims that when we consider the nature of the danger that an ox runs in its natural habitat the advantages of herding are readily apparent. When alone the ox is by no means defenceless, but it is too easily surprised by a predator. It is forced to spend much of its time grazing and ruminating, and then it cannot remain alert. But, taken as a whole a herd of such animals is always on the *qui vive*:

> 'To live gregariously is to become a fibre in a vast sentient web overspreading many acres; it is to become the possessor of faculties always awake, of eyes that see in all directions, of ears and nostrils that explore a broad belt of air; it is also to become the occupier of every bit of vantage ground whence the approach of a wild beast might be overlooked.'[2]

The survival value of such gregarious tendencies is so great that natural selection would favour their possession. Furthermore, a certain degree of gregariousness can be regarded as optimal: if the animals are too gregarious they will crowd one another too closely to graze efficiently; if they are less gregarious, they will disperse too widely for their mutual protection.

What is true of cattle is also, Galton believes, true of the native peoples in the same area. At the time of his visit the inhabitants were congregated into tribes at war with one another. Few of the tribes were very small or very large, and these extremes were unstable. The small tribe was in constant danger of being overrun by its larger neighbours, while the large tribe was likely to become fragmented owing either to its lack of central authority or to a deficiency in its local food supply.

Galton now develops the argument to explain the rarity of lead oxen. The incidence of the requisite independence is about one in fifty because one leader is sufficient in a herd of that size and that size is optimal for survival.

Applying the argument to the human group, there should likewise be an optimal size for such a group and an optimal ratio of leaders to led, these optima being again determined by their survival value. The medium sized tribes under one ruler in the region appeared to fit these criteria. Now according to Galton, there is no reason to suppose that our own primitive ancestors lived very different lives from those of the nineteenth century inhabitants of South West Africa and there is therefore reason to regard the above argument as applicable in their case.

He further develops the argument:

> 'The blind instincts evolved under these long-continued conditions have been ingrained into our breed, and they are a bar to our enjoying the freedom which the forms of modern civilisation are otherwise capable of giving us. A really intelligent nation might be held together by far stronger forces than are derived from the purely gregarious instincts. A nation need not be a mob of slaves, clinging to one another through fear, and for the most part incapable of self-government, and begging to be led; but it might consist of vigorous self-reliant men, knit to one another by innumerable ties, into a strong, tense and elastic organisation.'[3]

Having assumed an instinctual basis for the gregarious behaviour exhibited by modern man, Galton then concludes that the only way to bring about a change to more selfreliant behaviour is to breed gregariousness and its associated servility out of a nation.

At the time he provided no methods by which this desired goal might be achieved, but in the following year he returned to the theme of more general hereditary improvement with which he had been concerned in the closing chapters of *Hereditary Genius*. The paper, published in Frazer's Magazine, argues that as heredity has a major influence in determining a man's physical, mental and moral attributes it should be the prime duty of humanity to aid the process of natural selection in improving the race of the future.[4]

'It is no absurdity to expect, that it may hereafter be preached, that while helpfulness to the weak, and sympathy with the suffering, is the natural form of outpouring of a merciful and kindly heart, yet that the highest action of all is to provide a vigorous, national life, and that one practical and effective way in which individuals of feeble constitution can show mercy to their kind is by celibacy, lest they should bring beings into existence whose race is predoomed to destruction by the laws of nature. It may become to be avowed as a paramount duty, to anticipate the slow and stubborn processes of natural selection, by endeavouring to breed out feeble constitutions, and petty and ignoble instincts, and to breed in those which are vigorous and noble and social.'[5]

Galton's own scheme entails the building up of a sentiment of caste among the naturally gifted members of each social class and the procurement for these people of various social benefits. As a first step he advocates an extensive series of enquiries into the range of hereditary gifts within the nation. The very fact of conducting such investigations and notifying individuals of their talents will, he thinks, lead to more social contact among the gifted families with consequent intermarriages. Local registers should be drawn up of those who are 'hereditarily remarkable'. Then these selected in this manner would consider themselves members of a caste or guild and would expect to be treated with more respect and consideration than those without their merits. Galton even supposes that they might be preferred over common paupers as recipients of charity from the wealthy. He is not, however, so naive as to suppose no resentment on the part of those excluded from the guild. Their hostility would lead to a cohesion of the gifted caste who would live in cooperative associations in the country rather than the town, or, if further persecuted, might have to emigrate to found new colonies.

'The gifted race would be urged into companionship by the pressure of external circumstances, no less strongly than, as I have shown, they would be drawn togther by their own mutual attraction.'[6]

In time the gifted class would so increase its influence over the legislature that changes would be made in the laws affecting the inheritance of wealth, and no longer would heirs deficient in natural gifts be allowed to inherit vast fortunes. Ultimately, endowments would be assigned for the maintenance of the gifted who would live under better sanitary conditions and multiply more rapidly than the less able.

> 'I do not see why any insolence of caste should prevent the gifted class, when they had the power, from treating their compatriots with all kindness, so long as they maintained celibacy. But if these continued to procreate children, inferior in moral, intellectual and physical qualities, it is easy to believe the time may come when such persons would be considered as enemies to the State, and to have forfeited all claims to kindness.'[7]

Galton did not write again on the subject of 'viriculture', as he then termed it, until the 1880s. But in spite of the lack of public interest in his proposals he began to follow the programme he had outlined in his paper. The first requirement was for an exact stocktaking of the nation:

> 'We want to know all about their respective health and strength and constitutional vigour; to learn the amount of a day's work of men in different occupations; their intellectual capacity, so far as it can be tested at schools; the dying out of certain classes of families, and the rise of others; sanitary questions; and many other allied facts, in order to give a correct idea of the present worth of our race, and means of comparison some years hence of our general progress or retrogression.'[8]

Thus began his anthropological and psychological data collection. His first move was to submit a proposal to the Anthropological Institute, which received the sanction of the Council, to approach schools of all descriptions, from public to pauper, and to ask them to supply information about the heights and weights of the children attending them.[9]

He issued a few preliminary requests but received returns from only two schools, Marlborough and Liverpool College. The headmaster of Marlborough, Dr Farrar, later Dean of Canterbury, was extremely enthusiastic and enlisted the aid of the school medical officer and natural science master. Not only were all the 550 boys in the school weighed and measured for height, but several other bodily measurements were also taken, namely circumference of head, chest and limbs. The data were published by the school officers in the *Journal of the Anthropological Institute*, with a supplementary note by Galton indicating the methods to be employed when all the school data were obtained.[10] He obtained from the Marlborough returns arithmetical averages, or means, as well as medians of height for each group from 12 to 16 and thus produced a growth curve. He noticed an increase in variability at the older ages and suggested the possibility of deriving a formula from the data which would enable extrapolations to be made beyond the confines of the measured ages.

Two years were to pass before Galton had sufficient data from other schools to publish further results.[11] A paper entitled 'On the Height and Weight of Boys aged 14 in Town and Country Public Schools' was based on the relevant figures obtained from Clifton, Eton, Haileybury, Marlborough and Wellington (the so called 'country schools'), and from Christ's Hospital, City of London School, King Edward's School, Birmingham, and Liverpool College (the so called 'town schools'). Galton finds the country group to be $1\frac{1}{4}$ inches taller and 7lb heavier than the town group, a difference he ascribes not so much to the bad effects of town nurture on the boys themselves as to the town life of the boys' parents. But in 1876 such differences were almost certainly due to a class rather than rural–urban difference, the country schools attracting a higher proportion of upper class children.

Apart from these data on a few hundred boys at the upper end of the socio-economic scale nothing further of note was received from other schools. But Galton appears to have continued to nurse the hope of utilising the resources of these human laboratories. In a letter to *Nature* he points out that just as a hospital has two functions, the primary one of curing the sick and the secondary one of advancing our knowledge of pathology so might schools serve the double purpose of educating the young and advancing the sciences of anthropology and psychology.

'If a schoolmaster were now and then found capable and willing to codify in a scientific manner his large experiences of boys, to compare their various moral and intellectual qualities, to classify their natural temperaments, and generally to describe them as a naturalist would describe the fauna of some new land, what excellent psychological work might be accomplished? But all these great opportunities lie neglected. The masters come and go, their experiences are lost, or almost so, and the incidents on which they were founded are forgotten, instead of being stored and rendered accessible to their successors; thus our great schools are like mediaeval hospitals, where case-taking was unknown, where pathological collections were never dreamt of, and where in consequence the art of healing made slow and uncertain advance.'[12]

Disappointed by the lack of interest on the part of the schools, Galton cast around for other sources of data. He was intent on collecting more than the sparse physical measurements he had been sent by the schools. He made it quite clear in an address to the Anthropological Department of the British Association in 1877 that he believed anthropologists should not be content with physical anthropology alone but should study differences in mental characteristics.[13] Then, supposing one could obtain groups of different mentality, one could examine them for differences in their external appearance. One such group is provided by the criminal, whose mentality must be different from that of the law-abiding citizen. According to Galton, the 'ideal' criminal has a deficient conscience, weak self control and vicious instincts.[14]

An acquaintance with Sir Edward du Cane, Inspector of Prisons, gave Galton the opportunity he was seeking. Du Cane provided him with photographs of a large number of criminals convicted of certain classes of crime and serving long prison sentences. Galton divided them into three main groups: those convicted of murder and manslaughter, those convicted of felony and forgery, and those convicted of sexual offences. The problem now was to find some method of extracting those physical features peculiar to each type of criminality and of comparing them with each other and with non-criminals.

Herbert Spencer had already tried superimposing drawings made on tracing paper and holding them to the light to obtain an aggregate result, while a New Zealander, A. L. Austin, had written to Darwin suggesting the use of a stereoscope to combine two portraits, a technique which he thought might be relevant to the study of emotional expression.[15]

Galton at first tried Austin's stereoscopic method with the portraits of criminals. They combined readily, but he needed a method of super-imposing more than two portraits at once. His own solution was elegantly simple. It was to photograph the series of portraits one after another on the same photographic plate. He hung the portraits one in front of another so that they were exactly superimposed. He then copied them with a camera, giving each one an equal fraction of the normally adequate ex-posure. The print obtained was a composite of all eight portraits, the ordering of the exposures being irrelevant to the final result.

It is a characteristic of a composite that the individual peculiarities are lost while those aspects that are common to the greatest number of its components are emphasised.

'A composite portrait represents the picture that would rise before the mind's eye of a man who had the gift of pictorial imagination in an exalted degree. But the imaginative power even of the highest artists is far from precise, and is so apt to be biased by special cases that may have struck their fancies, that no two artists agree in any of their typical forms. The merit of the photographic composite is its mechanical precision, being subject to no errors beyond those inciden-tal to all photographic productions.'[16]

The quotation is taken from a paper Galton read a year after he had first outlined his technique. He was now able to exhibit composites of his criminal groups. In his discussion of the portraits he claims that the composites are better looking than the individual portraits :

'The special villainous irregularities in the latter have disappeared, and the common humanity that underlies them has prevailed. They represent, not the criminal, but the man who is liable to fall into crime.'[17]

Many of his audience at the Anthropological Institute were disappointed that no criminal types recognisable by the face had emerged in the composites. But the negative result was valuable in that it showed that if there were a criminal mentality it was certainly not associated with a particular physiognomy.

In this same paper Galton proceeds to describe several possible uses for composite photography. One obvious possibility would be to provide a racial photograph from a random and large number of individuals of a particular racial group. Another aim might be to obtain a really good likeness of an individual by combining portraits of him taken at various times and with various facial expressions. Similarly, the truest picture of an historical personage might be obtained from a composite derived from his representation on various medals and coins. Finally, the hereditary transmission of facial features might be investigated by means of composites. A composite of several members of the family as in Plate VI might be obtained. Or the children in the family might be compared with the composite of their parents, grandparents, etc. It would even be possible to assign different 'weights' to the individual constituents of the composite; for example, if each grandparent was given an exposure of one unit, each parent could be weighted by a factor of four. Composites on this principle might lead to better forecasts of the appearance of offspring and might prove useful to breeders of animals who needed to judge the desirability of a proposed mating.

Not all these ideas were pursued to fruition. Some of the best composites were those preserved by Karl Pearson from Galton's trials with medals and coins. Plate VII shows the results obtained in the case of Napoleon. This and several composites of Greek and Roman women were exhibited at a lecture to the Royal Institution in 1879.[18] The illustrations were merely incidental to the main theme of the lecture which was to discuss the analogy between the process of making a composite portrait and that of forming a general impression.

Galton begins his lecture by describing various everyday actions that are based on general impressions. For example, we have an impression that the day looks rainy, and we take an umbrella. The opinion on which we act is not, he thinks, formed by a process of reasoning but it is the effect of the blending together of a large number of similar experiences that we have had in the past.

'I shall try to prove that blended memories are strictly analogous to blended pictures, of which I have produced many specimens by combining actual portraits together; and I shall explain the peculiarities of the images by those of the portraits; then I shall show that the brain is incompetent to blend images in their right proportions. My conclusions will be that our unreasoned impressions are of necessity fertile sources of superstition and fallacy from which the child and the savage are never free, and with which all branches of knowledge are largely tainted in their prescientific stage.'[19]

Without following Galton through all the details of his argument and accepting that the process of forming generalised mental images has similarities to that of taking composite pictures, let us ask the question whether a person with perfect visualising power who put his eye in place of the camera during a series of shots would obtain an identical generic image to that on the photographic plate.

Galton answers this question in the negative, basing his view on two observations: a true photographic composite never appears true, and percepts often repeated may lead to only indistinct images while infrequent percepts may give rise to vivid images. In generic images undue consideration is given to the exceptional cases that we have encountered while the great prevalence of mediocre instances is overlooked. Composite portraits, on the other hand, include the features of every individual in the series. They are pictorial equivalents of statistical tables from which averages can be deduced.

Galton concludes his paper with the following fine paragraph:

'The human mind is a most imperfect apparatus for the elaboration of true general ideas. Compared with the mind of brutes, its powers are marvellous; but for all that they fall vastly short of perfection. The criterion of a perfect mind would lie in its capacity of always creating images of a truly generic kind, deduced from the whole range of its past experiences. General impressions are never to be trusted. Unfortunately when they are of long standing they become fixed rules of life, and assume a prescriptive right not to be questioned. Consequently, those who are not accustomed to original inquiry entertain a hatred and a horror of statistics. They cannot endure the idea of submitting their sacred impressions to cold-blooded verification. But it is the triumph of scientific men to rise superior to such superstitions, to devise tests by which the value of beliefs may be ascertained, and to feel sufficiently masters of themselves to discard contemptuously whatever may be found untrue.'[20]

Two other papers on the applications of composite photography are worthy of mention. The more substantial enquiry concerned the physiognomy of tubercular patients.[21] With the assistance of F. A. Mahomed, a physician at Guy's Hospital, Galton photographed 442 patients and made composites of various subgroups of different ages and disease duration. Two hundred patients suffering from other diseases acted as controls.

Conclusions were quite clear cut in spite of the technical difficulties in compounding as many as 200 photographs into a single composite portrait. As the authors put it,

'The results lend no countenance to the belief that any special type of face predominates among phthisical patients, nor to the generally entertained opinion that the narrow ovoid or "tubercular" face is more common in phthisis than *among other diseases*. Whether it is more common than among the rest of the *healthy* population we cannot at present say.'[22]

Thus, this paper can be seen as an illustration of Galton's previous contention that the generalisations made from our experiences of a particular series of events are likely to be biased and inaccurate.

The second paper demonstrated the source of a perceptual error to which artists had been liable in their conventional representations of a galloping horse.[23] It had just been shown by rapid photography that a galloping horse never had all four legs extended simultaneously. Why then should observant artists have represented horses in this incorrect posture?

To answer the question Galton made a composite from 20 successive photographs of a horse at full gallop. It resembled the artistic representation but was very confused. Finding from his own observation that it was difficult to watch the four legs at once and seeing that according to the photographic evidence the forelegs were extended for a quarter of the complete cycle and the rear legs for another quarter, he made separate composites of these groups. Uniting the two halves he obtained the conventional attitude.

'I inferred that the brain ignored one half of all it saw in the gallop, as too confused to be noticed; that it divided the other half in two parts, each alike in one particular, and combined the two halves into a monstrous whole.'[24]

It was while working with composites that Galton attempted the reverse process, that is, he tried to annul all that was typical in an individual portrait and to preserve only that which was peculiar. He published nothing until much later on the topic but, finally, in a letter to *Nature* he explained the method in detail.[25]

If a faint transparent positive plate is held face to face with a negative plate, they will neutralise one another and produce a uniform grey. But if the positive is a photograph of individual, A, and the negative a photograph of individual, B, then they will only cancel one another out where they are identical and a representation of their differences will appear on a grey background. Take a negative composite photograph and superimpose it on a positive portrait of one of the constituents of that composite and one should abstract the group peculiarities and leave the individuality.

Galton's experiments with the process were not extensive and he was dissatisfied with the result which did not clearly reveal the individual peculiarities he was looking for. In practice, problems arise because the negative does not wholly obliterate the positive unless the tones are of medium brightness. The idea appears never to have have been taken up and it is difficult to see any worthwhile application of the technique. As a party trick it had certain attractions : the combined positive of A and the negative of B will act as a 'transformer'. One has only to project a positive portrait of B on to the same screen to see it change as if by magic into a positive portrait of A.

Composite portraiture, on the other hand, has had occasional vogues.[26] Little work of scientific merit has appeared, although, following Galton's lead, attempts have been made to superimpose photographs of skulls for anthropological purposes.[27] One interesting practical possibility was suggested by Frazer who obtained composites of signatures in an endeavour to establish criteria by which a forger might be detected.[28] But we must conclude that in spite of his persistence with the technique Galton's efforts have led nowhere; the making of composites is a laborious business and the results appear to have little more than entertainment value. Galton's original conception of the method as a means of distinguishing people of different psychological makeup who might show their temperamental peculiarities in their faces died with him. The early twentieth century psychologists were able to show that there was no association between facial features and intellectual abilities, and although more recently temperamental and physique measures have been shown to be highly correlated this work has not included an examination of particular facial features and their possible linkage with behavioural traits.[29]

The main body of Galton's psychological work consisted of attempts to analyse the mental processes of himself and of others by introspection. The prevalent view held by the early psychologists was that this technique of selfexamination was the obvious approach to mental phenomena which could then be described and discussed. Galton followed their lead in adopting their technique, but soon broke new ground in the subject matter of his enquiries.

His first introspective attempts consisted of observations on himself alone. For example, on one occasion he tried to bring his breathing under solely voluntary control and in his reference to the episode in his auto-biography he claimed that the normal automatic power of breathing was so dangerously interfered with that for a period of half an hour he thought he would suffocate unless he continued to will each breath.[30]

An equally brave attempt to induce paranoia in himself is vividly described in his own words :

> 'The method tried was to invest everything I met, whether human, animal, or inanimate, with the imaginary attributes of a spy. Having arranged plans, I started on my morning's walk from Rutland Gate, and found the experiment only too successful. By the time I had walked one and a half miles, and reached the cabstand in Piccadilly at the east end of the Green Park, every horse on the stand seemed watching me, either with pricked ears or disguising its espionage. Hours passed before this uncanny sensation wore off and I feel that I could only too easily re-establish it.'[31]

The first published work utilising introspective methods was naturally of a more substantial kind and sprang directly from the associationist psychology of the day. Galton was interested in the automatic elicitation of ideas by association, ideas that come of their own accord and cannot normally be compelled to come.

> 'These associated ideas, though they are for the most part exceed-ingly fleeting and obscure, and barely cross the threshold of our consciousness, may be seized, dragged into daylight and recorded.'[32]

The first technique employed was to observe successive objects that caught his attention during a walk along Pall Mall. He allowed his atten-tion to rest on the object until one or two thoughts had arisen by direct association with that object, he mentally noted these thoughts and then passed on to the next object. Although unable later to recall the numerous associations aroused during the course of the walk he was sure that many bygone incidents had come to mind and that the associations had touched on many different periods of his life.

> 'I saw at once that the brain was vastly more active than I had previously believed it to be, and I was perfectly amazed at the unexpected width of the field of its everyday operations. After an interval of some days, during which I kept my mind from dwelling

on my first experiences, in order that it might retain as much freshness as possible for a second experiment, I repeated the walk, and was struck just as much as before by the variety of ideas that presented themselves, and the number of events to which they referred, about which I had never consciously occupied myself of late years. But my admiration at the activity of the mind was seriously diminished by another observation which I then made, namely that there had been a very great deal of repetition of thought. The actors in my mental stage were indeed very numerous, but by no means so numerous as I had imagined. They now seemed to be something like the actors in theatres where large processions are represented, who march off one side of the stage, and, going round by the back, come on again at the other. I accordingly cast about for means of laying hold of these fleeting thoughts, and submitting them to statistical analysis, to find out more about their tendency to repetition and other matters.'[33]

Galton now devised the technique later to be known as the word association test. He extracted from a dictionary 100 words, all beginning with the letter 'a', and wrote each word on a separate sheet of paper. Drawing one at random, Galton placed it so that it was partly obscured by a book. Leaning forward, he started a stopwatch as soon as the word came into view and allowed himself four seconds to produce as many associations to the stimulus word as possible. Occasionally only one idea came to mind, but more often three or four. These associations he noted down.

He found it repugnant and laborious work and was only able to complete the task by strong selfcontrol. His programme entailed four separate attempts at the list under very different circumstances, in England and abroad, and at intervals of about a month.*

The results were thrown into 'a common statistical hotchpotch' and the rate at which ideas arose was first examined. The average rate was about 50 associations per minute, which Galton thought miserably slow when compared with the rate that would have been attained if he had allowed one association to follow another as in reverie. Another factor slowing the rate was the abstract nature of many of his stimulus words.

The list of 75 words, gone over four times, gave rise to 505 associations

---

* Galton's published account of his experiments does not tally with the material preserved in the Galton Archives. He admits in his paper that he mislaid some of his stimulus material and was forced to derive his results from 75 out of the original 100 words. But even so, there appear to have been eight lists which vary in length from 20 to 87 stimulus words. The final experiment, dated 13th January 1879, entailed the use of most of the stimulus words common to the previous lists and it is these words that are given in Appendix II. There appears to have been no list of 75 words that was repeated on four occasions as he claims.[34]

and 13 cases of 'puzzle', that is, complete failure to produce a response. Of the 505 associations, 29 had occurred on all four trials, 36 on three, 57 on two, and 107 on one trial only. In short, there was much less variety in his associations than he had expected.

'[The mind] is apparently always engaged in mumbling over its old stores and if any one of these is wholly neglected for a while, it is apt to be forgotten, perhaps irrecoverably.'[35]

It did not seem to Galton sufficient merely to have paid keen attention to an episode for it to be subsequently retained, the subject must continue to have an abiding interest. On rare occasions during the experiments he recalled a memory which had lain dormant for many years, but even in such cases he believed it probable that he had recalled a memory of the incident rather than the incident itself, which in the process had been modified in unknown ways to become a condensation and transformation of the original. In this connection he cites the experience of meeting a childhood friend and comparing recollections of early events with him. In such a case each person retains a very different version of the same occurrence and their recollections do not tally.

'My associated ideas were for the most part due to my own unshared experiences, and the list of them would necessarily differ from that which another person would draw up who might repeat my experiments. Therefore one sees clearly, and I may say, one can see *measurably*, how impossible it is in a general way for two grown-up persons to lay their minds side by side together in perfect accord. The same sentence cannot produce precisely the same effect on both, and the first quick impressions that any word in it may convey, will differ widely in the two minds.'[36]

Galton found it possible in 124 cases to determine the period of his life at which each of the associated ideas had first become attached to the stimulus word. Table 11.1 is reproduced from his paper and best summarises his results.

He infers the greater fixity of the earlier associations by noting that a quarter of these occurred on all four trials, while of the associations formed in manhood only one sixth of them occurred as frequently, and none of the recent associations was similarly favoured.

'If the figures . . . may be accepted as fairly correct for the world generally, it shows, still in a measurable degree, the large effect of early education in fixing our associations. It will of course be understood that I make no absurd profession of being able by these very few experiments to lay down statistical constants of universal application, but that my principal object is to show that a large class of mental phenomena, that have hitherto been too vague to lay hold of, admit of being caught by the firm grip of genuine statistical enquiry.'[37]

TABLE 11.1. Relative number of associations formed at different periods of life.

Source	Total number of different associations	Percentages				
		Total	Occurring four times	Occurring three times	Occurring twice	Occurring once
Boyhood and youth	48	39	10	9	7	13
Subsequent manhood	57	46	8	7	5	26
Quite recent events	19	15	—	3	1	11
Totals	124	100	18	19	13	50

(Adapted from F. Galton, 'Psychometric experiments', *Brain*, 2 (1879), 157.)

Lastly, Galton attempted to divide both the stimulus words and his associations into classes. In the case of the associations he was able to distinguish three groups:

a. Those in which he responded in a parrot-like way by giving a phrase or quotation,

b. Those in which sense imagery, particularly visual imagery, occurred, and

c. A third group, made up of what he calls 'histrionic representations', where he acted a part in his imagination, or saw a part acted, or most commonly, where he was both actor and spectator at the same time.

'Thus the word "abasement" presented itself to me, in one of my experiments, by my mentally placing myself in a pantomimic attitude of humiliation with half closed eyes, bowed back, and uplifted palms, while at the same time I was aware of myself as of a mental puppet, in that position.'[38]

On the same principle the stimulus words were also divisible into three groups:

a. Those of the first group, he instances 'abbey', 'aborigines', 'abyss', could be experienced as visual images;

b. Those of the second group, e.g., 'abasement', 'abhorrence', 'ablution', could be given histrionic representation, while

c. The third group contained more abstract words, such as 'after-noon', 'ability', 'abnormal', which were variously dealt with, most often giving rise to purely verbal phrases and quotations. These catchphrases intruded themselves before Galton was able to appreciate the meaning of the stimulus word, and led him to conclude that his own generalising powers were very imperfect.

'Nothing is a surer sign of high intellectual capacity than the power of quickly seizing and easily manipulating ideas of a very abstract nature. Commonly we grasp them imperfectly, and hold on to their skirts with great difficulty.'[39]

Galton found that histrionic ideas most often occurred as the first response to a stimulus word while visual imagery was more prevalent as a second response. The verbal class of associations was often produced immediately as a rapid reaction.

Apart from a few extracts, such as those we have given, Galton never published the list of 75 stimulus words, and, in view of the point made earlier in connection with his notebooks on the topic, it seems probable that his published results were derived from some portion of his stimulus material. There appears to have been no reason for Galton to have deliberately falsified his results, and it is much more probable that he did more work on the topic than he saw fit to divulge. Support for this view is provided by correspondence between Kegan Paul, the publisher, and Galton.[40] In 1877 Kegan Paul offered Galton £50 on the first edition of a book to appear in the International Scientific Series entitled, *Psychometry, or the Measurement of Mental Action in Time and Quantity.* But after a lapse of two years, Galton wrote to refuse on the grounds that his net results were so full and the gross so bulky. Presumably the word association experiments were undertaken with the publication of the book in mind and it was a selection of his results that appeared in the published papers.

Neither did Galton divulge his associations to the stimulus words. His reticence is explained in his paper :

'It would be too absurd to print one's own singly. They lay bare the foundations of a man's thoughts with curious distinctness, and exhibit his mental anatomy with more vividness and truth than he would probably care to publish to the world.'[41]

The paper concludes with the following comment :

'Perhaps the strongest impression left by these experiments regards the multifariousness of the work done by the mind in a state of half-unconsciousness, and the valid reason they afford for believing in the existence of still deeper strata of mental operations, sunk wholly below the level of consciousness, which may account for such mental phenomena as cannot otherwise be explained.'[42]

The first account of Galton's work appeared in the March issue of the *Nineteenth Century* in 1879;[43] a substantially similar paper but with more statistical treatment was published in the July issue of *Brain* in the same year, and it is from this latter journal that we have quoted. Among the readers of this issue Sigmund Freud can almost certainly be included. Freud subscribed to *Brain* and in his writings makes explicit reference to papers by the neurologist, Hughlings Jackson, contained in the January and October issues.[44] However, he never referred to Galton's paper nor did he credit Galton with priority in suggesting the existence of unconscious mental processes.

It is perhaps unimportant whether Freud's subsequent adoption in the 1890s of the free association technique really sprang from his availing himself of Galton's discovery. What is of greater significance today is the way in which Freud put the discovery to work as the therapeutic tool of psychoanalysis. But then it was Freud's genius to explore the depths of the unconscious which Galton had glimpsed; it was Galton's genius to apply his creativity more widely if superficially over a variety of scientific disciplines.

'Human Faculty'

Galton's word association experiments were to bear other and more immediate fruits. In discussing his results with scientific colleagues he was amazed to find that many of them were at a loss to understand how a stimulus word could arouse imagery as they themselves had no experience of the phenomenon. On the other hand, many men without specialised aptitudes, and even more women, claimed that they habitually experienced imagery of a distinct and colourful kind. Variations in the intensity of imagery seemed a topic worthy of investigation and suitable for a question-naire approach.

Entitled 'Questions on visualising and other allied faculties', the questionnaire was issued in November 1879. At first he limited its distribu-tion to relatives and friends, but then contacted several educational establishments and had it distributed among the pupils. The published results were derived from one school, Charterhouse, where the science master succeeded in interesing all his 172 boys in the enquiry. Galton completed his sample with the returns from 100 adult men, of whom 19 were Fellows of the Royal Society.

In the questionnaire Galton directs the respondent's attention to his breakfast table of that morning and asks him to summon up a picture of it in his mind's eye. He then asks for an estimate of its brightness, defini-tion, colouring, and the extent of the field of view. A further series of questions refers to particular instances in which visual imagery may occur, and the questionnaire concludes with a request for ratings of the intensity of other sense imagery.

The variety of answers surprised Galton as they may still surprise the reader of today. They ranged from that of the respondent who stated :

> 'I can see my breakfast table or any equally familiar thing with my mind's eye, quite as well in all particulars as I can do if the reality is before me.'[1]

F

To the man at the other extreme who experienced no visual imagery :

'My powers are zero. To my consciousness there is almost no association of memory with objective visual impressions. I recollect the breakfast table, but do not see it.'[2]

Galton awaited the return from Charles Darwin with some impatience. Erasmus Darwin had reported unusually strong visual imagery himself and the possibility of the inheritance of such a peculiarity was naturally of interest to Galton. He himself had strong motor imagery, as we have seen in his responses in the association experiments, but his visual imagery was no more than moderate. In this latter respect Charles resembled his cousin more than his grandfather; he was able to see his breakfast table in part only and moderately illuminated, although some objects were well defined.[3]

As in the case of the association experiments, the results were published in two versions : one fairly statistical paper appeared in the journal *Mind*; the other, originally given as a lecture at the 1880 British Association meeting at Swansea, was published by the *Fortnightly* and was intended for a lay audience.[4]

Much of the *Mind* paper is taken up with an attempt to apply a statistical treatment to his returns. Galton succeeds in taking the replies to the several questions and ordering them in terms of the strength of imagery shown by his three groups of respondents. (His schoolboys were divided into those from the upper classes of the school and those from the lower classes.) In order to compare the vividness of imagery possessed by the three groups Galton takes the middlemost, or median, answer in each series and compares these. He goes further and examines the answers falling at various positions on either side of the median, namely the quartile, octile and suboctile points.

The application of ranking methods to his data does not bring much enlightenment; Galton is content to show that his two schoolboy groups are almost identical and very similar to the adults, except that among the young subjects there is a greater vividness of colour imagery. The adults' replies did not form as regular a series as did the boys', and Galton is undoubtedly right in attributing this irregularity to the heterogeneity of his adult sample. Some people replied to his questionnaire because they had particularly vivid imagery and seized the opportunity to write about it, others were his scientific friends, and yet others his and Louisa's relatives and friends.

For Galton there were two notable results :

'The one is the proved facility of obtaining statistical insight into the processes of other persons' minds; and the other is that scientific men as a class have feeble powers of visual representation. There is no doubt whatever on the latter point, however it may be accounted for. My own conclusion is, that an over-readiness to perceive clear mental pictures is antagonistic to the acquirement of habits of highly generalised and abstract thought, and that if the faculty of producing them was ever possessed by men who think hard, it is very apt to be lost by disuse.'[5]

A similar point is made more amusing in the *Fortnightly* where Galton describes an experiment in which he accosted a philosopher and his girl-friend with the words, 'I want to tell you about a boat.' The girl immediately visualised a large boat leaving the bank filled with men and women dressed in blue and white. The philosopher asserted that he held his mind in suspense and refused to allow himself to experience a visual image. Galton continues,

'A habit of suppressing mental imagery must therefore characterise men who deal much with abstract ideas; and as the power of dealing easily and firmly with these ideas is the surest criterion of a high order of intellect, we should expect that the visualising faculty would be starved by disuse among philosophers, and this is precisely what I have found on inquiry to be the case.'[6]

But he does not think that visualising powers should on this account be allowed to decay. The process of generalising can be helped by a fluid visual imagery. Visual imagery is also useful in many occupations, such as those of engineer, architect, mechanic, where spatial representation is involved. It can also bring pleasure in enabling faithful recall of scenery and works of art. Instead of starving it by disuse, it should be judiciously cultivated by as yet undiscovered educational techniques. Galton believes that conscious efforts to strengthen weak imagery are ineffective. The role of the will is to reject inappropriate ideas rather than to evoke or render more vivid appropriate ones.

In spite of the popular interest aroused by Galton's work he came in for some criticism from the early psychologists. For example, Alexander Bain pointed out that the range of visual imagery had been known since antiquity and that Galton's enquiry had done nothing to further our knowledge of the phenomenon. The lack of precision in Galton's questions resulted in a lack of precision in the replies and led, he believed, to under- and over-estimation at the extreme ends of the continuum. He therefore doubted the replies both of those who stated that they had never known what a visual image was and those who claimed that their images had an hallucinatory quality.[7] It is difficult to know how far Bain's criticisms are justified. Galton's wording did lack precision, but there is little doubt that the extremes of imagery do exist in a normal population and Bain's inability to comprehend the mental processes of others very different from himself is of common occurrence.

Further criticisms are of more recent date. The theory that people could be typed according to their predominant imagery seems to have been derived from Galton although he made no explicit suggestion to this effect. But subsequent work has shown that most persons do not have a discrete style; they use images of various sense modalities.[8]

Galton's use of a vividness scale directed later workers' attention to the one aspect of the imaginal process which appears to be of little functional importance.[9] The vividness with which imagery is experienced in one or another sense modality is a characteristic which has since Galton's day been widely regarded as of crucial significance.[10] But vividness is in a sense a side-effect. The use to which imagery can be put does not primarily depend on its faintness or vividness; imagery may be employed in problem solving even by those who cannot agree that they 'see' anything. Part of the confusion is undoubtedly semantic, but it can be justifiably maintained that Galton was too easily content with the superficial success of his statistical method and did not at the time push the enquiry as far as he might well have done.

One of Galton's respondents was George Bidder, son of a well known rapid calculator, who was gifted in much the same way as his father. Bidder drew Galton's attention to a peculiar way in which he visualised numbers. When a number occurred to him, he visualised it in the appropriate position on a spatial framework made up by the other numbers. Galton collected further instances of what he termed 'number forms' until he had enough material for a paper entitled, 'Visualised Numerals', which appeared in *Nature*.[11] Much correspondence ensued and to accompany a second paper of the same title read two months later to the Anthropological Institute, Galton was able to demonstrate 60 examples of number forms.[12] The matter continued to excite attention and a large collection was amassed by Galton of which only a selection was ever published. Some examples are shown in Figure 12.1.

It is easier to demonstrate than to describe the variety of number forms and it can be seen from these illustrations that the patterns in which numerals are visualised can assume a great variety of shapes. The drawings do not give an idea of their size; they cannot usually be visualised as a whole, but extend across the visual field.

As in the case of colour blindness, which remained undescribed until the time of Dalton, the ability to visualise numerals in this way had escaped notice until Galton discovered it. But, as he points out, the neglect of the phenomenon is understandable when we consider that the ability is even rarer than colour defect, being possessed by not more than about one man in 30, although twice as common among women.

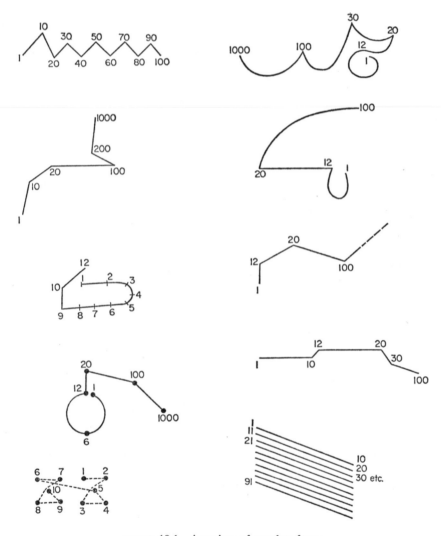

FIGURE 12.1 A variety of number forms

Galton was sufficiently unsure of himself before the Anthropological Society, that he invited six friends, including George Bidder, to attend the meeting (after a good dinner) to testify to the veracity of their reported number forms. His uncertainty was probably due to the fact that he did not visualise numerals in this way himself and he knew of the incredulity with which the majority would greet his secondhand assertions.

In spite of their great variety number forms do have certain points in common. They more frequently curve to the right than to the left and they typically plunge up and down in the vertical plane. Sometimes they are threedimensional and some of Galton's correspondents sent him wire models to illustrate this fact. They are more typically fixed in space with regard to the visualiser's position; for example, one person had a form which swept backwards high over his head to end in his pocket!

Galton believed that the reason behind the idiosyncratic shape of a number form lay in a 'natural fancy for different lines and curves', which was also evident in an individual's handwriting. Thus he thought he was able to discern a resemblance between handwriting and the general shape of the number form.

He thought it probable that number forms originate early in childhood, although they may be developed later to encompass the higher values and even negative numbers. Although historical dates, days of the week, months of the year, and letters of the alphabet may also be visualised in a spatial framework, it seems that these forms are of later construction, frequently being based on the number form or on diagrams used in class or derived from books. Being the oldest of all, the number form is of most interest; it seems to be developed as a natural mnemonic diagram when the child first learns to count, a diagram to which he refers the spoken words, 'one', 'two', etc. As soon as he begins to read, the child supplants the verbal sounds by the visual symbols of the figures which establish themselves permanently on the form. In a few cases children learn their numbers up to 12 from the clock face and the number form reveals this influence. (See Figure 12.1) The origin of some other forms can be traced to experience with dominoes, cards, the fingers, or other simple counting devices. The names that numerals are given appear to influence the form. In this respect Galton makes the interesting point that the numbers from 10 to 20 are spoken 'in defiance of the beautiful system of decimal notation in which we write these numbers.'[18] Our present usage may, he thinks, prove a serious hindrance to the ready adoption of a decimal system of weights and measures, and he proposes the replacement of our 'barbarous nomenclature' by one consistent with the higher numbers. Thus, we should say something like 'on(e) one, on(e) two, on(e) three,' instead of 'eleven, twelve and thirteen.' ('Onty' suggests itself as a more consistent term.)

Number forms do appear to provide evidence for a conflict between the visual and verbal systems, in that the 'teens nearly always show a deviation from the general shape of the form. A hitch usually occurs at 10 or 12 and the space devoted to the 'teens is usually greater than is their due. It is as though we see in the number form a pictorial representation of the efforts and ingenuity of the child in coping with this problem.

It was not until the publication in 1883 of his next book, *Inquiries into Human Faculty and its Development*, that Galton was able to add to his account of number forms. By then he had acquired several hundreds, including those from the members of 22 families where the tendency appeared to be hereditary. In some cases the number forms of relatives are very similar, in others they do not resemble each other, but when the incidence of the phenomenon in the general population is taken into account the familial link is certainly remarkable, although insufficient as sole evidence for the hereditarian viewpoint.

Galton reports that numbers are often personified by children. Although large differences are found with respect to the attributes assigned to most of the numbers, Galton found some unanimity in the case of 12. In agreement with its important position on many number forms it is typically regarded as an important and influential person. He gives these examples :

a. 'Good and cautious—so good as to be almost noble.
b. 'A more beautiful number than 10 from the many multiples that make it up—in other words, its kindly relations to so many small numbers.
c. 'A great love for 12, a large-hearted motherly person because of the number of little ones that it takes, as it were, under its protection.'[14]

Occasionally, number forms are themselves coloured but more frequently the numbers are coloured without being disposed in any particular form. Even more common among children is the association of the sounds of words with colour. Galton provides several full accounts from adults who have preserved this ability. For example, a scientist's wife who visualised the vowels :

'A, pure white, and like china in texture.
E, red, not transparent; vermilion with china-white would represent it.
I, light bright yellow; gamboge.
O, black, but transparent; the colour of deep water seen through thick clear ice.
U, purple.
Y, dingier colour than I.'[15]

He concludes from his data and from earlier reports that the association of colour with sound is as persistent as that of the number form with numbers. Those who experience the former imagery are invariably minute in their description of the precise hue of the colours and it is rare to find two individuals in agreement.

'Persons who have colour associations are unsparingly critical. To ordinary individuals one of the accounts seems just as wild and lunatic as another, but when the account of one seer is submitted to another seer, who is sure to see the colours in a different way, the latter is scandalised and almost angry at the heresy of the former.'[16]

A paper read in May 1881 to the Royal Institution has the title, 'The visions of sane persons.'[17] In it Galton classifies number forms and colour associations as primitive forms of the visionary tendency, remarkable for the fact that they occur in normal individuals. Various other kinds of subjective visual experience are discussed, ranging from patterns seen when the eyes are closed to actual hallucinations, or visions, experienced by normal persons in good health. His variety of cases leads him to accept a continuity among all forms of visualisation from the extreme of no imagery at all to the other extreme of a complete hallucination. The continuity is not a simple one of degree of intensity but of variations in the process itself. Some good visualisers who are also able to see visions claim that visions are different from vivid visualisations in that they characteristically appear and disappear suddenly and without warning and are quite involuntary.

In the draft of a letter, probably intended for *Nature* but apparently never published, Galton describes a near hallucination which he himself experienced when ill with influenza and bronchitis.

'When fancies gathered and I was on the borderland of delirium I was aware of the imminence of a particular hallucination. There was no vivid visualisation of it, but I felt that if I let myself go I should see in bold relief a muscular blood-stained crucified figure nailed against the wall of my bedroom opposite to my bed. What on earth made me think of this particular object I have no conception. There was nothing in it of the religious symbol, but just a prisoner freshly mauled and nailed up by a brutal Roman soldier. The interest in this to me was the severance between the state of hallucination and that of ordinary visualisation. They seemed in this case to be quite unconnected.'[18]

Galton's Royal Institution paper concludes with an attempt at explanation. The weirdness of visions lies in their vividness and in the suddenness with which they come and go. He draws an analogy with a common experience at the zoo when a seal is under observation. At one moment the water surface is unbroken, at another the head of the seal protrudes, and a little later the surface is again placid. If there is a sheen on the water the movements of the animal before and after its appearance are shrouded in mystery and one link in a continuous chain of actions stands isolated for our observation. Similarly in visions a single stage in a whole series of mental operations emerges into consciousness. The reason for this isolation Galton ascribes to an 'oversensitiveness' of certain brain tracts and an 'undersensitiveness' of others; thus, certain stages in a mental process are vividly conscious while other stages occur outside awareness.

He now examines the distinction normally made between hallucinations and illusions, the former being defined as due solely to the imagination, while the latter are misrepresentations of objects actually present to the senses. He believes that most hallucinations are of a hybrid nature as they are probably triggered off by the ever-varying visual patterns which can be seen when the eyes are closed but to which attention is not normally paid.

To understand the establishment of illusions he describes the process of trying to see faces in the fire or on wallpaper when confined to bed with illness. In health, the process is normally too rapid to observe, but illness may slow it down. The first essential is for the field of vision to be restricted so that a whole picture can only be made up by slow movements of the eyes. There are idiosyncratic contractions of the eye muscles which lead to certain preferred eye movements. The presence of these preferences is demonstrated in the individual peculiarities of the number form. There are also influences from the associations of the moment and from the subject's mood. The eye thus tends to follow a favourite course and dwells on the marks that coincide with that course. These marks are then strung together, with incongruities disregarded and with deficiencies supplied by the fantasy, until a picture is formed.

Visions are often patchworks of bits of recollections, which may be blended together to give an appearance of novelty. He compares the process with that seen in making a composite portrait when a 'new' face will emerge from familiar superimposed faces. Similarly in the case of the creative type of vision, many blended memories may be involved and the number of possible combinations is almost endless.

Galton believes that the visionary tendency has an hereditary foundation. In this way he explains familial and racial differences in the ability to have visions. Although inheritance will set the limits, illness, solitude, food and sleep deprivation may be necessary before a person may reach those limits. The number of great men who have been subject to hallucinations—he describes Napoleon's guiding star—is explained by the conditions of social isolation under which they must live.

'It follows that the spiritual discipline undergone for purposes of self-control and self-mortification has also the incidental effect of producing visions. It is to be expected that these should often bear a close relation to the prevalent subjects of thought, and although they may be really no more than the products of one portion of the brain, which another portion of the brain is engaged in contemplating, they often, through error, receive a religious sanction.'[19]

Similarly, social conditions may favour the production of visions :

'It is remarkable how largely the visionary temperament has manifested itself in certain periods of history and epochs of national life. My interpretation of the matter, to a certain extent, is this—That the visionary tendency is much more common among sane people than is generally suspected. In early life, it seems to be a hard lesson to an imaginative child to distinguish between the real and the visionary world. If the fantasies are habitually laughed at and otherwise discouraged, the child soon acquires the power of distinguishing them; any incongruity or non-conformity is quickly noted, the vision is found out and discredited, and is no further attended to. In this way the natural tendency to see them is blunted by repression. Therefore, when popular opinion is of a matter-of-fact kind, the seers of visions keep quiet; they do not like to be thought fanciful or mad, and they hide their experiences, which only come to light through inquiries such as these I have been making. But let the tide of opinion change and grow favourable to supernaturalism, then the seers of visions come to the front. It is not that a faculty previously non-existent has been suddenly evoked, but that a faculty long smothered in secret has been suddenly allowed freedom to express itself, and it may be to run into extravagance owing to the removal of reasonable safeguards.'[20]

The last of Galton's intensive introspective attempts took the form of systematic observations into his own decision-making which he published in *Mind* under the title, 'Free-will—observations and inferences.'[21] He explains in his autobiography that he had long been 'harassed with the old question of Determinism,' and it seems likely that a letter from Clerk Maxwell asking him if he was interested in the concepts of freewill versus fixed fate led to his selfexamination.[22]

His procedure was to examine every case of what might fairly be called free-will by recollecting what had occurred immediately beforehand. The selfexamination was carried on continuously over a period of six weeks and then occasionally over a subsequent period of several 'uneventful and pleasant months spent in the country.'[23]

He begins this interesting paper by pointing out that certain acts of 'will' did not come within his province. Thus, tenacity of purpose in achieving a goal is 'not popularly considered to be a high order of psychical activity.'[24] Galton instances the obstinate man who is vulgarly said to be as obstinate as a pig. He did not concern himself with acts that were determined by the appetites, nor those cases in which two motives of the same kind were in conflict and the greater prevailed.

'The events with which I did concern myself were those in which feelings of different quality had been in opposition, as when the

appetites of passions had been thwarted by alien influences, and I
endeavoured to infer from a comparison with past experiences, how
far the issue of each contest had really at any time been doubtful.'[25]

The rate of occurrence of these cases averaged about one a day, all
the remainder of his actions seeming to lie within the province of normal
cause and effect. Introspecting, Galton was able to his own satisfaction
to trace his motives in these rare cases backwards by orderly and continuous steps until they led 'to a tangle of familiar paths whose issues
were well known.'[26]

The cases of irresolution with which he concerned himself were of two
or three types. In the first, neither of two alternate plans was attractive
and the lack of attraction became stronger the longer he contemplated
either one. Then the attention would swing to the other alternative and
after a time back again. In the second, the growth of the desire to change
was fitful and characterised by frequent retrogressions, as was the waning
of the wish not to change. Resolution of the conflict was delayed until a
considerable waxing of the new desire corresponded with a sudden drop
of the old one. Galton provides as an example the daily act of waking up
and rising in the morning. The same process of rising may also illustrate
a third form of irresolution in which a change of Ego has to occur before
a decision can be made. Thus, although one may give intellectual assent
to a faint voice preaching the merits of early rising, before one can will
to rise,

> 'The Ego that is subsisting in content must somehow be abolished
> and a transmigration must take place into a different Ego, that of
> wide-awake life.'[27]

Various conditions could lead to this 'transmigration'. Sometimes a
momentary triumph of the waxing over the waning desire was adequate,
sometimes a slight accidental stimulus, such as a noise outside, might bring
about the change. A wrench of will is experienced at the moment of
making up the mind which is similar, although stronger, to the momentary
discomfort felt when an ambiguous visual pattern flips over to an alternative interpretation.

> 'I suspect that much of what we stigmatise as irresolution is due to
> our Self being by no means one and indivisible, and that we do not
> care to sacrifice the Self of the moment for a different one. There are,
> I believe, cases in which we are wrong in reproaching ourselves
> sternly, saying "The last week was not spent in the way you now wish
> it had been," because the Self was not the same throughout. There is
> room for applying the principle of the greatest happiness to the

greatest number; the particular Self at the moment of making the retrospect being not the only one to be considered.'[28]

Galton completes his analysis with a discussion of those cases in which 'incommensurable motives' are pitted against one another and in which the victor is not the one which is more keenly felt nor gives the greater pleasure. Such cases are typical of those in which the feeble voice of conscience may win. Social habits may also obtain easy victories in such contests. Galton cites a typical case from his own experience :

'An imperious old lady, infirm and garrulous, called at my house just as I had finished much weary work and was preparing with glee for a long walk. Hearing that I was at home, she dismissed her carriage for three quarters of an hour, so I was her prisoner for all that time. As she talked with little cessation, I had full opportunity for questioning myself on the feeling that supported me through the infliction. The response always shaped itself in the same way, "Social duties may not be disregarded; besides, this is a capital occasion for introspection".'[29]

He explains these cases by adopting a physiological frame of reference by which he claims one can gain as much as by adopting a Copernican rather than Ptolemaic view of the planetary system. Consciousness has a very limited view of the battles within our brain and can readily be deceived about the relative strengths of the opposing forces. Thus, there is no real occasion for surprise when the consciously-judged weaker force is the victor.

The remaining difficulty lies in the apparent spontaneity with which decisions can be made. He considers these as end products of an unconscious chain of ideas. Many of our ideas are but partially shaped when they are first perceived, while some are fully shaped. In the former case we may be able to trace the process of formation, but in the latter case the ideas will appear to have no antecedents. The conditions are similar to those under which hallucinations occur, and Galton thinks similar mechanisms are operative in both cases. By careful introspection one can find the causes of these apparently spontaneous images and thoughts.

'If these explanations are correct, as I feel assured they are, we must understand the word "spontaneity" in the same sense that a scientific man understands "chance". He thereby affirms his ignorance of the precise causes of an event, but he does not in any way deny the possibility of determining them. The general results of my introspective inquiry support the views of those who hold that man is little more than a conscious machine, the larger part of whose actions are predictable. As regards such residuum as there may be, which is not automatic and which a man however wise and well informed could not possibly foresee, I have nothing to say, but I have found that the more carefully I inquired, whether it was into the facts of hereditary similarities of conduct, into the life histories of like or of very unlike twins, or now introspectively into the processes of what I should have called by own Free-will, the smaller seems the room left for the possible residuum.'[30]

Most of the psychological work so far reported was reprinted in book form in *Inquiries into Human Faculty and its Development* to which reference has already been made. Unlike his previous books this small volume was a compilation of a variety of papers and traces of its fragmentary origin are very obvious. Galton's purpose in bringing this assortment of material together was made explicit in his introduction to the book.

'My general object has been to take note of the varied hereditary faculties of different men, and of the great differences in different families and races, to learn how far history may have shown the practicability of supplanting inefficient human stock by better strains, and to consider whether it might not be our duty to do so by such efforts as may be reasonable, thus exerting ourselves to further the ends of evolution more rapidly and with less distress than if events were left to their own course. The subject is, however, so entangled with collateral considerations that a straightforward step-by-step inquiry did not seem to be the most suitable course. I thought it safer to proceed like the surveyor of a new country, and endeavour to fix in the first instance as truly as I could the position of several cardinal points.'[31]

The book begins with a brief consideration of the physical characteristics of mankind and Galton shows how, by composite portraiture, one can obtain an idea of the typical facial features of a race or group. At the time of writing Galton was still sanguine that the method would be adopted by ethnologists in their examination of racial differences, but in this hope he was, as we have seen, to be disappointed.

With regard to physical build he does not deny the great importance of good nurture. But he warns his readers not to be misled in surveying their contemporaries: all the worst examples of misshapen and weakly individuals are hidden from sight in hospitals and asylums. Our civilised stock is far inferior through congenital imperfections to that of any other species of animal.

He now considers energy and sensitivity. From the results of his earlier enquiry into scientists and their antecedents he concludes that the leaders of scientific thought have generally been gifted with remarkable energy and that this capacity is inherited. Energy enables man to overcome environmental hazards and to perform hard and continuous work. It is the most important quality to favour in any scheme of eugenics.*

Sensitivity is treated in more detail. Galton claims that the intellectually able have greater sensitivity than the less able. He provides no real evidence for his claim, basing it on a report made by a surgeon at the Earlswood Asylum that two idiot boys felt no pain when their ingrowing toenails were excised. The supposition that sensory acuity bears some relationship to intellectual ability was destroyed by the work of Wissler and others at the turn of the century. Their research also showed that sensory measures do not themselves intercorrelate, so that one cannot argue from the acuity of one sense to that of another.[32]

The first sense Galton investigated experimentally was sensitivity to high notes. This work involved the use of what came to be known as the Galton whistle, a device for presenting extremely high pitched notes around and above the human auditory threshold. As early as 1875 Galton made preliminary enquiries of his acquaintance, Wheatstone, about the physics of producing high notes from closed pipes.[33] He then persuaded Tisley and Co. to manufacture whistles from his own design.

Various investigations carried out with this instrument and using both animal and human subjects are reported in *Human Faculty*. For his animal experiments Galton incorporated a whistle in a hollow walking stick with a rubber bulb under the handle that could be squeezed inconspicuously.

> 'I hold (the stick) as near as is safe to the ears of the animals, and when they are quite accustomed to its presence and heedless of it, I make it sound; then if they prick up their ears it shows that they hear the whistle; if they do not it is probably inaudible to them. Still, it is very possible that in some cases they hear but do not heed the sound.'[34]

A walk through Regent's Park Zoological Gardens was not very fruitful, although he tells us that he succeeded in annoying the lions. Of all the animals tested, domestic cats were found to be most sensitive to high pitched notes. Cats, Galton believed, would have been differentiated by natural selection until they could localise the high notes made by mice and other small prey. As well as cats, he was able to make all the small dogs turn around during a town walk, but

> 'At Berne, where there appear to be more large dogs lying idly about the streets than in any other town in Europe, I have tried the whistle

* The first use of the word. Galton derives it from the Greek, 'eugenes', which he defines as 'good in stock, hereditarily endowed with noble qualities'.

for hours together, on a great many large dogs, but could not find one that heard it . . . I once frightened a pony with one of these whistles in the middle of a large field. My attempts on insect hearing have been failures.'[35]

In the examination of the hearing of human subjects Galton used an adjustable whistle which enabled him to investigate the upper threshold at which the note became inaudible, but the calibration of the whistle was unreliable above 14 000 cycles per second.

Although it was known that people varied in their thresholds for high pitch, Galton was the first to put to experimental test the old saying that nobody over forty can hear a bat squeak. He found that the ability to detect high notes fell off sharply with age, that it was independent of the threshold for low notes, and that the elderly were usually unconscious of their deficiency and did not always welcome its demonstration. Galton found no difference between men and women in their sensitivity to high notes, but on all other tests of sensory acuity women were on the whole inferior to men.*

'I found as a rule that men have more delicate powers of discrimination than women, and the business experience of life seems to confirm this view. The tuners of pianofortes are men, and so I understand are the tasters of tea and wine, the sorters of wool, and the like. These latter occupations are well salaried, because it is of the first moment to the merchant that he should be rightly advised on the real value of what he is about to purchase or to sell. If the sensitivity of women were superior to that of men, the self-interest of merchants would lead to their being always employed; but as the reverse is the case, the opposite supposition is likely to be the true one.

'Ladies rarely distinguish the merits of wine at the dinner-table, and although custom allows them to preside at the breakfast-table, men think them on the whole to be far from successful makers of tea and coffee.'[38]

Galton's generalisation is too sweeping and ignores the possibility that men may vary more in their powers of sensory discrimination than do women. Thus, although there may be extreme cases of men with finer discriminations than any women—and from such men are selected the wine and tea tasters—nevertheless, the average for the sexes is probably alike. In most physical attributes men vary more than women and it is probable that the case is no different in sense discrimination.[39]

---

* A conclusion he later modified in claiming that women were more sensitive to touch on the nape of the neck.[36] But subsequent work has not confirmed this particular difference.[37]

Galton also ignores the role of learning in improving one's discriminative powers and, as is his wont, ascribes adult differences to heredity alone. A further point of criticism can be levelled at his failure to allow for the social conditions of the day which barred women from many occupations for which they have subsequently been found to be suited.

As well as investigating sex differences in sensory discrimination Galton examined the performance of a large number of blind children on tests of sensory acuity and in this respect his conclusions have stood the test of time. He found no evidence for the supposed superiority of blind over sighted boys of the same age.

'The guidance of the blind depends mainly on the multitude of collateral indications to which they give much heed, and not in their superior sensitivity to any one of them. Those who see do not care for so many of these collateral indications, and habitually overlook and neglect several of them.'[40]

Although he did not report the work in the book of his travels in South Africa, Galton tells us in *Human Faculty* that he made some tests of the Hottentot and Damara peoples but found that they were not superior in their sensory acuity to himself and his European companions, even in keenness of eyesight. The apparently extraordinary ability of these peoples to discern and identify distant objects he attributes to their familiarity with those objects.

In connection with colour blindness Galton makes the interesting point that it is nearly twice as prevalent among the Quakers as among the rest of the community. The reason for this difference lies, he thinks, in the nature of the original stock from which the Quaker sect originated. Few of them can have been of a temperament that found fine arts and coloured clothing attractive, and it is reasonable to presume that a large proportion of them must have been colour blind. As colour blindness is a sex-linked hereditary defect the community would slowly increase in colour blindness. We may note that Dalton, the discoverer of the anomaly, was himself a Quaker.

After a brief discussion of statistical methods he passes on to the subject of character, illustrated by those traits that distinguish the two sexes. Men are said to be more straightforward than women who are capricious and coy. He claims that these womanly characteristics are to be found in females of other species at the time of pairing and prevent mating with the first male who approaches. Thus competition among the males is encouraged and racial degeneration prevented.

'The willy-nilly disposition of the female in matters of love is as apparent in the butterfly as in the man, and must have been con-

tinuously favoured from the earliest stages of animal evolution down
to the present time. It is the factor in the great theory of sexual
selection that corresponds to the insistence and directness of the male.
Coyness and caprice have in consequence become a heritage of the
sex, together with a cohort of allied weaknesses and petty deceits,
that men have come to think venial and even amiable in women, but
which they would not tolerate among themselves.'[41]

Galton's conclusions appear to have been based on his own observations
but he is insistent on the need for more statistical enquiries. Schoolmasters
have enviable opportunities in this respect if they can train themselves to
approach the subject without prejudice and to look upon their pupils as
if they were 'the fauna and flora of an hitherto undescribed species in an
entirely new land.'[42]

The characteristics of criminals and the insane are briefly considered.
Galton depends mainly on the recently published pedigree of the infamous
Jukes family in arguing for the inheritance of criminality. Likewise insanity
is thought by Galton to spring from the 'neurotic constitution' although
it may be induced by certain environmental conditions. He instances the
enforcement by religious teachers of celibacy, fasting and solitude, which
restrictions largely succeed in inducing morbid mental conditions among
their followers.

The next section, entitled 'Gregarious and Slavish Instincts', is a reprint
of his paper on gregariousness which we have already considered. A major
portion of the book is now taken up with details of his investigations into
mental imagery, number forms, colour associations, visions, and word
association. These chapters are based on his previously published papers,
although expanded in places. To his chapter on word association a new
section is added which he entitles the 'Antechamber of Consciousness' and
from which we now quote.

'When I am engaged in trying to think anything out, the process of
doing so appears to me to be this : The ideas that lie at any moment
within my full consciousness seem to attract of their own accord the
most appropriate out of a number of other ideas that are lying close
at hand, but imperfectly within the range of my consciousness. There
seems to be a presence-chamber in my mind where full consciousness
holds court, and where two or three ideas are at the same time in
audience, and an antechamber full of more or less allied ideas, which
is situated just beyond the full ken of consciousness. Out of this antechamber the ideas most nearly allied to those in the presence-chamber
appear to be summoned in a mechanically logical way, and to have
their turn of audience.

'The successful progress of thought appears to depend first, on a a large attendance in the antechamber; secondly, on the presence there of no ideas except such as are strictly germane to the topic under consideration; thirdly, on the justness of the logical mechanism that issues the summons. The thronging of the antechamber is, I am convinced, altogether beyond my control; if the ideas do not appear, I cannot create them, nor compel them to come. The exclusion of alien ideas is accompanied by a sense of mental effort and volition whenever the topic under consideration is unattractive, otherwise it proceeds automatically, for if an intruding idea finds nothing to cling to, it is unable to hold its place in the antechamber, and slides back again.'[43]

He continues:

'It is very reasonable to think that part at least of the inward response to spiritual yearnings is of similar origin to the visions, thoughts, and phrases that arise automatically when the mind has prepared itself to receive them. The devout man attunes his mind to holy ideas, he excludes alien thoughts, and he waits and watches in stillness. Gradually the darkness is lifted, the silence of the mind is broken, and the spiritual responses are heard in the way so often described by devout men of all religions. This seems to me precisely analogous to the automatic presentation of ordinary ideas to orators and literary men, and to the visions of which I spoke in the chapter on that subject. Dividuality replaces individuality, and one portion of the mind communicates with another portion as with a different person.'[44]

Two reprints of earlier papers are now included to show the vast effects of nature over nurture. The history of twins has already been discussed; the other paper on the domestication of animals is a slight affair from which Galton derives the following conclusion:

'It would appear that every wild animal has had its chance of being domesticated, that those few which fulfilled the above conditions were domesticated long ago, but that the large remainder, who fail sometimes in only one small particular, are destined to perpetual wildness so long as their race continues. As civilisation extends they are doomed to be gradually destroyed off the face of the earth as useless consumers of cultivated produce.'[45]

He now turns to the role of nurture in implanting religious beliefs and in creating aversions in the mind of the child. Much of what is regarded as natural religious sentiment is taught in childhood. Galton cites the cases of deaf-mutes who learn to communicate only after their childhood is over. They report that the church services to which they were taken by their parents were completely unintelligible to them and no religious chord was touched by the ritual.

Although the substance of religious teaching varies from sect to sect, in one particular its form is identical:

'In subjects unconnected with sentiment, the freest inquiry and the fullest deliberation are required before it is thought desirous to form a final opinion; but wherever sentiment is involved, and especially in questions of religious dogma, about which there is more sentiment and more difference of opinion among wise, virtuous, and truth-seeking men than about any other subject whatever, free inquiry is peremptorily discouraged. The religious instructor in every creed is one who makes it his profession to saturate his pupils with prejudice.'[46]

Galton points out that good and wise men have belonged to many races and many creeds and that it will not do to believe that any one dogma would suffice them all. Besides, however eminent in goodness and in intellect, men may be deeply prejudiced and their judgements in matters of faith cannot therefore be trusted.

If we are told to trust in our conscience, we should understand that it arises from two sources: from inheritance, as Darwin claimed, and from early education. The inherited portion is the organised result of the social experiences of many preceding generations, but, as the doctrine of evolution shows, organisms are never perfectly adjusted to their environment and inherited conscience may be a bad guide to present conditions. The acquired part of conscience may under the influence of dogma be an even worse guide.

'Happy the child, especially in these inquiring days, who has been taught a religion that mainly rests on the moral obligations between man and man in domestic and national life, and which, so far as it is necessarily dogmatic, rests chiefly upon the proper interpretation of facts about which there is no dispute—namely, on those habitual occurrences which are always open to observation, and which form the basis of so-called natural religion.'[47]

Terror, Galton claims, is easily learnt and he cites the manner in which gregarious animals learn it one from another. In the case of man he mentions the ways in which in mediaeval times terror was inculcated by preaching about the torments of the damned, and he argues that such harsh treatment by the Deity did not appear to be incongruous with his supposed beneficence when revenge and torture were commonplace attributes of every mundane ruler.

Aversion is as easily taught as terror. Here he appeals to his own experience among Muslims when he was much impressed by what he calls
the manly conformity of their everyday actions to their creed, which he
contrasts to the Christian's protestations of unworldliness on one day of
the week and worldly behaviour on the other six. Although more than
thirty years have passed since he lived among Muslims he still finds many
of their customs remain with him—such as that of regarding the left hand
as unclean.

The three following sections are also devoted to religion. His main purpose in this part of the book is to consider the possibility of theocratic
intervention in human affairs. Intervention on the part of the Deity may
be on his own initiative or in response to prayer. Galton attempts to show
that there is only one mode of interference which could upset the statistical
comparison of the relative effects of nature and nurture, and that is by
God's attempting deliberately to mislead the scientific observer, a possibility Galton rejects. He, however, ignores the effects that would be produced by occasional and capricious interference, which could make for
little agreement between one statistical enquiry and another. The general
stability of statistical ratios is one of the best arguments against such a
possibility.[48]

Most of his previous paper on prayer is now reproduced and the conclusion reiterated that there is no objective evidence for its efficacy.

The third section is entitled 'Enthusiasm'. Galton does not employ the
word with its modern meaning as an equivalent to 'zeal' but as meaning
'the vain confidence or opinion of a person that he has special divine
communications from a Supreme Being or familiar intercourse with him.'[49]
He remarks that many able men are convinced of this fact and that many
of the enquiries reported in his book have sprung from his own attempts
to put such a supposition to test.

> 'The arguments scattered or hinted at throughout this book are
> negative so far as they go, but it must be borne in mind that they
> would be scattered to the winds by solid objective evidence on the
> other side, such as could be seriously entertained by scientific men
> desiring above all things to arrive at truth.'[50]

He thus clears the way for the final chapters of the book in which he
expounds his own religious belief. He begins with a consideration of the
part we may play in the universe as a whole. We do not understand how
consciousness is related to the billions of cells of which our body is
composed. Perhaps our part in the universe is analogous to that of the
cells in the body and our personalities may be 'the transient but essential
elements of an immortal and cosmic mind.'[51] In an obscure passage he
continues :

'It is difficult to withstand a suspicion that the three dimensions of space and the fourth dimension of time may be four independent variables of a system that is neither space nor time, but something else wholly unconceived by us. Our present enigma as to how a First Cause could itself have been brought into existence . . . may be wholly due to our necessary mistranslation of the four or more variables of the universe, limited by inherent conditions, into the three unlimited variables of Space and Time.'[52]

Putting these speculations to one side two indisputable facts are evident : the one is that the whole of the living world moves continuously towards the evolution of races that are progressively more adapted to their mutual needs and external circumstances; the other is that, considering it in human terms, this evolutionary process has been hitherto carried out with prodigious waste, little intelligence and complete disregard for individual wellbeing. Man has in the past furthered evolution, but half unconsciously and for his own personal advantage. Now, Galton proposes, he must rise to the conviction that it is his religious duty to do so deliberately and systematically.

'While recognising the awful mystery of conscious existence and the inscrutable background of evolution, we find that as the foremost outcome of many and long birth-throes, intelligent and kindly man finds himself in being. He knows how petty he is but he also perceives that he stands here on this particular earth, at this particular time, as the heir of untold ages and in the van of circumstance. He ought therefore, I think, to be less diffident than he is usually instructed to be, and to rise to the conception that he has a considerable function to perform in the order of events, and that his exertions are needed. It seems to me that he should look upon himself more as a free-man, with power of shaping the course of future humanity, and that he should look upon himself less as the subject of a despotic government in which case it would be his chief merit to depend wholly upon what had been regulated for him, and to render abject obedience.'[53]

Galton now sketches out methods by which man may implement eugenic ideals. Early marriage will, in general, lead to more offspring and must therefore be encouraged in the cases of those who possess favourable hereditary qualities. Modest steps may be taken in that direction by a system of endowments to be made available to selected young people. Another technique is favourably to handicap persons of superior heredity when they take competitive examinations for entry into permanent employment. He advocates extra marks to be awarded for 'family merit' so that the hereditary factor will not be ignored in the selection procedures. Even a small allowance for family merit might have a great effect in its social implications as it would make clear to every individual the importance of suitable marriage alliances if they wished their off-spring to be so favoured. But he is clear that even these small positive steps would be considered premature until popular discussion had established the desirability of the general programme.

Galton's attack on orthodox religion should be regarded in the light of his attempt in *Human Faculty* to develop a new and more rational religion, based on Darwinism and the eugenic improvement of mankind. That he was misunderstood by his family was not surprising; that he was savagely attacked by the critics of the day was equally to be expected.

The Anthropometric Laboratory

Inquiries into Human Faculty and its Development was published by Macmillan in the April of 1883 and had sold 247 copies by early June. The demand for the book was never great but just sufficient for the publishers to ask Galton to produce a revised edition in 1892. Galton refused on the grounds that the labour necessary to incorporate the later work originating from his research was too great for him to contemplate. He was probably referring in particular to research on sensation which had made great strides in the German psychological laboratories. Macmillan reprinted the book as it stood.

A further reprint appeared in 1901 in the Everyman Library with some significant omissions. The religious section, comprising the chapters on theocratic intervention, the efficacy of prayer and enthusiasm, was dropped. In his preface to this reprint Galton claims that he does not in any way recant his views but that he has been persuaded to omit the material on the grounds that the balance of the book would thereby be improved. It is, however, noteworthy that it was these particular chapters that had received most attention from his critics when the book was first issued.

The critic of the Church newspaper, the *Guardian*, wrote a long and swingeing attack, but completely missed the point of Galton's eugenic proposals.

'To say that it is our duty to influence the future of humanity and to further the evolution of a higher humanity is only another way of saying that we should obey the instinct which teaches us to care for those that come after us . . .

'Do not weak men have strong children, stupid ones wise, wicked good?—while, on the other hand, do we not find the weak emanating from the strong, and bad from good? The practical inferences which are the outcome of all this odd and very imperfectly worked out speculation are as much opposed to philosophy as they are to common sense and good feeling . . .

'The author cannot even refrain from trespassing upon the territory of those with whom he is at issue, a territory which for him is not matter, which cannot be seen, or touched, or measured, or weighed— and so cannot be proved (by his methods of proof) to exist. We are henceforth to apply ourselves to elicit the "religious significance" of the doctrine of evolution; whether if we substitute for religious *"anti-religious"*, Mr Galton would be able to demonstrate any difference in the meaning conveyed by the word he uses we take leave to doubt.'[1]

The *Spectator's* review revealed more understanding of Galton's purpose, but the reviewer could not resist again producing the argument against Galton's demonstration that prayer was ineffectual, namely that there was more than one type of prayer and that the prayers of individuals were private and beyond the reach of statistical investigation.[2]

The most favourable review was by George Romanes in *Nature*.[3] Romanes was an acquaintance of Galton's, a comparative psychologist and ardent Darwinian, who had had a popular success with his book *Animal Intelligence* in the previous year. His review provided a selective account of *Human Faculty* with little adverse comment. He was even able to recommend Galton's new religion on the grounds that it was based on honesty and commonsense. But he took issue with Galton over what he considered the untrustworthiness of the statistical method when applied to prayer. Romanes did not claim to know whether prayers for longevity were answered or not, but he pointed out that it was reasonable to assume that only a proportion of the clergy did pray for a long life for themselves. Supposing only one in every eight had such prayers answered, then the fact that as a group the clergy appear to live on the average two years longer than other groups may conceal the possibility that it is the pious eighth who live sixteen years longer, a not inconsiderable addition to their natural span!

Of Galton's immediate family, Emma alone appears to have commented on the book:

'When I wrote the other day, I had not then finished your book. I wished to read it slowly, and take into my mind so much that is interesting—the part on twins and the domestication of animals I was delighted with. Your similes are particularly happy—but I cannot help greatly deploring what you have said on Prayer. Whatever may be your ideas, I cannot see any reason for publishing the fact to the World. It is a grave responsibility on your part. I do hope in some of the later editions many of your friends will persuade you to abstract that part from your volume, which in other ways is so much to be appreciated. Forgive me dearest Frank for saying this, you know how dearly I love you and how proud I am of your talents.'[4]

It is possible, but unlikely, that Galton destroyed letters from his brothers and other sisters; he tended to keep all correspondence relevant to his work. Adèle was certainly in no condition to reply as she had fallen seriously ill at the beginning of 1883. Her married daughter, Millicent Lethbridge, wrote to thank Galton for his book.[5] Her critical comments were again reserved for the chapter on prayer. Galton replied immediately:

'My dear Milly,

From your very liberal standpoint, the arguments in the Chapter on Prayer have necessarily little value. They are directed to those who either (1) like the great majority of Puritans and theological writers assign a magical (? right word) power to prayer, or (2) whose ideas are habitually confused as to what they believe, what they doubt about, and what they disbelieve. I fear that everyone belongs in some degree to the last category and that it is most important for reasonable beings to extricate themselves as far as may be out of it . . . I want to knock away all fictitious supports, and to get the evidence *pro* and *con* that we possess clearly before us and to look at it fearlessly . . . It is of course cheering to the heart and ennobling to the mind if the belief be that of being a missionary, as it were, in a high cause affecting humanity. Beyond that I suspect there is little, and that each man puts a great deal of his own self into the ideal that he sets before him.'[6]

Mrs Lethbridge wrote again:

'Please remember that much as I value your letters, I do not want you to answer mine unless you have plenty of time and nothing to do, which I suppose is almost an unknown state of affairs with you! . . You say that the habitual confusion of the average mind "as to what it believes, what it doubts about, and what it disbelieves, is a state from which it ought to extricate itself." But if it is happy in that state . . . why not let it be? If you take away the "fictitious props" you speak of, what remains? Can you give the "Average Mind" strength to grasp an Abstract Idea?'[7]

Louisa's reaction to the book can be inferred from a letter she received from her friend Marianne North, the painter and traveller. Miss North wrote to say that she had read and liked all the book.

'You have been brought up amongst clericals all your life and have received the usual education of "don't think or ask questions on

many subjects—leave that to the priests and those who know better."
Reasonable or unreasonable on many subjects "faith" is the one thing
needful. I have never believed in Priests and have kept aloof from
them, and thought my own thoughts quietly. I know no more than
anyone else, but will not forswear myself by saying I believe that
which reason tells me is untrue. I do not know that there is much
good in stirring up disbelief in others—as if they do think, they seem
to get no nearer knowing the end—but the feeling of their own little-
ness of power of getting at the truth may make them more charitable
and reasonable towards those who do not believe their own narrow
views. And so it is good that such men as Mr Galton say what they
think frankly—and perhaps some generations hence may arrive at a
nearer insight into the future—at any rate can tell their views and
compare them without being called bad names or being burnt by
raving idiots.'[8]

It would seem from this letter that Louisa had complained to her friend
about the religious chapters of the book. Louisa remained a practising
Christian until her death, but there is no evidence that the divergence
between her beliefs and those of her husband led to friction. Nor is there
evidence of difficulties between Galton and Louisa's relatives. In spite
of the fact that three of her brothers had taken Holy Orders, visits to them
continued as before and Galton mentions attending church services at
Harrow conducted by Montagu.[9]

The decade from 1874 was a sad one for the Galtons, their otherwise
uneventful lives being punctuated by a series of deaths of those near to
them. These years can best be described through the medium of Louisa's
Record.

'1874. Uneasy from the very beginning about Mrs Galton. Frank went
to see her early in Feby and she died Feby 12th aged 90. This coming
so soon after my dear Mother made a sad blank, both homes gone.
We went to dear Emma at Easter for a week . . . Thompson [her
maid] left us in March, and was a sad loss to me . . . We paid many
visits during July and at the end went down to Cornwall spending
a fortnight with Adèle and Milly and visited Boscastle and Tintagel.
After this we went to N. Devon till September when we visited the
Groves near Blandford. On the 14th I broke a blood vessel and was
very near dying, but thro' God's mercy, I came back to life and felt
so peaceful and happy in my quiet sick room, that it was not a time
of misery. And all were so kind and good to me, and Frank especially,
that I felt sustained by love. We moved to Bournemouth as soon as
I was able and then in November to dear Emma and found her well
in her newly arranged house. We came home Novbr 18th. Very

severe weather soon set in and lasted to the end of the year. Frank was ill in December and had Dr A. Clarke. We had a quiet dull Xtmas, no going out and F. had to give up his promised lectures at Newcastle. His Book on the Nature and Nurture of Scientific Men came out in Decbr, occupied on inquiry about Twins. On the whole a year of sad memories.'

Louisa's illness was severe and she never fully recovered her health. It is noticeable that her handwriting changes, entries in her *Record* subsequent to 1874 being written in a larger and untidier hand.

Details of Dr Clarke's regimen for her husband have survived in notes made by Galton at the time.[10]

'On going to bed spunge with tepid water and rub quickly—never use cold water extensively. Clothe warmly—woollen underclothing; avoid damp and guard against chill in evening, particularly after a little excitement.'

Galton was advised to drop afternoon tea and to restrict his drinking to a pint of Bordeaux at dinner time. He had to avoid hearty meals and long fasts, and a variety of spices, cakes and coffee. The advice concluded :

'Walk at least half an hour twice a day. Do the most important head work after breakfast and *not* after dinner.'

Galton's complaint appears to have been minor and the chest pains of which he was complaining disappeared.

'1875. Rather an uneventful year owing to the remainder of my illness, which kept me pretty much a prisoner to the house all the winter and but for the cold Spring, we should have gone to Fontainebleau early and returned for May, but the cold kept us till May 10th when we started and were joined by Emma and Lucy [Bessy's daughter], our time at Fontainebleau was spoiled and shortened thro' Lucy's caprice and early in June we went on to Seelisberg and remained in Switzerland till Augt 19 when we returned to Paris and were met again by Emma. Frank went to the Brit Assoctn at Bristol and returned to us for ten days . . .'

'1876. Another year without great events to us. Frank worked again at the Sweet Peas helped by Miss Christie. We spent Easter at Leamington. Soon after our return I caught cold and was kept to the house nearly a month and lost the Geographical Soirée . . . Emma came to us on June 1 and Darwin's illness at the same time spoiled her visit . . . We left England on Aug. 23rd, met Emma at Calais and with her and Mr Broderick travelled thro' Bavaria, the Tyrol and to Venice and the Italian lakes. We returned Oct 23rd much better and stronger and had a quiet domestic settlement to my unspeakable comfort.'

'1877. A year of illness for me but marked by so much kindness, love and affection, that in looking back, it seemed full of sweetness and to have brought me nearer to Frank and to the dear friends who solaced me, especially to my very dear old and early friend E. Gurney. Amy Lowder too was full of help and in my own family, all were kind and sympathising and Montagu gave me many kind visits, but Frank was my great support throughout. I only fear, that I shall never be able to go about with him as heretofore, and that cuts off so many sources of happiness, but with so many blessings and comforts I will only look to the bright side of life. My illness lasted from Jan. 19 till June, on the 21st we went to Tunbridge Wells, Emma and Temple [Louisa's maid] with us and they were most kind in arranging every thing to save me and help Frank. After this we went to Bournemouth for 6 weeks, and Frank went to the Brit. Asstn. Meeting at Plymouth in Augt and made several short excursions on his return for the day only. Then in Sptbr we had dear Emma's kind hospitality for a fortnight and returned home the end of September. Few events to record. The Telephone is one of the great discoveries of the year, and Stanley's feat of crossing Africa. Arthur was married at Easter, just when I was at my worst and not expected to live. We have seen so little of him of late years, that his marriage makes little mark in our lives. Xtmas has been spent quietly at home.'

'1878. A year of no great mark for ourselves and families. My health has gone on improving, but greatly narrows our life or rather lives, as I lose so many opportunities of making friends and of mixing myself with the stirring events of the day by refusing all dinner invitations and yet I am so much stronger that I always hope I shall be able to resume old habits, still years go on. Frank had rheumatic gout in his knee last March and was a prisoner nearly 3 weeks, his great solace was working out his ideas about composite photographs, for which he has received great encouragement from men of note . . . We again spent Easter with Emma and returned intending to enjoy our friends and society, but the death of dear Mr R. Gurney May 31st greatly saddened our summer and Amy Lowder's engagement to Sir J. Pelly made another break in our society. The blank caused by Mr Gurney's death and dearest Emily's shattered life will never be filled up to me . . . We went to Vichy in July for the waters, and both of us benefited greatly but the aftercure was not successful, the weather was wet and I could never make any excursions, F. enjoyed his mountain walks . . .

'The winter began early and was severe all through Xtmas, and I have been chiefly kept to the house. We have had a few dinner parties but our life is much quieter than it used to be, as I go about so little with Frank.'

'1879. Very little of great moment to us. Gave more dinner parties but seldom able to go out. Dear Lady Grove died March 8th. We went to Bournemouth for a fortnight in April and after had visits from Lucy and Emma. Went to Vichy in July . . . We went to the Blk. Forest where I had great enjoyment of the lovely scenery and left a bit of my heart behind. Then we paid Emma a visit and Judge Grove and were at home the middle of October to London fogs and a most dismal winter. F. gave a lecture at the R. Institution on Generic Images in May and we paid C. Darwin a short Sunday visit . . .'

'1880. Gave many dinner parties for Frank's sake, but seldom went out to any. Visited Emma at Easter and Claverdon and no sooner settled at home than we were off to Vichy late in May and had no summer engagement after for we were both ill after and I could neither enjoy our visits nor eat. We went to Boulogne in Augt and F. returned for the B. Asstn. at Swansea . . . F. began to photograph at home. Busy arranging the house after its decoration.'

'1881. A quiet uneventful year and rather dull for my health puts a stop to so many things of interest and when I am without pain after eating, I am so thankful, that the fear of bringing it on makes me fearful of extending my small limit. Frank has been very much taken up by his Photography. The winter lasted long, we visited Emma at Easter and then Bessy and Lucy and others visited us and I was overdone, so as any pleasant engagements came, I had to give up nearly all in turn. We went to Stanmore in July, and to Bournemouth for a month waiting for the Brit. Asstn. Meeting at York. Frank went to Lord Wenlock's and we should have met in Devonshire, but constant pain for 6 weeks drove me again to Vichy and we were the last of the season and came home direct from Paris. Dean Stanley died in July and left a deep impression on me and for some time I did hope Montagu wld have been his successor. Teddie had a serious illness in the autumn and gave the greatest anxiety but thank God, he was restored. We spent Xtmas at home.'

'1882. Another year and now there seems so little to record, tho' a great deal to be thankful for and a good deal of quiet happiness. Cook bothers tormented me till summer and were a veritable torment, as my dear Frank can little understand, so he was not sympathetic . . . Frank began his book on Human Faculty early in the year and it has gone on thro' the year, and was a great pastime to him during our summer ramble on the Rhine, in the Blk Forest, Constance, and lastly Axenfels. Bad weather tormented us, but we were happy and I kept well and I began sketching again. It was such a boon not to be kept by a Brit. Asstn. meeting this summer. Mr Darwin's death in May cast a deep gloom over us. M. North's gallery at Kew was opened in June . . . Frank's Portrait was taken in June by Professor Graef and tho' a great consumer of time, the success was sufficient reward. I just scraped thro' summer in London without my old pain and by leaving early, but was very worn. Frank spent several days at Guy's Hospital about photographing the patients and seeing what Dr Mahomet had done . . . Cold weather began with our return from abroad and the cold and fogs brought on my pain and kept me in its grasp more or less for 6 weeks. Still it was less bad than often and I have been free from cook embroglios to my infinite joy . . . George was made Canon of Winchester in June and left Liverpool. The Harrow young ones growing up are a great pleasure . . .'

'1883. The last day but one of the year. It seems such a short one, events for me are fewer and fewer as health impedes my doing much, and this year has been an obstinate one for my pain. Early in Feby dear Georgina's illness took a serious turn and she died after five days severe suffering on the 12th. It was a frightful blow to all of us feeling the immensity of the loss to dear Montagu and his children besides the love we bore her . . . In May Spencer's 7th son was born. We remained in London till July 11th when we went to Stanmore. I was done up by London whirl and grief for Mr Spottiswoode's death on June 28 and the Funeral in the Abbey July 5th and became so unwell that we began our summer outing at Boscombe and Bournemouth and spent a pleasant month meeting pleasant people, all the time I was on starvation diet . . . Still I prefer foreign climates and think it suits my tiresome ailment better. We were kept very anxious about Mrs Bunbury [Adèle]. Frank went to see her and found her better, she has had many ups and downs since and is now in a very critical state . . . Frank went to the British Asstn at Southport in Sepbr. In the early part of the year he corrected proofs of his Inquiries into Human Faculty wh was published by Easter. He worked at means of measuring the sensations helped by Croom Robertson. In the Augt Fortnightly he wrote an Article on Medical Life Histories offering Prizes up to £500. Spent much time on the details. His Record of Family Faculties has just come out, also the Life History Album, which he edited . . .'

Louisa completed her entry for the year a little later :

'Dear Adèle Bunbury died on the 31st Dec. She hoped she would not live to see the New Year and her wish was granted. Thus I have lost two sisters-in-law this year, both dear to me, but of course dear Georgina's loss is the more grievous for Montagu's sake and the children.'

As Louisa indicates, in this year Galton began to pursue another line of approach to obtain hereditary data. In his *Fortnightly* article he suggests for the first time a system of monetary prizes to be given in this case to doctors for accounts of their own family histories.[11] It was proposed that these histories should include details not only of family illness but also of fertility, vigour, sensory capacity, intelligence, character and special gifts. Galton obviously thought that doctors would be less likely than laymen to avoid the unpleasant task of publicising their family secrets.

'Most men and women shrink from having their hereditary worth recorded. There may be family diseases of which they hardly dare to speak, except on rare occasions, and then in whispered hints or obscure phrases, as though timidity of utterance could hush thoughts and as though what they fondly suppose to be locked-up domestic secrets may not be bruited about with exaggeration among the surrounding gossips.'[12]

A further advantage of restricting the enquiry to medical men lay in the greater accuracy with which they would be able to record family ailments and causes of death. But the scheme never caught on and there appear to have been no submissions. The reasons for its lack of success are unknown. Galton gave a lecture on his proposals to a special committee of the British Medical Association but failed to secure their co-operation. The medical profession advised that the competition should be thrown open to laymen, and Galton accordingly devised the *Record of Family Faculties*, which was published by Macmillan in 1884.[13]

The prizes were now to be awarded to those members of the public who provided the most adequate answers to what was in effect a long questionnaire. Information was to be provided about the child, its parents, grandparents and great grandparents, and as far as possible the respondent was to include further facts about the brothers and sisters of each of these relatives.

The questions asked for information about the date and place of birth, residence, occupation, age at marriage of the individual and spouse, number and age of children, height, colour of hair and eyes, general appearance, bodily strength and energy, sensory acuity, mental powers and energy, character and temperament, favourite pursuits and special aptitudes, minor and major illness in youth and middle age, cause of death and age at death. In the appendices the respondent was asked to describe the hereditary peculiarities of body and mind of his parents and to discuss the possible combinations of these peculiarities in himself.

In his preface Galton remarks :

'Whatever may be the value of these results, the facts incidentally obtained during the course of the inquiry will form a separate document much prized by the family. The scientific importance of each investigation will, however, be soon appreciated by the author of it, for his researches will lay bare many far-reaching biological bonds that tie his family into a connected whole, whose existence was previously little suspected. Few, if any, have seriously studied the facts of heredity without being impressed by the conviction that no man stands on an isolated basis, but that he is a prolongation of his ancestry in no metaphorical sense, and I shall be surprised if the compilation of these registers does not extend this conviction very widely.'[14]

In the same year as the *Record of Family Faculties* appeared Galton edited the *Life History Album*.[15] A committee of the British Medical Association with Galton as Chairman was responsible for this publication. It was intended to be bought as a gift to parents on the birth of a child. The parents were supposed to fill in much the same kind of details as those required in the *Record* and to keep a current account of their child's development. Thus, it was primarily directed to the individual who would subsequently continue the record himself when old enough to do so. No prizes were offered and no returns seem to have been made, the book itself having an insignificant sale.

The response to the *Record of Family Faculties* was much better, with 110 people making returns. The respondents were drawn from various sections of the community although the majority came from the professional classes. The answers obtained were assessed by Galton who decided to divide the prize money among 85 of the competitors. Imperfect though much of the information was, it provided Galton with material on which to base several papers and the book, *Natural Inheritance*, which appeared in 1889.

Other data incorporated in that book were derived from Galton's anthropometric laboratory. Galton was not the first to open a laboratory devoted to the measurement of human subjects; in 1882 Bertillon had begun a similar venture in connection with the Parisian criminal investigation department, but in many ways the procedures adopted in the two laboratories were widely divergent, and Galton was probably unaware of Bertillon's early work which received no official recognition until 1888.[16]

The impetus for Galton's laboratory came from discussions with Croom-Robertson, the first editor of the periodical, *Mind*. Between them they

IX   Francis Galton, aged 71, photographed in Bertillon's laboratory

x   Francis Galton, aged 84, with Eva Biggs

drew up a pamphlet describing the current techniques for making anthropometric measurements and asking for details of any other equipment that might be in private use.[17] The pamphlet was circulated to a few English psychologists but drew a complete blank. The only equipment available was employed in the newly established German laboratories and Galton was left to use equipment mainly of his own devising.

He proceeded, at his own expense, to equip and open an anthropometric laboratory as part of the International Health Exhibition held in South Kensington in 1884. He fenced off an area 36 ft by 6 ft from the rest of the hall and arranged for visitors to enter at one end of this long passageway along which the various measuring instruments were placed. The payment of a threepenny admission charge covered the running costs and probably increased the interest-value of the procedure. Subjects passed one at a time through the laboratory while the staff of three, including Galton, led them through each of the tests and furnished them with a card of their results, a duplicate being filed for reference.

Measurements were taken of weight, sitting and standing height, arm span, breathing capacity, strength of pull and of squeeze, force of blow, reaction time, keenness of sight and hearing, colour discrimination and judgements of length. Snags were encountered from the very beginning as much of the equipment was untried. Galton complains of the 'coarse and inexperienced' persons who broke the device for recording the speed of a blow, which consisted of a pad connected to a stout deal rod on a spring, the subject being required to punch the pad. After replacing the deal rod with an even stouter one made of oak several people sprained their wrists. No other accidents were recorded, but it seems hardly credible that many of the measurements can have been very exact. Galton mentions the undesirability of asking people to remove their shoes when their height is taken. He preferred to measure the heel and to subtract the value from the overall height. No head measurements were taken as ladies would have had to remove their bonnets and their hair styles would have been disturbed. Considering that nearly 10 000 people passed through the laboratory, it must often have been crowded and conditions for exact measurement far from ideal. Trouble was experienced on a few occasions when 'rough persons entered the laboratory who were apparently not altogether sober.'[18] Nevertheless, Galton was so pleased with its popular success that he obtained permission to establish a more permanent laboratory in the South Kensington Museum and when the Health Exhibition closed in 1885 his equipment was moved to a room there. Improvements were then made in the techniques of measurement, a permanent superintendent, Sergeant Randall, was appointed and the laboratory continued to attract people, although not to the same extent, over the next eight years.

G

Visitors were mainly drawn from the middle and upper middle classes with a sprinkling of celebrities.

'Mr Gladstone was amusingly insistent about the size of his head, saying that hatters often told him that he had an Aberdeenshire head—"a fact which you may be sure I do not forget to tell my Scotch constituents." '[19]

Gladstone asked Galton if he had ever seen such a large head, to which Galton replied that Gladstone must be very unobservant as his head was in no way remarkable, being well shaped but of average circumference. Several versions of this encounter exist, the most unlikely being that provided by Hesketh Pearson who reports Galton saying uncharacteristically that he knew of one head superior to Gladstone's and that was his own.[20]

Apart from the improved accuracy of the equipment and the addition of head measurements to those taken in the first laboratory, Galton's main reason for continuing this work for so long lay in the value of the laboratory as a source of fingerprint data. As we shall see, he was to spend many years over the classification of fingerprints and the development of the technique as a means of personal identification.

Galton displayed his apparatus at several meetings of the British Association and when his laboratory finally closed in June 1894 he gave all the equipment to Professor Thompson at Oxford who established a laboratory there. Laboratories were also soon opened at Eton, Cambridge and Dublin. The Dublin laboratory was to be a mobile one, touring round Ireland every summer in order to record the measurements of small ethnic groups relatively isolated in the west.[21]

Galton was thus directly responsible for the increase in interest in anthropometry during the closing years of the last century. Unfortunately, as any glance at a current text book of anthropology will show, anthropologists have never pursued his dynamic approach to the subject but have remained content with relatively static structural measurements.[22] Reaction time, speed of movement, and general measures of physical efficiency have been excluded from their concerns and intellectual and personality measurement have been left to the psychologist, too often working in ignorance of the exact bodily characteristics of his subject.

Galton foresaw a much wider use of anthropometry as a supplement to the restrictions imposed by the then current examination system of candidates for the public service. The Armed Services and the Indian Civil Service selected entrants by means of a written examination alone; Galton proposed that, in the case of those near the borderline, physical fitness tests might be used to distinguish the allrounders and those who could best live under tropical conditions.[23]

The tests to be adopted were not to be those of athletic prowess, which might be susceptible to previous training, but were to be those of the kind he had already used in his laboratory, supplemented by some type of marking system during the standard medical examination, somewhat on the same lines as that adopted by slave dealers in assessing the value of their goods. The Council of the British Association took up Galton's suggestion, but the War Office turned it down, apparently on the unjustifiable grounds that physical tests were likely to be less reliable than written tests. Discouraged, Galton pursued the matter no further.[24]

The objective approach exemplified in the work of the laboratory was adopted in several psychological investigations Galton undertook at this time. Not all of this work was pursued to very definite or useful conclusions, but it is worthy of mention on account of Galton's method, which was to measure whatever and whenever he could. Sometimes his efforts in this direction appear slightly ludicrous and assume a kind of 'counting mania' common among those with obsessional difficulties. For example, one cannot help suspecting the involvement of a defensive mechanism in his attempt to construct a 'beauty-map' of the British Isles. He concealed in his pocket a cross of paper and a pricker. Every girl he passed who appeared above average in beauty was recorded by pricking a hole in the upper end of the cross, the average lookers were recorded on the cross arm and the ugly on the long lower arm. From a sample of various cities he reached the conclusion that the incidence of pretty girls was highest in London and lowest in Aberdeen![25]

Galton's attendance at many tedious scientific meetings must have been enlivened for him by his method of measuring the boredom of the audience. Two techniques were tried: the first stemmed from his observation that an intent audience sits upright with a roughly equal distance between their heads, but a bored audience sways from side to side and the intervals between their heads vary greatly. However, Galton could find no simple measure of this behavioural change and abandoned it in favour of counting fidgets. At a meeting of the Royal Geographical Society he watched a section of about 50 members of the audience and counted the number of distinct movements made per minute, which averaged about 45. As the use of a watch might have attracted attention, he reckoned time by the number of breaths taken: in his case 15 to the minute. In spite of the difficulty in carrying out this double count he was satisfied that the frequency of fidget was more than halved when the audience's attention was aroused and their fidgets were also of shorter duration, that is, they performed them more smartly.

'Let this suggest to observant philosophers when the meetings they attend may prove dull to occupy themselves in estimating the frequency, amplitude and duration of the fidgets of their fellow sufferers. They must do so during periods of both intenseness and indifference, so as to estimate what may be called natural fidget, and then I think they may acquire the new art of giving numerical expression to the amount of boredom expressed by the audience generally during the reading of any particular memoir.'[26]

Another and more controlled psychological investigation entailed the use of an experimental technique devised by Jacobs who had measured the ability of children of various ages on a test of immediate memory.[27] Jacobs had presented lists of letters, numerals and nonsense syllables to the children and recorded their memory span, i.e. the number of such items they could repeat back to the experimenter after a single presentation. His finding that the extent of the span depended on the age of the child led Galton to suggest the application of the method to subnormal children. In the company of two well known psychologists, Bain and Sully, he visited the Earlswood and Darenth Asylums. At Earlswood, Bain and Galton tested the higher grade 'idiots' who could read and write a little and who could do some housework. The selected children were incapable of simple addition and averaged no more than 4 digits in recall, although aged between 15 and 25.[28] In comparison, Jacob's group of normal eight-year olds averaged 6·6 digits. At Darenth, Sully and Galton found the children to be superior to the Earlswood group, being classed as four grades of 'imbeciles'. The top grade gave a span of 6, the second and third grades 4, and the lowest grade 3. The relationship between these results and estimates of the children's intellectual ability seemed marked and the test itself appeared reliable, the Earlswood children on the basis of their general accomplishments falling between the second and third grade Darenth children and recalling the same average number of digits.

Although Galton did not pursue this work any further, its significance was not lost on Alfred Binet who 20 years later was to devise the first successful intelligence scale in an attempt to distinguish those children who could not profit from ordinary educational methods.[29] Digit span was included as one of several simple memory tests in the original version of the Binet test and has been retained in successive revisions, a fact which testifies to its discriminative power at the lower intellectual levels. It is also included as one of the subtests in the more recent and widely used Wechsler Intelligence scales.[30]

In 1884 Galton was invited to give the Rede Lecture at Cambridge University. He devoted the lecture, most of which was reprinted in the *Fortnightly Review*, to a consideration of the ways by which one might proceed to assess differences in personality.[31]

An interesting sidelight on his lecturing technique is provided by a diagram attached to a notebook containing his script.[32] The drawing shows the signalling system to be adopted by a confederate in the audience, possibly Louisa, who was to raise the left arm to one of two positions to indicate that he should raise or lower his voice and to raise the right arm to signal that he should speak more rapidly or more slowly. The need for signals of this kind implies that he was unable to use the other more subtle feedback, such as the amount of fidget, which he had already advocated as a measure of the audience's boredom. His lack of empathy with others has already been remarked upon, and on the present occasion, which was the first on which he had spoken at his old university, whose high academic standards he continued to revere, it is probable that he was also more anxious than usual over his performance.

It cannot have helped his peace of mind to have had concealed under his coat a device known as Maret's pneumocardiograph. He divulged this information to his amused audience and pointed out that it would not have been a difficult matter to have had an assistant concealed beneath the table who would from time to time have opened the stopcock to the recording equipment and by this means would have obtained interesting samples of the speaker's emotional state.

Galton begins his lecture by pointing out that although no satisfactory theory of personality exists we do not have to wait until one has been elaborated. As in the case of intellectual capacity we can make progress by probing at roughly defined points. We can note definite acts that occur in response to definite emergencies, there being no need to wait for the natural occurrence of emergencies as they can be extemporised.

Differences in emotional behaviour supply obvious subject matter for investigation. Having devised situations that are likely to cause emotional reactions, such as undergoing the 'formidable ordeal' of the Rede Lecture, one can simultaneously record the subject's behaviour. In this connection Galton reports a bizarre attempt to record surreptitious information about the emotional states of guests at 42 Rutland Gate. He placed pressure tambours under the legs of his dining-room chairs in order to record the bodily movements of the diners, on the principle that when two people have an 'inclination' for one another they will in fact visibly incline or slope together when sitting side by side. But for one reason or another these experiments were discontinued.

Much, he thought, might be done by engaging people in conversation on certain specified topics. Galton instances a 'weather test', particularly appropriate in Britain, by which one notes the reaction of the subject to a comment on the weather; by such means it should not be difficult to distinguish the optimist from the pessimist!

Trite as these examples may be, they illustrate Galton's contention that current generalisations about personality tended to be recollections based on inexact observation.

'We want lists of facts, every one of which may be separately verified, valued and revalued, and the whole accurately summed. It is the statistics of each man's conduct in small everyday affairs, that will probably be found to give the simplest and more precise measure of his character.'[33]

It is only in the last few decades that some of the advances envisaged by Galton have occurred; at the time at which he was speaking, what is now commonplace was regarded as fantastic.

Although it is mainly on account of his emphasis on the differences among individuals that Galton holds an honoured place in the history of psychology, psychologists have more to be thankful to Galton for than the work reported in these chapters. Some of the apparatus he invented proved of use for many years in psychological laboratories, and his derivation of statistical measures supplied psychologists with powerful tools. For crude as his anthropometric data were, they supplied Galton with the means of testing the theoretical basis of the Bertillon system of personal identification and in conjunction with the data derived from his hereditary enquiries led him to one of his most important discoveries, the measurement of correlation.

14

The Statistics of Heredity

Galton's important statistical discoveries were made little by little in the context of his attempts to understand and above all to measure hereditary phenomena. He had never been satisfied with the qualitative assessments he had been forced to employ in writing *Hereditary Genius* and *English Men of Science*, but there had been no alternative if he were to restrict his dealings to human heredity. In the 1870s no measurable data from two generations of a human population existed and Galton was forced to turn his attention to nonhuman material.

Charles Darwin had asked Galton for help with the statistics involved in comparisons of cross and self fertilised plants,[1] and it was Darwin who suggested that Galton should try breeding sweet peas. Joseph Hooker, the botanist, concurred over the choice of plant, which was suitable on three counts, being hardy and prolific, having little tendency to cross fertilise, and having in each pod all the seeds of about the same size (unlike the common edible pea).

Galton began by weighing individually thousands of sweet pea seeds and selecting seven different weights. He also measured their diameters, which he found to be directly proportional to their weights. Ten specimen of each weight were packaged and the resulting sets of 70 seeds sent off to friends who had agreed to plant them for him under standard conditions. The method to be followed was for the gardener to prepare seven equal and parallel beds and to plant the ten seeds of each weight in each bed. Minute instructions were given with regard to the planting and harvesting of the seeds and little source of error was possible. Nine friends, including Darwin, co-operated and Galton's peas flourished from Nairn in the north to Cornwall in the south. However, two crops turned out to be failures and Galton was left with the produce of seven sets, or 490 parent seeds.

Results were embodied in a paper of 1877 entitled, 'Typical Laws of Heredity,' which he read at the Royal Institution.[2] Although there were snags in Galton's initial nonrandom selection of seeds of equal weight as representative of the parental character, the main point to be noted is his discovery that the daughter seeds were not as extreme as the parent seeds; he speaks of them as 'reverting' towards the average ancestral type.

Table 14.1 gives the essential data relating the *sizes* of the parent seeds with those of the daughter seeds.

TABLE 14.1

Diameter (in $\frac{1}{100}$ in) of parent seeds and their offspring

Diameter of parent seed	15	16	17	18	19	20	21
Mean diameter of filial seeds	15·4	15·7	16·0	16·3	16·6	17·0	17·3

For each increase of one unit on the part of the parent, there is an average increase of only about one third of a unit in the offspring. The offspring of the extreme dwarf and giant seeds are less dwarfish and gigantic than their parents.

'Reversion is the tendency of the ideal mean filial type to depart from the parental type, reverting to what may be roughly and perhaps fairly described as the average ancestral type. If family variability had been the only process in simple descent that affected the characteristics of a sample the dispersion of a race from its mean ideal type would indefinitely increase with the number of generations, but reversion checks this increase, and brings it to a standstill.'[3]

The mathematical analysis is now developed further as Galton attempts to find the relation between the reversion coefficient and the variability of the offspring for the population to remain unchanged. We need not try to follow him here, nor in his difficult discussion of differential fertility and natural selection, but may pass on to the later elaborations of the reversion concept.

Galton appears to have had doubts about his reversion assumption and published nothing further on the subject for eight years. Further advances were to await more data, this time those of human stature, which were now available from family records. As Galton expressed the need :

'It was anthropological evidence that I desired, caring only for the seeds as means of throwing light on heredity in man. I tried in vain for a long and weary time to obtain it in sufficient abundance, and my failure was a cogent motive, together with others, in inducing me to make an offer of prizes for family records, which was largely responded to, and furnished me last year with what I wanted.'[4]

Several papers were based on the material extracted from the *Record of Family Faculties,* but it will be most convenient to take the paper in which Galton's exposition is clearest and least mathematical. This paper appeared in *Anthropological Miscellanea* and was an amplified version of one read as a Presidential Address to the Anthropological Section of the British Association which met in Aberdeen in 1885.[5]

The term 'reversion' is now replaced by the present statistical term 'regression', and on this occasion Galton provides a graphical representation of the finding that human offspring tend to regress in stature towards the average. He first converts each female stature into its equivalent male stature by multiplying it by 1·08; he then takes the mean of the statures of the mother and father to provide the stature of what he terms the 'mid-parent'.

This step can only be valid if there were no assortative mating, i.e. differences in stature between male and female must not be involved in marriage choice. Galton examined his data derived from 205 males and 205 females but was able to dismiss this possibility.

In Figure 14.1 the line AB shows the mid-parents' statures, while CD is a line drawn to fit the children's statures at maturity. It can be seen

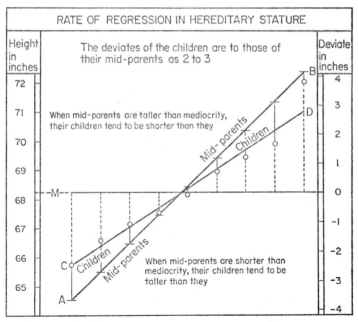

FIGURE 14.1. Regression in hereditary stature. (Reproduced from the *Journal of the Anthropological Institute*, **15** (1885), pp. 248, 249.)

that the children of tall parents are not on average as tall as their parents, nor are the children of short parents as short. The deviation in height of the offspring from the average is two thirds of the deviation of its mid-parentage. From this finding Galton concludes that the physical characteristics of the parents do not fully define those of the children.

'The explanation of it is as follows. The child inherits partly from his parents, partly from his ancestry. Speaking generally, the further his genealogy goes back, the more numerous and varied will his ancestry become, until they cease to differ from any equally numerous sample taken at haphazard from the race at large. Their mean stature will then be the same as that of the race; in other words, it will be mediocre.'[6]

The ancestors will then impart an averaging tendency to the parental contribution and the children will regress towards mediocrity.

'This law tells heavily against the full hereditary transmission of any gift, as only a few of many children would resemble their mid-parentage. The more exceptional the amount of the gift, the more exceptional will be the good fortune of a parent who has a son who equals, and still more if he has a son who overpasses him in that respect. The law is even-handed; it levies the same heavy succession-tax on the transmission of badness as well as of goodness. If it discourages the extravagant expectations of gifted parents that their children will inherit all their powers, it no less discountenances extravagant fears that they will inherit all their weaknesses and diseases.'[7]

Galton now makes clear that one cannot argue backwards by merely converting his estimate into its numerical opposite. It does not follow that if a child deviates only two thirds as much as his mid-parent, that the mid-parent will deviate $\frac{3}{2}$ as much as his child. When he examines what is in effect the correlation table relating the statures of mid-parents and offspring and, instead of averaging the children's stature for each mid-parental value, averages the mid-parental statures for each child's value, he finds that the mid-parents deviate only one third as much as their children.

Galton was somewhat worried over this apparent paradox and his worries were only dispersed when he had mathematical confirmation of his statistical conclusions. He relates in his autobiography that he was pondering over his data while waiting for a train at a wayside halt near Ramsgate when he suddenly perceived a certain regularity in his results. When the data were smoothed and diagrammed in the way shown in Figure 14.2 and lines drawn through entries of the same value, a series

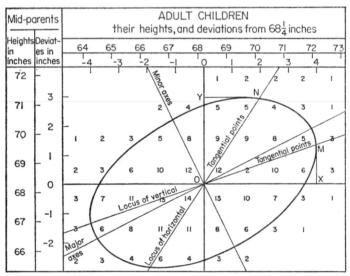

FIGURE 14.2 Galton's elliptic contour. (Reproduced from the *Journal of the Anthropological Institute*, **15** (1885), pp. 248, 249.)

of concentric and similar ellipses were obtained, of which one is shown in the diagram. These ellipses are in fact contour lines drawn on a surface, the shape of the surface being moulded by the relation between the two normal distributions of mid-parental and children's heights. The common centre of the ellipses lay at the intersection of the vertical and horizontal axes that corresponded to the means of 68·25 inches. The axes of the ellipses were all at the same inclination.

Galton now drew horizontal tangents to each ellipse (YN on the ellipse shown). Joining the points where each ellipse was touched by its horizontal tangent he obtained the line ON, which was inclined to the vertical in the ratio of ⅔. Drawing vertical tangents to each ellipse (XM on the ellipse shown) and joining these tangential points, he obtained the line OM, which was inclined to the vertical in the ratio of ⅓. These ratios confirmed the regression values obtained by the different method, namely those of ⅔ from mid-parent to offspring and of ⅓ from offspring to mid-parent. That the two methods must correspond is obvious because the place on each horizontal array where an ellipse touches must be the point of maximum value on that array. The same is true of the vertical arrays.

Galton also obtained from his contours the ratio of the axes of this ellipse system and the inclination of the major axis to the horizontal. These relations could now be subjected to mathematical verification. With a knowledge of the variability of the heights of mid-parents and of offspring and the average regression ratio it would be possible to investigate the resulting surface and the particulars of sections cut in that surface, one of which would form the ellipses Galton had drawn. He thought at first of attempting the mathematical analysis himself, and having forgotten the formulae for conic sections he visited the Royal Academy library to consult the relevant texts. The President, Sir James Dewar, advised him not to bother his head with it and referred him to a brother-in-law, Hamilton Dickson, a Cambridge mathematician, to whom Galton submitted the problem.

'I may be permitted to say that I never felt such a glow of royalty and respect towards the sovereignty and magnificent sway of mathematical analysis as when his answer reached me, confirming, by purely mathematical reasoning, my various and laborious statistical conclusions with far more minuteness than I had dared to hope, for the original data ran somewhat roughly, and I had to smooth them with tender caution. His calculation corrected my observed value of mid-parental regression from $1/3$ to $6/17\cdot6$, the relation between the major and minor axis of the ellipses was changed 3 per cent., their inclination was changed less than 2 degrees.'[8]

Thus he was satisfied that the various results of his statistics were not casual and disconnected determinations, but strictly interdependent.

In his paper he now proceeds to discuss the separate contribution of each ancestor to the heritage of the offspring.

'When we say that the mid-parent contributes two-thirds of his peculiarity of height to the offspring, it is supposed that nothing is known about the previous ancestor. We now see that though nothing is known, something is implied, and that something must be eliminated if we desire to know what the parental bequest, pure and simple, may amount to. Let the deviate of the mid-parent be a, then the implied deviate of the mid-grandparent will be $\frac{1}{3}a$, of the mid-ancestor in the next generation $\frac{1}{9}a$, and so on. Hence the sum of the deviates of all the mid-generations that contribute to the heritage of the offspring is $a(1 + 1/3 + 1/9 + \text{etc.}) = a3/2$.'[9]

If this is the total 'bequeathable property', he now asks whether each ancestor contributes equally to it. Under the supposition that they do so, it can be argued that as the total property of $a3/2$ yields an effective heritage of $a2/3$, it must follow that each piece of property must be reduced, as it were by a succession tax, to $4/9$ths of its original amount (i.e. $3/2 \times 4/9 = 2/3$).

A different supposition of successive diminution with the property being taxed afresh on each transfer leads to an effective heritage of

$a(1/r+1/3r^2+1/3^2r^3+\text{etc.})=a(3/3r-1)$, and this must, as before, be equal to $2/3$, whence $1/r = 6/11$.

As the two suppositions lead to values close to $\frac{1}{2}$, he accepts this figure. Then, without comment or reason, he accepts the second supposition of a geometric progression and states that the influence of the mid-parent is $\frac{1}{2}$, of the mid-grandparent $\frac{1}{4}$, of the mid-great-grandparent $\frac{1}{8}$, and so on. The influence of a single parent would then be $\frac{1}{4}$, of a single grandparent $1/16$, of a single great-grandparent $1/64$, and so on.

Thus we reach Galton's *Law of Ancestral Inheritance*, as it was later termed by Karl Pearson.[10] Pearson was, however, well aware of the several mathematical fallacies involved in Galton's neat formulation and introduced enormous complexities in his own attempts to verify the law.[11] Galton's idea that because a grandparent is the parent of a parent his regression must be $1/3 \times 1/3 = 1/9$ appears commonsensical but is in fact erroneous. Regression coefficients cannot be obtained from one another in this manner. It can be noted now that Galton compounds the error in *Natural Inheritance* where he proceeds to compute the regression of various degrees of family relationship by multiplicative means.

In Galton's comparison of his two suppositions that the ancestors either contribute equally or in a geometric progression, his two constants of $4/9$ and $6/11$ are derived from different equations in that the $4/9$ refers to the equal contribution of each ancestor while the $6/11$ refers to the mid-parental contribution which has to be raised to higher powers for the earlier ancestors.[12] Galton's preference for the geometric progression was a fortunate one as it gave Pearson the starting point for his work on multiple regression, but it was not based on any logical decision. It seems rather to have stemmed from a conclusion reached in his very first paper on an hereditary topic, that entitled 'Hereditary Talent and Character' which appeared in *Macmillan's Magazine* in 1865. There he states quite categorically

'The share that a man retains in the constitution of his remote descendants is inconceivably small. The father transmits, on an average, one-half of his nature, the grandfather one-fourth, the great-grandfather one-eighth; the share decreasing step by step, in a geometrical ratio, with great rapidity.'[13]

He characteristically illustrates his contention by calculating that if a man who can claim descent from one of William the Conqueror's barons should weigh 14 stone the part of him that may be ascribed to the baron will not exceed $1/50$ grain.

This early version of the law also does not depend on any previous argument. The statement, of course, does not refer to mid-parents but to the father alone. The omission of the mother is presumably a slip, but if she were included the characteristics of the offspring would be grossly overdetermined. As the figures are similar to those adduced later, it is almost certain that Galton meant to write 'parents' where he wrote 'father'. But, even so, whence could he have derived the figures? The date was too early for him to have knowledge of Darwin's theory of pangenesis which could have been mathematicised in this form. (Darwin's manuscript was written at least six months later; the theory was not published until 1869.[14]) He probably inferred the law *a priori*. To support this view there is his much later claim that there exist good grounds for such an argument.[15] Here he points out that it is a matter of common observation that each ancestor *may* contribute something of his own peculiarity to an offspring and that the more remote the ancestor the less he appears to contribute. Furthermore it is reasonable to suppose that the contributions of parents to children are in the same proportion as those of grandparents to parents and so on. The total amount which must equal 1 can then only be expressed by an infinite geometric series diminishing to zero, i.e. $\frac{1}{2} + (\frac{1}{2})^2 + (\frac{1}{2})^3$, etc.

Although there are fallacies in this argument it is reasonable to suppose that Galton was convinced by this chain of reasoning as early as 1865 and when he came to deal with his later data he fitted his statistical analysis to a foregone conclusion. He did not, however, completely convince himself that he had discovered a fundamental law of heredity until he had more data than those of stature.

The second type of data was also derived from the family records and took the form of the respondents' reports on the eye colour of their relations. When contrasted with stature Galton had what appeared to be two very different hereditary qualities.

'Speaking broadly parents of different statures transmit a blended inheritance to their children, but parents of different eye-colour transmit an alternative heritage. If one parent is as much taller than the average of his or her sex as the other parent is shorter, the statures of their children will be distributed in much the same way as those of parents who were both of medium height. But if one parent has a light eye-colour and the other a dark eye-colour, the children will be partly light and partly dark, and not medium eye-coloured like the children of medium eye-coloured parents.'[16]

Thus he believed that if he could show that the law held for these data as it did for stature, the demonstration would widen the law, possibly to universal applicability.

His method was to construct a prediction table for eye colour in the offspring when facts were known about certain of their ancestry. Three cases were taken: the case in which the eye colours of both parents are known, that in which the eye colours of the four grandparents are known, and a combination of these two cases where the eye colours of parents and grandparents are known. He supposed, as with height, that each parent contributes $\frac{1}{4}$ and each grandparent $1/16$ of the individual's heredity. In the case of height the statement implied that the contribution of $\frac{1}{4}$ of a parent's deviation in height would be handed on to his offspring; in the case of eye colour it means that the parent's eye colour will be contributed to $\frac{1}{4}$ of his offspring.

The predicted values were compared with the obtained values with quite extraordinary results. As expected, the more hereditary information included, as in prediction of the third type, the closer the predicted to the observed values. For example, out of a total of 183 children, all of whose parents and grandparents were light-eyed, 172 were predicted to be light-eyed; the number found was 174.

Criticisms have been made of Galton's mathematics in this paper, errors which make the accuracy of the predictions surprising.[17] He was himself clear that the observations on which the paper was based were too few and too uncertain to make a more rigorous analysis worthwhile. Nevertheless, he felt justified in concluding that his law had stood this further test extremely well.

But he was still unsatisfied. The family records had provided data from no more than three generations, and longer pedigrees could only be obtained from breeding experiments. He therefore turned to animal breeding and decided that a type of moth that bred twice a year might speedily provide sufficient information. With the help of an entomologist, F. Merrifield, he began breeding the Purple Thorn moth, *Selenia illustraria*, with a view to investigating the inheritance of the wing length.

A great deal of trouble was taken with these experiments which began in 1887 and which were to have continued for six years.[18] All the moths were photographed by an assistant, Miss Reynolds, and temperature, feeding and other environmental variables were to be held constant. Unfortunately the fertility of the largest and smallest moths fell off, and when Merrifield increased the temperature to force more frequent broods they became completely sterile and the experiments had to be begun again. Food supplies next became too low and irregularities in wing size were produced which became so great that the experiments finally had to be discontinued in 1889.

Although Galton now appears to have toyed with the idea of breeding mice his plans came to nothing and he had to wait for more data until 1897 when he had access to Sir Everett Millais' large compilation giving details of the coat colour of a pedigree stock of basset hounds. There were only two varieties of colour, either white with blotches of red or yellow, known as 'lemon and white', or with the addition of black, known as 'tricolour'. He thus had only two types to deal with and nearly 1000 examples over several generations.

His paper on this material consists of calculations of the proportions of the two types in any generation expected in terms of his law. He found very close agreement between the expected and observed proportions and felt satisfied at last with the accuracy of his law.[19] A paper to *Nature* in the following year[20] provided a diagrammatical representation of the law and is shown in Figure 14.3.

All even numbers in the diagram represent males and odd numbers females. 2 and 3 are the parents who together contribute one half of the total heredity; 4, 5, 6 and 7 are the four grandparents who contribute

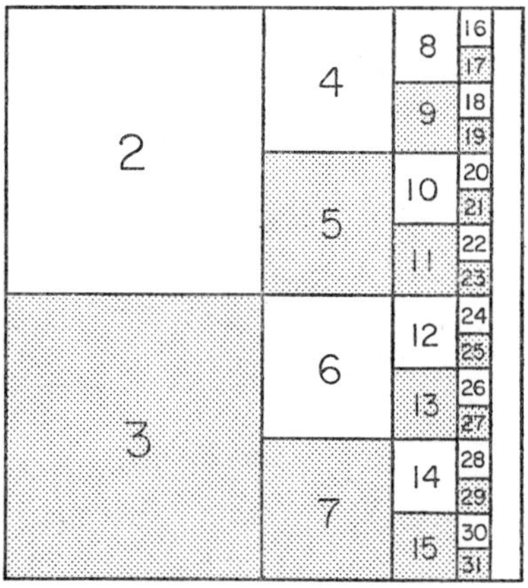

FIGURE 14.3 Diagrammatic representation of Galton's ancestral law. (Reproduced from *Nature*, **57** (1898), p. 293.)

one quarter, and so on with the eight great grandparents and more remote ancestors. The numerical code enables one to assign a number to each ancestor, however remote.

Galton appears to have had few doubts about his law after this date and did not believe it to have been rendered false by the rediscovery of Mendel's work in 1900. As much as possible he tried to remain above the controversy that then opened between his lieutenants, Pearson and Weldon, and the Mendelians, notably Bateson. But this bitter battle and the many difficulties over the newly-founded Eugenics Society nevertheless disturbed the tranquillity of his final years.

Galton's attempts to measure the resemblance between parent and offspring had led him, as we have seen, to the regression slope. His puzzlement over the two regression lines did not last long. He realised as the data from his anthropometric laboratory were tabulated that he had a similar problem with this material. How were the separate measures of stature, sitting height, length of arm, etc. related? Each measure was on a different scale, and when other possible associations were to be examined, such as that between strength of pull and breathing capacity, the units of measurement appeared even more disparate. The idea that the regression coefficient for inheritance could be applied as a measure of the relationship between two anthropometric variables, *provided each variable was measured on a scale of its own variability,* came to Galton as an insightful flash of inspiration. He had in the summer of 1888 been invited to ramble in the grounds of Naworth Castle.

'A temporary shower drove me to seek refuge in a reddish recess in the rock by the side of the pathway. There the idea flashed across me, and I forgot everything for a moment in my great delight.'[21]

By December of that year he had prepared a paper which he read to the Royal Society on the 20th of the month.[22] Entitled 'Co-relations and their Measurement Chiefly from Anthropometric Data,' this paper contains details of his technique for calculating the correlation coefficient and presents coefficients obtained from the measurements of 350 adult males.

He begins this important paper with a definition of correlation.

' "Co-relation or correlation of structure" is a phrase much used in biology, and not least in that branch of it which refers to heredity, and the idea is even more frequently present than the phrase; but I am not aware of any previous attempt to define it clearly, to trace its mode of action in detail, or to show how to measure its degree.

'Two variable organs are said to be co-related when the variation of the one is accompanied on the average by more or less variation of the other, and in the same direction. Thus the length of the arm is said to be co-related with that of the leg, because a person with a long arm has usually a long leg, and conversely. If the co-relation be close, then a person with a very long arm would usually have a very long leg; if it be moderately close, then the length of his leg would usually be only long, not very long; and if there were no co-relation at all then the length of his leg would on the average be mediocre. It is easy to see that co-relation must be the consequence of the variations of the two organs being partly due to common causes. If they were wholly due to common causes, the co-relation would be perfect, as is approximately the case with the symmetrically disposed parts of the body. If they were in no respect due to common causes, the co-relation would be *nil*. Between these two extremes are an endless number of intermediate cases, and it will be shown how the closeness of co-relation in any particular case admits of being expressed by a simple number.'[23]

Galton takes as an example the relation between the length of the forearm, or cubit, and the stature, which is such that for every inch that the cubit deviates from its average, the stature will deviate 2·5 inches from its average. That is, cubit : stature = 1 : 2·5. Conversely for each unit of deviation of stature, the average deviation of the cubit will be 0·26 inch. That is, stature : cubit = 1 : 0·26. These relations are not numerically reciprocal, just as the regression of children on parents and parents on children were not. However, if the inches of the cubit and stature are now expressed as units of their own variability a different state of affairs will exist. As a measure of variability Galton employs the probable error, which he obtains in the following manner : the measures of stature are marshalled in order of magnitude and a note taken of the measures in the series which fall at the first, second and third quarterly divisions. The second quarterly division is the middlemost value, or median, which is taken as the average. Calling the first quarterly point Q_1 and the third quarterly point Q_3, then $\frac{1}{2}(Q_3 - Q_1) = Q$, which is the probable error. This is in practice the same as saying that one half of the deviations fall within $\pm Q$ from the average.

In the case of stature the Q value is 1·75 inch, while in the case of cubit it is 0·56 inch. Now in order to transmute the measurements of stature into the new scale each unit will be 1·75 inch, and the new cubit unit will be 0·56 inch. The relationships then become :

$$\text{Cubit : stature} = \frac{1}{0\cdot56} : \frac{2\cdot5}{1\cdot75} = 1 : 0\cdot8$$

$$\text{Stature : cubit} = \frac{1}{1\cdot75} : \frac{0\cdot26}{0\cdot56} = 1 : 0\cdot8$$

The correlation is thus 0·8 between stature and cubit.

Galton now provides a table of median and Q values for head length, head breadth, length of left middle finger and height of right knee. From this table he calculates some of the correlations between these measures, which are as follows :

Cubit and stature	$r = 0\cdot8$
Head length and stature	$r = 0\cdot35$
Middle finger and stature	$r = 0\cdot7$
Cubit and middle finger	$r = 0\cdot85$
Head breadth and head length	$r = 0\cdot45$
Knee height and stature	$r = 0\cdot9$
Knee height and cubit	$r = 0\cdot8$

These are the first correlations ever calculated. It will be observed that as his symbol of correlation Galton employs the letter r, originally abbreviated from 'reversion' and then from 'regression', and still used today.

The statures of kinsmen are also correlated variables. In most cases there is no need when dealing with kinships to reduce the measure to units of Q, because the Q values are alike in all kinsmen, being of the same value as that of the general population. However in the case that Galton first examined, the statures of mid-parents and children, this general case did not hold and the regressions have to be calculated in Q units to obtain the correlation. The Q of the mid-parental statures is now found to be 1·2 and that of the children 1·7. Thus,

$$\text{Children : mid-parents} = \frac{1}{1 \cdot 2} : \frac{2}{3} \times \frac{1}{1 \cdot 7} = 1 : 0 \cdot 47$$

$$\text{Mid-parents : children} = \frac{1}{1 \cdot 7} : \frac{1}{3} \times \frac{1}{1 \cdot 2} = 1 : 0 \cdot 47$$

The correlation then between the statures of mid-parents and offspring is 0·47.

Galton's method of obtaining correlation is different from that employed today. He uses medians instead of means and quartile measurements instead of standard deviations. His results depend on the assumption that all his data fit a normal distribution, which certainly does not appear to have been the case in his sample of stature measurements.[24] He also does not seem to have appreciated the possibility of the existence of negative correlations. But the importance of this paper lies in Galton's demonstration that the statistical apparatus he had evolved for the treatment of hereditary data had a much wider significance. Karl Pearson, who was largely responsible for extending the work and for placing it on a much sounder mathematical basis, sums up Galton's contribution in the following words :

'Galton's very modest paper of ten pages from which a revolution in our scientific ideas has spread is in its permanent influence, perhaps, the most important of his writings. Formerly the quantitative scientist could only think in terms of causation, now he can think also in terms of correlation. This has not only enormously widened the field in which quantitative and therefore mathematical methods can be applied, but it has at the same time modified our philosophy of science and even of life itself.'[25]

The final expression of Galton's ideas on heredity and regression is to be found in his book *Natural Inheritance* (1889).[26] Galton was aware of the stylistic problems involved in writing a book of this technical nature for a general readership. As he says in his introductory chapter :

'I have a great subject to write upon, but I feel keenly my literary incapacity to make it easily intelligible without sacrificing accuracy and thoroughness.'[27]

The book is concerned to offer a solution to three main questions : how do the characteristics of parents relate to those same characteristics in the offspring, what is the relative contribution of each ancestor to the nature of the offspring, and how is it possible to measure the nearness of kinship. The first two of these problems had already been dealt with in the papers we have discussed and much of Galton's treatment in the present volume is a restatement of his earlier views.

The second and third chapters are devoted to his general conception of the hereditary process. He deals briefly with 'natural' and 'acquired' peculiarities and expresses doubt about the inheritance of the latter although stressing the necessity for well devised experiments to settle the issue. He describes inheritance as 'particulate', that is, we seem to inherit bit by bit, one element from one ancestor and another element from another. An individual may possess some elements that have not appeared in his parents; for example, he may suffer from a disease that is said to have skipped a generation. To explain this phenomenon he uses his earlier postulate of 'latent' elements, which are not revealed in the individual but which are available for transmission to the offspring. He believes it to be sheer chance whether a particular element, either in latent or patent form, finds its way into the sample that makes up an individual. To provide a clue as to the nature of the latent elements present in a single case, he advocates an examination of the differences among brothers of a large fraternity whose total heritages must have been alike but whose personal structures are often very different.

In his lack of recognition of dominance Galton is, of course, at variance with subsequent genetic thought. Galton also confuses the broader issue by postulating here what appears to be a physiological basis for the hereditary mechanism and yet a little later explicitly denying that he is propounding a theory of heredity. Rather, he claims, he is describing statistically the overt characteristics of people, that is, their phenotypic resemblance. We must assume that this is how he viewed his work although he certainly succeeded in misleading some of his readers.[28]

A section on organic stability now follows. He illustrates his notion by means of a model of a polygonal slab that can be made to stand on any of its edges upon a flat surface.

'The model and the organic structure have the cardinal fact in common, that if either is disturbed without transgressing the range of its stability, it will tend to re-establish itself, but if the range is over-passed it will topple into a new position . . . The ultimate point to be represented is this. Though a long-established race habitually breeds true to its kind, subject to small unstable deviations, yet every now and then the offspring of these deviations do not tend to revert but possess stablility of their own.'[29]

Thus a distinction has to be made between variations from the mean of a race, which will tend to regress according to the Ancestral Law, and 'sports' which do not. Sports can lead to the establishment of new races while variations cannot. It follows that evolution must take place by jumps and not by minute steps. The view that evolution must be discontinuous was to be worked out in detail in a paper of 1894 when he had finger-print data to support his conviction; it was this kind of evidence that was to convince Bateson and others of the importance of mutations in forwarding the evolutionary process.

The whole section of Galton's book devoted to organic stability is marred by the frequent use of analogy. Thus, he appeals to contemporary experience of hansom cabs, in breeder's terms a 'sport', to argue that the sudden appearance of a new type may be stable! His excuse that he wished to avoid entanglement with hereditary theory is inadequate in view of his earlier formulations.

Chapter 4 is concerned with schemes of distribution and frequency. He had discussed in previous papers his method of ranking subjects in terms of percentiles or grades. He now supplies data from his anthropometric laboratory showing the values obtained at the different percentile points for the various anthropometric measures. A comparison of the relevant performance of the two sexes leads to the interesting conclusion that,

'Very powerful women exist, but happy perhaps for the repose of the other sex such gifted women are rare. Out of 1,657 adult women of all ages measured at the laboratory, the strongest could only exert a squeeze of 86 lbs, or about that of a medium man.'[30]

A chapter on normal variability stresses the point that the distribution can be described by two constants, the median and the quartile. By their use the charms of statistics become evident.

'It is difficult to understand why statisticians commonly limit their inquiries to Averages, and do not revel in more comprehensive views. Their souls seem as dull to the charm of variety as that of the native of one of our flat English counties, whose retrospect of

Switzerland was that, if its mountains could be thrown into its lakes, two nuisances would be got rid of at once. An Average is but a solitary fact, whereas if a single other fact be added to it, an entire Normal Scheme, which nearly corresponds to the observed one, starts potentially into existence.

'Some people hate the very name of statistics, but I find them full of beauty and interest. Whenever they are not brutalised, but delicately handled by the higher methods, and are warily interpreted, their power of dealing with complicated phenomena is extraordinary. They are the only tools by which an opening can be cut through the formidable thicket of difficulties that bare the path of those who pursue the Science of man.'[31]

Chapter 6 details the sources of his data and includes an account of his sweet pea and moth breeding experiments, the *Record of Family Faculties*, the anthropometric laboratory, and a special enquiry into the variations in stature among brothers conducted by questionnaire. This latter source is considered more trustworthy than the *Record of Family Faculties*, and the data from it enable Galton to calculate a value for fraternal regression of $\frac{2}{3}$ which is similar to that obtained for the regression of sons on mid-parents.

He now takes the appropriate regression coefficient as an expression of the nearness of kinship. Thus, brothers are as closely related to one another as mid-parents are to sons. Fathers and sons give a coefficient of $\frac{1}{3}$. As a nephew is the son of a brother, his regression on his uncle must be $\frac{1}{3} \times \frac{2}{3} = \frac{2}{9}$. But, as we have pointed out, this procedure is not legitimate. In any case it leads to contradictions. If a brother is considered to be the son of a midparent he should have a regression $\frac{2}{3} \times \frac{2}{3} = \frac{4}{9}$, instead of Galton's observed value of $\frac{2}{3}$. One may equally well compute the regression of a nephew on his uncle by other routes and arrive at different figures.[32] The numerical values he provides are thus little more than suggestive and cannot replace the results of direct observation. The remainder of Chapter 7 is taken up with a discussion of the results from stature measurement and covers much of the same ground as that reported earlier. A discussion of the data of eye colour in Chapter 8 also corresponds to the earlier account.

A consideration of the Artistic Faculty makes up Chapter 9. The information was obtained from the *Record of Family Faculties* in answer to a question about an individual's favourite pursuits and artistic aptitudes. In some cases Galton found the exact nature of the artistic interest difficult to identify from the questionnaire entry and he is therefore forced to consider musical and painting abilities in a single group.

Galton supposes that if artistic aptitude could be measured in some way the resulting distribution would be normal. Furthermore, if the law of inheritance holds, the value of filial regression should be ⅔ as it was in the other cases.

Pearson has shown the fallacies in Galton's treatment.[33] Galton claims that if the matings of artistic and nonartistic couples are examined there is apparently a slight disinclination for like to marry like. He interprets this finding to mean that although highly artistic people maintain a caste apart from the general population the very much larger group of slightly artistic people do not.

'A man of highly artistic temperament must look on those who are deficient in it as barbarians; he would continually crave for a sympathy and response that such persons are incapable of giving. On the other hand, every quiet unmusical man must shrink a little from the idea of wedding himself to a grand piano in constant action, with its vocal and peculiar social accompaniments; but he might anticipate great pleasure in having a wife of a moderately artistic temperament, who would give colour and variety to his prosaic life. On the other hand, a sensitive and imaginative wife would be conscious of needing the aid of a husband who had enough plain common-sense to restrain her too enthusiastic and frequently foolish projects.'[34]

Galton's data do not however support this supposition. Pearson calculated the correlation between husband and wife and found it to be low but positive.[35] As a 'quiet unmusical man' himself, married to a woman with moderate artistic interests, Galton was perhaps generalising from his own life situation in describing such marriages as common.

When the percentage of artistic offspring of various kinds of parents is examined Galton obtains the figures given in Table 14.2.

The calculated percentages, using a regression value of ⅔(0·67), are very close to the observed percentages and Galton concludes that the same law of regression must apply to the artistic faculty as to stature and eye colour. But his calculation makes no allowance for the assortative mating we have noted and he also assumes equal inheritance from both parents. Taking the correlations into account, Pearson has shown that the regression value should be 0·56 and not 0·67, which is a significant difference.[36]

TABLE 14.2
Percentage of artistic offspring

	Both parents artistic	One parent artistic	Neither parent artistic
Observed	36	39	21
Calculated	40	38.5	17

Thus, although there is a definite resemblance between parents and off-spring, Galton was unjustified in concluding that the regression value was similar in this and the earlier enquiries.

Another descriptive characteristic assessed from family records was the tendency for the person to be good- or bad-tempered. Galton relegates his account of this work to an appendix, which is in fact a reprint of a paper published two years previously.[37] The methods adopted in investigating the possible inheritance of temper are necessarily cruder than those used with other characteristics. However, it does not follow that they are accordingly unreliable. In a passage reminiscent of his Rede lecture Galton states :

> 'The accurate discernment and designation of character is almost beyond the reach of any one, but, on the other hand, a rough estimate and a fair description of its prominent features is easily obtainable; and it seems to me that the testimony of a member of a family who has seen and observed a person in his unguarded moments and under very varied circumstances for many years, is a verdict deserving of much confidence.'[38]

Galton is content to deal with the percentages of good- and bad-tempered individuals, assigning a variety of 15 descriptions to the former and 46 to the latter category. When the percentages of parents and offspring thus categorised are compared, the results favour the view that it is an hereditable quality. Where both parents were good-tempered, 30% of the children were classified likewise and only 10% were described as bad-tempered. Where both parents were bad-tempered, 54% of the children were classified likewise and only 4% were described as good-tempered.

Galton claims that no evidence of assortative mating was to be found in the case of temper, but again Pearson reworked his data and obtained a slight negative correlation.[39] Galton's lack of consideration of the environmental influence of the home is an obvious shortcoming in the case of a behavioural characteristic such as temper.

He now turns to the inheritance of disease. He works here with the causes of death provided by the family records. Probably from ignorance of the exact cause of death only one third of the returns were satisfactorily completed and he had to rest content with 2000 records. This was quite insufficient to determine, as he wished, whether a parent who died at a given age of a specific illness gave rise to an offspring dying of the same or another specific illness at a given age.

The one disease treated in detail is tuberculosis, a condition from which about one in six of the population of England died at that time. In sorting his cases, he included under the heading of consumption various epithets probably used to describe the condition, such as 'lungs affected' and 'decline'. Other descriptions were even less precise and he was forced to use three categories of doubtful cases: highly suspicious, suspicious, and somewhat suspicious.

There were 66 marriages in which one parent was consumptive and they produced a total of 413 children, of whom 70 were actually consumptive and 37 others who were suspiciously so in various degrees. In other words, 26% of the children could be classified as probably consumptive. When neither parent was consumptive, 18% of the children died of the illness, a figure slightly in excess of the 16% found in surveys of the general population.

Galton arranges the returns to show the percentage of cases having various percentages of consumptive taint. (See Table 14.3.) From this table and from some additional figures he ascertains that consumptive traits are not normally distributed.

'They make a distinctly double-humped curve, whose outline is no more like the normal curve than the back of a Bactrian camel is to that of an Arabian camel.'[40]

TABLE 14.3

Percentage of cases having various degrees of consumptive taint

	Percentages of taint				
	0–9	10–19	20–29	30–39	40+
66 cases, one parent consumptive	27	20	9	15	29

Consumption, he concludes, tends to be transmitted strongly or not at all. It is partly acquired by infection and is partly an hereditary malformation. In so far as it is hereditary either parent may transmit it; in so far as it is acquired the mother appears to be responsible, a conclusion inferred from the greater tendency of mothers to die of the illness at an average age of 58 compared with the fathers who die from other causes at an average age of 73. But these averages are calculated from only 13 families and the variance is so great that the difference is in fact statistically insignificant.

Galton now returns in the next chapter to a discussion of latent elements which he believes follow the same law as personal ones. That is, only one quarter of the characteristics of the ancestry lies latent in each parent and can be contributed to the offspring, the remainder drop out.

The final chapter summarises the book. He makes one new point here which is worthy of mention. He distinguishes between two couples whose personal attributes may be naturally alike.

'If one of the couples consist of two gifted members of a poor stock, and the other of two ordinary members of a gifted stock, the difference between them will betray itself in their offspring. The children of the former will tend to regress; those of the latter will not. The value of a good stock to the well-being of future generations is therefore obvious, and it is well to recall attention to an early sign by which we may be assured that a new and gifted variety possesses the necessary stability to easily originate a new stock. It is its refusal to blend freely with other forms. Some among the members of the same fraternity might possess the characteristics in question with much completeness, and the remainder hardly or not at all.'[41]

Thus it is not that there is less mediocrity in the ancestry of a given stock that leads to the absence of regression; it is rather that the new stock has arisen from a mutation, that is, it has fallen into a fresh position of stability.

Galton appears to have written *Natural Inheritance* in some haste, as there are numerous errors. If he had only delayed the book a little longer it would have been vastly improved by the incorporation of his correlational discoveries. However he had begun writing late in 1887 and was correcting the proofs by September 1888, while his paper on correlation was not ready until the December of that year.

The major defect in *Natural Inheritance* arises from Galton's misinterpretation of regression. It is not that the offspring have been forced towards mediocrity by the pressure of their mediocre remote ancestry, but a consequence of a less than perfect correlation between the parents and their offspring. By restricting his analysis to the offspring of a *selected* parentage and attempting to understand their deviations from the mean Galton fails to account for the deviation of all offspring. By arguing that the reason for the regression to mediocrity was the weight of the mediocrity of the ancestors more remote than the parents, he leaves open the question of what would be the result of having ancestors who deviated as much as the parents. Surely he should infer that the return to mediocrity should cease and a new line should be established. But Galton's conclusion is that regression is perpetual and that the only way in which evolutionary change can occur is through the occurrence of sports.

The paradoxical result of Galton's work was to help to create two rival schools of heredity.[42] *Natural Inheritance* had led directly to the formation of the Biometric School, who continued in Galton's steps with their application of statistical methods to heredity. But the rival school of neo-Mendelians, with their stress on the mutational mechanism of evolutionary change, received their initial stimulation from the same source.

Personal Identification

Galton's anthropometric work brought him immediate recognition from the Anthropological Society who in 1885 invited him to be their President, an office he accepted for a period of four years. In the same year he was also nominated for the Gold Medal of the Royal Society. But Thomas Huxley pressed the claims of E. R. Lankester in biology, and it was Lankester and not Galton who received the medal that year.[1] Galton's name was again put forward in 1886 and on this occasion he was unopposed.

Louisa conveyed the good news to Emma in a letter of 4 November:

'Dearest Emma,
   See the Telegram has just come, quite unexpected but not the less welcome. I am so glad. Frank works on patiently and quietly, there is less to bring him to the front than with many who do less. He is very pleased but do not talk about it for a few days, as the President of the Royal Society puts "private" till confirmed by the Queen (a mere farce). It is given for his Statistical inquiries and investigations in Biology. You will be pleased, I know, more than anyone next to ourselves.'[2]

Louisa had been in poor health during the previous two years, a fact she attributed to her enforced stay in Britain without continental holidays, which had been prevented by outbreaks of cholera in both France and Italy. Accordingly in 1886 the Galtons determined on a Spring tour abroad and made an early start, as Louisa records:

'We left England on Feb. 25th for Paris and escaped it and had a delightful time at Hyères first, then Mentone, Rome and Sorrento. We were so happy there, every passing hour had its tale of keen enjoyment and we felt to grudge each day as it passed. We returned by Amalfi and Florence where we spent another week to be remembered, such beauty and loveliness in art and nature.'

The vacation produced an astounding improvement in Louisa's condition, but her husband was suffering from gout and they spent a few extra weeks in Contrexeville for him to take the waters. The local physician must have made a favourable impression—Galton preserved a copy of his dietary and other recommendations:

'White meat and plenty of vegetables except those containing oxalic acid . . . Little and light wine, preferably red. Wholly avoid champagne.
'Get rid of uric acid by (*a*) intestines (*b*) kidneys (*c*) skin.
a. Saline physic (mineral waters) now and then.
b. Diuretics.
c. Sponge bath, friction.
'Spring and autumn are critical times . . . He said I had mentally overworked myself (possibly a little).'[3]

The following year he again felt need of a cure:

'About July 16th we went to Homburg for Frank to take the waters and staid 3 weeks, we enjoyed the fresh air, the music out of doors, the pleasant setting under trees, but were glad to leave.'

They left to begin a long tour in Switzerland but Galton fell ill with gastric fever, bronchitis and then typhlitis and remained in poor health until the summer of 1888.

'1888. Frank was ill all the early part, congestion of the lung and I felt very anxious about him and overtired myself, as when he recovered, I fell ill and that brought on my old pain, which never left me until we had recourse to Vichy in Septbr . . . Montagu* took us by surprise in June by the announcement of his engagement to Agnata Ramsay the Senior Classic of 1887 and the wish to be at his wedding modified our summer plans. We staid in England visiting the Lethbridges at Clifton and then Marianne North, at the end of a fortnight, we returned to London for Montagu's wedding Augt 9th. It was a very interesting gathering and picturesquely arranged at St. Margaret's, Westminster . . . We went [to Vichy] Sept 1st and had 3 weeks of glorious weather, a flood of sunshine on our rooms from early morning, it just gave me fresh life and we basked in the dry warmth and were happy. Frank was busy about his Book, "Natural Inheritance" correcting Proofs and I led a quiet life, as suited the cure, taking the waters and we did so enjoy the fresh morning air. The late season prevented our meeting pleasant people and the last week, Frank was a sufferer from a bad fall on

* Montagu Butler had become Master of Trinity College, Cambridge in 1886.

his right arm and this hurried us home after 3 days in Paris, instead of making a stay at Compiègne, as I hoped, so we were back the end of Septbr and soon comfortably settled and the home rest was a good conclusion to Vichy cure.'

During his few days in Paris, Galton visited the Department of Judicial Identity where Bertillon demonstrated his photographic and anthropometric techniques and took Galton's measurements and photograph (See Plate IX).*

Upon his return to England, Galton was invited to lecture at the Royal Institution on Bertillon's work.[5] In his lecture he gives a short description of Bertillon's method which involved measuring head length and breadth, middle finger length, forearm length, foot length and up to seven other bodily proportions. Each measurement was classified as long, medium or short, the criteria for these groupings being so arranged that an equal number of persons fell into each group. Thus, the operator first measured the length of the subject's head which was then classified as large, medium or small. The measurement of head breadth served as a second subdivision, making nine classes in all. The third subdivision gave 27 and so on. With five main measurements Bertillon had 243 subdivisions, all of roughly equal size. A cabinet with 243 drawers was used to hold the cards containing photograph and details of bodily peculiarities, scars, etc., which would enable the final indentification to be made. As the numbers of subjects involved grew so one could classify more finely, and Bertillon's method could easily cope with several millions.

The advantages of anthropometric measurement were quite apparent to Galton and not only in the case of those who had committed a crime. The Tichborne trial was very much in the public mind at the time and Galton alluded to the enormous waste of money, effort and anxiety which might have been spared had Roger Tichborne been measured accurately before leaving the country. It would then have been a matter of minutes to check the credentials of the claimant to the name.†

But Galton was not convinced that Bertillon had the best solution.

---

* Galton's visiting card survives with the written note, 'Vendredi vers $2\frac{1}{4}$ heures ayant grand désir de voir vos appareils photographiques.'[4]
Bertillon was renowned for his fine photography.

† An interesting side light on the Tichborne case is thrown by a letter from Galton to *Nature* in 1884.[6] It had been proposed that a campaign should be mounted on behalf of the claimant in which use would be made of 'identiscopes'. This device appears to have been a type of stereoscope, in one field of which a drawing of Roger Tichborne was presented, while the other field contained a drawing of the claimant. The result of looking into the instrument was to see a combined portrait, which it was claimed was proof of their identicality in real life. But as Galton points out no proof is afforded by this demonstration, as one might choose portraits of many different individuals that would harmonize with that of the genuine Roger Tichborne, including that of an eminent member of the Royal Household!

There were several possible sources of error: those on the part of the operator, both in measuring and classifying, those due to variations in the subject, and those due to the fact that some of the bodily proportions measured may not be independent of others and may therefore be unnecessary for purposes of identification. (This latter hypothesis was to be confirmed within the next few months when Galton applied his new correlational technique to his anthropometric data.)

Individual differences can be clearly seen in more minute particulars. He instances the handwriting, the shape of the ears, the variation in the markings in the iris of the eye, the variation in the patterns of superficial veins, and the patterning of the ridges on the hands and feet. Galton was obviously at this time sceptical of the value of fingerprints and he mentions the difficulty of taking durable impressions of the finger tips. He spoke from experience, as from March of that year he had been using a inked plate to take fingerprints at his anthropometric laboratory. These early trials owed nothing to Bertillon's influence; it was Galton who later persuaded Bertillon to add fingerprinting to his system. Galton's interest was probably aroused by a faint memory that someone had written on the topic previously. He wrote to *Nature* requesting information, but the letter was never published. It is probable that the Editor dealt with the matter privately and referred Galton to two letters on the topic that had appeared in the 1880 volume.

One of these letters Galton had seen before. It was from Henry Faulds, a medical missionary in Japan, who had written from that country, the letter dated 16 February 1880, to Charles Darwin mentioning that there might be racial differences in fingerprints and enclosing two specimen prints.[7] Darwin's health was failing at the time—he died two years later —and he was not able to do more than to forward the letter to Galton suggesting that it might be of interest to anthropologists. Galton gave the letter to the Anthropological Institute where it remained in obscurity until it was returned to Galton in 1894.

Galton had obviously paid little attention to the letter in 1880, although the fact that it was sent on his birthday might have made an impression. He had also overlooked the letter when it appeared in *Nature* later in that year, although he himself had a letter in the same volume.[8] But there is nothing very surprising in this lack of interest. At the time he was involved in his visualising experiments and his anthropometric interests were at a very early stage.

What is less excusable is the error Galton made in referring to Faulds' letter during his Royal Institution lecture. Instead of giving Faulds priority, Galton suggests that Faulds wrote to support the views of Sir William Herschel who had originated the method; Herschel had in fact written to *Nature* in reply to Faulds. Thus, Galton unwittingly implied that Herschel was the first and more important contributor. A small error, but one which was to sour relationships between Faulds and Galton and which was to result in an acrimonious debate maintained for many years after the deaths of the principals.[9]

Although incidental to Galton's own work with fingerprints, it is worth describing the relative contributions of Faulds and Herschel for the light thrown on Galton's inclination to prejudice. Galton's relationships were always of the black or white variety with no shades of grey. Faulds suffered, as Stanley had done in earlier years, from being categorised as black, while Herschel was credited with more than his due.

In his *Nature* letter Faulds explained how his interest had been directed to fingerprints by finding impressions on ancient Japanese pottery that had apparently been intended to identify the potter.[10] He had taken inked impressions from Japanese and Europeans and thought that racial differences were apparent. He briefly described three types of pattern, arch, loop and whorl, and found instances of close familial resemblance in such patterns. Finally, he was convinced of the potential usefulness of fingerprints in identifying criminals and provided two examples from his own experience. In the first, greasy finger marks on a bottle of rectified spirit identified a thief, while in the second a suspect was exonerated from a study of sooty finger marks on a white wall.

Herschel, who was then chief administrator of a district of Bengal, immediately added his observations to those of Faulds in a letter published a month later.[11] He had been taking 'sign-manuals by means of finger marks' for more than twenty years in order to render attempts at personation and repudiation of contract less frequent. He had also introduced fingerprinting into jails where, on commitment, each prisoner 'had to sign with his finger.' By comparing the prints of persons then living, with their prints taken twenty years previously, he was satisfied that they were unchanging characteristics.

If the two letters are examined dispassionately it seems clear that although Faulds merits recognition as the first person to draw general scientific attention to fingerprints, Herschel had worked more extensively with the method. He had collected several thousand prints although he had not attempted to classify them. Faulds had suggested the basis of the obvious classificatory system in terms of arch, loop and whorl patterns, one which Galton was to adopt. Herschel had used the method to prevent fraud but Faulds had seen its potentialities in the detection of crime. Herschel had obtained evidence for the persistence of prints which Faulds had mentioned but without supporting his statement.

But Galton did not take a dispassionate view. In his major contribution, *Finger Prints* (1892), which will be discussed shortly, Mr Fauld [*sic*] is dismissed in a couple of lines while Herschel is given a laudatory review.

'If the use of finger prints ever becomes of general importance, Sir William Herschel must be regarded as the first who devised a feasible method for regular use, and afterwards officially adopted it.'[12]

Galton's second book on fingerprints, his *Finger Print Directories* (1895), was dedicated to Herschel. But the final blow to Faulds' prestige occurred ten years later when Galton reviewed for *Nature*, Faulds' own text book, *Guide to Fingerprint Identification*. The review was very severe on Faulds. For example :

'Dr Faulds in his present volume recapitulates his old grievance with no less bitterness than formerly. He overstates the value of his own work, belittles that of others, and carps at evidence recently given in criminal cases. His book is not only biased and imperfect, but unfortunately it contains nothing new that is of value.'[13]

Galton points out that Faulds' attempts to introduce fingerprints for legal purposes fell flat when he proposed them. The reasons for the then lack of interest Galton ascribes to Faulds' inability to demonstrate that the patterns were permanent, that they were of great variety in their minute detail, and that they were amenable to a precise method of classification.

Understanding 'permanence' to mean 'persistence', the first point is well taken. Faulds had conducted experiments in which the surface skin had been shaved off the finger and prints taken before the injury compared with those taken after the skin had grown, but he had no evidence of persistence over long periods of time. Neither Herschel's nor Faulds' evidence taken alone was sufficient, but together they demonstrated that fingerprints were permanent in the sense (1) that they persisted over a period of twenty years, and (2) that they regenerated after superficial injury in the same pattern that they had prior to the injury.

Galton is right in criticising Faulds for basing his arguments on inadequate material; he never had at his disposal the variety Galton obtained from his anthropometric laboratory. But Faulds had devised a method of classification and had tried between 1886 and 1888 to interest Scotland Yard in his system. He had even offered to work a small bureau free of charge in order to test its practicality. But Scotland Yard rejected his offer and Galton may never have heard of the report on Faulds' work received by the Commissioner of the Metropolitan Police in 1887.[14] Whether the rejection occurred because of the inadequacies to which Galton drew attention in his review is not known. According to Faulds Scotland Yard regarded him as a crank, an attitude which he could probably do little to dispel, as he was by temperament aggressive and aloof.[15]

The origin of Galton's dislike of Faulds and his constant disparage-

XI   Francis Galton, aged 87, with Albert Gifi

XII   Sister Adèle

ment of Faulds' work can best be understood if Herschel and Faulds were seen by Galton as contestants for the honour of originating the use of fingerprints for purposes of identification. Galton never met Faulds, who had neither the wealth nor social position to move in the same circles of stratified Victorian society. On the other hand, he did know Herschel who figures in *Hereditary Genius* as one of the eminent descendants of Sir William Herschel, the astronomer, from whom he derived his title. We have earlier glimpsed Galton's unbounded admiration for those of high scientific and social status who came from gifted families. Herschel was the perfect example of the kind of person Galton was liable to overestimate. If a choice had to be made between the relative achievements of Faulds and Herschel there could be little doubt in Galton's mind to whom the credit should be given.

Galton's own work with fingerprints can now be considered. His systematic collection of fingerprints from the Anthropometric Laboratory was at first mainly restricted to thumb prints of which he had about 2500 before he began to realise that the distribution of patterns was peculiar to a finger and that one could not apply the results from the thumb to the other fingers. From 1890 he began to take prints from all ten fingers and by 1893 he had enough material to produce his first and major contribution to the subject, a 200 page book entitled simply, *Finger Prints*.

The book is worthy of examination in detail as with it Galton established the importance of fingerprints in biological and criminological investigation. His subsequent work on classification and indexing represented little advance on the system put forward in this book.

After a general introductory chapter and a necessarily brief historical survey Galton proceeds to discuss the various methods he has employed to obtain clear fingerprints. He had observed that a beautiful impression, but without the advantage of permanence, could be obtained by the simple expedient of running the fingers through the hair and then pressing them on a window pane. By this means they were very slightly oiled and the hardness of the glass ensured that only the ridges left an impression. After many trials, he found that the best way to secure a permanent impression was to spread ink very thinly on a copper plate by means of a printer's roller, and then to roll each finger in turn on the plate and on to white card. It was in this form that fingerprints were filed in the Anthropometric Laboratory and it is in this way that they are taken today. The rolling of the finger ensures that the complete pattern is registered.

It is difficult to do justice to the ingenuity revealed in this the longest chapter of the book. It is reminiscent of the *Art of Travel* or even earlier inventiveness. He tells us how to construct a pocket apparatus and how to manage if we have left it behind, how to send inked slabs by post, how to use water colours and dyes, how to print from wax or soot-blackened

H

plates. Apparently after blackening the finger it has to be pressed on to an adhesive surface. Galton found stamp edging, luggage labels, pastel, glue, isinglass, size and mucilage all suitable. He continues :

'It was my fortune as a boy to receive rudimentary lessons in drawing from a humble and rather grotesque master. He confided to me the discovery, which he claimed as his own, that pencil drawings could be fixed by licking them; and as I write these words, the image of his broad swab-like tongue performing the operation, and of his proud eyes gleaming over the drawing he was operating on, come vividly to remembrance. This reminiscence led me to try whether licking a piece of paper would give it a sufficiently adhesive surface. It did so. Nay, it led me a step further, for I took two pieces of paper and I licked both. The dry side of the one was held over the candle as an equivalent to a plate for collecting soot, being saved by the moisture at the back from igniting (it had to be licked two or three times during the process), and the impression was made on the other bit of paper. An ingenious person determined to succeed in obtaining the record of a finger impression, can hardly altogether fail under any ordinary circumstances.'[16]

The function of the ridges is Galton's next concern. He points out that the ridge system runs over the whole of the hand and foot and does not exactly accord with the creases of the hand which are of interest to the palmist. The creases appear to be due to the characteristic flexing of the fingers and are more variable over a period of time and thus less reliable as means of identification.

At first Galton thought that the end organs for touch might be congregated more closely under the ridges than under the furrows; the power of tactile discrimination would then depend on the closeness of the ridges. He invoked the aid of the American psychologist, E. B. Titchener, who was then training at Wundt's psychological laboratory in Leipzig, to test this supposition, but the results were completely negative.

It seemed that the ridges might subserve another aspect of touch, namely that of enabling one to perceive the surface texture of an object. If a person is asked to close his eyes and to ascertain the nature of a surface by touch alone, he will rub the surface in different directions and with different pressures. Galton appeals to introspection :

'The ridges engage themselves with the roughness of the surface, and greatly help in calling forth the required sensation, which is that of a thrill; usually faint, but always to be perceived when the sensation is analysed, and which becomes very distinct when the indentations are at equal distance apart, as in a file or in velvet.'[17]

But the ridges' prime function was in connection with the sweat glands. In his autobiography Galton tells a story characteristic of Herbert Spencer who visited the Anthropometric Laboratory and had his fingerprints taken. Spencer began speculating on the role of the ridges in protecting the delicate mouths of the sweat ducts which he supposed to emerge in the furrows. Galton allowed him to argue his ingenious hypothesis at great length before gently pointing out that the ducts emerge not in the furrows but on the ridges.[18]

This raising of the exit of the ducts led, Galton thought, to the more efficient removal of sweat, but it is now considered that it leads to an efficient moistening of the skin, which, with the corrugation of the surface and lack of hair, serves as an antislipping device when grasping.[19]

Galton now turns to the patterns provided by the ridges on the digits. Any visual search of the patterns tends to be biased by imperfections in the printing process leading to some ridges appearing more prominent than others. The first necessity is to establish one or more points of reference in the patterns. What is now generally referred to as the 'triradius' is taken by Galton for this purpose. The triradius is located at the meeting point of three opposing ridge systems. Galton suggests tracing the ridges that emerge from the triradius with a fine pen in order to delineate the type lines of the pattern (See Figure 15.1).

The figure shows the three basic patterns of whorl, loop and arch adopted by Galton. These categories had been mentioned by Faulds in his original letter to *Nature* and provide the most obvious method of classification.

The typical *whorl* is distinguished by a concentric design with the ridges circuiting the core of the pattern. Any pattern with two or more triradii would fall into this category.

The *loop* is simpler in construction, there being one triradius and the ridges flowing out to the border of the digit instead of circling the core.

The *arch* has no triradius and is the simplest of the three patterns.

It must not be thought that all patterns fall into one of those three distinct categories. Galton discusses a fourth and fairly common compound pattern of whorls within loops and supplies drawings of various transitional forms that could be a source of difficulty.

Whorl   Loop   Arch

FIGURE 15.1 Galton's basic classification of fingerprints

A variety of cores may be found at the centre of whorls and loops. Galton enumerates the various possibilities, e.g., circles, ellipses, spirals, twists, plaits, single, double and multiple rods, plain and parted staples, and many more.

These details by no means exhaust the minutiae contained in a fingerprint. Each ridge runs its own particular course : it may join with another ridge, divide into two, begin or end abruptly and so on. It is these minutiae rather than the gross patterning which provide Galton with evidence for the permanence of a fingerprint.

This evidence is nearly all derived from Sir William Herschel's collection and consists of successive prints taken from 15 persons at various stages in their life span. Overall the prints cover the period from age 2 to age 80, the intervals between successive prints varying from 12 to 31 years. Galton marked 700 minutiae in these prints and in only one case was a change observed where a bifurcated ridge at age 2 became a single ridge by age 14. He concludes from his massive accumulation of evidence :

> 'There appear to be no external bodily characteristics, other than deep scars and tattoo marks, comparable in their persistence to these markings . . . The dimensions of the limbs and body alter in the course of growth and decay; the colour, quantity, and quality of the hair, the tint and quality of the skin, the number and set of the teeth, the expression of the features, the gestures, the handwriting, even the eye colour, change after many years. There seems no persistence in the visible parts of the body, except in these minute and hitherto too much disregarded ridges.'[20]

The value of fingerprints as a means of identification depends not only on the persistence of minutiae but also on the fact that the complex of these minute ridge details in a single fingerprint is not replicated by any other finger. It is unnecessary to follow Galton in his attempt to put a numerical value on the odds of obtaining two similar fingerprints from different fingers. His conclusion has never been seriously questioned that the odds are so enormously great against such a likelihood that confronted with two identical fingerprints no further corroboration is needed to accept their unitary origin.

The influence of heredity on fingerprint patterns was an obvious focus for Galton's interest and in two chapters of the book he reports the results of his investigations into family similarities and racial differences. Although Faulds must again be given the credit for mentioning both possibilities, it was Galton who obtained the first factual data.

In one typical investigation he examined the right index finger of 105 paired siblings and noted the incidence with which the nine possible combinations of pattern occurred (arch, loop, whorl, versus arch, loop, whorl). Comparisons were then made with unrelated persons paired at random. In this control series the frequency of the nine combinations was found to be almost exactly similar to chance expectation. The concordance of patterns in the case of the siblings was above chance and therefore must be due to the inheritance of pattern type.

Using similar techniques he examined parent–child resemblances and those of twins. He found a strong tendency to resemblance in the ridge patterns of twins, although there was no danger of mistaking the fingerprints of one twin for that of the other; however alike the patterns, the minutiae were quite different.

For his work on racial differences Galton had the co-operation of colleagues who provided him with Welsh and Negro fingerprints although he took prints from Basques and Jews himself. The only outstanding difference to emerge was between his English collection and the Jews, the latter having fewer arches and more whorls.

This finding has subsequently been confirmed, and with larger samples variations among the European populations as well as among more widely-separated peoples have been revealed.

Galton points out that differences among the educational and social classes within a culture might still exist in the absence of racial differences. But he found nothing.

> 'I have prints of eminent thinkers and of eminent statesmen that can be matched by those of congenital idiots. No indications of temperament, character, or ability are to be found in finger marks, so far as I have been able to discover.'[21]

Before fingerprints can be used for personal identification one further requirement is necessary : it is essential to have a method of indexing such that one can compare as readily as possible the print under inspection with one in the index. Galton's system entails classifying each finger into whorl, loop or arch (w, 1 or a). In the case of loops on the forefingers, the category is further subdivided into inner or outer (i or o) depending on the side of the digit to which the loop opens.

A person's formula can now be written by a sequence of ten letters, but the digits are not taken in order from thumb to little finger. It is more convenient to group them as follows : (1) the fore, middle and ring fingers of the right hand, (2) the fore, middle and ring fingers of the left hand, (3) the thumb and little finger of the right hand, (4) the thumb and little finger of the left hand.

Thus, the formula for Galton's own fingers would read : *wlw, oll, wl, wl.*

One hundred specimens taken at random from Galton's collection of five hundred were indexed by the method and Galton uses this material to illustrate the advantages of recording the direction of loops on the forefingers alone instead of either omitting it entirely or recording it for loops on all digits. In the first case too many entries would be recorded under the same heading, while the tedium of registering loop directions on all digits could lead to errors.

The largest group of persons (9%) had loops on all their fingers. By the method of recording loop directions on forefingers this category was broken down somewhat, but even so 4% fell in the category, *oll, oll, ll, ll*. Galton realised that a problem would occur with larger samples and suggests the classification of loops cores, or a count of the ridges between core and upper limit of the loop as further aids in distinguishing individuals within this common group. But he did not pursue the possibilities of such secondary classifications at the time. *Finger Prints* was the first extensive survey of the whole area and not a fingerprint indexing manual. Its deficiencies in the latter respect were to be remedied in the near future, but not by Galton.

The final chapter of the book is entitled, 'Genera'; in it Galton expounds his view that the different types of fingerprint pattern, loop, arch and whorl, can be considered similar to the genera or species of plants and animals.

> 'It has been shown that the patterns are hereditary, and we have seen that they are uncorrelated with race or temperament or any other noticeable peculiarity, inasmuch as groups of very different classes are alike in their finger marks. They cannot exercise the slightest influence on marriage selection, the very existence both of the ridges and of the patterns having been almost overlooked; they are too small to attract attention, or to be thought worthy of notice. We therefore possess a perfect instance of promiscuity in marriage, or, as it is now called, panmixia, in respect to these patterns. We might consequently have expected them to be hybridised. But that is not the case; they *refuse to blend*. Their classes are as clearly separated as those of any of the genera of plants and animals.'[22]

Galton shows that the variation about a typical loop takes the form of a normal distribution. He also claims, without supplying any evidence, that whorls also have a typical central form. But he makes no claim with regard to the arch pattern as he was unable to identify any distinct point of reference.

Now natural selection need play no part in influencing the construction of genera, 'internal conditions' acting by themselves being sufficient. When the internal conditions are in harmony with the external ones, as in long-established races, their joint effects will be to curb individual variability to a greater extent than either could do alone. But the normal distribution will not then be altered, the amount of variation will merely be reduced.

Galton's contention is that natural selection acts by favouring small mutations. Mere varieties will blend in the offspring who will regress towards their typical central form. Sports, on the other hand, will not blend; they provide new typical centres from which the offspring will radiate.

'A mere variety can never establish a sticking-point in the forward course of evolution, but each new sport, affords one. A substantial change of type is effected, as I conceive, by a succession of small changes of typical centre, each more or less stable, and each being in its turn favoured and established by natural selection, to the exclusion of its competitors. The distinction between a mere variety and a sport is real and fundamental. I argued this point in *Natural Inheritance*, but had then to draw my illustrations from non-physiological experience, no appropriate physiological ones being then at hand: this want is now excellently supplied by observations of the patterns of the digits.'[23]

One cannot accept the argument of this chapter in its entirety. His demonstration that certain aspects of the loop design are in rough accordance with the normal law of error is irrelevant to his contention that the three main types can be considered as genera. He needs to show that these same aspects belong to the other types as well. As the differences among the types appear to be qualitative and not quantitative he is unable to do this.

Secondly, it is not true that the different types never blend: the difficulty in classifying intermediate types is witness to this fact.

Lastly, the misinterpretation of regression is again an obvious shortcoming.

In October of the same year as Galton's book was published an official enquiry opened to consider the possible introduction into Britain of Bertillon's system of identification. On the suggestion of Sir Edmund Du Cane, the terms of reference of the Asquith Committee, as it was called, were extended to include a consideration of fingerprints. The committee of three were remarkably prompt in submitting their report which appeared in February 1894. In the four months they had visited Bertillon's and Galton's laboratories and conducted an exhaustive enquiry into Galton's techniques.

Galton's evidence to the committee takes the form of answers to over 100 questions posed by members of the committee who also asked him to supervise the taking of fingerprints at Pentonville Prison and to find particular fingerprints in his index system. Although he appears to have passed these tests with flying colours the committee was cautious in its recommendations; it was clear to them that his classificatory system was not easily capable of dealing with large numbers. If 25 000 prints were involved, as many as 1500 might fall into one class (all loops), while there would be several other classes each containing between 500 and 1000 prints.

'The sub-classification of the largest class, which Mr Galton at our suggestion carefully worked out, is very elaborate, and in the matter of the counting of the number of ridges in the loops, it seems to us open to some uncertainty; and we believe we are only following Mr Galton's own opinion in saying that it would not be desirable to adopt it for a very large collection if any better system is available.'[24]

No better classification was available at the time and the committee compromised. As the Bertillon system had, it was agreed, as nearly perfect a primary basis of classification as possible, it was to be introduced for that purpose. But Bertillon's secondary classification was less satisfactory. Height, length of little finger, and eye colour were involved in this further breakdown. Now measures of height are notoriously subject to unreliability; little finger length correlates with middle finger length, one of the primary measures; the classification of eye colour into one of the seven possible varieties requires much practice.

In view of these difficulties the committee advised the abandonment of Bertillon's secondary classification and its replacement by Galton's fingerprint index. Thus prisoners were to be measured according to the Bertillon system and their measurements and fingerprints entered on a card. The cards were to be sorted into Bertillon's 243 classes and placed in order within their class by means of Galton's fingerprint index.

This restricted application of Galton's index system was seen by the committee as possibly no more than an interim measure. They recommended the appointment of a scientific officer to the Convict Office whose duties were to include further investigation of the possibilities inherent in fingerprints.

However, Dr Garson, the anthropologist who obtained this appointment was in Galton's words, 'somewhat biased towards bertillonage', and little was done to follow the committee's recommendations.[25]

Nevertheless fingerprint records began to accumulate in the criminal files and Galton began to try to improve his method of classification. By 1895 he was ready to publish again and *Finger Print Directories* embodied his final thoughts on classification based on more than 2000 sets of prints.

The book is disappointing. The earlier classification of whorl, loop and arch is retained, with loops being subdivided into radial and ulnar, terms that now replace inner and outer. The order in which the digits were to be 'read' is changed to the natural order running from left little finger to right little finger. This change is designed to reduce errors but it leads to a reduction in the variety of initial letters in the index, as the little finger has less variety than the forefinger.

The troublesome group of all loops is now broken up by ridge counting which he had demonstrated earlier to the Asquith Committee. He claims that by this means his index can cope with 1000 sets of prints.

When the number is increased towards 3000 a secondary classification becomes necessary in order to deal with the large classes both of loops and whorls. Galton adds subscripts to the letters of the primary classification to indicate peculiarities in the core, ambiguities in classification, scars, etc. As there are 28 possible subscripts the process of classification becomes a fairly tedious operation and one liable to error.

This involved method was still to be used in conjunction with Bertillon's primary classes, so Galton had now achieved the possibility of classifying 243×3000, or approximately 700 000 individuals. (He would have been surprised to hear of the extent of modern fingerprint systems. In 1964 there were over 173 million sets of fingerprints contained in the files of the F.B.I.)[26]

Although Galton retained an interest in fingerprints until his death, his publications after 1895 were mainly of a popular nature. No change in the official criminal identification system resulted from *Finger Print Directories*, but then Galton had proposed none. The shift from bertillonage to fingerprints occurred first in India where the need for an efficient identification office was of course very great. In a semi-popular account of the trials of the colonial administrator in that country and in Egypt, Galton wrote:

'. . . while the natives of India and of Egypt have beautiful traits of character and some virtues in an exceptional degree, their warmest admirers would not rank veracity among them. It is not insinuated that false testimony is unknown in English courts of justice, or in England generally; indeed I find, on a rough attempt at a vocabulary (made for quite another purpose), that more than fifty English words exist which express different shades and varieties of fraud; but if a map of the world were tinted with gradations of colour to show the percentage of false testimony in courts of law . . . England would be tinted rather lightly and both Bengal and Egypt very darkly.*[27]

E. R. Henry, Chief of Police in Bengal, visited Galton's laboratory during leave in 1894. On his return to India he introduced the combination of bertillonage and fingerprints recommended for Britain by the Asquith Committee. Numerous letters from Henry to Galton culminate

* In another place Galton proposes Salonika as the centre of gravity of lying![28]

in a proposal to drop bertillonage and to classify all Indian criminals by fingerprints alone using a new classificatory system. The Indian government's agreement was secured in 1897. In 1900 Henry published details of his system and saw its introduction into England in 1901, prior to his appointment as Chief Commissioner of the Metropolitan Police. In the Henry system there are four main types of pattern : arches, loops, true whorls and composites. The *primary* classification depends on the distribution of whorls on the ten fingers. It is expressed in a most ingenious numerical formula. The *secondary* classification depends on the pattern type of the index fingers and more subordinate divisions are made using ridge counts.[29]

Unlike Garson, Henry was extremely active in conducting an efficient fingerprint bureau which served as a model for the police forces of other countries. The worldwide adoption of Henry's classificatory system has led to his identification with the discovery of the fingerprinting technique, while Galton's didactive role has been forgotten.

Another man who is popularly believed to have originated the practice of taking fingerprints for purposes of identification is Bertillon. It is a strange reversal of fortune that any credit should go to the Frenchman who appears never to have trusted the uniqueness of a fingerprint. Galton had written to Bertillon in 1891 suggesting the possibility of including fingerprints in the French system. Three years later Bertillon introduced the prints of thumb and three fingers of the right hand on the identification card, without attempting to classify them but treating them in the same way as scars or moles as possible supporting evidence of identity.

An error in Bertillon's textbook gives 1884 instead of 1894 as the date of his adoption of fingerprints and many readers may have been under the erroneous impression that fingerprints were in use in Paris previous to their use in England.[30] Furthermore an arrest of a murderer was made by Bertillon's department through fingerprint evidence as early as 1902, and this fact may have drawn publicity to Bertillon.[31]

Galton was unfair in claiming that Bertillon finally adopted fingerprints as his chief stock-in-trade and played the showman wherever he went, until people began to suppose the discovery had been Bertillon's.[32] On the contrary, it seems certain that Bertillon never accepted nor promulgated the view that fingerprints were superior to anthropometry as a means of identification.

A certain amount of ill-feeling existed between Galton and Bertillon. In a draft of a letter dated 19th May 1889 Galton writes with reference to a paper that Bertillon had published in April of that year :

'It was with no little surprise that I failed to find in your article the slightest allusion to my previous work although it covered almost the same ground as your own and was certainly not inferior to it either in its scope or its completeness of treatment. I trust that when you next publish upon the same subject, as I am pleased to see that you propose to do, the existence of my earlier memoir (5 December 1888) will not be entirely ignored.'[33]

It is not known whether the letter was sent or not. Bertillon appears to have been so involved with his method of classification that he was loath to give credit elsewhere however much it might be due. On the other hand, Galton may have felt some resentment over Bertillon's initiative in establishing an anthropometric laboratory prior to his own. It is, perhaps, poetic justice that Galton should have suffered at Bertillon's hands the same disregard that he had shown to Faulds.

It is impossible to single out any one man as essential to the development of the fingerprint system as a means of personal identification. Faulds was the first to publish anything on the matter and to draw attention to the use of fingerprints in tracing criminals from the scene of their crime. Herschel was the first European to put a system into operation and to produce evidence for the persistence of a fingerprint over long periods of time. Henry was responsible for the improvement in classification that led to its adoption by Scotland Yard, while Galton's own contribution was to bring together and strengthen the evidence that fingerprints could provide an ideal technique for personal identification. Although not in this field an originator, no unbiased examination of his publications can fail to allow him the status of a pioneer.

16

The 1890s

Finger Prints was Galton's last major technical book. He later somewhat regretted the amount of attention he had devoted to that topic, and it is clear that it drained much of his creative energy. The decade prior to 1893 had been a very productive one with an average rate of publication of eleven papers per year, but from that date his research output begins to decline and his writings fall off both in frequency and in extent.

Louisa's *Record* continues much as before with the old complaints about her health and narrowing social circle. Her brother, George, died in 1890 and her friend, Marianne North, in 1891. In 1892 Galton lost his colleague, H. W. Bates, who had served as Assistant Secretary of the Royal Geographical Society since shortly after the contretemps with Norton Shaw. Galton had always found Bates congenial, and many friendly letters were exchanged over a period of some twenty years. During this time Galton had been active in the work of the Society and it is now necessary to sketch in the background to his involvement in order fully to understand why he resigned from the Society in 1894.

We have seen something of Galton's many contributions to geographical affairs, and in particular his desire to further geography as a reputable science. One move to that end had been the institution of the medal scheme for schools; another was the promotion of lectures and research by a system of yearly awards. The situation within the Society when this latter scheme was put into effect is best described in Clements Markham's words:

'The "doctrinaire" element which had caused so much trouble in the time of Norton Shaw gained great strength under Sir Rutherford Alcock's weak rule. Francis Galton, through his activity and regular attendance, had once more acquired considerable influence in the Council of the Society. His aims were good but he had no tact and no idea of adapting his theories to the actual conditions. He had been reinforced by another doctrinaire in the person of Colonel Richard

Strachey, a retired Indian engineer officer who was a member of the Council of India . . . With all his scientific knowledge he was not sociable and did not understand how to adapt his theories to the actual conditions with which he had to deal any more than Galton did. So Galton and Strachey put their heads together and got Sir Rutherford Alcock to consent to a scheme intended to give a more strictly scientific turn to the Society's work. There was to be £500 a year set apart for scientific purposes; there was to be a Scientific Purposes Committee to spend it and there were to be lecturers on abstruse scientific subjects to cost £50 a piece.'[1]

Galton produced a pamphlet inviting requests from persons competent to engage in geographical research, map and instrument making.[2] £250–300 per annum was to be devoted to their support, the remaining money was to be used to pay for lectures in physical geography. Strachey gave the first introductory lecture and was followed by Dr Carpenter, who lectured on sea temperature, and Alfred Wallace, who discussed the comparative antiquity of the continents. But the lectures were not popular, and it was with some satisfaction that Markham reported the short life of 'this unpractical scheme' which was abandoned after two years.

Several futile attempts had been made by Galton and his earlier Presidents to interest the universities in geographical teaching. In 1886 a conference was finally arranged between Oxford University and R.G.S. representatives, including Galton, which led to the election of a Reader in Geography at that university. The Society agreed to pay half the stipend of the Reader, whose salary was to be £300 per annum, and in this manner a foothold was gained. The step into Cambridge did not occur until 1892 when the Society entered into a similar arrangement by helping to support a lectureship. Thus geographical teaching on a modest scale began at the older universities, although geography was still not recognised as an independent subject which could be read for a degree.

With Strachey's assumption of the Presidency in 1887 the 'doctrinaires' took complete control of the Society. It was Queen Victoria's jubilee year and the question of the eligibility of a woman as Patron of the Society was in many members mind. Strachey made a move to propose the election of women to the Society but Council could not agree and after eight months of discussion the topic was dropped. Markham now felt unable to continue as Secretary when so much out of sympathy with the Society's policy and he resigned in 1888. Douglas Freshfield, the other Secretary, continued in office and lent his support to Strachey and Galton. Grant Duff, another progressive, assumed the Presidency and all was ready to reopen the question of the admission of women.

The 'Duffer Council', as Markham termed it, now became involved in a long and complex wrangle over this issue which split the Society from top to bottom. Grant Duff proposed the election of fifteen well-qualified women as Lady Fellows. The motion was passed by a majority on the Council with Galton, Strachey and Freshfield supporting the President, and Markham and George Curzon in vociferous opposition. The dissentients refused to accept the Council decision and asked for a general meeting of Fellows at which a vote might be taken. They gauged the general opinion accurately, for at a general meeting on 24th April 1893 the motion that women should be eligible was negatived by 147 votes to 105. The Council thereupon decided that no more women should be admitted but that the twenty two who had by now been granted Fellowship should be retained. This compromise pleased neither side as was evidenced by the correspondence that ensued in *The Times*. As an example of the level of the debate, Curzon, later to be Viceroy of India and then President of the Society, wrote as follows :

'We contest *in toto* the general capability of women to contribute to scientific geographical knowledge. Their sex and training render them equally unfitted for exploration, and the genus of professional female globe-trotters with which America has lately familiarised us is one of the horrors of the latter end of the 19th century.'[3]

It is unnecessary to follow the intricacies of the ensuing moves and countermoves. A general referendum of all Fellows resident in the British Isles brought a decision to admit women. But the Council were reluctant to proceed without another general meeting, and when this was called the dissentients organised themselves so well that they carried the day. Grant Duff resigned in anger and was followed by Galton and Freshfield. Strachey retired and Markham was handed the Presidency. He offered Galton the Trusteeship of the Society, but Galton declined and took no further part in Society affairs.[4]

Markham successfully avoided becoming involved in the sex war, and it was not until 1913 that Curzon, having changed his mind in the interval, succeeded in having women admitted to the Society.

In his autobiography Galton makes no mention of this controversy but gives as the sole reason for his resignation his increasing deafness which made attendance at meetings useless. However, this disability did not provoke his resignation either from the Meteorological Council or from the Kew Observatory Committee. Indeed he served as President of the latter body from 1889 until 1901 and only retired when the Observatory was absorbed by the National Physical Laboratory. It seems much more probable that it was the controversy over the admission of women with the consequent destruction of the power of the progressives that led directly to his resignation from the R.G.S. It is difficult to believe that

Galton felt very strongly that women had a right to Fellowship of the Society, but he was led to vote as he did by his fellow progressives with whom on other issues he had so much in common. That he did not feel in accord with them on the present issue is clear from the fact, reported by Markham, that he fell out with Freshfield, who was the strongest advocate for the admission of women, prior to their resignation from the Society. Details of this quarrel are not, however, available.[5]

Galton's support for Lady Fellows is in any case hard to reconcile with his general attitude to women expressed or implied on other occasions. Having secured evidence from his anthropometric laboratory that women were inferior to men in their muscular powers and sensory acuity, Galton inferred from the supposed correlation between the latter ability and intellectual power that they were comparatively deficient in this respect also. It is therefore no surprise to find him extolling the virtues of separate educational establishments for women while denying them the right to universities as they were then conceived. Thus, in a letter to Edward Thorndike, Professor of Psychology at Columbia University, he states that the higher education of women either selects those who have a small probability of marriage or creates in them qualities which lessen that probability.[6] As under any eugenic programme the main function of intelligent women must be to bear children any factor preventing the exercise of that function could not be favourably regarded.

Galton was also antipathetic to women's involvement in political issues. He joined the Anti-suffrage Society and was even opposed to Louisa's sister-in-law, Josephine Butler, in her attempts to have the Contagious Diseases Act repealed.[7] As he commented in a letter to George Darwin:

'Josephine Butler joined her husband at Positano last night. Well, well! One can't talk to her about her favourite topics, holding as I do most diametrically opposed views in nearly every particular of faith, morals, and justifiable courses of action.'[8]

Aided by the average Victorian woman's conviction that she belonged to the weaker sex Galton had no difficulty in showing unfailing courtesy to women, and his denigration of their capacities perhaps went no further than was usual on the part of Victorian men.

His attitude to homosexuality may be mentioned at this point. Hesketh Pearson has reported a conversation he had with Galton about the merits of Oscar Wilde. Pearson asked Galton whether he had ever met Wilde.

'As a rule my uncle spoke in a gentle urbane manner, but there was almost a note of intolerance in his reply: "I used to see him occasionally, but I never wanted to make his acquaintance. He annoyed me by posing in elegant attitudes at a club I sometimes frequented. Everything about him seemed to denote a lazy boredom. I believe he was utterly insincere."

'This was the first time I had ever known him speak harshly of anyone, and his manner surprised me . . . Hamlet's words came to mind. "There is something in this more than natural, if philosophy could find it out".'[9]

What was in it was probably a reflection of Galton's whole attitude to femininity. His admiration for masculine men, whether explorers or scientists, has been hinted at earlier in these pages. Any man with feminine traits would be likely to arouse his hostility. But whether this dislike covered a deep fear of his own repressed femininity can only be conjectural.

During the year in which the troubles at the R.G.S. were at their height Galton's research work centred mainly around his fingerprint data. He did, however, fleetingly return to certain psychological topics that had been long in his mind. Thus we find him delivering a lecture at the Royal Institution on 'The Just-Perceptible Difference'.[10] The title refers to the unit employed to measure sensation, that is, the smallest difference in intensity that can be perceived between two sensations. He begins this lecture by referring to the work of Weber who had shown that each increment in sensation that was perceptible was a constant fraction of the absolute stimulus. Thus, a small increase in brightness can be detected if a light is dim, but a very large increase in brightness is required before a bright light can be seen to have changed. Characteristically Galton extrapolates from such simple situations as judgements of weight, brightness and the like to the more complex human condition.

'The result of all this is, that although the senses may perceive very small stimuli, and can endure very large ones without suffering damage, the number of units in the scale of sensation is comparatively small. The hugest increase of good fortune will not make a man who was already well off many degrees happier than before; the utmost torture that can be applied to him will not give much greater pain than he has already suffered. The experience of a life that we call uneventful usually includes a large share of the utmost possible range of human pleasures and human pains. Thus the physiological law which is expressed by Weber's formula is a great leveller, by preventing the diversities of fortune from creating by any means so great a diversity in human happiness.'[11]

Galton now turns to a problem that had escaped the attention of other psychologists. How do 'internal factors' affect our sensory experience? Imagination appears to be capable of magnifying weak external stimuli until they exceed the threshold of awareness. He illustrates this point by a personal experience. He had noticed in church that his deafness prevented him hearing the clergyman reading a prayer unless he followed the words in the prayer book. It was difficult to move to a nearer pew once the service had begun so he restricted his experiments to scientific meetings where a copy of the speaker's script was available to him. He tried moving forward until he was able to hear the speaker without having recourse to the printed version of the lecture. He found that he had to approach one quarter of the total distance separating him from the speaker to achieve this result. As the relative loudness of speech at the two positions would be as 9 is to 16, he concluded that his auditory imagination must be to a just perceptible sound as 7 (i.e. 16–9) is to 16. Thus the effect of imagination was to reach nearly halfway to the level of consciousness; if his imagination had been a little more than twice as strong it would have been able by itself to produce an effect indistinguishable from an actual sound, that is, he would in that case have experienced an hallucination.[12]

He now applies the idea of the just-perceptible difference to visual material. It is possible to imitate a drawn line by a series of dots; if these dots are spaced at a frequency of 300 to the inch a person of normal visual acuity at a viewing distance of 12 inches will perceive them as a continuous line. Galton tried reducing the number of dots and found that with as few as 50 dots to the inch he could produce an accurate representation of a facial profile. By this means he is then able to express the profile in code. For this purpose it is necessary to indicate the position of each dot in respect to its predecessor, which Galton achieves by means of a compass notation. Thus, if the second dot is immediately above the first it is said to be 'north'. Galton suggests the representation of sixteen compass points by the letters from 'a' to 'p', north to be represented by 'a', north-north-east by 'b', north-east by 'c', and so on.

He uses this system to provide an excellent copy of the profile of a Grecian woman copied from an ornament. Her profile was reduced to a string of 400 letters, or, for the purposes of a telegram, 80 words, which he reckons would cost about £8 to send from London to New York at that date.

Attempts to codify profiles continued to exercise Galton's ingenuity for the remainder of his life and he published twice more on the subject. In the first of these papers he adopts a completely different approach to that outlined above.[13] Certain cardinal points are now to be identified on a drawing of a profile: the hollow between nose and brow, the tip of the nose, the meeting of nose and upper lip, the upper lip, the lower lip, and the point of the chin. The distance between the first and last of these points, i.e. the brow to chin distance, is taken as a standard, and all subsequent measures are expressed in terms of this distance. Two axes are now drawn on the profile, the horizontal axis at the chin, the vertical axis from brow to chin. (See Figure 16.1.) The four remaining cardinal points can now be measured from these two axes, that is, their coordinates are drawn.

Using the coordinates of only two cardinal points, the nosetip and nose–lip junction, Galton was able to code 68 profiles with no two profiles having identical numerical values. He speculates that two additional points, the upper and lower lips, would have to be included to ensure the separation of 1000 profiles.

One problem in this system of coding arises from the omission of any information about the directions taken by the delineating lines between one cardinal point and another. Two people might be given very similar numerical classifications and yet look totally unalike with, say, noses of quite different shapes.

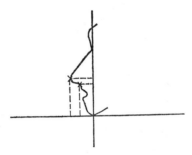

FIGURE 16.1   Profile coordinates

Galton provides a partial solution to this problem in his final paper on the subject written at almost the end of his life.[14] He retains the second system of numeralising with only a slight change : coordinates are obtained from the nose, nose–lip junction, and from the parting of the lips, instead of separately from upper and lower lip. Thus, he now has three cardinal points and six coordinates using the same axes as before.

The profile is now divided into seven sections from the brow to the point of the chin and a table is provided showing the variety of shapes that may be encountered in each section. He was satisfied with nine varieties for most sections of the profile, although ten were required for the bridge of the nose. The varieties in each section are numbered from 1–9, or 1–10, and the judge has to select the appropriate variety for each of the seven sections. He then expresses the result in a formula which consists of the six coordinate numbers followed by the seven sectional variety numbers.

It would obviously be an easy matter to arrange an index system based on these numerals, and Galton's claim that it would reduce the time spent in identifying criminals from a series of photographs was doubtless justifiable but never put to practical test. Indeed, it should be stressed that the system was never applied to photographs but only to drawings and its discriminatory powers were never investigated. The limitations are not surprising when Galton's age of 88 is taken into account!

In spite of the immense amount of patient trial and error that went into Galton's profile coding it must be regarded as one of his least successful pursuits.[15] Yet at the time it must have appeared to have at least as much practical potential as his earlier work with fingerprints. The construction of the recent Identikit picture probably owes its origin more to Bertillon's similar technique of the *portrait parlé*, where acquaintances of a suspect select from a more extensive collection of possible facial features the relevant items from which a portrait is built up.

To return to 1893, Galton gave his 'Just-Perceptible Difference' lecture in January of that year. In May another opportunity for psychological enquiry presented itself. A Signor Ercole called at Galton's house with a letter from the French psychologist, Alfred Binet. Ercole was acting as publicity manager to Inaudi, a young Piedmontese, who had an extraordinary facility in mental arithmetic and who had already been a subject of investigation by Binet and by the neurologist, Charcot. Galton arranged to test Inaudi in the presence of a few friends, who included George Romanes and Oliver Lodge. During the session Inaudi demonstrated his favourite feats of mentally subtracting two long rows of numbers and extracting square and cube roots from seven-figure numbers. Several techniques were tried to discover if Inaudi was using visual or motor imagery but the general consensus was that he was not and that Binet's conclusion, based on much more extensive investigation, was correct in ascribing his ability to an abnormally developed auditory imagination. Sums had to be given to Inaudi in the form of so many millions, billions, hundreds of thousands, and so on before he could work on them.

Galton does not appear to have been unduly impressed by Inaudi: his notes of the 'séance', as he called it, describe Inaudi as the possessor of calculating powers that do not exceed those of many bank clerks, although Galton admits that his memory for figures is prodigious. An interesting final observation in the notebook refers to the wearied look in Inaudi's eyes and brow, which Galton claims to have seen in other boy calculators.[16]

These scanty findings were never published; Galton must have known that Binet was about to publish on the matter and he was content to report his own findings in the context of a review of Binet's book which he wrote for *Nature*.[17]

The review also contains a reference to another psychological investigation completed a few months previously, details of which Galton had published in the first issue of the *Psychological Review*.[18] The purpose here was to discover whether arithmetic could be performed without the aid of visual, auditory or motor imagery. In preference to touch or taste, Galton chose to work with smells, hence the curious title of the paper, 'Arithmetic by Smell'.

He devised an apparatus by which a whiff of scented air could be presented to the nostril. He then taught himself to associate two whiffs of peppermint with one of camphor, three of peppermint with one of carbolic acid and so on. Next he practised small additions with the scents themselves and then with recalled imagery of them. He found he could easily abolish all visual and auditory associations and perform perfectly.

With these minor enquiries Galton's interest in psychology terminated. More substantial writings from the same year (1894) are concerned with the evolutionary process. In his 'Discontinuity in Evolution' he retraces much of the ground already covered in *Natural Inheritance* and in *Finger Prints* where he declared his opinion that evolution proceeds through the occurrence of sports. Two quotations from this paper will suffice.

'No variation can establish itself unless it be of the character of a sport, that is, by a leap from one position of organic stability to another, or as we may phrase it, through *"transilient"* variation. If there be no such leap the variation is, so to speak, a mere bend or divergence from the parent form, towards which the offspring in the next generation will tend to regress; it may therefore be called a *"divergent"* variation. Thus the unqualified word variation comprises and confuses what I maintain to be two fundamentally different processes, that of transilience and that of divergence, and its use destroys the possibility of reasoning correctly in not a few important matters.'[19]

That Galton felt himself to be alone up to this time in stressing the importance of mutations in bringing about evolutionary change is clear from his further comment.

'These briefly are the views that I have put forward in various publications during recent years, but all along I seemed to have spoken to empty air. I never heard nor have I read any criticism of them, and I believed they had passed unheeded and that my opinion was in a minority of one. It was, therefore, with the utmost pleasure that I read Mr Bateson's work bearing the happy phrase in its title of "discontinuous variation", and rich with many original remarks and not a few trenchant expressions.'[20]

The second paper is concerned with the part played by religion in human evolution.[21] It was published in the *National Review* in August 1894 and is noteworthy for its forcible argument and exemplary prose.

It was written as an answer to Benjamin Kidd's recent book *Social Evolution*, which had achieved wide popularity. Kidd had argued that human evolution had been brought about by the blind action of natural selection which involves a strenuous struggle for existence, a struggle that is pitiless to the individual and therefore repugnant to his reason. The paradox then arises that reason, which is an end of man's evolution, teaches him to withstand the law of the survival of the fittest and is thus anti-evolutionary in its effect. The solution of the paradox Kidd considered to lie in the interposition of altruistic sentiments, that is in the preference shown for the welfare of others to our own. These sentiments he ascribes to the result of religious belief which provides an ultra-rational sanction for moral conduct.

Galton takes issue with Kidd's definition of religion as being necessarily ultra-rational. In Galton's view there are three ways in which we can understand the word:

'A is that of J. S. Mill: "The essence of Religion is the direction of the emotions and desires towards an ideal object, recognised as rightly paramount over all selfish objects of desire." B is that of Kant: "Religion consists in our recognising all our duties as Divine commands." C is that of Gruppe, namely: "A belief in a State or Being which properly speaking, lies outside the sphere of human striving and attainment, but which can be brought into this sphere in a particular way, namely, by sacrifices, ceremonies, prayer, penances, and self-denial." '[22]

Kidd would refuse to accept A as sufficient and his paradox arises because he insists on the conditions contained in B or C. Galton, on the other hand, is content with A. Thus the paradox vanishes because

'the direction of the emotions and desires towards *the furtherance of human evolution*, "recognized as rightly paramount over all objects of selfish desire," can justly merit the name of a religion.'[23]

Although he does not mention the word 'eugenics' the remainder of his argument is devoted to an elaboration of the view put forward in *Human Faculty* that a eugenic programme may be invested with all the emotional impetus of a religious faith.

In order better to appreciate the part that a religion of this kind might play in human evolution Galton supposes the existence of a nation that has become disillusioned about its established B or C religion. He further supposes that the existing social arrangements are acknowledged to be failures and that various socialistic experiments had been tried but had been found to be ineffective owing to the moral and intellectual incompetence of the average citizen.

'There would then be a widely-felt sense of despair; there would be ominous signs of approaching anarchy and of ruin impending over the nation, while a bitter cry would arise for light and leading. A state of things like this is by no means impossible in the near future, even here in England, and therefore, it deserves some consideration as being something more than a merely academic question. In the imagined event, preachers of all sorts of nostrums would abound, mostly fanatics who could see only one side of a question, and on that account they would be all the more earnest in their opinions and persuasive to the multitude. I will endeavour to present in a clear light what one of these, a professed agnostic, might say.'[24]

With certain unstated reservations Galton now expresses his own views through the medium of his imaginary agnostic preacher :

'The mystery is unfathomed as to whence the life of each man came, whether it pre-existed in any form or not. The mystery is equally great, as to what will become of his life after the death of the body; whether it will be perpetuated in a detached form as some creeds say, whether it will be absorbed into an unlimited sea of existence, as other creeds assert, or whether it will cease entirely. As regards this life, there are also mysteries. Every act may or may not have been determined by previous conditions, but man has the sense of being free and responsible : he is accustomed to do and to be done by as if he were so, therefore we may provisionally believe that he is free and should act on that supposition. There is a further mystery as regards the cosmic conditions under which we live, for no assurance can as yet be obtained of any supernatural guidance, the facts alleged in evidence of its existence being more than counterbalanced by those that point the other way. We cannot, in consequence, tell with certainty whether human life is subject to an autocracy, or whether, at least for practical purposes, it exists as an isolated republic; but the latter appears at present to be the more probable, and should, therefore, guide our conduct. Each man's destiny during his life may then be viewed with propriety as depending entirely on his own physiological peculiarities and on his surroundings. He has, consequently, to conduct himself as a member of a free executive committee during his brief life, guiding his actions by whatever he can learn of the tendencies of the cosmos, in order to cooperate intelligently with what he cannot in the longrun resist.'[25]

Galton believes that the adoption of such a view would brace the character, just as dependence on an autocratic power would enfeeble it. Galton's political opinions now become apparent when he states that the main disadvantage of a socialist form of government springs from its paternalistic overconcern with the wellbeing of its citizens who learn to expect everything to be done for them and as a result have their faculties but half-developed.

'On the foregoing basis our agnostic might say, Let us consider what is peculiarly profitable and proper for man to attempt. One of the most prominent conditions to which life has been hitherto subject, is the newly discovered law of the survival of the fittest, whose blind action results in the progressive production of more and more vigorous animals. Any action that causes the breed or nature of man to become more vigorous than it was in former generations is therefore accordant with the *process* of the cosmos, or, if we cling to teleological ideas, we should say with its *purpose*.

'It has now become a serious necessity to better the breed of the human race. The average citizen is too base for the every day work of modern civilisation. Civilised man has become possessed of vaster powers than in old times for good or ill, but has made no corresponding advance in wits and goodness to enable him to direct his conduct rightly. It would not require much to raise the natural qualities of the nation high enough to render some few Utopian schemes feasible that are necessary failures now.'[26]

Before any form of artificial selection could be applied to the human race national customs would have to be modified. This step may not be as difficult as commonly supposed: an historical perspective reveals that national customs have changed to an incredible extent over periods of time; no custom that has ever prevailed in the past in a contented nation can be regarded as repugnant to human feeling; a custom established by a powerful authority soon becomes looked upon first as a duty and then as an axiom of conduct that is rarely questioned.

The following general programme is finally urged which may suffice as the basis of a national religion:

'(1) Of steadily raising the natural level of successive generations, morally, physically, and intellectually, by every reasonable means that that could be suggested; (2) of keeping its numbers within appropriate limits; (3) of developing the health and vigour of the people. In short, to make every individual efficient, both through nature and by nurture.'[27]

Another ten years were to pass before Galton's eugenic proposals were to attract attention; in 1894 they were completely ignored. Louisa closes her account of that year on a sombre note.

'With us a quiet but happy decline, blessed in our home when so many around us of our intimates are bereft of their dearest. I often feel a dread of what may come to either of us after 41 years of happy unison, but let us trust our heavenly Father that he will help us at all times, as he has hitherto helped us.'

The following year was unusually barren for Galton. *Finger Print Directories* appeared in May and completed his fundamental contributions to the subject. A book review, two letters to *Nature*, and a circular to naturalists requesting information about the transmission of strongly marked peculiarities, these constitute the whole year's output. He was ill for the first quarter of the year and had not yet come to terms with his increasing deafness which made him reluctant to attend public meetings. A few extracts from Louisa's very long entries for 1895 and 1896 will provide an outline of this and the following year.

'1895. Always it costs an effort to record the year till I am ashamed of my idle procrastinations and now I am determined to begin the task. The beginning of the Year 95 began with great cold and we had a trying time. Frank fell ill Jan 10 and kept half invalided till the 21st when Dr Chepmell came and advised rest and quiet. He attended the Meteorological Council on Feb 6 and became worse on the 9th, with Gastric Catarrh Dr C. called it, any way, he was very miserable and thought himself very bad and for a few days I was very uneasy about him as he got weaker and made no progress, so he went on better and worse up to March 7th when the weather and he both improved and he began to go out and about in a careful way and was able to attend a Kew Comttee on the 29th . . . Cambridge gave Frank a D.Sc. Degree and Montagu gave us his delightful hospitality for the event, May 13–16, two of the days were perfection of Spring, Cowslips, Buttercups, Blue Sky etc. . . . We left England on July 3 for Nauheim to see Arthur and Emily, who were taking a course of Baths, and thence to Garmisch . . . We staid more than a month, the scenery was very fine, but there was a drawback, i.e. so little shade and the weather was very hot with frequent clattering storms, still I enjoyed it and so did Frank. We left Garmisch on Aug 12th for Munich, caught cold there and had no heart for Munich sights . . . We thence travelled to Nüremberg, which we both loved . . . We were nearly baked there and nearly burnt at Rothenburg our next place, both were full of old world mediaeval life, with Churches and Fountains and Rath Haus and Picturesque bits of Buildings . . . Only being able to get food uneatable for hardness, we gave but 2 nights to Rothenburg, tho' full of interest and sketches to attract, but we frizzled and journeyed on to Frankfort and Bonn and home on Aug 27. I soon fell sick from the great heat and a horrid crossing and we had to give up Corby to our sorrow and spent a prosaic fortnight at Tunbridge Wells, again very hot, but we had nice drives in the fair English country. Hop Gathering going on everywhere. We went to Emma on Sept 21 till the 30th and then home to a clean arranged house, soon to be disarranged by the Installation of the Electric Light, which has been a great boon to us thro' the dark winter days . . . The year has ended sadly for England threatened by United States, Venezuela, the Ashantis and War rumours from the Transvaal. Well we have a strong government under Lord Salisbury and favourable auguries for Public working since the summer Elections . . .

'So ends the year, I feel towards it as a real friend; having learned to withdraw from many pleasures and attractions, I find great happiness in the quiet enjoyment of home life, in Books, in Home Duties and friends and in the promise of success and useful distinction of the young members of the family and in the hope of keeping their love. One great regret is the barrier Frank's increasing deafness occasions in our intercourse and of this he had little idea; it also makes society difficult, so that we are not fit to mix in any large circle.'

'1896. In the early year, Frank had a good deal of cold and cough and thought himself very bad, so we went to Hastings . . . and to Emma for Easter. Soon after our return Darwin announced his engagement to Miss Cumberland, which gave me a pang to think how soon a dear life companion can be forgotten for the sake of comfort and companionship.* . . . Frank fell ill on the 19th June with Gastric Catarrh like he had before, but much milder and it might have been nothing, had he not gone to Kew with Temperature 102 so with guests and nursing I was nearly done for. Chepmell advised Wildbad as a cure and tho' still very weak but in perfect summer weather, he and I left England July 10 and began the treatment July 14.'

It was while undergoing the course of hot baths at Wildbad with 'its relaxing accompaniments' that Galton wrote his one substantial paper of the year. Four years previously the planet Mars had made a near approach to earth and the newspapers had been full of speculation over the possibility of exchanging visible signals with that planet. The general conclusion was that little could be learned about the Martians other than that they were intelligent enough to make signalling equipment. Galton believed at the time that such a limitation in our knowledge of the planet

---

* This was Darwin Galton's third marriage, his second wife having died in November 1894.

was unjustifiable and thought out the ground plan of the article he finally wrote up at Wildbad. It was published in the *Fortnightly Review* under the title, 'Intelligible Signals Between Neighbouring Stars.'[28] His original manuscript exists in the *Galton Archives* and consists of sixty pages of notes, reduced to eight printed pages in the published paper. The reduction in length involves the omission of much humorous fantasy about the appearance and behaviour of the Martians; the *Fortnightly* article is restricted to an account of a signalling code that could be used to provide this and much other information.

Galton begins with the assumption that a similar knowledge of mathematics is possessed by the two communicating parties, and it is on this basis that he describes a method whereby pictures can be constructed from a series of flashed signals. Three lengths of signal are involved, which are termed 'dot', 'dash' and 'line', and by their use he shows how a system of numerals can be communicated. The simple operations of addition, multiplication, etc., are next transmitted. These are followed by an astronomical message giving three series of numbers, which are speedily interpreted by the observers to refer to the mean distances between the sun and the five major planets, their respective radii and their times of rotation on their axes. This message leads to comprehension of the code word for 'radius', and the Martians now proceed to send the value of 'π' and then to embody the two symbols in the familiar groupings of 'πr^2' and '$2\pi r$'. The code words associated with these formulae are those for 'area' and 'perimeter'.

Now came eight new words, the names of various regular polygons, proceeding from triangle, square, pentagon up to a 24-sided figure. The nomenclature of the polygons is communicated by prefacing their names with the number that corresponds to the number of their respective sides in conjunction with the word for perimeter. So that there will be no mistake, numbers corresponding to their areas are presented in a separate sequence.

We now reach the final stage where Galton shows how pictures may be transmitted using the technique he had devised for his earlier paper on just-perceptible differences. The 24-sided polygon has each side labelled with a letter and these letters are then used to indicate direction to the nearest 15 degrees, thus a = 0°, b = 15°, c = 30° and so on. With this technique the Martians are able to send pictures made up of equal length 'stitches', each one at a particular angle to its predecessor. A picture of the planet Saturn requires 105 stitches, while their outline of the North American continent is sufficiently accurate for recognition with 88 stitches.

Galton calculates that this stage could be reached in less than $2\frac{1}{2}$ hours of actual signalling time. When once picture-writing has been achieved the list of named objects could be indefinitely extended. Symbols for parts of speech other than nouns would be more difficult to communicate : for example, the past tenses of verbs would have to be explained by pictures of objects in motion.

'It would be tedious, and is unnecessary to elaborate further, for it must be already evident to the reader that a small fraction of the care and thought bestowed, say, on the decipherment of hiero-glyphics, would suffice to place the inhabitants of neighbouring stars in intelligible communication if they were both as far advanced in science and arts as the civilised nations of the earth at the present time. In short, that an efficient inter-stellar language admits of being established under those conditions, between stars that are sufficiently near together for signalling purposes.'[29]

Modern attempts to devise a 'celestial syntax' are similar to Galton's in that they begin with elementary arithmetical concepts although they typically develop into more sophisticated forms employing symbolic logic.[30]

Before leaving the subject, a sample from Galton's notes contained in his Wildbad notebook may be quoted.[31] Although his description of the Martians and their life is obviously based on the appearance and behaviour of ants, it is hardly necessary to read between the lines to perceive the personal relevance of much of his fantasy. His description of the Martians might almost be a self-description :

'Their sense of hearing is almost deficient but their eye power is acute and ample. Their senses of taste and especially that of smell are highly discriminative and so is that of touch.'

He continues,

'But above all the rest in delicacy of touch are the antennae which during conversation between social equals and friends are in constant movement and touch. They convey not only as much as ordinary men and women can convey by grasps, squeezes and gentle pressures of the hand, but quite as much as any "thought reader", or rather any gesture interpreter, can make out from them . . . Their public utterances are by gesture language like that of deaf mutes who may be seen in operation any Sunday in the pulpit in the Deaf Mute Chapel in Oxford Street.'

Besides males and fertile females there are neuter females whose responsibility it is to look after the eggs and subsequent larvae and who perform a eugenic selection at various stages in the growth of the off-spring. Galton describes the characteristic behaviour of each type :

'The fertile females queen it over the males. They are far superior to any of them in size and strength and such is the constitution of the sex that while their figures and imposing demeanour excite some fear in the weaker males they also invoke their chivalrous loyalty and attachment. The fertile females rarely associate; they do not necessarily dislike one another but they are too jealous and self-contained for friendship.

'The neuter females possess no quality that we should call loveable : they are devoid of generosity and they have but little originality, but they continually occupy themselves with work of some sort however petty and cannot keep still for a moment. Whatever passion they possess is socialistic—they certainly care little for themselves and much for the community, and though very obstinate in small things are practically directed by the males with the concurrence of the queens, towards whom their attitude of mind is peculiar. It is one neither of personal love nor of personal loyalty but rather one of respect for the temporary representative of a necessary institution which prevents the community from becoming extinct.

'The males are warriors. They have all the truly male virtues and all the male defects of our race; they are the salt of the community, both morally and intellectually. They look on the neuters as "hands" in a factory, not particularly disliking them, but as members of a different social stratum, who have to be dealt with in matters of business but not as friends.'

It is a pity that Galton never worked up these rough notes to write a more detailed account of his Martian fantasy. The exercise served as a preliminary to a later long Utopian novel which was refused publication but which survived in fragmentary form.

After the efficacious Wildbad treatment Galton felt very well; his only complaint, at the age of 74 was that his brain power was not as vigorous as formerly and that he could not work so quickly. He and Louisa now felt able to undertake a long tour in Switzerland and Germany and did not return home until September. Louisa closes her account of 1896 with these words, the last she was to write in her *Record* :

'We have alas lost our good friend Dr Chepmell, he has resigned and left London for good, we shall miss him sadly; in Frank's illnesses, I felt his support firm and satisfying, indeed after 22 years of his wise advice, I cannot imagine how we can live without him and his kind wife. So surely do good things come to us and pass from us, and I try to be thankful enough for the innumerable blessings we have had even with the pain of feeling them gone. So ends our year, not an eventful one, but a calmly happy one ending with a merry Xmas at Spencers', the young folk full of life and ambition.'

The following year's entry is in Galton's handwriting and with it the *Record* concludes.

'1897. It is with painful reluctance that I set down the incidents of this fatal year, and do so on Jan 6, the anniversary of the day when I first became acquainted with dear Louisa at the Dean's house, next door to our own, at Dover in 1853.

'In the early part of the year I was more of an invalid than she was, but we had some pleasant outings together, as to Nansen's great meeting on Feb 8. Chiefly on account of my persistent asthmatic cough, we went to Bournemouth, partly to be near Dr Chepmell. He told me to go to Cauterets or Royat . . . We had had alarming news from time to time of Emma, from middle of Feby onwards. At length she was better and we went to her April 20–23. Louisa was well enough for some small festivities, a tea party, her last, on May 7, and the military tournament. June 21 Jubilee day, we went with Mrs Lyell to the Athenaeum and had excellent places and Louisa was not overtired. Next day Bessy came to tea and Mrs Lyell. 26th I went to Naval Review, L. not strong enough to go with me. July 14 left for Royat, slept at Boulogne: next day, a weary waiting till 10 p.m. at Lyons Station but night journey comfortable, Louisa not suffering at all. July 24th Puy de Dôme with Mr Livett and a young lady. L. remained in the garden at the auberge while we went up and she had luncheon set out. I never saw her more pleased and nicer as a hostess than when we came down . . . Aug 3 L. awoke with diarrhea—we all had it—but recovered. Very sultry. On Sunday 8th she was apparently quite well and half packed for a start next morning. Monday 9, she had had bad diarrhea and sickness in night, not worse than frequently before. Tuesday Aug 10 was worse, I had Dr Petitin, who made light of it, but said he wd. come the next morning. Wed 11th she was very ill . . . L. wrote a postcard to prepare Chumley in case she was wanted. In afternoon very weak indeed, continual vomiting. Thursday 12 worse and in a very serious state. That night, or rather on Friday morning early at 2 h ¾, she quietly passed away.'

At 5 a.m on the Friday morning Galton wrote to his sister Emma:

'I had a nurse to sit up through the night who woke me at 2½ a.m. when dear Louie was dying. She passed away so imperceptibly that I could not tell when, within several minutes. Dying is often easy! . . . I cannot yet realise my loss. The sense of it will come only too distressfully soon, when I reach my desolate home . . . Dear Louisa, she lies looking peaceful but worn, in the next room to where I am writing, with a door between. I have much to be thankful for in having had her society and love for so long. I know how you loved her and will sympathise with me.'[32]

The next letter is dated two days later.

'Dearest Emma,

I hardly know how much time has really passed since I wrote, for each day has been divided into two or three by intermediate dozes or sleeps and the last week has been terribly long. Dear Louisa was buried with simple decorum yesterday in the cemetery of Clermont-Ferrand. The day was lovely, the mountains looked singularly imposing, the English Chaplain officiated, and a most kindly and tactful clergyman, Mr Jennings . . . came with me to the grave . . . You will easily understand how desolate I have felt, but thanks largely to Mr Jennings' tact, consideration and manly sympathy I have already perhaps gone through the bitterest period, though I look forward with dread to the most painful task of distributing her well known clothes etc. Dearest Louisa, I have very much to be grateful for, but our long-continued wedded life must anyhow have come to an end before long. We have had our day, but I did not expect to be the survivor. . .

'Of course Bessy will understand that in writing to you I write also to her . . . I had not written either to Darwin, Erasmus or Milly, but have done so today. Excuse more for I must husband strength.

Ever very affectionately,
Francis Galton.'[33]

Louisa was 75 when she died. The postmortem examination revealed that her stomach was barely one third the natural size and the outlet was extremely constricted, the result, it was thought, of her serious illness 19 years previously.[34]

However, there is little doubt that she vastly exaggerated her own ill-health during almost the whole of her married life. That was the opinion of her younger relatives who became so tired of her periodical preparations for death that they did not immediately accept the reality when it occurred.[35] Louisa inevitably found relief from her complaint whenever she was able to escape to the Continent, the result she thought of a change of food and increased sunshine. But when she was abroad she was also free of domestic responsibilities and she had her husband's constant companionship, a state of affairs that did not exist in London where he was perpetually busy with scientific meetings and club life. Galton also enjoyed their foreign tours, mainly because they provided the leisure in which he could draft out new projects. But the intellectual life of a foreign spa could not bear comparison with that of the Athenaeum, and after a month or two of undemanding routine he looked forward more eagerly than did Louisa to a resumption of town life.

Her bouts of illness and his were typically sequential: Louisa would fall ill when her husband was busily occupied away from home; he would relinquish his work to stay at home with her; Louisa would then improve while he would begin to sicken. Like two yoyos out of phase they would alternate into and out of sickness. Strong though the psychological component must have been, it served a different function in their two cases: Louisa used illness as an attention-seeking device; her husband's bodily symptoms appeared whenever he was prevented from working. The story of his married life is largely a story of his work, and every psychiatrist is familiar with the obsessive-compulsive patient whose constant temptation is to overwork and whose illness is exacerbated by a more leisurely routine.

It is probably true that the marriage would have been happier if they had had children. Louisa was obviously fond of her nephews and nieces, although the feeling was not always reciprocated. Thus, one nephew has claimed that none of the children liked Aunt Louisa as she was so mean with her money. At Christmas time when Uncle Frank would slip each of them a newly-minted sovereign he would have to warn them not to mention it before their aunt.[36] But outside the family Galton himself was not in the least generous and although his largesse to his young relations may have led them to like him, he showed little interest in them. He never took a child on his lap, while Louisa's frustrated maternity led her to mother the young ones and take a real interest in their development.

As an intellectual companion Louisa was in the early years ideal, but she was unable to follow and to encourage him in his later statistical and hereditary research. Galton's enjoyment of literature, other than fiction, was shared by his wife whose literary opinions were valued by writers and poets.[37] They appear to have had few other interests in common. Some of the entries in Louisa's *Record* bear witness to her visual sensibility which was much greater than her husband's. He seems after his marriage to have abandoned sketching, in which he had shown some talent, and he was never interested in art. (When his portrait was painted, he spent his time counting the number of brush strokes made by the artist, the result being reported in yet another letter to *Nature*!)[38] Louisa also enjoyed music, which Galton actively disliked. Their political opinions were similar and strongly conservative. In religion they were fundamentally at variance, but Galton never let his disbelief in Christianity obtrude and he attended church and conducted daily prayers for the household without demur.[39]

His kindness of heart and unselfish disposition were possibly worked on by Louisa to gain her own ends. But no hint was ever dropped by Galton to indicate that the marriage was not happy. He rarely referred to the personal in conversation or in correspondence, and Karl Pearson, who knew both marriage partners, maintains a similar reticence in his biography, although his scanty references to Louisa imply a certain disapproval.

In her later years her invalidism must have exacerbated her self-concern and his deafness increased her isolation. Thus her death broke what had become a loose tie, and after the initial shock Galton took on a new lease of life in the company of an ideal companion.

XIII Sister Emma

XIV   Sister Bessy

17

Eugenics

Galton did not return from Louisa's funeral to an empty house: his nephew, Frank Butler, agreed to live with him until some more permanent companion could be found. The obvious choice was Eva Biggs, the grand-daughter of his late sister Lucy. Eva was unmarried and quite prepared to take on the role. Before plans were made final Galton took her on a probationary two month holiday to Spain in early 1899, followed by a long stay in Egypt from December of that year until the summer of 1900. Both tours were highly successful and more exciting than those holidays of the recent past, marred as they were by Louisa's semi-invalidism.

Eva was a great success from the very first, as Galton makes clear in a letter from Granada to his sister Emma.

'Eva is a capital companion, always cheerful and punctual and interested; moreover she always sees the good side of things and of persons.'[1]

In an enclosed note, Eva tells how her uncle is faring:

'I don't suppose he ever mentions his cough, so I will tell you about it. It has never actually gone yet, but it is much better and he looks very well and is tremendously energetic, the Spaniards all ask me his age, and won't believe it when I tell them [77] . . . He is really a perfect person to travel with, because he never fusses or gets impatient *or* grumbles if we are kept waiting ever so long for food or luggage.'

Galton's letters from Spain to his sister are long, detailed and cheerful. In one he describes a bull fight in Madrid:

'In the bull fight here, that I saw, one of the six bulls leaped over the barrier twice, among the people behind it. Also two of the bull-fighters were knocked over and one of them hauled himself clear of danger by laying hold of the animal's tail and coming out between his hind legs. It was a terrible looking business, but neither were really hurt and both did some very plucky feats after a little rest. Two of the horses were lifted wholly in the air with their riders, *all* four legs being in each case off the ground at the same time. A bull when he has been tired is not so quick as the *quickest* of the men, who will let him rush at them without any red cloak or other thing to distract attention, but he seemed to me quicker than most of the men. Many bulls jump and bound in the air like buck rabbits. It is a very strange scene altogether, and certainly a fascinating one . . . How I wish you had health and strength still to enjoy travel . . . I trust that Darwin's betterment continues.'[2]

Darwin Galton had recently suffered a stroke and his health remained precarious until his death at the age of 89 in 1903. Emma may not have been able to travel abroad but she was still extraordinarily active—another letter refers to a bicycle tour she had just undertaken at the age of 88. She was following Galton's Spanish tour in Bradshaw's Continental Railway Guide and on a map, and writes :

'Your letters are most interesting—but let me hear about your cough. I do hope you find Louisa's grave, all nice and tidy.'[3]

Galton's route took him through Clermont-Ferrand, where he visited the grave, and he reached London in May. He immediately obtained medical opinion about his throat, as he reports in a letter to Emma.

'The people I have talked to, insist that I ought to spend future winters in sunny lands; that my throat and cough are well-known ailments of advanced life, and that there is no option but to go. Of course, I shall inquire further, but this prospect has to be faced, so I have arranged gradually to drop my only two scientific ties to London, and to keep myself free to go next winter. Then again, of the brief six months between now and then, I may be ordered to Royat to give the throat more strength, for though all regular cough has long since gone, I feel the tendency is still there, and I might have a bad attack of it if I got a cold. One must submit. Forgive this long story. I am quite well now and full of engagements.'[4]

Summer was spent at Royat, as predicted, and in touring Switzerland with Eva as a companion. He returned in time for the British Association meeting at Dover where he contributed a short paper.[5] Entitled 'The Median Estimate', the paper is concerned with a method by which the proper damages to be awarded by a jury can best be estimated. Galton applies a technique he had devised earlier by which one can obtain the median and the quartile from any two percentiles.[6] Galton requires the jury to vote with regard to two possible sums of money that might be appropriately awarded as damages. The jury would not vote for actual amounts but for a sum less than the smaller, greater than the larger, or for an amount in between. Assuming a normal distribution of judgements Galton then shows how a median can be calculated.

The application of statistics to judicial matters was little more than a passing interest of Galton's but he had written one or two short communications on this topic which should not escape all mention. Thus, a paper in *Nature* on the variations in terms of imprisonment showed quite clearly that there were marked preferences among judges for sentences of certain lengths.[7] In over 10 000 sentences made in terms of months the maxima occurred at 3, 6, 9, 12, 15, 18 and 24 months with none at 17 and few at 11 or 13. Judges seem to calculate in quarterly units and to vary among themselves in their personal fancies for particular numbers. Galton concludes that justice will not be done if the sentence passed on a criminal is determined by the judge's unconscious preferences rather than the criminal's deserts.

In a contribution to a debate on corporal punishment in the correspondence columns of *The Times* Galton has more to say on making the punishment fit the crime.[8] He claims, without citing evidence, that there is a correlation between the bluntness of moral feelings and those of bodily sensation; thus the 'worse' the criminal the less sensitive he will be to pain. Weber's law can be applied to pain : a blow would have to be quadrupled in force in order to double the pain experienced.

'In a Utopia the business of a Judge would be confined to sentencing a criminal to so many units of pain in such and such a form, leaving it to anthropologists skilled in that branch of their science to make preliminary experiments and to work out tables to determine the amount of whipping or whatever it might be that would produce the desired results.'

Finally, a short comment on capital punishment may be noted. Galton appears to have been an advocate of death by hanging and he took the opportunity provided by the death of Samuel Haughton, the originator of the modern method, to write a piece for *Nature*.[9] Haughton, as a mathematically-trained Divine with medical qualifications, was a peculiarly well qualified person to determine the length of the 'long drop' necessary to break the neck without decapitating the victim. But Galton found an error in his formula, which had omitted to take into account the increased girth of the neck muscles in fat men, an error which he repairs in this note to *Nature*.

He spent the autumn after the British Association meeting at home, but the next letter to Emma, dated 15th December 1899, was written from the Hotel Karnak at Luxor in Egypt. He and Eva were now comfortably cabined on a large Nile steamer en route to Aswan.

'Some of the people, indeed most of them, are nice or fairly nice. Today we had an excursion of seven hours including about 14 miles of donkey ride. I was lucky in beast and in saddle, and enjoyed it as much as any horse ride that I can recollect. The wonders are just unspeakable . . . the only drawback here is that we are aloof from the natives. In a dahabieh one lived among them. On the other hand the convenience of river steaming is great.'[10]

In January they spent a week with Professor Flinders Petrie, whose party was excavating a site 100 miles away. Living quarters were in mud huts and food was restricted to tinned meat and jam with native bread. In spite of his age Galton enjoyed it immensely and in a lively letter to Emma and Bessy describes the experience as one of the most interesting he has ever had. The heat during the day was no problem but the intense cold at night necessitated sleeping in socks, jersey, drawers and pyjamas. A sketch of his sleeping arrangements shows that he had to use three double blankets, a thick rug, a thick morning coat, a dressing gown, a shawl, an Ulster coat, an overcoat and a pillow on top in order to feel comfortably warm.

'The Nile is so low and shrinking so fast, that it will possibly stop the running of the steamers soon. It has shrunken in width, since we left a week ago, to about that of the Thames at Westminster, if I judge rightly; during the inundation it must be quite seven miles broad. Such a difference! There are very few English tourists on account of this terrible war, very few Americans and hardly any of other nations. The church today was not $\frac{1}{4}$ full . . . Eva is painting studies of the changes in colour of the only remaining chameleon [a pet which Galton brought back to London] . . . I feel very painfully the contrast between my enjoying myself lazily in this glorious climate and the sufferings of our countrymen at the Cape, but cannot think of anything I can *now* do usefully, except get thoroughly well.'[11]

Two more letters survive, written from Luxor and Helouan, from which the following extracts are taken.

'We are all right, and have taken a bit of a walk this morning; only four miles, but the roads are *very* dusty and tiring. Donkey riding is the correct thing, but we wanted exercise . . . We have had no war news today. How glad Bob [a son of Millicent Lethbridge, Galton's

niece] must be that he was not fatter, else the bullets that went
through his clothes might have gone through his body. Nelson's
cocked hat was once shot through; had he been a taller man, he
would have died long before Trafalgar.'[12]

'We are quite well, but are bothered by the difficulties in the
way of simply camping out in the Desert, which I thought had been
overcome, but are still going on. According to what an excellent
dragoman now assures us, there is always a risk with the Bedouins
unless elaborate and costly arrangements are made . . . There is something of interest nearly every day since I wrote. On Friday I drove
with Professor Schweinfurth in one carriage, and Admiral and Mrs
Blomfield in another, across the desert and along the valleys for two
or three hours. Then we picknicked, botanised and geologised for
four hours and then returned, after seeing (1) an ancient barrage, built
of stones, in the time of the Early Pharaohs, to dam the water when
it ran down the creek, (2) some *true* Jericho roses, of which I send a
a few. If you dip them in water they begin to expand, almost
instantly, into a true flower . . . From my window I can see at least
seven large Pyramids (including those of Gizeh). I am told that it is
possible to count seventeen of them . . . We went in the evening to
an Arab concert. The singers were five Syrian Jewesses. The room
had a gallery round it with muslin draperies, behind which the
native ladies sat. The few European ladies and all the men sat below.
Eva was taken up to see the native ladies and says they had very
good and pleasant manners and some were very picturesque. They
were all powdered on the faces, and the eyes and eyebrows were
much painted; not much perfume . . . I am anxious for home news
of all sorts, for Gifi is a little later than usual with his letter; so also
is Frank Butler. I only know that Chumley [the maid at Rutland
Gate] has been successfully operated on. I hope that Darwin is
recovering steadily, and that you, Bessy, have lost your cough at last.
Mine is practically gone for present purposes, but I know that bad
English weather would soon bring back that particular abomina-
tion. As for you dear Emma you do not often tell me about yourself, so I imagine ups and downs. I hope Erasmus is now quite
right.'[13]

By summer Galton was back in London and arrangements were made
with Eva's father for her to take up permanent residence at Rutland Gate.

'My dear "chattell" Eva,
   I am delighted that you are now to be altogether transferred to
me and to take charge of my household henceforth. You weren't
transferred *quite* as a "chattell" (I don't know how many *t*'s or *l*'s

there are in the word) as I said in my letter to your father "if she acquiesces . . . " So you will now have "42 Rutland Gate" at the bottom of your visiting cards. I am very glad we shall meet so soon.'[14]

The summer was mainly spent in preparing a lecture for the Royal Anthropological Institute. The Institute had invited him to give the second Huxley Lecture and to receive the Huxley Medal, which he did in the October. He took the opportunity provided by this forum to return to eugenics and to add what was essentially a further chapter to his books on heredity. He begins with a familiar theme : the application of the normal curve to human variation. On this occasion he divides the population with regard to their 'civic worth' into five classes (R, S, T, U, V) above mediocrity and five classes (r, s, t, u, v) below mediocrity. He now compares his own grading with the figures produced by Charles Booth in his study of the population of London. Booth's lowest two classes of criminals, loafers, and casual earners, who are 'inevitably poor from shift-lessness, idleness or drink,'[15] constitute Galton's classes t, u and v, classes whom Galton considers to be made up of 'undesirables'.

'Many who are familiar with the habits of these people do not hesitate to say that it would be an economy and a great benefit to the country if all habitual criminals were resolutely segregated under merciful surveillance and peremptorily denied opportunites for producing offspring. It would abolish a source of suffering and misery to a future generation, and would cause no unwarrantable hardship in this.'[16]

Booth's most worthy class encompasses all of Galton's T, U, V and above. The problem, as Galton sees it, is to distinguish these individuals when they are children. If one accepts Dr Farr's estimate that the child of a country labourer is worth £5 to the nation, then one might calculate the worth of a high-grade baby in thousands of pounds. Galton now introduces the concept of regression to show how a population reproduces itself. In spite of his usual and unlikely assumption that the ancestors would have been more mediocre than the parents, his general conclusion can stand : that is, if we wish to increase the output of, say, V-grade offspring the most profitable parents to encourage will be those of the V-class. While it will take 35 V-class parents to produce 6 V-class sons, it will take 5000 R-class parents to do likewise. Thus, to economise our eugenic endeavours we should concentrate on the superior grades.

Galton sees no serious difficulty in classifying and giving diplomas to young people if there were a strong demand for it. But the correlation between youthful promise and mature performance had never at that time been established.

'Neither school-masters, tutors, officials of the Universities, nor of the State department of education, have ever to my knowledge taken any serious steps to solve this important problem, though the value of the present elaborate system of examinations cannot be rightly estimated until it is solved.'[17]

Galton thinks it likely that the mental powers of a youth will continue with him until old age, but other faculties may arise and 'alter the balance of his character'. Assuming that the correlations are high, Galton suggests the encouragement of early mating by the provision of low cost housing for promising young couples, the requisite financial aid being derived from new charitable organisations and wealthy patrons.

'All I dare hope to effect by this lecture is to prove that in seeking for the improvement of the race we aim at what is apparently possible to accomplish, and that we are justified in following every path in a resolute and hopeful spirit that seems to lead towards that end . . . To no nation is a high human breed more necessary than our own, for we plant our stock all over the world and lay the foundation of the dispositions and capacities of future millions of the human race.'[18]

Once again there was little response to his proposals, either among the anthropologists or among the general public. The Anthropological Institute was content to publish an abstract of his lecture and the full version in *Nature* attracted no attention.[19] He had to wait until 1904, when the newly founded Sociological Society provided him with a platform and an eminent series of co-contributors, before he received some of the publicity he desired.

One further event of 1901 may be briefly noted : the founding of a new journal, *Biometrika*. The proposal came from Weldon and was enthusiastically received by Pearson who enlisted Galton's support as a consulting editor. The need for the journal was obvious as the Royal Society, following the lead of their main referee, Bateson, had rejected an important paper by Pearson, who was probably correct in his assumption that most biological work on statistical lines would suffer a similar fate in the future.[20]

Galton gave £200 to help the journal off the ground[21] and contributed a short introduction to 'Biometry' for the first issue. Here he explains that the journal is intended for those interested in the application to biology of the modern methods of statistics.

'The new methods occupy an altogether higher plane than that in which ordinary statistics and simple averages move and have their being. Unfortunately the ideas of which they treat, and still more the many technical phrases employed in them, are as yet unfamiliar. The arithmetic they require is laborious, and the mathematical investigations on which the arithmetic rests are difficult reading even for experts; moreover they are voluminous in amount and still growing in bulk. Consequently this new departure in science makes its appearance under conditions that are unfavourable to its speedy recognition, and those who labour in it must abide for some time in patience before they can receive much sympathy from the outside world. It is astonishing to witness how long a time may elapse before new ideas are correctly established in the popular mind, however simple they may be in themselves. The slowness with which Darwin's idea of natural selection became assimilated by scientists generally, is a striking example of the density of human wits.'[22]

The journal was envisaged as a clearing house for ideas, by means of which research workers could receive assistance and criticism. Galton even proposed the provision of a data depository in which authors should lodge their raw results to enable others to check their conclusions and to rework the material in different ways.

He concludes with this definition of the goal of the new science :

'The primary object of Biometry is to afford material that shall be exact enough for the discovery of incipient changes in evolution which are too small to be otherwise apparent. The distribution of any given attribute, within any given species, at any given time, has to be determined, together with its relations to external influences. This affords a standard whence departures may be measured and the direction and rate of their progress ascertained . . . The organic world as a whole is a perpetual flux of changing types. It is the business of Biometry to catch partial and momentary glimpses of it, whether in a living or in a fossil condition, and to record what it sees in an enduring manner. It is an after-process to combine these glimpses into a continuously changing scene, much as some tumultuous procession is made to live and move again by means of a "biograph". . . Biology could soon be raised to the status of a more exact science than it can as yet claim to be, if each of many biometricians would thoroughly work out his own particular plot, although these plots may be very far indeed from occupying the whole of the area that admits of being directly explored.'[23]

The journal was a most successful venture and served as an outlet for many important contributions by Karl Pearson and his students. In later years it lost its biological applications and became the pre-eminent vehicle for statistical theory.

Galton contributed one technical paper to *Biometrika* in 1902. In it he calculates the relative value that should be proportioned to first and second prizes in any competition. He bases this calculation on a knowledge of the average interval between the first, second and third man in a competition between n individuals. As Pearson points out in a comment[24] after Galton's paper this was the first occasion on which a population was considered not as a continuous distribution but as one in which there were finite differences between its members when they were arranged in order of intensity on a given characteristic. In a group of 100 individuals the difference between, say, the 50th and 51st will be only one tenth of the difference between the 1st and 2nd. That is, the mediocre are crowded together, the extremes are widely separated.

Galton finds that the ratio of first prize to second prize should be about 3 : 1, the greater the number of competitors the more accurate this ratio. Little attention appears to have been paid to this finding; prizes continue to be allocated on the basis of some subjective estimate of their suitability.

Galton wrote little else in 1902. The year passed quietly with the winter being spent in Italy in order to recuperate from bronchitis. While on holiday there he received both good and bad news. First, came the news that he had been awarded the Darwin medal of the Royal Society for his 'numerous contributions to the exact study of heredity and variation'.[25] Hard on the heels of this letter came more good news, this time from his brother-in-law, Montagu Butler, Master of Trinity College, Cambridge.

'My dear Frank,

Many happy duties have come to me in my life, but few happier than that of now informing you, by the direction of our Council, that we have today elected you an Honorary Fellow of the College under the provisions of our Statute XIX, as a "person distinguished for literary and scientific merits". . . .

'Need I say how it delights me to think that all your long and brilliant services in the cause of many a science should again link you in the later years of your life with the College, to which, as I know, you have always been so loyal?'[26]

Galton's delight was evident in the letter he immediately wrote to Emma.

'I was sure that you and Bessy and Erasmus would all be glad to hear of the Darwin Medal. But there is even more to tell, of even yet more value to myself. They have elected me Honorary Fellow of Trinity College, Cambridge, which is a rare distinction for a man who has not been previously an ordinary fellow, or who is not a professor resident in Cambridge. The beautifully conceived and worded letter of Montagu Butler, the Master of Trinity, of which Eva has made a copy for you to keep, will explain much of this . . .

Is it not pleasant? This is the sort of recognition I value *most* highly. All the more so, as I did so little academically at Cambridge, in large part owing to ill health. But I seem to owe almost everything to Cambridge. The high tone of thought, the thoroughness of its work, and the very high level of ability, gave me an ideal which I have never lost.'[27]

It will be noted that Darwin Galton was excluded from the members of the family who would be delighted at the news. Although Darwin took little interest in his youngest brother's career, the probable reason for his exclusion on this occasion was his precarious state of health. He lived less than two months longer. Galton writes to Millicent Lethbridge in the January of 1903:

'The post has this instant brought me tidings from Emma of Darwin's death. It is more of a shock to me than I could have expected, for many happy incidents of early days crowd the memory. His was a complex character, veins of clay and veins of iron and gold. He was loved by many and admired by many—not, as you know, by all . . . Darwin used to have a terror of death and was extremely moved if he heard unexpectedly of the death of any one he knew. Now he is initiated into the secret and has passed the veil. He is well out of suffering and the sense of incapacity with absence of hope for a better bodily condition . . . When you write—after Darwin's funeral is over—please tell me what your family news is, and what seems the consensus of opinion about Darwin. Emma will I am sure send me Leamington newspapers.'[28]

Among other obituaries Galton received a cutting from *The Warwick and Warwickshire*. Darwin's wealth and position as Deputy-Lieutenant and magistrate for the county had made him a dominant local figure:

'Perhaps the most familiar recollection the villagers of Claverdon have of him is his riding past their houses wearing the well-known white felt hat and carrying in his hand the umbrella which he always took with him in his constitutionals on horseback. The extreme courtliness of his manner and speech did not, however, prevent him from occasionally seeming arbitrary in his action and it was well for him and for them that his dependents were able to thoroughly appreciate the noble qualities he possessed. Eccentricities he was guilty of, meanness never.'[29]

Galton returned home in the Spring of 1903 to a house that had been radically changed in his absence. Convinced that stuffy rooms exacerbated his asthmatic cough he had ordered the house to be stripped of wallpaper and carpets in the hope that he might be able to spend more of the year in London. But by the autumn the cold and fog drove him abroad again and he left with Eva for a first visit to Sicily.

He had been able to do little work in London, although an article he contributed to the *Daily Chronicle* is worthy of mention. Entitled 'Our National Physique : Prospects of the British Race. Are We Degenerating ?' it contains an amusing account of Sandow's competition for the best developed of his pupils which Galton surprisingly witnessed. But Galton's serious purpose in writing the article was to ask whether the British race was equal to its 'Imperial responsibilities' and how far it might be capable of improvement.

> 'There is no question that the pick of the British race are as capable human animals as the world can at present produce. Their defects lie chiefly in the graceful and sympathetic sides of their nature, but they are strong in mind and body, truthful and purposive, excellent leaders of the people of the lower races.
>
> 'The lower middle class of Britons are quite as efficient by nature . . . but they are of coarser fibre than the Latins. Our average holiday-maker and cheap-excursion tourist is proverbially unprepossessing.'[30]

Even the physiques on display in the Sandow competition were a source of disappointment to Galton, who considered them ill proportioned and too heavily muscled to be aesthetically pleasing. Before the State should allocate money for the improvement of the physical condition of the nation, extensive enquiries needed to be made. Perhaps an improvement in nurture would bring about the desired change. That possibility should be tested in the light of research into child development. On the other hand, it might be that nature was of pre-eminent importance. And that view must be tested by a programme of eugenic research. It was in this cautious vein that Galton concluded his article.

No details remain of his Sicilian tour, but in a letter to Weldon he mentions a plan to spend a few days in the Lipari Islands among pumice-stone, active volcanoes and members of the Mafia who had been convicted of murder, a visit to which both he and Eva were looking forward with the keenest interest.[31] It is easy to imagine what Louisa's reaction would have been to this proposal.

Galton kept the last letter he was ever to receive from Emma which she wrote to him just before Christmas. It typically contains financial and domestic news :

> 'My House smells of Puddings and Cakes—and now the Mincepies will be made. Bessy will have a large Party on Xmas Day . . . The

Darwin family have had to pay some duty on Breadsall Lodge left by Sir F. Darwin to his unmarried daughters. He died 40 years ago, and Aunt Darwin 34 years ago and they know nothing about any receipts. They should write, as Annie Sykes did, to the Papers.'[32]

By April 1904 Galton and Eva were back at Rutland Gate and he was preparing to visit Emma and Bessy, aged 92 and 96 respectively, at Leamington. But the cold was almost more than he could bear and the visit was cancelled as he was confined to bed. He occupied himself by preparing a lecture on eugenics at the request of V. Branford, the very active Secretary of the newly-formed Sociological Society. A large and distinguished audience was attracted to the meeting which was held at the London School of Economics on 16th May. Galton persuaded Karl Pearson to take the chair and felt well enough to deliver the lecture in person. Entitled 'Eugenics, its Definition, Scope and Aims,' the lecture was a very clear exposition of what was meant by the term and of what was initially involved in the practice. He defines eugenics as 'the science which deals with all influences that improve the inborn qualities of a race; also with those that develop them to the utmost advantage.'[33] However, in his lecture he restricts himself to a consideration of the former alone and omits discussion of the broader environmental issues.

The essentials of eugenics are easily determined: Galton claims that all would agree that it was better to be healthy than sick, vigorous than weak, well fitted than ill fitted for one's part in life. That is not to say that there should be uniformity. There are conflicting ideals which must be allowed expression within a Society.

'Society would be very dull if every man resembled the highly estimable Marcus Aurelius or Adam Bede. The aim of Eugenics is to represent each class or sect by its best specimens; that done, to leave them to work out their common civilisation in their own way.

'A considerable list of qualities can be easily compiled that nearly every one except "cranks" would take into account when picking out the best specimens of his class. It would include health, energy, ability, manliness and courteous disposition.'*[34]

Galton optimistically foresaw one of the functions of the Sociological Society to be the active furtherance of eugenics through various specified procedures. They might disseminate knowledge of the laws of heredity, especially those of an actuarial kind. They might conduct enquiries into

* The inclusion of the latter two qualities strikes one as a little odd until one recalls Galton's usual omission of any reference to womanly virtues. Sir Francis Darwin subsequently made the perceptive comment that Galton's list of attributes might have served as a self-description.[35]

the fertility rates of different social groups, for there was reason to suppose that these relative fertilities were associated with national rise and decline. One very appropriate function of the Society would be to collect data from large and thriving families to discover the circumstances under which they had originated. A 'Golden Book' containing the names of these eugenically favoured individuals might in time rival *Who's Who* or Burke's *Peerage*. A study of the influences that affect marriage was badly needed. Galton thought social influences and not personal preferences were of pre-eminent importance in marriage choice, a topic to which he was to return in his next address to the society.

Finally, the Society would need to be persistent in arguing for the national importance of eugenics. Three stages would need to be passed through: the first that of familiarising the public with the topic, the second that of persuading people of the importance of implementing eugenic proposals and the third that of introducing eugenics into the national conscience like a new religion.

'What Nature does blindly, slowly, and ruthlessly man may do providently, quickly and kindly. As it lies within his power, so it becomes his duty to work in that direction; just as it is his duty to succour neighbours who suffer misfortune. The improvement of our stock seems to me one of the highest objects that we can reasonably attempt. We are ignorant of the ultimate destinies of humanity, but feel perfectly sure that it is as noble a work to raise the level in the sense already explained, as it would be disgraceful to abase it. I see no impossibility in Eugenics becoming a religious dogma among mankind, but its details must first be worked out sedulously in the study. Over-zeal leading to hasty action would do harm, by holding out expectations of a near golden age, which will certainly be falsified and cause the science to be discredited.'[36]

Galton's paper was followed by a long and general discussion in which Galton did not take part on account of his deafness. Among the speakers were Weldon, Benjamin Kidd, and H. G. Wells. Written contributions came from Bateson, G. B. Shaw and many others.

Wells made a most thoughtful if critical contribution. He pleaded first for a much fuller analysis of 'human faculty' to provide us with true hereditary elements. Galton's assumption that energy and ability were unitary qualities may not be correct; they may be analysable into simpler constituents. Wells took particular issue with Galton over the latter's implication, in his discussion of differential fertility rates, that criminals should not be allowed to breed. In Wells' views the criminal might well prove to be the most energetic and intelligent member of his family, the one who was attempting to escape from an impossible environment.

Of the other contributors, Shaw was predictably the most controversial :

'[Men and women] select their wives and husbands far less carefully than they select their cashiers and cooks'.

Whereas in the eugenic future, polygamy would be in order for the outstanding male :

'It seems a natural loss to limit the husband's progenitive capacity to the breeding capacity of a single woman.'[37]

Shaw's later proselytising of the eugenic cause was not to be looked upon by Galton with much favour : he was too extreme and deliberately provocative, while Galton was preaching caution to elicit public acceptance.

Galton's dismissal of this discussion, which he read later in print, as 'wishy-washy' was perhaps an immediate response to what was on the whole a negative reception to his paper.[38] But although the sociologists were no more persuaded into action than the anthropologists had been, the meeting was a success in drawing a response from many eminent men, which in turn led to good press coverage.

Galton spent the summer of 1904 at Royat in the company of Millicent Lethbridge. Mrs Lethbridge includes a short account of this trip in her 'Recollections of Francis Galton' which she prepared for Karl Pearson on Galton's death.[39]

'The heat was terrific and I felt utterly exhausted but seeing him perfectly brisk and full of energy in spite of his 82 years, dared not, for very shame, confess to my miserable condition. I recollect one terrible train journey, when, smothered with dust and panting with heat, I had to bear his reproachful looks for drawing a curtain forward to ward off a little of the blazing sun in which he was revelling. He drew out a small thermometer which registered 94°, observing : "Yes, only 94°, Are you aware that when the temperature of the air exceeds that of blood heat, it is apt to be trying." I could quite believe it! By and by he asked me whether it would not be pleasant to wash our face and hands. I certainly thought so, but did not see how it was to be done. Then, with perfect simplicity and sublime disregard of appearances, and of the astonished looks of the other occupants of our compartment, a very much "got-up" Frenchman and two fashionably dressed French-women, he proceeded to twist his newspaper into the shape of a washhand-basin, produced an infinitesimally small bit of soap, and poured some water out of a medicine bottle, and we performed our ablutions—I fear I was too self-conscious to enjoy the proceeding, but it never seemed to occur to him that he was doing anything unusual.

'He half-killed me by his energy at Royat. We used to sally forth at 4 a.m. and take a walk before the heat of the day. That was really enjoyable, but I felt by no means enthusiastic when we started off again when the sun was at its highest, and walked and trammed wheresoever it was hottest. He always chose the sunny side of the road, but occasionally I rebelled and left him to his sun while I walked in the shade. He really was a salamander! I can see him now, sitting at his work-table in the window at Royat, with the broiling sun streaming down upon his bald head. Even to think of it is almost enough to give one a sunstroke.'

A few weeks after their return from Royat Galton received the news of the death of his sister, Emma. According to Mrs Lethbridge, Emma's death was a great blow to Galton, who described the remainder of the family as like a wheel that had lost its tyre. Emma with her weekly letters had certainly kept them all in touch, and her domesticity and continuous support had a maternal quality that Galton had long appreciated.

After much discussion between Galton and Millicent Lethbridge a design and inscription for Emma's grave was decided, and an unsuccessful attempt was made to grow South African hyacinths there. This flower, *Hyacinthus Candicans*, was an appropriate choice, it had been named the *Galtonia* by a French botanist in Galton's honour—and to Galton's amusement as he had no claim to the association.[40]

Galton was still active in research. He followed up his lecture to the Sociological Society with an investigation into the abilities of the kinsfolk of Fellows of the Royal Society.[41] The results of a questionnaire sent to all F.R.S.'s requesting information about any 'noteworthy' kinsfolk confirmed Galton in his old belief that exceptionally gifted families did exist and that it would be feasible to make a register of such families, as he had proposed in his lecture.

But Galton knew that he was no longer capable of the sustained effort needed for comprehensive data collection and analysis. He needed more direct assistance than could be provided by Weldon or Pearson, who in spite of their enormous energy were too heavily committed to their academic duties to do little more than correspond. For some years Galton had been putting aside a reserve of money to be used for scientific purposes after his death; he now determined to draw on this fund to endow a research fellowship. He called on his acquaintance Sir Arthur Rücker, who was Principal of the University of London, and in a sequence of events which must be unparalleled for speed of execution by any large academic institution Galton's proposals were put into writing, passed by the Academic Council, modified by a small committee and confirmed by the Senate within the course of a week.

Karl Pearson was a member of the small committee which modified Galton's original proposals. He recalls that most of their time was spent in redefining what Galton had termed 'National Eugenics'. Galton favoured a broad definition similar to that contained in his lecture to the Sociological Society, but the committee preferred a narrower definition to which Galton finally agreed and which he later adopted himself. By 'National Eugenics' the committee meant :

'The study of the agencies under social control that may improve or impair the racial qualities of future generations either physically or mentally.'[42]

Galton gave the University £500 a year for three years, but with the possibility of a permanent endowment if the plan proved satisfactory. A Research Fellow was to be appointed at £250 a year (a comparable stipend to that of a good College Fellowship), an Assistant at £100 a year, and the remainder was to be used to cover expenses. University College provided rooms in Gower Street, the premises being called at Galton's request the 'Eugenics Record Office'.

A problem arose over the formal standing of the Research Fellow *vis-à-vis* Karl Pearson who was conducting a vigorous research programme in his Biometric Laboratory at University College. Rücker was quite explicit in a letter to Galton that if the Fellowship was to be established at University College Pearson would either dominate the holder or quarrel with him.[43] The problem was solved by keeping the Biometric Laboratory quite separate from the Eugenics Record Office, and Galton was careful never to consult Pearson about the eugenic research he was undertaking. A small Advisory Committee was formed to help Galton run the office but Pearson was not included.

The advertisement for the Fellowship attracted six applicants* and, although the man Galton most favoured was not appointed, he was well pleased with the Committee's choice of Edgar Schuster, who took up the appointment in January 1905. By February Galton had drawn up a programme of subjects for eugenic enquiry and was prepared to read it to the 'So-so,' as he called the Sociological Society, with Schuster to stand by in case he broke down. But Galton's main purpose in addressing

* Whether any of the applicants were misled by the strange wording of the advertisement is unknown. Rücker had altered the Committee's definition of eugenics by the substitution of the word 'moral' for 'mental' and thus it appeared in the advertisement.[44]

the Society on this second occasion was to contribute his views on the factors influencing marriage choice, an obvious fundamental in any eugenic scheme. This paper was entitled 'Restrictions in Marriage' and that is how Galton conceptualised it : marriage was never a matter of the free choice of a member of the opposite sex; societal restrictions were universal.[45] There was nothing very original about the anthropology contained in the paper, Galton relied heavily on Frazer and Westermarck, but the message was timely in the eugenic context.

Galton begins with an acount of various marriage customs : some societies are monogamous, some endogamous, some exogamous, some have even more complicated restrictions. Our own society have various degrees of kinship within which marriage is prohibited. None of these restrictions can be considered instinctual, but each is based on social expediency, hallowed by religion and enforced by law.

'Persons who are born under their various rules live under them without any objection. They are unconscious of their restrictions, as we are unaware of the tension of the atmosphere. The subservience of civilised races to these several religions, superstitions, customs, authority, and the rest, is frequently as abject as that of barbarians.'[46]

Galton points out that as we are impelled by similar motives to other races, a knowledge of their customs can help us. When the objects of eugenics become recognised as worthy goals it should not prove difficult to instil the view that non-eugenic unions are taboo and should be looked upon with an abhorrence similar to that with which we regard incestuous relationships.

However, Galton does not believe that eugenics can ever receive the sanction of recognised religion. In that respect it is similar to certain other cardinal features of modern civilisation.

'Religious precepts, founded on the ethics and practice of olden days, require to be reinterpreted to make them conform to the needs of progressive nations. Ours are already so far behind modern require-ments that much of our practice and our profession cannot be recon-ciled without illegitimate casuistry. It seems to me that few things are more needed by us in England than a revision of our religion, to adapt it to the intelligence and needs of the present time. A form of it is wanted that shall be founded on reasonable bases and enforced by reasonable hopes and fears, and that preaches honest morals in unambiguous language, which good men who take their part in the world and who know the dangers of sentimentalism may pursue with-out reservation.'[47]

The memorandum outlining a programme for eugenic enquiry was also communicated to the Sociological Society at the same meeting*. Without going into detail we may note that the first item on Galton's list was the compilation of a biographical index to gifted families, and it was with this particular task that Edgar Schuster began his term as Research Fellow. Galton further suggests the importance of collating biographical material from families distinctly below average in health, physique and intelligence, including those with members in prison. The latter line of enquiry would serve to establish whether the breeding of habitual criminals should be restricted, as he had averred in his Huxley lecture.

Other actions by the State and by public institutions were to be examined carefully for their eugenic significance. Besides criminals, the feeble minded were an obvious source of concern.

'Aid given to institutions for the feeble minded are open to the suspicions that they may eventually promote their marriage and the production of offspring like themselves. Inquiries are needed to test the truth of this suspicion.'[49]

Public funds used to subsidise higher education should not be wasted on those intellectually unable to profit by it. The expectation that aid given to the more capable would have a eugenic effect needs to be checked. A further wide field for enquiry is into the effects of indiscriminate charity which Galton believes to be notably non-eugenic.

In advocating detailed research into the influences furthering or restraining marriage Galton omits to distinguish between marriage and procreation, as though the latter is an inevitable consequence of the former. In all his eugenic writings he avoids any reference to contraception, probably because he found the subject distasteful but possibly because he did not wish eugenics to be associated with the struggles of the pioneers of birth control.

Galton's two papers were again the centre of vigorous discussion. The four anthropologists who commented on his marriage paper were in agreement with his views that the most varied restrictions in marriage have been contentedly accepted. Westermarck wished to go further than Galton and to prohibit all marriages that did not have the approval of a doctor! But the twenty six contributors of written comments on the papers were not so favourable. Many doubted the efficacy of imposed marriage restrictions, love being too strong a passion to be restrained. In his reply on this point Galton regrets that he did not distinguish in his lecture between two

---

* Only Havelock Ellis saw the joke in making public a programme of eugenics on 14th February, St Valentine's Day.[48]

stages, that of slight inclination for another person and that of falling in love, for it was the first of these with which he was concerned.

> 'Every match-making mother appreciates the difference. If a girl is taught to look upon a class of men as tabooed, whether owing to rank, creed, connections, or other causes, she does not regard them as future husbands and turns her thoughts elsewhere. The proverbial "Mrs Grundy" has enormous influence in checking the marriages she considers indiscreet.'[50]

The other main source of discontent was with the broader issue involved in any positive eugenics programme, the issue discussed in Galton's 1904 paper, namely that of deciding on the qualities for which people should be bred. Galton answers the objections simply by stressing that he seeks 'all round efficiency in physical, intellectual (including moral), and hereditary qualifications.' In any case, he believes that the best qualities are largely correlated.

> 'The youths who became judges, bishops, statesmen and leaders of progress in England could have furnished formidable athletic teams in their time. There is a tale, I know not how far founded on fact, that Queen Elizabeth had an eye to the calves of the legs of those she selected for bishops. There is something to be said in favour of selecting men by their physical characteristics for other than physical purposes. It would be decidedly safer to do so than to trust to pure chance.'[51]

Galton took a break in Italy during the Spring of 1905. On his return home he found a letter requesting him to serve as President of the British Association in 1906. But he had no hesitation in refusing.

> 'I cannot stand even a moderate amount of flurry. It is of no use for me to fight against impossibilities. Long since I have learned to renounce many tempting pleasures, and must do so now. The only chance I have of doing useful work during the remainder of my life lies in doing it quietly and living very simply much like an invalid, and in never undertaking to tie myself to a day when I might prove quite unfit.'[52]

He was kept fairly busy throughout the summer superintending the work of the Eugenics Record Office. Schuster was finding the administrative load too heavy to handle on his own, and an assistant, Miss Elderton, was appointed with the title of Secretary. Galton was a little uneasy about entrusting any form of academic work to a woman, although he was to change his mind with regard to Miss Elderton, who later made substantial contributions to research in eugenics.[53]

Schuster's main occupation was to sort through the questionnaires returned in Galton's earlier study and to select those from F.R.S.'s who had at least three noteworthy kinsmen. He then compiled brief biographies of these sixty-six families while Galton wrote a long preface for the resulting book, *Noteworthy Families*. The manuscript was ready for the publisher in September, as Galton explains in a letter to Millicent:

> 'My little book is as troublesome as an ague. I thought it was off my hands but it has bothered me up to this instant, when I sealed up the MS in a packet to go by post to Murray. And still there are odds and ends left and revises to come, etc., etc. But it is comparatively calm now. And it is such a small book after all. My friend F. H. Collins, who is a prince among proof correctors but cannot now leave his arm-chair, has been giving all his working time last week to putting Schuster's contribution into better shape. The material was good but the arrangement too higgledy-piggledy.'[54]

By October Galton was ready to escape the English winter and was preparing to leave for the French resort of Pau.

> 'I had a stern reminder not to delay, in the form of a sudden severe shivering for nearly a couple of hours on Wednesday morning. The *amplitude* of the shiver was remarkable and interesting, my hands shook through a range of fully 7 if not 8 inches.
>
> 'I think now, what with Schuster's willing help and Miss Elderton's business-like ways and the Advisory Committee, the Eugenics Office ought to run on its own legs while I am away . . . I dare not give a previous day to Leamington [to visit Bessy]. Every ounce of strength must be reserved for the Pau Journey, but Eva will go to Bessy for a day.'[55]

No sooner was he settled in Pau then he was planning to write a book on eugenics. Dr C. W. Saleeby, an ardent eugenicist and a member of the Eugenics Office Advisory Committee, was instrumental in arranging matters with Methuen, and Galton was happy with the royalty of 20% on a selling price of six shillings.[56] But by December he had changed his mind: it was too difficult a job to do creditably and the climate at Pau was so enervating that it seemed to sap his resolve. He and Eva left for Biarritz where they spent the remainder of 1905.

It had been a good working year for Galton. He had been well enough to address the sociologists, he had completed a book, and plans for eugenics research seemed in good hands. With Bessy and Millicent as his weekly correspondents, with Eva as his constant companion, with his old servant Gifi to run his household, Galton now entered the final phase of his long life. But the five years left to him were not to be free of troubles.

The Final Years

As a correspondent Bessy had done her best to replace Emma. She had neither the domestic nor maternal qualities of her sister, but no one could call her letters dull; they reflect a lively interest in contemporary affairs and her brother must have found them amusing. For example:

'Here the whole talk is about Lord and Lady Warwick, whose property is to be turned into the Warwick Estate Co. and people are asked to take shares ! ! ! What next? . . .

'The Duke of Beaufort wants to sell those lovely castles. He ought to be hanged.'[1]

'I want to ask you a question. Does lightning affect the electric trams? Will they draw down the lightning upon them? I know very little about electricity but should not like to be in one in a thunder storm.'[2]

'I have been reading "The Russian and Japanese War". Very interesting. How nicely the Japanese behaved when the Russian Admiral was blown up—all lowered their flags. I only hope we shall not teach them too much, now to make war on us.'[3]

'I am very sorry that Amy [Millicent's daughter] has become R.C. although I quite expected she would, but it is a trial for Millicent. How strange that in our Quaker family so many have become Catholics! I quite agree with you it is much better than ultra High Church. I remember Lady Cartwright when talking of ultra High Church said "it does not do playing at being R.C.".'[4]

Now in the autumn of 1905 at the age of 98 Bessy was confined to a sofa and obliged to take her meals upstairs. But she was hopeful that Francis would call:

'I know that your throat and my deafness do not suit but you can do as Lucy [her daughter] always does—*write* instead of speaking. I quite hope to get rid of my rheumatics soon and in all aspects I am very well.'[5]

Her optimism over her health was not justified and while Galton was in Biarritz he received news that she had been taken seriously ill with the family ailments of bronchitis and asthma. Her sufferings were not protracted and she died after a few days' illness in January of 1906. In a letter to his niece, Millicent, Galton remarks:

'It is the last link with my own boyhood, for Erasmus was at sea, etc., and knew little about me then. So much of interest to myself is now gone irrecoverably. But it was time according to the order of nature, and I feel sure it will give longed-for liberty to Edward and M.L. [Bessy's son and his wife] to see distant parts. They were so devoted to Bessy and made their arrangements so subservient to hers, that the liberty *must* be welcome. But how they will feel the loss. Bessy's was a stoical life for a long time, not only after her widowhood but long before when her and her husband's income was very small. She battled bravely then.'[6]

Millicent kept all Galton's weekly letters to her and they comprise an interesting record of the lighter side of his personality. Whereas Eva devoted herself to him as a nurse companion, Millicent, an older woman, played the role of confidante. She and Galton had had an important formative element in common: Sister Adèle, who had educated her young brother, Francis, had also educated her own daughter, Millicent. Galton writes more familiarly to her than to Bessy; he discusses his research plans, his state of health, his acquaintances, he tells jokes and comments on life in general.

Extracts from his letters of 1905–6 illustrate their general content:

'My Eugenics Research Fellow has been grinding on, but possibly he needs more *go*. Statisticians, like the children of Israel in Egypt, have not only to make bricks but to collect materials. Here it is that men differ so much in their success.'[7]

'I wish I could get information about the principal Eugenic *centres* or *districts* in England. I mean those that are reputed to turn out the best sort of people, however the phrase "best sort" may be interpreted. The finest men come from Ballater in Scotland or thereabouts. I am trying to get an inquiry into this made. I suppose the "best sort" of persons are those who have so much energy that they are fresh after finishing their regular day's work to get their living, and who employ their after hours in some *creditable* way.'[8]

'Why don't they use false webbed soles for swimming? They ought to get through the water much faster if they did. A neat patented design might bring in lots of money, if brought *well* out, just before the bathing season.'[9]

'Explain the relationship between (1) a gardener, (2) a billiard-player, (3) an actor, (4) a verger. The gardener attends to his p's (peas), the billiard player to his q's (cues), the actor to his p's and q's and the verger to his keys and pews . . .'

'This Biarritz is an excellent place for carriages but driving is usually too cold now to be pleasant. I want vicarious exercise, like being tossed in a blanket (of course, not occasionally bumped on the floor as in school-boy days). Some mechanism ought to be devised for shaking elderly people in a healthful way, and in many directions.'[10]

Much of Galton's winter vacation was spent in villages in the Basque country, one of his favourite regions. As he explained to Karl Pearson :

'The Basque orderliness, thorough but quiet ways, and their substantial clean-looking houses, tug at every Quaker fibre in my heart, and I love them so far. As to their wonderful language unlike in syntax to any other, the virtue of these parts is accounted for by the legend that Satan came here for a visit, but finding after six years that he could neither learn the Basque language, nor make the Basques understand him, he left the country in despair.'[11]

Being housebound by the cold weather Galton took up a research topic he had long toyed with, the measurement of resemblance. His purpose was to be able to measure the similarity of two objects, especially faces. Such a measure might, he thought, have a use in eugenic enquiries where one might need to assess family or racial likeness, possibly with the aid of composite photographs.

The essence of the idea is contained in a letter he sent to Millicent.[12] When a person is walking towards you, you see his head at first as a dot, then you see its general shape, then the general markings of the face, and lastly the individual features. These grades of resemblance can be well seen in a photograph of a crowd, and each grade is associated with a critical distance.

Now if you wish to compare the similarity of two objects, you must bring them to the critical distance at which they can just be distinguished and measure their apparent size, i.e. their angular size at the eye. For this purpose Galton thought a telescope without magnifying lenses might be constructed, what he termed an 'isoscope', and by its means a fine graticule made up of little squares could be visually imposed on the objects. By counting the number of squares that covered the images a measure of their area could be obtained and this in turn could serve as a numerical expression of their similarity.

A characteristic touch was Galton's proposal to use as his unit the visual angle subtended by the sun's disc. His graticule was to be made up of squares whose sides were one 'sol' in length.

Theoretically the idea seemed sound, and, after criticism and encouragement from Pearson, Galton submitted a note to *Nature*.[13] On his return to London in April he had an isoscope constructed and was able to utilise a visit to Millicent to sit in her garden protected by a canvas screen and to test out the practicality of the scheme. He kept encountering difficulties and it appears that he soon gave up the experiment. Other matters were in any case obtruding.

The sudden death of his biometric colleague, Weldon, occurred at this time. Pearson was probably incorrect in ascribing Galton's rather rapid decrease in selfreliance to the effect on him of Weldon's death. It is clear from Galton's correspondence, and Millicent was of this opinion, that it was Emma's death that he felt most strongly and the further loss of Bessy left him with a heightened sense of isolation.[14] Weldon's death was a greater blow to Pearson; the two men had been close friends and had supplied much mutual support. Pearson now found it difficult to continue with his work and had to lean on Galton for sympathy and advice. A month after Weldon's death Pearson felt he could no longer continue the struggle to have biometric work published outside his own *Biometrika*. The Royal Society had again rejected a biometric paper and in despair Pearson wrote to Galton to ask whether he should resign his fellowship.[15] Galton's reply was a model of sound advice.

'Dear Karl Pearson, I fully understand and sympathise with your feelings. It is a disgrace to the biologists of the day, that their representatives in the Royal Society are incapable of understanding biometric papers, and of distinguishing between bad and good statistical work. To that extent I am entirely at one with you, but I do not on the above grounds see that your resignation would mend matters. It is a very general rule of conduct *not* to withdraw when in a minority, because a vantage ground is surrendered by doing so. It is far easier to reform a society while a member of it than when an outsider . . . So I should say *don't resign*, but abide your time, and give a good and and well-deserved slash now and then to serve as a reminder that your views are strong, though not querulously and wearisomely repeated.'[16]

Pearson next consulted Galton about a memorial to Weldon and received further advice and material support.[17] Again, in the preparation of his memoir of Weldon, Pearson depended on Galton for criticism. If Galton had become less selfreliant, it is not obvious in retrospect.

One change in Galton's domestic life occurred not long after Weldon's death. Eva had requested that daily prayers should be reintroduced at

Rutland Gate. Galton's reaction to this suggestion has been recorded in a letter he wrote to Eva.

> 'I should be *glad* to have family prayers as of old. The household needs a few minutes of daily companionship in reverent thought and ritual. The first morning when I returned home after dear Louisa's death, we the remainder of the household reassembled as usual, but —oh the pitifulness of it—when half-way through the prayers, I lost all control of my voice, and fairly broke down, and dismissed the household. I never recommenced the custom; partly shrinking from its memories; largely because I felt at least one of the heads should be able to join in the prayers *without any reservation*. This as I understand from your letter you would do now.'[18]

Eva's subsequent conversion to Roman Catholicism also had Galton's approval, he believed that it would better suit her temperament and he made no attempt to interfere.[19]

Noteworthy Families had appeared in print in March. In June, Murray wrote to tell Galton that only 80 copies had been sold, 869 being left on his hands; he was accordingly £32 out of pocket.[20] The poor sales were not surprising, the book could never conceivably have had much general appeal. Only half the Fellows of the Royal Society who had been approached had replied to Galton's questionnaire and it was impossible to know whether the results were of general significance. This limitation ruined Galton's long prefatory arguments, and the bulk of the book merely presented Schuster's potted biographies, of little interest except to those included, from whose numbers the sales were doubtless derived. The intention had been to make this the first of a series of books to be devoted to families eminent in a variety of fields, but no proper attempt was made to follow it up. Schuster was instead engaged, not very happily, on an enquiry into the inheritance of mental characteristics. He was living in Oxford for half the week and working in the Eugenics Office for the other half, an unsatisfactory arrangement and one that symbolised his attitude to Galton's work to which he was only half committed. During his tenure of the Fellowship he had produced two papers of his own and was now feeling uncertain whether he was fulfilling his contractual obligations or not. A tentative resignation in May 1906 was followed by a definite and immediate resignation in October.[21] Galton had by then moved to Plymouth for the winter, a trip abroad being beyond his powers, and felt incapable of further supervision of the Eugenics Office. He wrote to Pearson :

> 'I am not fit now for effort and am inclined to ask the Senate not to fill the vacant appointment yet. I wish that somehow it could be

worked into your Biometric Laboratory, but I am far too ignorant of the conditions to make a proposal. If any feasible plan occurs to you, pray tell me; it is almost sure to have my hearty acquiescence.'[22]

A plan did occur to Pearson, although it was with some reluctance that he proposed it. He was willing to direct the office on condition that it published the results of relevant biometric research as it accumulated in the Biometric Laboratory.[23] Galton most willingly agreed, and on this occasion Sir Arthur Rücker appears not to have raised any objection to Pearson's role as director. Galton made clear his intention of continuing the £500 per annum for the remainder of his life, and furthermore divulged that under the terms of his will provision would be made to endow a professorship of eugenics.[24] Pearson now appointed a new Research Fellow and promoted Miss Elderton to Research Scholar. The Eugenics Record Office was henceforth to be called the Francis Galton Laboratory for the Study of Natural Eugenics.

Thus after a bad beginning the year ended on a more hopeful note. Galton recovered his normal optimism and good humour, witnessed by a letter to *Nature* in which he explains how to cut a round cake scientifically.[25] He had adopted the method himself as it suited his 'modest wants'. The aim was to preserve the cake as well as possible for three days by leaving a minimum of exposed surface to become dry. The first day's section was to be cut across the cake, the second day's section at right angles to the first, and on the third day the four remaining pieces, mostly outside rind, were to be consumed. An elastic band was to be used to keep the segments together.

An earlier domestic experiment can be mentioned here. Very early in Galton's married life he had experimented with tea-making. The experiments had been conducted morning and evening for a period of two months and concerned the temperature of the water and of the teapot, the amount of tea, the time allowed for infusion and various categories of judgement of the resulting brew! But this was before the days of *Nature* and the results remained unpublished.[26]

The Spring of 1908 was spent alone at Rutland Gate. In a letter to Millicent, Galton describes his current occupation.

'I have been busy with an old method of mine, adopted only at long intervals, of *stock-taking* of my own character, and grieve to find it has somewhat deteriorated in two particulars. The process may interest you, and if on this occasion I can elaborate it further, it may be worth publishing. Its essence is (1) to catch oneself unawares and to consider carefully the thoughts and moods that were at that moment in the mind, and (2) to note them. The (1) is not difficult at *first*, but after a while it becomes very difficult without independent aid such as a person calling out or a machine striking. (2) requires a good deal of thought and experiment to make a *logical* classification, and yet a *brief* one, of moods and subjects of thought. I based mine originally on the Ten Commandments (leaving out the 2nd, 3rd and 4th as archaic), but find this division can be much improved on for the present purpose. Thus, it is convenient to have a preliminary division into *vigorous* virtues and vices, and into *subservient* ones . . . Where I have deteriorated is firstly in a general *weakening* of the moods—perhaps this is merely the result of age. The second failure is more easily remedied; it is the want of frequent *withdrawal into one's self* and of looking at and directing one's own conduct as if it were that of an alien, together with all that action connotes, such as communion with a higher power. The fact is, I used to *overdo* this, and feeling myself becoming priggish, thought that simple naturalness, for a bout, would be good. But I have over done this phase too, and must revert to the old one, which it will be grateful now to do. If you have ever attempted anything of this kind or heard of anyone doing so briefly (not by gushing outpourings and self-revelations), do tell me.'[27]

Unfortunately, Galton made his notes in code, committed them to memory and then destroyed the notes, leaving us in ignorance of the results of his introspections. The only personal document from this period of his life is a diary from 1904–6.[28] There is very little in the way of a record of his life here, but the end pages have been used for a few notes indirectly illustrative of his current concerns.

He records the following epitaph, heard in 1906. Galton admits in a letter to Millicent that he is obsessed with the last two lines.[29]

> 'He revelled 'neath the moon,
> He slept beneath the sun,
> He lived a life of *going to do*
> And he died with *nothing done*.'

Another quotation, almost true of himself, has been taken from a sun-dial :

> 'I can do nothing unless the sun shines.'

A page is devoted to mementos of 1897, the year of Louisa's death. He records the hotel rooms they occupied, the nurse and doctor, the sculptor of her gravestone, the position of her grave and the person responsible for its upkeep. Twelve francs a year was the cost of the latter service, last paid in 1903.

Finally, a note for dinners at home :

'Walnuts without shells go excellently with cheese. Why not serve chestnuts without shells?'

Galton was becoming increasingly infirm. He refused the Oxford Vice-Chancellor's invitation to give the Herbert Spencer lecture in June 1907, on the grounds of uncertain health. But he recanted when assured that it would be in order for a substitute to read it in his absence.

In May, he submitted his script to Pearson for comment. There would have been little time to incorporate any radical changes that Pearson might have proposed, for the paper had been sent to the printers two days after Pearson received it. Presumably, Galton never did intend to change much. Even if he had wished, he could not follow one suggestion of Pearson's, namely that he should leave his text and speak informally to his audience during part of his lecture. He was, as he had feared, unable to give the lecture himself. It was not ill health that prevented him but an awkward fall in his bedroom.

'It was about midnight, and getting up I rested on the edge of a three-legged table with "invalid comforts" on it. It tipped over and came down with a crash of crockery, and I fell with it, heavily, on to the floor. I was so bruised and battered that I had not strength to lift myself up, so there I lay helpless till $6\frac{1}{2}$ a.m. when the united forces of the awakened household lifted me, in no small pain, on to my bed. Things are mending one by one, and I can already almost get out of or into bed unaided. Hibbert, the nurse-housekeeper, sleeps in my dressing room, and Gifi and she are most anxious to help . . .

'Here is an *Art of Travel* experience. It has twice occurred to me for want of better accommodation to sleep on a billiard table. I now find that an oak floor is less hard, also that it carries off the body heat less quickly.'[30]

Galton's lecture does not merit detailed treatment. It was entitled, 'Probability, the Foundation of Eugenics', and it was the quantitative nature of eugenics research which was stressed by Galton.[31] He begins with a short history of eugenics, from his own coining of the word in 1883 until the foundation of the Eugenics Laboratory directed by Pearson. The main body of the lecture sets out to consider the application of theories of probability to eugenics but degenerates into a series of simple lessons in statistics.* The final section is the most interesting as it supplements the view that probability will provide a firm foundation for eugenic action:

'The stage on which human action takes place is a superstructure into which emotion enters, we are guided on it less by Certainties and

---

* Pearson had suggested that this part of the lecture should be expanded into a primer of biometry; Miss Elderton and her brother were to follow up his suggestion and Galton was to write a foreword.[32]

Probabilities than by Assurance to a greater or lesser degree. The word Assurance is derived from *sure*, which itself is an abbreviation of *secure*, that is of *se-cura*, or without misgiving. It is a contented attitude of mind largely dependent on custom, prejudice, or other unreasonable influences which reformers have to overcome, and some of which they are apt to utilise on their own behalf. Human nature is such that we rarely find our way by the pure light of reason, but while peering through spectacles furnished with coloured and distorting glasses.'[33]

Although Galton believes that we may begin by enlightening individuals, we shall succeed in influencing their behaviour only through public opinion. Galton sees no difficulty in directing public opinion by 'opportune pressure', but he does not enlarge on what would be an important aspect of the programme. He then refers to his paper on marriage and discusses these and other customs that are commonly thought to be unchangeable—he cites the customs of growing hair on the face and of athletes performing naked in public. He concludes that once public opinion is roused in favour of eugenics it will lead to action, however contradictory that may be to previous custom and sentiment. But that moment is not yet. More quantitative information is needed to justify legislation.

'When the desired fullness of information shall have been acquired then, and not till then, will be the fit moment to proclaim a "Jehad" or Holy War against customs and prejudices that impair the physical and moral* qualities of our race.'[34]

In spite of its long and tedious statistical section, the lecture apparently held the attention of the audience, a feat Galton was unlikely to have achieved if he had had to deliver it himself.[35]

He left London later in the summer for Haslemere where he hoped the climate might suit his by now chronic bronchitis. In November he was approached by Methuen who asked him to consider writing his autobiography. He readily agreed and began intensive work at once. As he wrote to Millicent :

'This will keep my hands very full indeed for months to come. Have you any old diaries or letters or documents that would help as to ancient dates? Now that Bessy and Emma are gone I feel singularly at sea about much. I *have* Louisa's diaries, but they refer little to myself; however, they should be very helpful.'[36]

His first notebook is headed with a cautionary quotation : 'Lord. How we old men are subject to lying.' His main error, however, was to prove

* Probably a slip for 'mental'.

to be one of omission, which is not surprising considering the rapidity with which he worked. By the following August he was reading proofs and the book was published in October of 1908, within a year of beginning work. Under the title, *Memories of My Life*, it was one of his most successful books, with good reviews and a first edition sold out within a month.[37]

The first half of the book takes us as far as Galton's marriage and is roughly chronological. He then abandons chronological order and takes the subjects of his interest one by one. This decision to write the second half of the book in this way probably sprang directly from the effect on him of dwelling on his memories, which made them as vivid as contemporary happenings.

> 'The consequence has been an occasional obliteration of the sense of Time, and to replace it by the idea of a permanent panorama, painted throughout with equal vividness, in which the point to which attention is temporarily directed becomes for that time the Present. The panorama seems to extend unseen behind a veil which hides the Future, but is slowly rolling aside and disclosing it. That part of the panorama which is veiled is supposed to exist as vividly coloured as the rest, though latent. In short, this experience has given me an occasional feeling that there are no realities corresponding to Past, Present and Future, but that the entire Cosmos is one perpetual Now . . . Philosophers have often held this creed intellectually, but I suspect that few have felt the possible truth of it so vividly as it has occasionally appeared to my imagination through dwelling on these "Memories." '[38]

The book is not a self-revealing document. With his usual reticence about personal matters Galton preferred to pack it with reminiscences and anecdotes of the many eminent men he had the good fortune to know. A rough count of the names in the index gives a total of more than 260, with the men outnumbering the women by 13 : 1. This imbalance may not itself require comment, taking into account the Victorian scientific circles to which Galton was limited, but the lack of any reference to the work of his sister-in-law, Josephine Butler, to George Eliot, a frequent visitor to Rutland Gate, and to Florence Nightingale, with whom he had considerable correspondence, seems again to reflect the prejudice to which we have earlier referred.[39]

After the detailed account of his travels and social life the book deals with his contributions to geography and meteorology and the work of the British Association and Kew Observatory. In less than 100 pages he compresses the remainder of his life's work, which he divides into anthropometry, human faculty, heredity and race improvement. There is little here that we have not already covered in greater detail, but two of his more recondite enquiries have escaped our notice and may be mentioned now.

He tells us that he frequently attended the Derby, even persuading Herbert Spencer to accompany him. The subjects of Galton's observation were as much the onlookers as the horses. On one occasion while waiting for the race to begin, he amused himself by studying the prevalent tint of the faces of the crowd in the distant stand. The race began and as the horses neared the winning post Galton observed a curious sight: the average tint of the faces became a sea of dark pink under the flush of excitement. A short note on this experience found its way to *Nature*.[40]

An experiment to gain insight into the feelings of an idol worshipper remained unpublished until described in his autobiography.

'I had visited a large collection of idols gathered by missionaries from many lands, and wondered how each of those absurd and ill-made monstrosities could have obtained the hold it had over the imaginations of its worshippers. I wished, if possible, to enter into those feelings. It was difficult to find a suitable object for trial, because it ought to be in itself quite unfitted to arouse devout feelings. I fixed on a comic picture, it was that of Punch, and made believe in its possession of divine attributes. I addressed it with much quasi-reverence as possessing a mighty power to reward or punish the behaviour of men towards it, and found little difficulty in ignoring the impossibilities of what I professed. The experiment gradually succeeded; I began to feel and long retained for the picture a large share of the feelings that a barbarian entertains towards his idol, and learnt to appreciate the enormous potency they might have over him.'[41]

One wonders whether Louisa was party to the procedure! According to one acquaintance of Galton's, he conducted several even stranger experiments but unfortunately these were never divulged.[42]

While he was engaged on his autobiography a new development in eugenics came to Galton's notice. Certain members of the Moral Education League had met in November 1907 and had under the chairmanship of Dr Slaughter formed the provisional council of a new society, the Eugenics Education Society.[43] Galton agreed to help, but then withdrew his offer upon receiving a complaint from Miss Elderton who had attended a meeting chaired by Dr Slaughter in which sexual problems were discussed. Matters became worse in March 1908 when Slaughter was convicted of indecent assault, a conviction that was, however, quashed on appeal.

Neither of these occurrences reflected well on the emerging Society and

Galton was content to remain at a distance while warily watching its progress. By May of 1908 he was much more sanguine :

> 'The Eugenics Education Society promises better than I could have hoped. Crackanthorpe is serious about it and Professor Inge has joined it ! . . . I have not *yet* ventured to join it, but as soon as I am assured it is in *safe* management, shall do so.'[44]

Montague Crackanthorpe had become very active in the affairs of the Society and Galton was convinced of his soundness. He knew Crackanthorpe quite well; they were neighbours in Rutland Gate, and Galton had had previous correspondence with him. Thus, he had few misgivings when Crackanthorpe persuaded him to become Honorary President. He also agreed to read a paper on eugenics to a small group at Crackanthorpe's house in June.

The main object of the paper was to describe the origins of eugenics. He explains to his audience that his attention was drawn to the inheritance of mental and physical abilities by his experiences as an undergraduate at Cambridge, that his speculations were later put to statistical test in *Hereditary Genius*, and that he then came to the conclusion that the procedures adopted so successfully by the breeders of plants and animals would have similar results if applied in a more gentle manner to man; thus, eugenics was born.

In a few paragraphs he summarised the main tenets of eugenics, and concludes with the by now familiar plea for the redirection of charity :

> 'Families which are likely to produce valuable citizens deserve at the very least the care that a gardener takes of plants of promise. They should be helped when help is needed to procure a larger measure of sanitation, of food, and of all else that falls under the comprehensive title of "Nurture" than would otherwise have been within their power. I do not, of course, propose to neglect the sick, the feeble, or the unfortunate. I would do all that available means permit for their comfort and happiness, but I would exact an equivalent for the charitable assistance they receive, namely, that by means of isolation, or some other less drastic yet adequate measure, a stop should be put to the production of families of children likely to include degenerates.'[45]

The paper was printed in full in the *Westminster Gazette* and helped to draw more attention to the Society, which was now becoming properly organised with a programme of monthly meetings. Galton's opening address as Honorary President was scheduled for October, but it seemed unlikely that he would be strong enough to give it. Karl Pearson reports that he was very weak at a public ceremony in July of 1908

xv   Brother Erasmus

XVI   Millicent Lethbridge

when he was one of the recipients of the Darwin–Wallace Medal of the Linnaean Society. He had to leave the meeting early and to be helped from the platform in a fatigued state.[46] His arthritis was now becoming restrictive of all movement, and walking any distance unaided was impossible. He writes to Millicent :

'I am about now to be trundled in my sister Bessy's bath-chair into the park, which I find very pleasant. Sometimes Mrs Simmonds (his nurse-housekeeper) sometimes Gifi, pushes it, and I have lost all sense of oddity in the matter and enjoy it without drawback.'[47]

He was hard at work on his address during the August and September and submitted a draft to Crackanthorpe for criticism.

'It has been typed and then much cut up by the skilled hand of Crackanthorpe, and is now being typed in a shrunken and disembowelled form, but made much more suitable thereby. It is a delight to me to put myself again to school, as it were, under a competent critic. Generally my friends are diffident and won't *slash*, but I have two excellent friends who happily feel no compunction in performing that operation, and I learn much thereby.'[48]

The other critical friend was undoubtedly Karl Pearson who did not hesitate to speak his mind to Galton and who was already concerned that his supervision of the Eugenics Laboratory was leading to research of a less popular kind than that envisaged by Galton. The first signs of strain emerge in their correspondence at the beginning of 1908 when Pearson suggested that he should resign, a suggestion that Galton would not entertain.[49]

They diverged again over the use of technical terms in *Biometrika*, Galton suggesting that glossaries should be appended to papers in which there appeared biological terms, such as 'chromosome' and 'zygote', to encourage the statisticians to read them, and that the mathematics of statistical papers should be simplified to aid their comprehension by the biologists.[50]

In his biography, Pearson makes the point that Galton had lost touch with the technical advances in the many sciences to which he had contributed in earlier years and that he was perhaps unconsciously harking back to the era of Victorian Science when the nonspecialist could flourish. Galton's disquietude over the way in which scientific papers were now being presented led him to write a paper in which he proposed methods for the literary improvement of scientific writing. The paper was read for him to the Royal Society of Literature.[51] It contained the suggestions that referees should assess not only the scientific content of a paper but also the adequacy of its literary style, and that scientific societies should occasionally publish extracts from submissions that were conspicuous for their literary shortcomings.

'The comparative rarity among the English of a keen sense of the difference between good and bad literary style is a great obstacle of the reform I desire. It is especially notable among the younger scientific men, whose education has been over-specialised and little concerned with the "Humanities". The literary sense is far more developed in France, where a slovenly paper ranks with a disorderly dress as a sign of low breeding.'[52]

The differences with Pearson were minor; Galton continued as a strong advocate of the merits of Pearson's research, a position that was shortly to lead him into controversy with some of the prominent members of the Eugenics Education Society. The affairs of that society were still troubled, as Galton explains in a letter to Millicent.

'The idea of your troubling to join the Eugenics Education Society! I never meant to cajole you into it. Still, it is not a bad thing to do, and a few of us are taking pains about it. I shall understand "the ropes" better after next Wednesday's meeting. The absurd part of it is that the proper President of it, Sir James Crichton-Browne, has wholly absented himself for ever so long, and won't answer the letters of the Secretary to him. It was this that *obliged* me to take the lead, which I did not at all want to do.'[53]

The meeting to which Galton refers was the occasion of his Presidential Address.[54] Pearson attended the meeting, the last time Galton was to speak in public, and was surprised and impressed by the clarity and force of Galton's presentation.

The original content of the lecture is slight. Galton deals with the role that might be played by local associations of eugenists in furthering the cause of eugenics. He suggests that branches of the Society should develop their own programme of popular lectures on the subject, with local worthies being invited to contribute to the discussions. These local men of merit would be chosen from various classes of society, and details of their backgrounds and abilities would be recorded in local registers. Thus a fund of information would become available and could be communicated to the central office.

'A danger to which these Societies will be liable arises from the inadequate knowledge joined to great zeal of some of the most active among their probable members. It may be said, without mincing words, with regard to much that has already been published, that the subject of eugenics is particularly attractive to "cranks". The councils of local Societies will therefore be obliged to exercise great caution before accepting the memoirs offered to them, and much discretion in keeping discussions within the bounds of sobriety and common sense.'[55]

The writing was already on the wall and Galton was not blind to the future dangers. He reiterates his note of caution :

'The basis of eugenics is already firmly established, namely, that the offspring of "worthy" parents are, *on the whole*, more highly gifted by nature with facilities that conduce to "worthiness" than the offspring of less "worthy" parents. On the other hand, forecasts in respect to particular cases may be quite wrong. They have to be based on imperfect data. It cannot be too emphatically repeated that a great deal of careful statistical work has yet to be accomplished before the science of eugenics can make large advances.'[56]

Feeling tired and bronchitic after his lecture, Galton lost no time in leaving London for Betchworth in Surrey where he spent the winter reading novels (*Waverley* and *Guy Mannering* are mentioned in a letter to Millicent[57]) and in driving a donkey cart :

'You say I have a kindly heart towards donkeys. You recollect perhaps Coleridge's not very wise ode to a *young ass* and Byron's comment on it : "A *fellow-feeling* makes us wondrous kind" ! An ass is certainly a mysterious animal, and the continual and usually independent movements of his long ears testify to the busy thoughts or perceptions of the beast. But its obstinancy ! What a martyr an ass would make to any cause that it pleased to favour.'[58]

Eva provided the stimulus for an amusing letter to *Nature* which is all he wrote for publication during the winter.[59] She had expressed a belief in the efficacy of a curse on church property that had been sequestrated at the time of the Reformation. The curse was said to extinguish the line of the owner before the inheritance by his eldest son. With Edgar Schuster's aid, Galton compiled statistics which showed that an equal percentage of eldest sons owned church and non-church property, and that the mean length of tenure was identical in the two cases. He did find, however, that church property changed hands more frequently, an effect he ascribed to the discovery after purchase of the unsuitability of the property for dwelling purposes. Theocratic intervention was, to Eva's chagrin, an unnecessary postulate.

In January 1909, Galton received the news that his surviving brother, Erasmus, had fallen and broken his thigh. He wrote to Millicent :

'Poor Erasmus! He is so very stoical. When he felt "something give" as he was about to enter the tram and fell on the road, the the first thing he said to those who picked him up was, "It's all arranged, and mind I'm to be cremated"! I hear that he is as free from pain and as comfortable as may be, but that the broken bone can never heal, so all his habitual walks and independencies must end. I am extremely sorry for him. He somehow seems to me to have failed to get as much interest and "go" in life as his circumstances might have given him.'[60]

The injury was serious for a man of 94 and complications followed, which led to his death the following month. Galton was himself 87 and on consulting *Whitaker's Almanack* found that his expectation of life was reduced to three years. He was feeling keenly his own physical limitations. When he returned to Rutland Gate in the spring he wrote to Millicent:

'I feel sure that I shall never be able to climb the stairs of this house again. I am carried up every night by Gifi and the man-nurse, Charman, who find me heavy, but I walk downstairs in the morning.'[61]

The arrangement of the house was now changed, with Galton's bedroom brought down to the drawingroom floor, but he had still to be carried upstairs from the diningroom which was on the ground floor. He reports to Millicent:

'I don't think that I am a bit better, though Eva and the doctor insist that I am. Anyhow, I do *not* gain in muscular strength, nor do the rheumatic cramps leave me.'[62]

Very little work was done during 1909: a short essay was written advocating the segregation of the feeble-minded and a foreword to the first issue of the *Eugenics Review*.[63] This latter publication was the organ of the Eugenics Education Society and Galton's foreword is notable in that it attempts to clarify the relative spheres of action of the Society and the Laboratory.

'The *Eugenics Review* emphatically disclaims rivalry in any form with the more technical publications issued from time to time from the Eugenics Laboratory of the University of London now located at University College. On the contrary it proposes to supplement them. There are two sorts of workers in every department of knowledge—those who establish a firm foundation, and those who build upon the foundation so established. The foundation of Eugenics is, in some measure, laid by applying a mathematics–statistical treatment to large collections of facts, and this, like engineering deep down in boggy soil, affords little evidence of its bulk and importance. The superstructure requires for its success the cooperation of many minds of a somewhat different order, filled with imagination and enthusiasm; it does not require technical knowledge as to the nature of the foundation work.'

Pearson was grateful for Galton's clear statement of the position, although critical of the insubstantiality of much of the remainder of the journal.[64] The Eugenics Laboratory was now producing work at a great rate. Galton continued to maintain his financial support of £500 per annum and was corresponding with Pearson over the codicil to his will by which the Professorship of Eugenics was to be established. He did not, however, divulge to Pearson the final clause under which the post was first to be offered to Pearson on condition that he should be given the liberty to continue to direct the Biometric Laboratory which Galton knew was so close to his heart. Galton was also insistent that more permanence should be given to the positions of Miss Elderton and other research workers in the Laboratory. There was one proviso :

'In fixing the future titles of Heron [The Galton Fellow], Miss Elderton and Miss Barrington, if you can get in a word to absolve us from granting pensions on retirement, it might be well. I have known much grievance created on the parts of those who had "expectations" in other Societies and Offices.'[65]

In the June of 1909 Galton received a further honour. He wrote to Eva, who was away for a few weeks :

'Yesterday a letter came by post with "Prime Minister" printed on the cover and "Confidential" written inside. At first, I thought it must be some wine-merchant's circular, but its contents were "*Confidential*. My dear Sir, I have the pleasure with the King's approval of proposing that you should receive the honour of Knighthood on his Majesty's approaching birthday. Yours faithfully, (signed) H. H. Asquith." So I shall have to live till November 9 and then shall blossom. Don't make any fuss about it. I told Gifi and Mrs Simmonds, as they would both like to know.'[66]

Galton wrote back to Asquith pointing out that he would certainly be unfit to attend the ceremony and received the reply that the patent of Knighthood would be sent to him. There is no evidence that he was particularly pleased with the distinction. As he wrote to Pearson :

'A precious bad *knight* I should make now, with all my infirmities. Even seven years ago it required some engineering to get me on the back of an Egyptian *donkey*! and I have worsened steadily since.'[67]

Meanwhile, Saleeby had completed a book on eugenics, a substitute for the book he had tried to persuade Galton to write in 1905. Galton comments on it in a letter to Millicent :

'I am just beginning Saleeby's new book, *Parenthood and Race Culture*. He dedicates it to me as "The August Master of all Eugenists". I read it in proof and, though there is much I would myself strike out, expect it will do good. He has eminently the art of popular writing with fluency.'[68]

Saleeby's book was fairly restrained compared with some of his other writings. Certain idiosyncrasies were apparent, notably in his stress on the deleterious effects of alcohol, which he classified as a 'racial poison' likely to produce feeble-mindedness in the offspring. He also omitted reference to Galton's Ancestral Law, believing it to be incompatible with Mendelian principles, a fact which Galton never recognised.

Galton must have been surprised to learn from Pearson that during this same year Saleeby had been writing a series of attacks on the work of the Eugenics Laboratory. By November, Pearson could contain himself no longer. He explained to Galton :

'I feel the time has come when it is necessary for me to reply to the sort of charges Saleeby scatters . . . If you feel, *as I do*, that any attack on a member of the Council of the Eugenics Education Society is incompatible with my official relationship to your Eugenics Laboratory, I will resign officially as from the end of the year . . . I had hoped that the Eugenics Education Society would do its own work and leave us to do ours, but some members of the Council think otherwise, and as they choose to throw down the gauntlet, I must take it up, though I do so very reluctantly, and particularly because I feel it can but pain you. Still, I think you will, if you imagine yourself trying to work the Laboratory in my place, admit that you could not pass by charges of what really amounts to wasting the founder's money.'[69]

Galton makes no reference in his reply to Pearson's threatened resignation, the third occasion on which this had occurred.

'It is painful news to me about Saleeby, whose articles I have not seen. Of course, if he attacks your work directly or otherwise, the right to reply rests with you and I do not see that the closeness of his connection with the Eugenics Education Society need deter you. It is of course, bad for the progress of Eugenics when two workers in it disagree, and gives an opening to ill wishers to say nasty things, but all that must be faced.'[70]

Galton was to some extent embarrassed over the situation as Saleeby had just arranged to issue abbreviated versions of four of Galton's books in a series entitled *The World's Great Books*. Pearson's comment on this venture was to wish the books were in other hands :

'The men you want to interest will be repelled, not knowing how far the rhetoric and froth lies in the account or in the original !'[71]

Letters continued to pass between Pearson and Galton, with the latter continuing to take a lighthearted attitude towards the controversy and advising Pearson to adopt a bantering reply. Pearson finally cooled sufficiently to let the matter drop. It was not, however, to rest there. In May 1910, Elderton and Pearson published their research on the children of alcoholic parents (as an Eugenic Laboratory Memoir)[72]. The memoir reported the results of two enquiries made into the mental and physical development of the children of alcoholic parents who were compared with the children of sober parents. The results of the statistical analyses showed that there was no relationship between the intelligence, physique or tendency to disease of the offspring and the alcoholism of the parents; indeed, the general health of the children of alcoholic parents was better than that of the children of sober parents. These rather startling conclusions aroused the wrath of the temperance movement, among whose most vigorous advocates were Saleeby and Sir Victor Horsley. Another group of critics were the Cambridge economists, notably Keynes and Marshall, whose attacks were to be directed mainly at the unrepresentative nature of the working-class samples investigated in the study.

The controversy began in the correspondence columns of *The Times*, which had carried a favourable leader on the results of the research, but then spilled over into various technical journals. Pearson vigorously defended the research and, without consulting Galton any further, produced two supplements to the Memoir in which he effectively, if acrimoniously, demolished his critics.[73]

Galton's own response was more dignified. A sober letter to *The Times* in response to criticism of the biometric method when applied to complex problems was followed by further letters to that newspaper and to the *British Journal of Inebriety*, where Saleeby had hinted that Galton was not in sympathy with the work of the Eugenics Laboratory.[74] Galton made it quite clear that Saleeby did not speak for the whole of the Eugenics Education Society which he did not consider was antagonistic to the Laboratory.

'If it were, I could not occupy the post I now hold of its honorary presidency, because so far from depreciating the work of the Laboratory, I hold it to be thoroughly scientific and most valuable, and I rejoice that I was its founder.'[75]

According to Pearson, Galton was undecided towards the end of the year whether the Society was not doing more harm than good, and mentioned that he might resign. But Pearson was careful not to influence him, in spite of Eva's urging. Eva wrote to Pearson following his visit to Galton :

> 'I don't believe the devil leaves you Protestants and Agnostics alone, but he doesn't torture you as he does Catholic communities . . . who but the devil prevented you from doing what I asked, namely persuading Uncle Frank off that worrying Eugenics Education Society. You and your pupils do not let your names appear among that tiresome crowd, so why should Uncle Frank's name be put at the head of them? The Doctor has been and keeps Uncle Frank in bed all day to rest, but this is the rule now once a week.'[76]

Thus, Galton continued to act as honorary president, probably on the grounds that his resignation would destroy the Society. He continued to nurse the belief that the popularisers were as necessary to eugenic progress as the researchers, but it was no easy matter to remain supportive of both parties when their views and personalities were so divergent.

Troubled by these difficulties and by his infirmities, 1910 was not a productive year. The paper on numeralised profiles discussed in an earlier chapter appeared in *Nature*, and two short articles were published in the *Eugenics Review*. One of these was a reiteration of his view that a change in public opinion in favour of eugenics could be brought about by small and persistent nudges in the right direction.[77] The other was more noteworthy in its argument that civic prosperity depended on a large capacity and eagerness for labour, both physical and mental, among the general population. In vivid words, Galton contrasts prosperous and decaying communities :

> 'A prosperous community is distinguished by the alertness of its members, by their busy occupations, by their taking pleasure in their work, by their doing it thoroughly, and by an honest pride in their community as a whole. The members of a decaying community are, for the most part, languid and indolent; their very gestures are dawdling and slouching, the opposite of smart. They shirk work when they can do so, and scamp what they undertake. A prosperous community is remarkable for the variety of the solid interests in which some or other of its members are eagerly engaged, but the questions that agitate a decadent community are for the most part of a frivolous order. Prosperous communities are also notable for enjoyment of life,

for though their members must work hard in order to procure the necessary luxuries of an advanced civilisation, they are endowed with so large a store of energy that, when their daily toil is over, enough of it remains unexpended to allow them to pursue their special hobbies during the remainder of the day. In a decadent community, the men tire easily and soon sink into drudgery; there is consequently much languor among them and little enjoyment of life.'[78]

Galton's attempt to characterise a prosperous community also found expression in a novel which he began in the early summer of 1910. This project was kept secret from all but his nearest relatives, and Pearson only learnt of it through Eva, who asked him to advise Galton to suppress the love episodes as they were absurdly unreal. Pearson did not feel justified in giving such advice and Galton did not ask for comment. It was, perhaps, the inclusion of these passages that led Methuen to reject the manuscript when Galton submitted it to him in December. Galton made no attempt to seek another publisher; he wrote to Millicent :

'*Kantsaywhere* must be smothered or superseded. It has been an amusement and has cleared my thoughts to write it. So now let it go to "Won't-say-where." '[9]

Fragments of the novel came into Pearson's possession after Galton's death, his executors having ordered its destruction. The niece responsible for destroying most of the story, including the love scenes, felt that the eugenic proposals were innocuous and might be of interest to Pearson, who published all he received.[80]

Galton's Utopia of *Kantsaywhere* is conceived as a community in which eugenics is firmly established and which is effectively and benignly governed by the trustees of the Eugenics College. The thread of the story concerns a professor of vital statistics who visits the country, where he falls in love with a Miss Allfancy. He determines to submit himself to the college examiners to obtain as high a degree in eugenics as possible, a necessary step before he will be allowed to marry the high-ranking Miss Allfancy.

In some detail Galton describes the examination procedure. The candidate is required to spend an hour in an anthropometric laboratory, strongly reminiscent of the South Kensington laboratory, then proceeds to a strict medical examination, submits himself to an examination in aesthetics and literature, and finally the papers relating to his ancestry are critically scrutinised.

Those candidates who fail the Poll examination are regarded as undesirables and are assisted to emigrate. If they remain, they are subjected to surveillance and prevented from propagating. The professor obtains a good honours degree in spite of losing marks on account of the insufficiency of the information available about his ancestry. He is now willingly accepted by *Kantsaywhere* society.

'I was greatly impressed by the tone and manner at the social gatherings that I attended, which were at first those of the more cultured class. The guests were gay without frivolity, friendly without gush, and intelligent without brilliancy; they were eminently a wholesome set of young people, with whom one could pass one's life, not only in serenity but with satisfaction and even a large share of keen pleasure. The physique of the girls reminded me of "Aurora" by Guido in Rome. It is a favourite picture of mine and I recall it clearly. The girls have the same massive forms, short of heaviness, and seem promising mothers of a noble race* . . . As for the men they are well built, practised both in military drill and athletics, very courteous, but with a resolute look that suggests fighting qualities of a high order.'

The professor is particularly impressed by his visit to the Kantsaywhere photographic workshops. An obligatory custom requires everyone to be photographed at fixed intervals of time under standardised conditions. From these individual portraits, various family composites are made, including one of both parents and the four grandparents in which half the exposure time is allowed to the grandparents. This composite representation of one's inheritance on the Galtonian model is seen as providing a personification of an individual's conscience. The 'peculiar superstition' of the people consists of a belief in a spirit world, made up of such composite beings who may themselves merge into super-composites of racial and universal spirits. Reverence is paid to these spirits in a kind of superior version of ancestor worship.

It can be seen that, in spite of his own agnosticism, Galton believed it necessary for the inhabitants of his Utopia to possess a creed to give them 'a unity of endeavour and a seriousness of action'. Other extracts might be quoted to illustrate how he brought together many apparently disparate strands of his earlier research to enrich his Utopian picture. There is reference to eugenic charities and hereditary registers, methods of marking physical efficiency, and the prevalence of visionaries. There are also significant omissions unlikely to have been included in the missing chapters. There is little about the method of government, which appears to be authoritarian rather than democratic.† There is no reference to the

---

* In point of fact it is difficult to distinguish male from female in Guido Reni's picture, both sexes being heavily muscled.

† The Galton Archives contain a list of anti-democratic quotations from Shakespeare that Galton compiled, possibly when he was writing his novel.

economic structure of the society, its relation to other states, its military. In short, it is a naive, simplistic, and untroubled Utopia.

This last winter of 1910–11 was spent at Haslemere. In October Galton received the news that he had been awarded the Copley Medal of the Royal Society. He wrote to Millicent :

> 'It is the "blue ribbon" of the scientific world, and I am of course deeply gratified. One is awarded annually, without distinction of *nationality* or of *time* when the scientific work was done, whether lately or some years back . . . About five other living Englishmen have it. People are always very kind to me, but I wish my Father and Emma were alive. It would have given them real pleasure.'[81]

Each week he continued to write to Millicent reporting in a light-hearted way on his deteriorating health.

> 'I am vegetating pretty happily, only vegetables don't cough in spasms and require cigarettes either of haschisch or stramonium to allay them, as I do.'[82]

> 'I pull on—sometimes rather badly, often rather well, but very infirm always, and am wheeled about and carried up and down stairs. But I have nothing to complain of. I sleep like Morpheus and enjoy a chastened dietary, and have had my day.'[83]

The occasional joke is still included :

> '*Scene*. Breakfast table, a small boy and his nurse who is reading the *Christian Herald. Boy* : "Nanny, I don't like this egg." *Nurse*, without looking up : "Be a good child and eat it." *Boy*, after a while : "May I leave half of it?" *Nurse* : "No, be good, eat it all up." *Boy*, after another pause : "Nanny, must I eat the *beak*?" '[84]

His asthma was now very bad, especially after any form of fatigue. A move to a different house in November led to his confinement to bed and he was unable to venture out of doors for a month. He seems to have realised that he might not survive the winter in view of his comment when being carried to his bedroom that the corridor would be difficult to negotiate with his coffin.[85]

January 1911 was foggy but he insisted on being taken outside to get air. The result was a severe attack of bronchial asthma. On the 15th Eva wrote to Pearson :

> 'Uncle Frank is one degree better to-day but still in danger. He is not the least worried about Laboratory affairs. I only told him the teetotallers were attacking you, and that a good leading article in *The Times* had snubbed them. He was much interested. He is quite

easy in his mind and very clear when he speaks, but too weak to speak more than a word or two. My cousin Edward Wheler, a very dear nephew of his, is here—we never leave him a minute.'[86]

On the 17th he was very weak and smilingly refused food with a quotation from Burns :

> 'Some hae meat and canna eat,
> And some wad eat that want it.'

When almost too feeble to speak, he was given oxygen, and struggled to ask his nephew to explain to the doctor that he had once experimented with it. An hour later he was dead.

He died a rich man. Under the terms of his will, £45 000 went to the University of London to endow a Chair of Eugenics, £15 000 went to Edward Wheler, and smaller sums to other relatives. To Gifi, in return for 40 years' devoted service, he left £200. Francis Galton was not only a genius, he was also unmistakably a Victorian.

Appendix I

Inventions

No account of Galton's life would be satisfactory without some detailed indication of his ingenuity in devising mechanical, optical and other contrivances.

Apart from a drawing of some kind of flying machine propelled by steam, entitled 'The Aerostatic Project', which he made at the age of 13, the earliest indications of his aptitude for inventions were apparent during his first year at Cambridge.

In November 1840, in a letter to his father, he discusses the rationale behind hot oil lamps in which the flame of the lamp heats up a reservoir of half-concrete oil and renders it quite fluid and easily inflammable, the oil being then fed to the flame. During December he designed his own version of this lamp which gave an exceedingly bright light, but in January of the following year he explains that he has been superseded.

> 'Captain Basil Hall aided by Wheatstone has hit upon the same idea a short time since and has since been making experiments. The light appears not advantageous as regards illuminating rooms though it is useful for lighthouses.'[1]

At about the same time he invented a lock of which no details survive. It was commended by the locksmith, Bramah, who, however, considered that Galton's lock would be too expensive to manufacture and, as the key consisted only of a piece of bent wire, it could too easily be copied. Although Galton took his advice and did not attempt to patent his own lock, he dis–concerted Bramah by offering to make a false key to Bramah's own patent lock in the space of five minutes.

> 'I got 10 knitting pins 5 large and 5 small and one wooden one which was central the others surrounding it. On pressing the central one down the bore of the key the other ones were variously depressed according to the teeth in the key . . . The knitting pins are of course clumsy but with a little contrivance a perfect picklock can be made (the breadth of the slits is of no consequence only the depth). Bramah was very fierce. I told him that I had some intention of patenting the picklock and advertising Important to Thieves, Housebreakers and others!'[2]

Another minor invention was a device to improve the efficiency of any balance. It consisted merely of a vertical steel bar to be attached to the centre of the scale beam, the top of the bar ended in a point which was held by the pole of a magnet. Thus, the beam was suspended from the minute surface of the point and friction was reduced to a minimum. If the method of double weighing was used, a very accurate balance would result for, Galton estimated, a total outlay of ten shillings.[3]

A more substantial invention was described and sketched in another letter to his father, dated 3rd February 1841. This was a design for a rotatory steam engine for which he lists the following advantages:

'Advantages being: 1st the whole power being available, cranks being absent. 2nd the momentum of the piston increasing the effect and therefore the rapidity of working being unlimited, 3rd consequently very small cylinder, 4th no flywheel, 5th exceedingly light.'[4]

It consisted of an outer box (A in Figure 1), which is like a pillbox in shape, in which another pillbox (B) revolves having a vane (D) which moves steam-tight inside the outer box. On either side of the vane are two bands (W, W'), which are instrumental in opening and closing the valves (V, V') as the vane approaches and passes them. Steam is admitted under pressure into the outer box through S and S' and can escape through E and E'.

He describes the operation of the engine as follows:

'Let the position of B be as in the diagram [Phase 1 in Figure 1]. S is open, E' is open. There is no exit for the steam in the direction V, therefore B must rotate in the direction of the arrow. As D approaches V', the band (W) raises V' before it passes under E' [Phase 2]. E' shuts and E opens. As now there is free communication on both sides of V', the vane (D) drives the steam before it through E'. D then passes under V' and as it goes on V' slides down the band (W') on the other side of it. But V' does not close completely until D is on the other side of S', when S' opens and S shuts, and so on. It is to be remembered that W are merely bands of metal.'

The remainder of the letter is taken up with a calculation of the power of the engine. Galton calculates that, with an outer box of diameter 6 in and an inner box of diameter 2 in and a height of 1 in and a steam pressure of 4 atmospheres, 1 h.p. would be produced. But to produce 1 h.p. his engine would have had to run at 50 000 rev/min, even at 100 per cent efficiency. It was not until about 1880 that speeds as high as 20 000 rev/min were achieved. At such speeds the problems involved in sealing become major sources of difficulty, and if Galton's engine had been constructed he would have found that the resources were not then available to solve these problems.

However, the date is a very early one for a rotating vane steam engine and Galton must receive credit on the score of originality. The Wankel motor-car engine developed one hundred years later has a rotor with seals not unlike Galton's although it is designed so that the area swept out by the rotor varies at different points in its rotation. Galton's design can be criticised on the grounds that it is thermodynamically extravagant because the steam is used non-expansively, i.e. the pressure behind the vane remains at boiler pressure until it is exhausted, and less work is thus available for a given flow of steam.[5]

The idea for another engine arose some thirty years later when Galton was transferring from a small boat to a larger ship. It occurred to him that the movement of the two vessels relative to one another, which could be considerable if any sea were running and which made transfer difficult, could be made responsible for driving a mechanism. In its simplest form this 'Wave Engine' could consist of an arm linking the two vessels which could activate a pump. A more complex arrangement links the two vessels by a sliding arrangement, so that they could approach or separate from one another, and a Hooke's joint at either end of the slider would permit the vessels to roll and yaw independently.

Galton's notebooks contain detailed drawings of the various complex

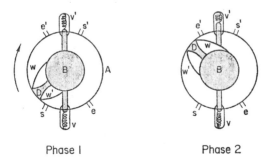

Phase I   Phase 2

FIGURE 1.   Rotatory steam engine

mechanical systems which would convert the yawing, pitching and rolling of each vessel into a rotatory motion to drive the double vessel along. He calculates the horsepower produced by various size waves of various frequencies and points out that if insufficient power is generated to drive the vessels it could still, with the hulks moored, be usefully employed.[6]

Galton consulted friends about his idea, but although they were generally agreed about its ingenuity they were less sanguine about its practicality. He accepted their advice and let the matter drop.

However, his interest in the action of waves was again aroused a few years later during a visit to Fawley in Hampshire, and in an unpublished note of 1876 he describes a method of measuring the height of waves which eliminates the effects of tidal movement.[7] The device is shown in Figure 2, which is modified from Galton's original drawing.

Below the surface of the water are two iron tubes (t and t') of sufficient length to cover the greatest rise and fall of tide, plus the height of any wave above that level, plus the length of the float. For the conditions at Fawley, Galton reckoned the tubes should be about 27 ft in length. There are two valves (v and v′) at the bottoms of the tubes, the former opening inwards and the latter outwards. The valves leak to provide a gradual readjustment. Two floats (f and f′) within the tubes indicate, by their difference in height, the height of the wave. That is, when a wave passes one float will rise and the other fall, pulleys (a and a′) and (b and b′) will turn to allow the connecting wire to move the pointer on the dial to register the height of the wave. In order to cancel out the changes in tide level, the pulley system (b and b′) is attached to a float which will move up and down independently of the rest of the system.

We now turn to the first of Galton's inventions to be published, his printing

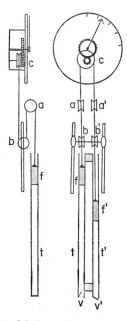

FIGURE 2.   Method of wave measurement

telegraph or *Telotype*. His interest in signalling had been first aroused during a vacation from Cambridge spent in the Lake District. On reaching the summit of Skiddaw he found a party of surveyors attempting to flash sun-signals to another group on the peak of Snowdon. The heliostats used by the Ordnance Survey were large and cumbersome and Galton saw the need for a small portable instrument that could be carried in the waistcoat pocket. It was some years before he began contriving a series of prototypes and it was not until 1859 that he exhibited his final design at a British Association meeting. In the interval he became interested in signalling by electrical means. The electric telegraph had been invented by Cooke and Wheatstone in the late 1830s. In its earliest form it consisted of five lines of wire and five magnetic needles arranged to point to various letters of the alphabet. Improvements occurred rapidly and by 1850 several thousand miles of telegraph wires had been installed by various commercial companies in Great Britain. It was at that time that Galton published his proposals for a telegraph that would print messages.[8]

The pamphlet describing this instrument attracted very little notice and Galton was not in a position to publicise it any further as he had left on his voyage to South Africa. As described, there appears to be nothing very original in Galton's method of transmitting signals: three wires connect sending and receiving stations, each wire being capable of sending one of three signals. These signals suffice to turn a galvanometer needle to the left, or to the right, or to leave it unaffected. Thus, the whole system can transmit 27 different signals, enough to cover the letters of the alphabet.

To magnify the weak movement of the receiving needles in order to print from them, Galton proposes an elaborate mechanical system which cannot easily be described here. Galton summarises the process in this account.

'Suppose a telegraphic needle of the most delicate construction conceivable having the three possible movements of right, neutral, left, to be momentarily lifted off its support by an arm that squeezes it against a little cushion above. However delicate the needle may be, its projecting ends will be stiff enough to push another freely suspended (but non-magnetic) needle of a much stronger and heavier build, in the same direction as itself. The process may be repeated on a third needle of considerably larger size and greater strength; and if desired, on a fourth. The force required to keep all this going is independent of that which moves the first needle, and is applied by a reciprocating beam worked by ordinary power.'[9]

Some parts of the Telotype were certainly constructed. Galton had cells in a drawer of his study table with wires leading from them through holes in the woodwork so that he could perform desk-top experiments. He mentions in his pamphlet the fascination of watching the power of the delicate needle being amplified by the means described above until printing can be achieved. But in view of its complexity it appears unlikely that he ever constructed the complete machine.

To return to his sun-signalling system. This instrument was completely successful in that it was manufactured by Troughton and Simms under the name of *Galton's Sun-Signal*; it was subsequently adopted by the Admiralty and used as late as 1908 in nautical surveys where shore parties needed to indicate their exact position to those on a ship.[10]

The problem in designing a small heliostat was to find a means of aiming the flash accurately. Galton's method was to intercept a small part of the flash from the mirror to create an image of the sun in the field of view of a small telescope attached to the side of the mirror. This mock sun could then be thrown by the operator on to the desired part of the landscape with the assurance that the flash would then be visible to a person in the target area.

The pocket instrument was very compact being less than 5 inches in length.

A larger version of the instrument consisted of a theodolite telescope and a finder, the whole being mounted on a camera tripod.[11]

Galton's meteorological work involved him in the design of automated weather stations, and his membership of the Kew Observatory committee led to his further involvement in the testing and improvement of a variety of instruments from sextants to thermometers.[12]

In the automated weather stations recordings were made on photographic paper. For instance, in the case of barometric records, a light source was placed behind a column of mercury and cast a shadow on to the light-sensitive paper which was moved continuously along by a clockwork mechanism. Similar arrangements were made to record from the other instruments. The resulting tracings were cumbersome and it was necessary to reduce them in size to enable them to be published in compendious yearly volumes. This meant that the reduction had to be greater in width than in height as the horizontal scale was very coarse on the photographic paper.

Galton's solution took the form of a compound pantagraph which would reduce the tracings in height independently of the reduction in length.[13] In essence the equipment worked by separating the vertical and horizontal movements of the tracing stylus and conveying the former by a pantagraphic linkage to the recording pencil, and the latter by a similar means to the drawing board itself, on which the reproduction was to appear. Galton was able to reduce the horizontal extent of the tracings in the ratio of $6:1$, while the vertical extent was reduced $2:1$. Drills and zinc plates could replace the pencil if casts were required for printing. The pantagraph proved successful in practice and was used over a period of twelve years to print the daily records from seven weather stations.

A second instrument designed in conjunction with meteorological recording was a 'trace computer'. This device enabled an operator to obtain a vapour-tension curve directly from the curves of dry and wet bulb thermometers. Again the essence of the technique was to separate the contribution of the two curves towards the final tracing. This trace computer was described in the 1871 Report of the Meteorological Committee,[14] but was never manufactured commercially, although it would have had wider application than for its specific purpose.

Galton's optical inventions were very simple. One device, which never caught the public fancy, consisted of special spectacles to be worn by divers to give clear vision under water.[15] In his description Galton points out that the eyeball, being convex, 'stamps' a concave lens in the medium of the water, which effect can be neutralised by a strong convex lens or system of lenses. He had experimented with various combinations of lenses in his bath until he found one that enabled him to read a newspaper under water. As he describes the incident in his autobiography :

'I amused myself very frequently with this new hobby, and being most interested in the act of reading, constantly forgot that I was nearly suffocating myself, and was recalled to the fact not by any gasping desire for breath, but purely by a sense of illness, that alarmed me. It disappeared immediately after raising the head out of water and inhaling two or three good whiffs of air.'[16]

He must also have tried the spectacles in the sea for he promises swimmers a material addition to their enjoyment :

'It is no slight pleasure to live in some degree the life of a mermaid, keeping below water for a minute at a time, and seeing everything in one's immediate neighbourhood as clearly as it could be seen by leaning over the gunwahl of a boat on a still day, when the glare from the water was perfectly shaded.'[17]

The extent of clear vision was limited to about 8 ft, and although Galton thought such spectacles might be useful to sponge and pearl divers, they would appear to have several disadvantages compared with the simple face mask worn by free–divers today.

In connection with this paper, Galton made extensive notes, which remained unpublished, on the possible visual mechanisms of diving birds and of aquatic mammals, such as seals and water-rats, which must adapt their vision from air to water. He suggests the keeping of water-rats in a tank from which the water is drawn and replaced alternatively while the convexity of the cornea is measured.

Being but a little above average height Galton had his view of public ceremonies, which he enjoyed, frequently obscured by the heads of those in front of him. His method for seeing comfortably under these conditions was to employ a small periscope—merely a square-sectioned cardboard tube with two inclined mirrors, similar to those obtainable in toy shops today. Galton constructed many of these 'hyperscopes', as he generally termed them, and even used them in lecture halls when his view of the lecturer was obscured. He last used one (which on this occasion he referred to as 'hypergynescope— for seeing over women's bonnets !') to observe Queen Victoria opening the Victoria and Albert Museum, when the Brompton Road was thickly crowded. According to his niece, on that, as on earlier occasions, he supplemented the periscope with a wooden brick and a piece of string concealed in a brown paper parcel.

'This he carried under his arm, and if a tiresome tall person stood before him, he would gently and slowly drop his brick and stand on it with one foot, and when it was time to go, draw it up by its string, and no one noticed anything.'[18]

Galton's inventiveness in devising anthropometric and psychological equipment was demonstrated in his successful Anthropometric Laboratory at the International Health Exhibition. But the apparatus exhibited there represents only a portion of his work in this general field.

He was one of the first to introduce standard scales for eye and hair colour. Printed tints had been devised by Broca and Chevreuil but they were unsatisfactory as they tended to fade. Galton used a series of artificial glass eyes against which the laboratory attendant matched those of the subject.

In the case of hair, samples were exhibited of flaxen, light-brown, brown, dark-brown, fair red (golden), red, dark-red (chestnut auburn), and black hair, but no attempt was made to judge the colour of the subjects' hair,

'for the reason that what with the darkening effects of pomades, and of dyes, and the misleading appearance of false hair, no useful results could be arrived at.'[19]

Later, Galton suggested the use of spun glass for hair matching and Horace Darwin prepared specimens for him, but no use was made of them, and it was not until the turn of the century that the German anthropologists produced reliable colour standards for hair by this means.

No attempt was made to estimate skin colour in the Laboratory, but for this purpose Galton made an interesting proposal. On a visit to the Vatican in 1869 he had been impressed by the extent of its collection of mosaics, 25 000 bins filled with cakes of mosaic material, each bin housing a different colour. If samples could be obtained from the whole range by some such body as the South Kensington Museum, a standard scale of colours might be selected for exhibition,

'by reference to which a person's meaning might be expressed with precision whenever he desired to designate a particular hue or tint.'[20]

Furthermore the scale could be copied in mosaic (to cover an area 10 ft × 1 ft) and distributed among the art schools of the United Kingdom.

In a letter to the Museum authorities he suggested that they should apply to the Pope for samples, but although his suggestion was pursued the price asked was too high. On a second visit to the Vatican in 1886, Galton, who was now deeply immersed in his anthropometric work, saw that the 500 or so flesh tints needed to match the varieties of Caucasian skin were amply covered by the Vatican series. In spite of the fact that the Vatican now appeared to be collaborating with outside bodies—he saw a sample being taken—he did not directly request tablets from that source but suggested that other factories might be induced to make them. Mosaics for matching skin colour were widely adopted at a later date, but have been superseded by the Munsell colour charts and photoelectric techniques.

Much of the equipment in Galton's Laboratory was designed to measure the acuity of the various senses and would today be found in the psychological laboratory. Most of these devices were extremely simple but do not deserve exclusion on that account.

Visual acuity was measured by simply noting the greatest distance at which a person could read a passage from a prayer book printed in very small ('diamond') type. The eyes were tested separately, the subject applying his eye to an eye-hole opposite which sentences were exposed at various distances from 7–41 inches. The sentences were posted on to wooden blocks attached to a curved frame in such a way that each stood clear of the next. It was unfortunate that the material was familiar to many of the subjects; Galton realised his mistake and proposed the use of logarithm tables in future work. He admitted too that the light in the laboratory was not constant, a necessary pre-requisite for this test. A later improved test for use with a non-literate population was never employed. It consisted of a series of white cards with a black dot near one corner. The subject's task was to indicate in which corner the dot lay. The size of the dot could be varied and an occasional trap laid, when a blank card would be exposed.[21]

Two types of visual judgement were also measured : judgements of length and judgements of 'squareness'. In the former, the subject moved a slider along a bar until he considered he had trisected it. His accuracy was checked against a scale etched on to the hidden side of the bar. In the case of 'squareness', the subject had to set a horizontally-rotating bar at right angles to a line drawn on the table. A hidden protractor supplied a measure of the accuracy of the setting. These tests were used less for the intrinsic value of the results than as examples of the way in which a large class of tests might conveniently be conducted. The examiner did not have to wait while the judgements were made but could return from other business when the subject had finished and in a few seconds take a reading.

To examine colour vision Galton devised two techniques. The first and simplest required the subject to examine reels of variously coloured wool and to indicate which of the reels contained wool of any shade of green. As the response was made by inserting a peg opposite the appropriate reel, it was again possible for the examiner to be otherwise occupied during the period of choice and later to check the result. This test was a variation of Holmgren's light-green test and was inadequate as a measure of colour weakness in other parts of the spectrum.

Another simple technique was described by Galton in 1890 in a report to a special committee of the Royal Society, of which Lord Rayleigh was chairman.[22] Nine boxes, each powered by a policeman's bull's eye lantern, could be set to produce red, green, or neutral hues. The investigator was apparently to set in advance three boxes of each colour and to present the nine in random order to the subject, who had to turn a lever attached to the box to indicate which hue he saw. The experiment was to take place in the dark, and Galton thought that the conditions were sufficiently similar to those under which sailors and engine drivers had to discriminate colours as to serve as a quick test to prevent the selection of red-green colour blind persons for these occupations. The apparatus was never put to practical use.

An instrument described as a test of the perception of tint can best be considered in the present context.[23] It appears primarily to have been a device for measuring the sensitivity of the observer to apparent brightness. At the end of a blackened viewing tube two square windows could be seen, which were illuminated by reflecting a light source off a white card. A square frame opposite each window was arranged to rotate in the horizontal direction, the rotation being controlled by a graduated wheel. Gratings of fine wire could be inserted into these frames, one of which was set to a particular position by the experimenter. The effect of the inclined grating was to dim the brightness of one of the windows, and the subject was required to adjust the other wheel until both windows were of the same apparent brightness. Sensitivity to brightness in different parts of the spectrum could be investigated by inserting sheets of coloured glass into the two frames. The instrument was never developed beyond the experimental stage. Galton exhibited it to the Anthropological Institute, but pointed out that further work was required to determine the calibration of the control wheels.

Galton's whistle for examining the threshold for high-pitched notes is perhaps the best-known item of his sensory equipment. The whistle was manufactured by at least two instrument makers (Hawksley and Tisley), and it was used in psychological laboratories for many years until replaced by the modern audiometer. It consisted of a narrow tube the length of which could be varied by screwing a plug in or out. A scale was arranged to register the number of turns made by the screw and was calibrated in cycles per second. The scale ran from 6461 c.p.s. to 84 000 c.p.s., but Galton considered the calibration to be unreliable over 14 000 c.p.s. The unreliability arose from the very narrow bore of the whistle (0.16 in) which was necessary to ensure that the length was always more than $1\frac{1}{2}$ times the diameter, which is critical for the formula giving the frequency.[24]

At higher frequencies the whistle gave a very weak note and Galton tried various means to produce notes that were both shrill and powerful. One interesting variation involved the use of hydrogen rather than expelled air. Hydrogen, being 13 times lighter than air, will give rise to many more vibrations per second, the period of vibration being inversely proportional to the square root of the specific gravity. By the attachment of a gas bag of hydrogen to the whistle Galton hoped to reach frequencies of 173 000 c.p.s.[25] In view of the failure of the air whistle in the examination of the hearing of insects, he proposed the use of the hydrogen whistle instead, but whether he made any trials is unknown.

Galton exhibited in his Anthropometric Laboratory a model of a test for measuring the delicacy of the pressure sense, but he did not use it as the procedure was slow. The subject placed a finger on one pan of a balance while the weight in the other pan was increased or decreased at a chosen rate. This was achieved by placing on the pan a light glass cylinder half filled with water, with a broad plunger suspended above it. When the plunger was depressed, the water rose in the graduated cylinder, and the effect was the same as if water had been poured in. Raising the plunger decreased the weight of water in the cylinder.

Experiments made on the pressure sense on other occasions employed the well-known series of graded weights used by earlier German investigators. Galton made his weights from cartridge cases filled with different amounts of lead shot. Eleven series of three weights in each were presented to the subject who tried to place the weights within a series in the correct order of magnitude. The items in the various series varied from very different to very similar to one another, and the point in the graded series beyond which the subject failed was taken as his threshold.

If, as in earlier work, the weights were placed on the palm which was then simply lifted up from a table, the judgement might be based on pressure or on the sense of muscular effort. In order to distinguish between these two cues, Galton arranged a stirrup, held by a counterbalance over a pulley, on which the subject's outstretched hand was placed. The weight was placed on the palm and an exactly equal weight on the pan of the counterbalance; the subject made his initial report from the pressure sensation alone. The stirrup was then suddenly depressed and the subject made a second judgement from the additional muscular cues. This equipment of Galton's represented the first attempt to effect a separation between the pressure and muscular sensations involved in weight judgement.[26]

The more dynamic anthropometric measurements involved recording (i) the speed of a person's reaction to a sound or to a flash of light, and (ii) the speed with which a punch could be delivered. Reaction time equipment had been devised in Germany and it was this German equipment that was later widely adopted by psychological laboratories until superseded in modern times by electronic time measures. Galton's own device was not used in his Anthropometric Laboratory and no results were published in this connection although the apparatus was certainly constructed. It was very much a 'Heath Robinson' affair. A pendulum released by the experimenter, either brushed against a small mirror which reflected a light on to a screen and thus gave the subject a light signal, or knocked off a small weight which fell on to a hollow box and provided a sound signal. Upon receiving the signal the subject reacted as quickly as possible by pressing a telegraph key which clamped a thread stationary, which until that moment had been pushed forward by the motion of the pendulum. The motion of the pendulum itself was not checked abruptly because the thread was stretched horizontally by two elastic bands which gave with the impact. The position at which the thread was clamped could be noted on a scale at the side of the instrument and the time which had elapsed between the stimulus and the response could be inferred.[27]

Several arrangements were devised for measuring the speed of a blow. The earliest equipment consisted of a rod, padded at one end, which ran freely betwen two guides. The rate of progress of the rod under the impact of a punch was measured by a pencil attached to a vibrating spring that had been bent to one side and retained by a catch which was set free by the moving rod. But, as mentioned in Chapter 13, this equipment was unsatisfactory in practice as the blow had to be a straight one.

To overcome this restriction Galton reversed the action of the equipment and replaced the pad at the end of the rod with a stirrup. The subject now faced the other way, put his hand in the stirrup and punched into space dragging the rod behind him. A final improved version worked on the same principle.[28]

Several pocket counters were devised by Galton for the surreptitious recording of events. The simplest was merely a thimble with a spike on the end which could be used to prick holes in a piece of paper. It was with this device that Galton started to record data for his Beauty Map (See Chapter 13).

Perhaps the neatest registrator consisted of a cotton glove with a pricking device sewn into the thumb. A visiting card could be inserted into a pocket in the glove across the palm at the base of the finger. By pressing the thumb against the base of any finger a prick could be made in the card. Thus, four different classes of event could be counted. One snag with this arrangement was the possibility that one would prick the same hole more than once and register too few counts. Another difficulty lay in keeping the registration of the different classes of event sufficiently separate.

The most complete pocket registrator was manufactured for Galton by Hawksley. It employed five keys to be operated by the fingers and thumb of one hand. When a key was pressed, a pointer was moved one division around one of five small dials. The instrument was only four inches long and less than two inches wide and it could be easily used in the pocket or under the cover of a mitten.

'It is possible by its means to take anthropological statistics of any kind among crowds of people without exciting observation, which it is otherwise exceedingly difficult to do.'[29]

Psychologists and others taking naturalistic observations could well find a use for a modern version of this instrument.

A few miscellaneous inventions remain to be discussed. When lecturing to Army personnel at Aldershot, Galton became interested in the possible protection of a rifleman from enemy fire.[30] His device consisted of a metal screen placed just above the line of sight of a prone rifleman. It relied on the fact that with the then available firearms, the trajectory at the beginning of an outward shot would be flatter than that at the end of an incoming shot and the screen would therefore interfere with the one and not with the other. To be effective the device depended on the unlikely circumstance that only one opponent would be involved and that he would maintain a fixed position. Presumably because of these limitations the invention did not find favour with the military authorities; in any case improvements in the rifle led to flatter bullet trajectories and soon rendered the device obsolete.

A bicycle speedometer was described in a letter to *Field* in 1877. It merely consisted of a small sand-glass carried by the rider who had simply to count the number of pedal revolutions before the sand ran out. This number gave the speed in miles per hour. Different sand-glasses were needed for different wheel diameters. Galton mentions a 10-second sand-glass for use with a wheel of a diameter of 4 ft 8 in !

A card selector, of which many variants have since appeared, was devised by Galton in order to select individual cards from a large card-index.[31] The cards had up to six notches cut out of their edges, corresponding in the case of the Bertillon system to certain measurements of the individual. The bottom of the box was replaced by a system of wires so arranged that the pressing of levers would cause all those cards without those particular notches to rise. Thus, the card with the combination of measurements needed would remain in place and could be readily extracted.

Finally, we will mention an item of perceptual interest described in a paper to *Nature* in 1882.[32] This 'rapid-view instrument' was a type of *tachistoscope*, that is, a device for presenting visual material for very short durations of time. Galton's apparatus differed from other versions in that it was intended to give a rapid glance not of a stationary drawing or photo-graph but of a moving object. His original purpose was to verify by eye the recent advances in photography which had, for the first time, enabled the photographer to arrest the motion of animals.

The device consisted of a box with a hole to which the observer applied his eye. When a stud on the top of the box was pressed, a horizontal slit moved rapidly in front of the eye allowing a momentary glimpse of the desired scene. Upon releasing the stud, a second view was obtained as a rubber band drew the slit upwards and past the view-hole again. Galton computed the duration of the second exposure to be 1/350th second under the action of the spring; the duration of the first exposure varied somewhat depending on the tap given to the stud.

'The power exists, and can be utilised, of seeing bodies in motion by a rapid-view instrument, showing them in apparent stillness, and leaving a sharply defined image on the eye, that can be drawn from visual memory, which in some persons is very accurate and tenacious.'[33]

Thus, Galton claims, it is simple to arrest the movement of animals, such as a galloping horse or a crow in flight. He thinks that naturalists might find the instrument useful in observing animals and that physicists could employ it in their investigations of fluids in motion.

A variation of the instrument utilised prisms and two horizontal slits, one above the other. The prisms deflected the first image 4° to the left and the second image 4° to the right. Thus, the observer saw two apparently simul-taneous pictures side by side.

Other and more elaborate versions of the instrument, employing multiple levers and revolving discs, were manufactured for Galton by Tisley. But Galton never again refers to these devices which might still be of use in preliminary field work.

Although today only a little of value remains from among these various practical manifestations of Galton's creativity, this brief account of the more important of them may help to emphasise the fact that Galton was a practical scientist. Not only did he attempt to put theoretical formulations to the test but he devised the apparatus to enable him to do so.

Appendix II

Stimulus Material
for Word Association Experiments

Final (eighth) list of 86 stimulus words contained in Galton's notebook, 'Psychometric Inquiries', dated 13th January 1879.

Abasement	Acerbity	Advance
Abbey	Acheron	Advantage
Abcess	Achievement	Advantageous
Abduction	Acid	Adventitious
Abhorrence	Acoustics	Adversity
Ability	Acquaintance	Advice
Ablution	Acquirement	Advocate
Abnormal	Acquisition	Aeriform
Abominable	Acrobat	Aesthetics
Aborigine	Activity	Affable
Abrasion	Actor	Affection
Abreviation [sic]	Actuality	Affiance
Absence	Actuary	Affinity
Absolute	Adage	Affliction
Absolution	Adder	Affluence
Abstemious	Addition	Affront
Abstract	Adequate	Afternoon
Abstruse	Adhesive	Agent
Abundance	Adjective	Ague
Abyss	Adjudication	Aide-de-Camp
Academy	Adjunctive	Aigle
Acceleration	Adjutant	Albino
Accepim	Administration	Album
Acceptable	Admiral	Alderman
Accidental	Admission	Alembic
Acclamation	Adoption	Alluvium
Accomodation [sic]	Adoration	Almananack [sic]
Accoutrement	Adulation	Animal
Ace	Adulteration	

Appendix III

Bibliography of Galton's published work

The Telotype: a Printing Electric Telegraph. J. Weale, London (1850).

Extract from a letter of 16 August 1851. *The Times*, 1 January (1852).

'Recent expedition into the interior of South-Western Africa.' *Journal of the Royal Geographical Society*, **22** (1852), pp.140–63.

Tropical South Africa. John Murray, London (1853). Second edition, under the title *Narrative of an Explorer in Tropical South Africa*, Ward, Lock and Co., London (1889).

'List of astronomical instruments, etc.' In 'Hints to travellers.' *Journal of the Royal Geographical Society*, **24** (1854), pp.1–13.

'Notes on Modern Geography.' In *Cambridge Essays contributed by Members of the University.* J. W. Parker (ed.), J. W. Parker, London (1885), pp.79–109.

The Art of Travel; or, Shifts and Contrivances Available in Wild Countries. Murray, London (1855). Second edition (1856). Third edition (1860). Fourth edition (1867). Fifth edition (1872). Sixth edition (1878). Seventh edition (1883). Eighth edition (1893). (David and Charles Reprints (1971), the 1872 edition reprinted under the title *Francis Galton's Art of Travel*, with an introduction by Dorothy Middleton.)

Arts of Campaigning. John Murray, London (1855).

Ways and Means of Campaigning. Privately printed (1855).

Arts of Travelling and Campaigning. T. Brettell, London (1856).

Catalogue of Models Illustrative of the Arts of Camp Life. T. Brettell, London (1858).

'The exploration of arid countries.' *Proceedings of the Royal Geographical Society*, **2** (1858), pp.60–77.

[Review of *Western Africa*, Hutchinson,] *Proceedings of the Royal Geographical Society*, **2** (1858), pp.227–9.

'A hand heliostat for the purpose of flashing sun signals, from on board ship or on land, in sunny climates.' *Report of the British Association* (1858), pp.15–7. Also in *The Engineer*, 15 October (1858), p.292.

'A description of a hand heliostat.' *Report of the British Association*, (1858), pp.211–2.

'Sun signals for the use of travellers (hand heliostat).' *Proceedings of the Royal Geographical Society*, **4** (1859), pp.14–9.

English Weather Data. February 9, 1861, 9 a.m. Privately printed (1861).

'Meteorological charts.' *Philosophical Magazine,* **22** (1861), pp.34–5.

Circular Letter to Meteorological Observers. Synchronous Weather Charts. Privately printed (1861).

Weather Map of the British Isles for Tuesday, September 3, 1861, 9 a.m. Privately printed (1861).

'Visit to North Spain at the time of the eclipse.' In *Vacation Tourists and Notes of Travel in 1860.* F. Galton (ed.), Macmillan, London (1861), pp.422–54.

'On a new principle for the protection of riflemen.' *Journal of the Royal United Services Institute,* **4** (1861), pp.393–6.

'Additional instrumental instructions to Mr Consul Petherick.' *Proceedings of the Royal Geographical Society,* **5** (1861), pp.96–7.

'Zanzibar.' *The Mission Field,* **6** (1861), pp.121–30.

'On the "Boussole Burnier", a new French pocket instrument for measuring vertical and horizontal angles.' *British Association Report* (1862), p.30.

'European weather charts for December 1861', *British Association Report,* (1862), p.30.

Meteorological Instructions for the Use of Inexperienced Observers Resident Abroad. Meteorological Society, (1862).

'Recent discoveries in Australia.' *The Cornhill Magazine,* **5** (1862), pp.354–64.

'Report on African explorations.' *Proceedings of the Royal Geographical Society,* **6** (1862), pp.175–8.

[Preface to] *Vacation Tourists and Notes of Travel in 1861,* F. Galton (ed.), Macmillan, Cambridge and London (1862).

'Explorations in Eastern Africa.' *The Reader,* **1** (1863), p.19, pp.42–3. (Signed F. G.).

'The sources of the Nile,' *The Reader,* **1** (1863), p.615. (Unsigned).

'A development of the theory of cyclones.' *Proceedings of the Royal Society,* **12** (1863), pp.385–6.

Meteorographica, or Methods of Mapping the Weather. Macmillan, London and Cambridge (1863).

'The climate of Lake Nyanza. Deduced from the observations of Captains Speke and Grant.' *Proceedings of the Royal Geographical Society,* **7** (1863), pp.225–7.

'The avalanches of the Jungfrau.' *Alpine Journal,* **1** (1863), pp.184–8.

[Preface to] *Vacation Tourists and Notes of Travel in 1862–3,* F. Galton (ed.), Macmillan, London and Cambridge (1864).

The Knapsack Guide for Travellers in Switzerland. Murray, London (1864).

'First steps towards the domestication of animals.' *British Association Report,* (1864), p.93–4.

'Captain Speke's new volume.' [Review of *What led to the Discovery of the Source of the Nile,* J. H. Speke,] *The Reader,* **4** (1864), pp.125–6. (Unsigned).

'Burton on the Nile sources.' [Review of *The Nile Basin,* Richard Burton and James McQueen,] *The Reader,* **4** (1864), p.728. (Unsigned).

'Grant's Africa.' [Review of *A Walk Across Africa,* James Grant,] *The Reader,* **4** (1864), p.792. (Unsigned).

'Table for rough triangulation without the usual instruments and without calculation.' *Journal of the Royal Geographical Society*, **34** (1864), pp.281–4.

'On spectacles for divers, and on the vision of amphibious animals.' *British Association Report*, **35** (1865), pp.10–11.

[Letter to Major General Sabine on magnetic observations at Tiflis,] *British Association Report*, **35** (1865), pp.316–7.

[Review of *Frost and Fire, Natural Engines, Tool Marks and Chips*, J. F. Campbell, and of *Ice-caves of France and Switzerland*, C. F. Browne,] *The Edinburgh Review*, **250** (1865), pp.422–55. (Unsigned).

[Discussion of Nilotic discoveries,] *Proceedings of the Royal Geographical Society*, **9** (1865), pp.10–11.

'On stereoscopic maps, taken from models of mountainous countries.' *Journal of the Royal Geographical Society*, **35** (1865), pp.99–104. Summary in *Proceedings of the Royal Geographical Society*, **9** (1865), pp.104–5.

Hints to Travellers, edited by G. Beck, R. Collinson and F. Galton. Revised edition, Royal Geographical Society, London (1865). Third edition (1871). Fourth edition, edited by Galton alone (1878).

'The first steps towards the domestication of animals.' *Transactions of the Ethnological Society of London*, **3** (1865), pp.122–38.

'Hereditary talent and character.' *Macmillan's Magazine*, **12** (1865), pp. 157–66, pp. 318–27.

'On an error in the usual method of obtaining meteorological statistics of the ocean.' *British Association Report*, **36** (1866), pp.16–7. Also in *The Athenaeum*, **2027** (1866), p.274.

'On the conversion of wind-charts into passage charts.' *British Association Report*, **36** (1866), pp.17–20. Also in *Philosophical Magazine*, **32** (1866), pp.345–9.

'Hereditary genius.' [Letter in] *Notes and Queries on China and Japan.* August (1868).

Hereditary Genius. Macmillan, London (1869). Second edition (1892). Third edition, Watts, (1950). Second edition, reprinted with an introduction by C. D. Darlington, Collins, London (1962); and World Publishing Company, New York and Cleveland (1962).

'Description of the pantagraph designed by Mr Galton.' *Minutes of the Meteorological Committee* (1869), p.9.

'Barometric predictions of weather.' *British Association Report*, **40** (1870), 31–3. Also in *Nature*, **2** (1870), pp.501–3.

'Mechanical computer of vapour tension.' *Report of the Meteorological Committee* (1871), p.30.

'Experiments in pangenesis, by breeding from rabbits of a pure variety, into whose circulation blood taken from other varieties had previously been largely transfused.' *Proceedings of the Royal Society*, **19** (1871), pp.393–410. Also, Taylor and Francis, London (1871).

'Pangenesis.' [Letter in] *Nature*, **4** (1871), pp.5–6.

'Gregariousness in cattle and in men.' *Macmillan's Magazine*, **23** (1871). pp.353–57.

'Statistical inquiries into the efficacy of prayer.' *Fortnightly Review*, **12** (1872), pp.125–35. Also in *The Prayer Gauge Debate*, J. O. Means (ed.), Congregational Publishing Co., Boston (1876).

'The efficacy of prayer.' [Letter in] *Spectator*, 24 August 1872, p.1073.

'On blood-relationship.' *Proceedings of the Royal Society*, **20** (1872), pp.394-402. Also in *Nature*, **6** (1872), pp.173–6.

[Opening address by the president to the Geographical Section.] *British Association Report*, **62** (1872), pp.198–203. Also, in *Nature*, **6** (1872), pp.343–5. Also William Clowes and Sons, Brighton (1872).

'Memorandum on the construction of "isodic charts", by which the average length of a day's sail by any particular class of vessels, in any direction, at any place, and in any season, may be readily found, and the average duration of passages along suggested tracks determined and compared.' *Minutes of the Meteorological Council*, 2 December (1872).

[Letter in] *Daily News*, 7 September (1872).

'Lieutenant Dawson and his barometers.' [Letter in] *Daily News*, 18 September (1872).

'Barometer tubes.' [Letter in] *Daily News*, 20 September (1872).

'On the employment of meteorological statistics in determining the best course for a ship whose sailing qualities are known.' *Proceedings of the Royal Society*, **21** (1873), pp.263–74.

Hereditary im provement.' *Fraser's Magazine*, **7** (1873), pp.116–30.

'On the extinction of surnames.' *Educational Times* (1873).

'On a proposed stable state.' *Nature*, **9** (1873), pp.342–3.

'The relative supplies from town and country families to the population of future generations.' *Journal of the Statistical Society*, **36** (1873), pp.19–26.

'On the causes which operate to create scientific men.' *Fortnightly Review*, **13** (1873), pp. 345–51.

'Africa for the Chinese.' [Letter in] *The Times*, 6 June (1873).

English Men of Science: their Nature and Nurture. Macmillan, London (1874), Second edition, with an introduction by Ruth Schwartz Cohen, Frank Cass, London (1970).

'On men of science, their nature and their nurture.' *Proceedings of the Royal Institution*, **7** (1874), pp.227–36. Also in *Nature*, **9** (1874), pp.344–5.

'On a proposed statistical scale.' [Letter in] *Nature*, **9** (1874), pp. 342–3.

'Nuts and men.' [Letter in] *Spectator*, 30 May (1874), p. 689.

'Proposal to apply for anthropological statistics from schools.' *Journal of the Anthropological Institute*, **3** (1874), pp. 308–11.

'Notes on the Marlborough School statistics.' *Journal of the Anthropological Institute*, **4** (1874), pp.130–5.

'On the excess of females in the West Indian Islands, from documents communicated to the Anthropological Institute of the Colonial Office.' *Journal of the Anthropological Institute*, **4** (1874), pp.136–7.

[Prefatory remarks to 'On the probability of the extinction of families', H. W. Watson,] *Journal of the Anthropological Institute*, **4** (1874), pp.138–9.

[Review of *Heredity; a Psychological Study of its Phenomena, Laws, Causes, and Consequences*, Th. Ribot,] *The Academy*, 30 January (1875).

'Statistics by intercomparison with remarks on the Law of Frequency of Error.' *Philosophical Magazine,* **49** (1875), pp.33–46.

[Discussion of 'Ultra-Centenarian Longevity', G. D. Gibb,] *Journal of the Anthropological Institute,* **5** (1875), pp.98–9.

'The history of twins, as a criterion of the relative powers of nature and nurture.' *Fraser's Magazine,* **12** (1875), pp.566–76. Revised version reprinted in *Journal of the Anthropological Institiute,* **5** (1875), pp.391–406. Summary in *Nature,* **13** (1875), p.59.

'Short notes on heredity etc., in twins.' *Journal of the Anthropological Institute,* **5** (1875), pp.324–9. Extracts reprinted under the title 'Twins and fertility'. *The Live Stock Journal and Fanciers' Gazette,* **3** (1876), p.148.

'A theory of heredity.' *Contemporary Review,* **27** (1875), pp.80–95. Also, under the title 'Théorie de l'hérédité'. *La Revue Scientifique,* **10** (1876), pp.198–205. Revised version reprinted in *Journal of the Anthropological Institute,* **5** (1875), pp.329–48. Summary in *Nature,* **13** (1875), p.59.

'On the height and weight of boys aged 14, in town and country public schools.' *Journal of the Anthropological Institute,* **6** (1876), pp.174–80.

[Report on measurement in] *The Effects of Cross and Self-Fertilization in the Animal Kingdom,* C. Darwin, Murray, London (1876), pp.16–8.

'Whistles for determining the upper limits of audible sound in different persons.' In *Physics and Mechanics, South Kensington Museum Conference.* Chapman and Hall, London (1876).

'Typical laws of heredity.' *Proceedings of the Royal Institution,* **8** (1877), 282–301. Also in *Nature,* **15** (1877), pp.492–5, pp.512–4, pp.532–3; and under the title 'Les lois typiques de l'hérédité', *La Revue Scientifique,* **13** (1877), pp.385–93.

'Considerations adverse to the maintenance of Section F.' *Journal of the Statistical Society,* **40** (1877), pp.468–73.

'Address to the Department of Anthropology, Section H.' *British Association Report,* (1877), pp.94–100. Summary in *Nature,* **16** (1877), pp.344–7. Also, under the title *Address to the Anthropological Department of the British Association.* W. Clowes and Sons, London (1877); and under the title 'La psychophysique', *La Revue Scientifique,* **13** (1877), pp.494–8.

'Bicycle speedometer.' *Field* (1877).

'Description of the process of verifying thermometers at the Kew Observatory.' *Proceedings of the Royal Society,* **26** (1877), pp.84–9. Also in *Philosophical Magazine,* **4** (1877), pp.226–31.

'On means of combining various data in maps and diagrams,' in *Chemistry, Biology, etc., South Kensington Museum Conference.* Chapman and Hall, London (1878), pp.312–5.

'Letters of Henry Stanley from Equatorial Africa to the *Daily Telegraph.*' *Edinburgh Review,* January (1878), pp.166–91. (Unsigned).

'Composite portraits made by combining those of many different persons into a single figure.' *Journal of the Anthropologival Institute,* **8** (1878), pp. 132–48. Also, under the title 'Les portraits composites', *La Revue Scientifique,* **15** (1878), pp.33–8; and *Nature,* **18** (1878), pp.97–100; and Harrison and Sons, London (1878).

'On the advancement of geographical teaching.' *Nature*, **18** (1878), p.337.

'Psychometric facts.' *Nineteenth Century*, March (1879), pp.425–33.

'Psychometric experiments.' *Brain*, **2** (1879), pp.149–62. Also William Clowes & Sons, London (1879).

'Generic images.' *Proceedings of the Royal Institution*, **9** (1879), 161–70. Also, William Clowes and Sons, London (1879). With additions, under the title 'Les images génériques', *La Revue Scientifique*, **17** (1879), pp.221–5.

'Generic images.' *Nineteenth Century*, **6** (1879), pp.157–69.

'The average flush of excitement.' [Letter in] *Nature*, **20** (1879), p. 121.

'The geometric mean, in vital and social statistics.' *Proceedings of the Royal Society*, **29** (1879), pp.365–7.

'Statistics of mental imagery.' *Mind*, **5** (1880), pp.301–18.

'Mental imagery,' *Fortnightly Review*, **28** (1880), pp.312–24.

'Visualised numerals.' *Nature*, **21** (1880), pp.252–6, 494–5.

'Visualised numerals.' [Letter in] *Nature*, **21** (1880), p.323.

'Visualised numerals.' *Journal of the Anthropological Institute*, **10** (1880), pp.85–102. Also Harrison and Sons, London (1880).

'The opportunities of science masters at schools.' [Letter in] *Nature*, **22** (1880), pp. 9–10.

'On determining the heights and distances of clouds by their reflexions in a low pond of water, and in a mercurial horizon.' *British Association Report*, **50** (1880), pp.459–61.

'On a pocket registrator for anthropological purposes.' *British Association Report*, **50** (1880), p.625. Summary in *Nature*, **22** (1880), p.478.

'The visions of sane persons.' *Fortnightly Review*, **29** (1881), pp.729–40. Reprinted with slight variations in *Proceedings of the Royal Institution*, **9** (1881), pp. 644–55.

'Composite portraiture.' *Photographic Journal*, **5** (1881), pp.140–6.

'Composite portraiture.' *Photographic News*, **25** (1881), pp.316–7, pp.332–3.

'On the application of composite portraiture to anthropological purposes.' *British Association Report*, **51** (1881), p.3.

[Tables and discussion of range in height, weight and strength] in Report of the Anthropometric Committee, *British Association Report*, **51** (1881), pp.225–72.

'On the construction of isochronic passage charts.' *British Association Report*, **51** (1881), pp.740–1. Also, *Proceedings of the Royal Geographical Society*, **3** (1881), pp.657–8. (A chart appears as frontispiece to *Hints to Travellers*, fifth edition, 1883.)

[Discussion on 'On the laws affecting the relations between civilized and savage life as bearing on the dealings of colonists with aborigines', H. Bartle Frere] *Journal of the Anthropological Institute*, **11** (1881), pp.352–3.

'Burials in the Abbey.' [Letter in] *Pall Mall Gazette*, **27** December (1881).

'Photographic chronicles from childhood to age.' *Fortnightly Review*, **181** (1882), pp.26–31.

With F. A. Mahomed. 'An inquiry into the physiognomy of phthisis by the method of "composite portraiture".' *Guy's Hospital Reports*, **25** February (1882).

'The late Mr Darwin: a suggestion.' [Letter in] *Pall Mall Gazette*, 27 April (1882).

'Conventional representation of the horse in motion.' *Nature*, **26** (1882), pp.228–9.

'A rapid-view instrument for momentary attitudes.' *Nature*, **26** (1882), pp.249–51.

[Discussion on 'Analysis of relationships of consanguinity and affinity', A. McFarlane,] *Journal of the Anthropological Institute*, **12** (1882), pp.61–2.

'The anthropometric laboratory.' *Fortnightly Review*, **183** (1882), pp.332–8.

Inquiries into Human Faculty and Its Development. Macmillan, London (1883). Second edition, Macmillan (1892). Third edition, Dent (1907). Fourth edition, Eugenics' Society (1951).

'Hydrogen whistles.' *Nature*, **27** (1883), pp.491–2. Also, corrected, in *Nature*, **28** (1883), p.54.

'Method of determining the distance and height of clouds and the direction and rate of their motions parallel to the earth's surface.' *Meteorological Council*, April (1883).

'The American trotting-horse.' *Nature*, **28** (1883), p.29.

[Reply to Romanes' review of *Human Faculty and Its Development*,] *Nature*, **28** (1883), pp.97–8.

'Arithmetic notation of kinship.' [Letter in] *Nature*, **28** (1883), p.435.

Outfit for an anthropometric laboratory. Privately printed (1883).

'On apparatus for testing the delicacy of the muscular and other senses in different persons.' *Journal of the Anthropological Institute*, **12** (1883), pp.469–77.

[Obituary: William Spottiswoode.] *Proceedings of the Royal Geographical Society*, **6** (1883), pp.489–91.

'Final Report of the Anthropometric Committee.' *British Association Report* (1883), pp.253–306.

'Report of the Local Scientific Societies Committee.' *British Association Report* (1883), pp.318–45. Partly reprinted in *Nature*, **28** (1883), pp.135–6.

'Family records.' [Letter in] *The Times*, 9 January (1884). Also in *Nature*, **30** (1884), p.82.

'The weights of British noblemen during the last three generations.' *Nature*, **29** (1884), pp.266–8.

[Discussion on 'On the races of the Congo and the Portuguese colonies in Western Africa', H. H. Johnston,] *Journal of the Anthropological Institute*, **13** (1884), pp.478–9.

Anthropometric Laboratory. William Clowes and Sons, London (1884).

'On the Anthropometric Laboratory at the late International Health Exhibition.' *Journal of the Anthropological Institute*, **14** (1884), pp.205–18. Also Harrison and Sons, London (1885).

'Some results of the Anthropometric Laboratory.' *Journal of the Anthropological Institute*, **14** (1884), pp.275–87.

Record of Family Faculties. Macmillan, London (1884).

L

Life-History Album. Macmillan, London (1884). First edition edited by F. Galton. Second edition, rearranged by F. Galton (1902).

'Free-will—observations and inferences.' *Mind*, **9** (1884), pp.406–13.

'Measurement of character.' *Fortnightly Review*, **36** (1884), pp.179–85.

'The identiscope.' *Nature*, **30** (1884), pp.637–8.

'The cost of anthropometric measurements.' [Letter in] *Nature*, **31** (1884), p.150.

'Anthropometric percentiles.' *Nature*, **31** (1885), pp.223–5.

'Hereditary deafness.' [Review of 'Upon the formation of a deaf variety of the human race', Alexander Bell,] *Nature*, **31** (1885), pp.269–70.

'Photographic composites.' *Photographic News*, **29** (1885), pp.234–45.

'A common error in statistics.' *Jubilee Volume of the Statistical Society*. Edward Stanford, London (1885), p.261.

'The application of a graphic method to fallible measures.' *Jubilee Volume of the Statistical Society*, Edward Stanford, London (1885), pp.262–5.

'The measure of fidget.' *Nature*, **32** (1885), pp.174–5.

[Presidential address, Section H, Anthropology,] *British Association Report*, **55** (1885), pp.1206–14. Also, under the title *Address to the Section of Anthropology of the British Association*. Spottiswoode, London (1885); and, *Nature*, **32** (1885), pp.507–10.

'Regression towards mediocrity in hereditary stature.' *Journal of the Anthropological Institute*, **15** (1885), pp.246–63.

[Opening remarks by the President, and discussion on 'Experiments in testing the character of school children,' Sophie Bryant,] *Journal of the Anthropological Institute*, **15** (1885), pp.336–8, p.350.

'Exhibition of composite photographs of skulls by Francis Galton.' *Journal of the Anthropological Institute*, **15** (1885), pp.390–1.

'Conference of delegates of corresponding societies of the British Association held at Aberdeen.' *Nature*, **33** (1885), pp.81–3.

'Hereditary Stature.' [Extracts from Presidential address to the Anthropological Institute.] *Nature*, **33** (1885), pp.295–8.

'Hereditary Stature.' [Letter in] *Nature*, **33** (1885), p.317.

[President's address,] *Journal of the Anthropological Institute*, **15** (1886), pp.489–99. Also, extracts in *Nature*, **33** (1886), p.295.

'Hereditary stature.' [Letter correction in] *Nature*, **33** (1886), p.317.

'On recent designs for anthropometric instruments.' *Journal of the Anthropological Institute*, **16** (1886), pp.2–8.

'Family likeness in stature.' *Proceedings of the Royal Society*, **40** (1886), pp.42–63.

[On *American Family Peculiarities in the Eighteenth Century*, J. Boucher,] *Journal of the Anthropological Institute*, **16** (1886), pp.98–9.

'Notes on permanent colour types in mosaic.' *Journal of the Anthropological Institute*, **16** (1886), pp.145–7. Also, Harrison and Sons, London (1886).

'Family-likeness in eye-colour.' *Proceedings of the Royal Society*, **40** (1886), pp.402–16. Also, summary in *Nature*, **34** (1886), p.137.

[Opening remarks by the President,] *Journal of the Anthropological Institute*, **16** (1886), pp.175–7, pp.189–90.

'The origin of varieties.' *Nature*, **34** (1886), pp.395–6.

'Supplementary notes on "Prehension in idiots".' *Mind*, **12** (1886), pp.79–82.

[Galton's speech at the Royal Society dinner after receiving the Gold Medal of the Society,] *The Times*, 1 December (1886).

'Chance and its bearing in heredity.' *Birmingham Daily Post*, 7 December (1886).

Pedigree Moths. On a Proposed Series of Experiments in Breeding Moths. Privately printed (1887).

[Address delivered at the anniversary meeting of the Anthropological Institute of Great Britain and Ireland,] *Journal of the Anthropological Institute*, **16** (1887), pp.387–402. Also Harrison and Sons, London (1887).

'Thoughts without words.' [Letters in] *Nature*, **36** (1887), pp.28–9, pp.100–1.

'North American pictographs.' *Nature*, **36** (1887), pp.155–7.

List of Anthropometric Apparatus. Cambridge Scientific Instrument Company, Cambridge (1887).

'Good and bad temper in English families.' *Fortnightly Review*, **42** (1887), pp.21–30.

'Photography and silhouettes.' [Letters in] *Photographic News*, **31** (1887), pp.429–30, p.462.

'Pedigree moth-breeding as a means of verifying certain important constants in the general theory of heredity.' *Transactions of the Entomological Society*, Part I (1887), pp.19–34.

[Discussion on 'On an Ancient British Settlement excavated near Rushmore, Salisbury', Pitt Rivers,] *Journal of the Anthropological Institute*, **17** (1887), 199–200.

'The proposed Imperial Institute: geography and anthropology.' [Letter in] *The Times*, 6 October (1887).

[Address delivered at the anniversary meeting of the Anthropological Institute of Great Britain and Ireland,] *Journal of the Anthropological Institute*, **17** (1887), 346–54. Also Harrison and Sons, London (1888).

'Note on Australian marriage systems.' *Journal of the Anthropological Institute*, **18** (1887), 70–2. Also Harrison and Sons, London (1888).

'Composite portraiture. A communication from Francis Galton.' *Photographic News*, **32** (1888), 257.

'On head growth in students at the University of Cambridge.' *Journal of the Anthropological Institute*, **18** (1888), 155–6. Also in *Nature*, **38** (1888), 14–5.

'Remarks on replies by teachers to questions respecting mental fatigue.' *Journal of the Anthropological Institute*, **18** (1888), 157–68. Also Harrison and Sons, London (1888).

'Personal identification and description.' *Nature*, **38** (1888), 173–7, 201–2. Also in *Journal of the Anthropological Institute*, **18** (1888), 177–91; and revised version in *Proceedings of the Royal Institution*, **12** (1888), 346–60.

[Discussion on 'On a method of investigating the development of institutions applied to laws of marriage and descent', E. Tylor,] *Journal of the Anthropological Institute*, **18** (1888), p.270.

[Remarks on the 'Exhibition of an ancient Peruvian gold breastplate',] *Journal of the Anthropological Institute*, **18** (1888), p.274.

'Co-relations and their measurement, chiefly from anthropometric data.' *Proceedings of the Royal Society*, **45** (1888), pp.135–45. Also in *Nature*, **39** (1889), p.238.

'Table of observations.' *Journal of the Anthropological Institute*, **18** (1889), pp.420–30. Also Harrison and Sons, London (1889).

Natural Inheritance. Macmillan, London (1889).

[Address delivered at the annual meeting of the Anthropological Institute of Great Britain and Ireland,] *Journal of the Anthropological Institute*, **18** (1889), pp.401–19. Also in *Nature*, **39** (1889), pp.296–7; and Harrison and Sons, London (1889).

'The sacrifice of education to examination.' *Nineteenth Century*, **25** (1889), pp.303–8.

'Exhibition of instruments (1) for testing the perception of differences of tint, and (2) for determining reaction-time.' *Journal of the Anthropological Institute*, 19 (1889), pp.27–9. Also Harrison and Sons, London (1889).

'Head growth in students at the University of Cambridge.' [Letter in] *Nature*, **40** (1889), p.318.

'On the advisability of assigning marks for bodily efficiency in the examination of candidates for public services.' *British Association Report*, **59** (1889), pp.471–3.

'On the principle and methods of assigning marks for bodily efficiency.' *British Association Report*, **59** (1889), pp.474–8. Also in *Nature*, **40** (1889), pp.631–2, pp.649–52.

'Feasible experiments on the possibility of transmitting acquired habits by means of inheritance.' *British Association Report*, **59** (1889), pp.620–1. Also in *Nature*, **40** (1889), p.610.

'An instrument for measuring reaction time.' *British Association Report*, **59** (1889), pp.784–5.

'Head measures at Cambridge.' [Letter in] *Nature*, **40** (1889), p.643.

'Why do we measure mankind?' *Lippincott's Monthly Magazine*, **45** (1890), pp.236–41.

'Cambridge anthropometry.' *Nature*, **41** (1890), p.454.

Tests and Certificates of the Kew Observatory. Kew Committee of the Royal Society (1890).

'Dice for statistical experiments.' *Nature*, **42** (1890), pp.13–4.

[Review of *The Criminal*, Havelock Ellis,] *Nature*, **42** (1890), pp.75–6.

'A new instrument for measuring the rate of movement of the various limbs.' *Journal of the Anthropological Institute*, **20** (1890), 200–4. Also, summary in *Nature*, **42** (1890), p.143.

'Physical tests in competitive examinations.' *Journal of the Society of Arts*, **39** (1890), pp.19–27.

[Remarks following 'Mental tests and measurements', J. McK. Cattell,] *Mind*, **15** (1890), pp.380–1.

Anthropometric Laboratory. Notes and Memoirs No. 1. Richard Clay, London (1890).

[Obituary: The Reverend G. Butler, D.D.,] *Proceedings of the Royal Geographical Society*, **12** (1890), pp.236–7.

[Discussion on 'An apparent paradox in mental evolution', Lady Welby,] *Journal of the Anthropological Institute*, **20** (1890), pp.304–23.

'The patterns in thumb and finger marks.' *Proceedings of the Royal Society*, **48** (1890), pp.455–7. Also in *Journal of the Anthropological Institute*, **20** (1890), pp.360–1; and *Nature*, **43** (1890), pp.117–8.

[Obituary: Miss North,] *Journal of the Anthropological Institute*, **20** (1891), p.302.

'Methods of indexing finger-marks.' *Proceedings of the Royal Society*, **49** (1891), pp.540–48. Also in *Nature*, **44** (1891), p.141.

'Meteorological phenomena.' [Letter in] *Nature*, **44** (1891), p.294.

'Identification by finger tips.' *Nineteenth Century*, **30** (1891), pp.303–11.

'Retrospect of work done at my anthropometric laboratory at South Kensington.' *Journal of the Anthropological Institute*, **21** (1891), pp.32–5. Also Harrison and Sons, London (1891).

'The patterns in thumb and finger marks.' *Philosophical Transactions*, B, **182** (1891), pp.1–23.

[Reminiscences of Henry Walter Bates, F.R.S.,] *Proceedings of the Royal Geographical Society*, **14** (1892), pp.255–7.

[Presidential address to the Division of Demography,] *Transactions of the Seventh International Congress of Hygiene and Demography*, **10** (1892), pp.7–12.

'Finger prints and their registration as a means of personal identification.' *Transactions of the Seventh International Congress of Hygiene and Demography*, **10** (1892), pp.301–3.

Finger Prints. Macmillan, London (1892). Reprinted, Da Capo Press, New York (1965), with an introduction by H. Cummins.

[Sections on 'Causes that limit population', 'astronomy', 'communications', 'statistics', 'population',] in *Notes and Queries on Anthropology*, Pitt-Rivers (ed.), second edition. British Association for the Advancement of Science (1892), pp.204, 208, 221, 226, 229.

'The just-perceptible difference.' *Proceedings of the Royal Institution*, **14** (1893), pp.13–26. Also, extracts published under the title 'Measure of the imagination.' *Nature*, **47** (1893), pp.319–21; and 'Optical continuity.' *Nature*, **47** (1893), pp.342–5.

'Enlarged finger prints.' *Photographic Work*, 10 February (1893).

'Identification.' [Letter in] *The Times*, 7 July (1893).

'Identification.' [Letter in] *Nature*, **48** (1893), p.222.

'Recent introduction into the Indian Army of the method of finger-prints for the identification of recruits.' *British Association Report* (1893), p.902. Also under the title 'Finger prints in the Indian Army.' *Nature*, **48** (1893), p.595.

Decipherment of Blurred Finger Prints. Macmillan, London (1893).

'Payments through telegram by P.O. Savings books.' [Letter in] *The Times*, 27 December (1893).

'Arithmetic by smell.' *Psychological Review*, **1** (1894), pp.61–2.

'A plausible paradox in chances.' *Nature*, **49** (1894), pp.365–6.

'Results derived from the natality tables of Korosi by employing the method of contours or isogens.' *Proceedings of the Royal Society*, **55** (1894), pp.18–23. Also in *Nature*, **49** (1894), p.570.

'The relative sensitivity of men and women at the nape of the neck, by Weber's test,' *Nature*, **50** (1894), pp.40–2.

'Discontinuity in evolution.' *Mind*, **3** (1894), pp.362–72.

Physical Index to 100 Persons Based on their Measures and Finger Prints. Privately printed (1894).

'The part of religion in human evolution.' *National Review*, **23** (1894), pp.755–63.

'Acquired characters.' [Letter in] *Nature*, **51** (1894), p.56.

'Psychology of mental arithmeticians and blindfold chess-players.' [Review of *Psychologie des Grands Calculateurs et Joueurs d'Echecs*, Alfred Binet,] *Nature*, **51** (1894), pp.73–4.

'A new step in statistical science.' [Letter in] *Nature*, **51** (1895), p.319.

'Questions bearing on specific stability.' *Transactions of the Entomological Society of London* (1895), pp.155–7. Also in *Nature*, **51** (1895), pp.570–1.

Finger Print Directories. Macmillan, London (1895).

'Terms of imprisonment.' *Nature*, **52** (1895), pp.174–6.

'Personality,' [Review of *The Diseases of Personality*, Th. Ribot,] *Nature*, **52** (1895), pp.517–8.

'The wonders of a finger print.' *Sketch*, 20 November (1895).

'Prints of scars.' [Letter in] *Nature*, **53** (1896), p.295.

[Obituary notices of Fellows deceased: Dr John Rae,] *Proceedings of the Royal Society*, **60** (1896), pp.5–7.

'Les empreintes digitales', *Comptes-rendus du IVe Congres International d'Anthropologie Criminelle*. Sessions de Genève (1896), pp.35–8.

'Three generations of lunatic cats.' *Spectator*, 11 April (1896).

'A curious idiosyncrasy.' *Nature*, **54** (1896), p.76.

'Intelligible signals between neighbouring stars.' *Fortnightly Review*, **60** (1896), pp.657–64.

'The Bertillon system of identification'. [Review of *Signaletic Instructions*, Alphonse Bertillon,] *Nature*, **54** (1896), pp.569–70.

Private circular of Committee for Measurement of Plants and Animals. Royal Society, 30 November (1896).

'Rate of racial change that accompanies different degrees of severity in selection.' *Nature*, **55** (1897), pp.605–6.

'Note to the memoir by Professor Karl Pearson, F.R.S., on spurious correlation.' *Proceedings of the Royal Society*, **60** (1897), pp.498–502.

'Retrograde selection.' *Gardiners' Chronicle*, 15 May (1897).

'The average contribution of each several ancestor to the total heritage of the offspring.' *Proceedings of the Royal Society*, **61** (1897), pp.401–13. Also, summary in 'A new law of heredity.' *Nature*, **56** (1897), pp.235–7.

'Hereditary colour in horses.' *Nature*, **56** (1897), pp.598–9.

'Relation between individual and racial variability.' [Unsigned review of 'A measure of variability and the relation of individual variation to specific differences', E. T. Brewster,] *Nature*, **57** (1897), pp.16–7.

'The late Dr. Haughton.' [Letter in] *Nature*, **57** (1897), p.79.

'An examination into the registered speeds of American trotting horses, with remarks on their value as hereditary data.' *Proceedings of the Royal Society*, **62** (1897), pp.310–5. Also in *Nature*, **58** (1898), pp.333–4.

'Photographic measurement of horses and other animals.' *Nature*, **57** (1898), pp.230–2.

'A diagram of heredity.' [Letter in] *Nature*, **57** (1898), p.292.

'Temporary flooring in Westminster Abbey for ceremonial procession.' [Letter in] *The Times*, 25 May (1898).

'Evolution of the moral instinct.' [Review of *The Origin and Growth of the Moral Instinct*, Alexander Sutherland,] *Nature*, **58** (1898), pp.241–2. (Signed F.G.).

'The distribution of prepotency.' [Letter in] *Nature*, **58** (1898), pp.246–7.

'Photographic records of pedigree stock.' [Letter in] *Live Stock Journal*, 30 September (1898).

'Corporal punishment.' [Letter in] *The Times*, 4 October (1898). (Signed F.G.).

'Photographic records of pedigree stock.' *British Association Report*, (1898), pp.597–603. Summary in *Nature*, **58** (1898), p.584.

'The photography of the premium horses.' *Appendix G, 7th Report of the Royal Commission on Horse Breeding*, (1899), pp.12–3.

'A measure of the intensity of hereditary transmission.' [Letter in] *Nature*, **60** (1899), p.29.

'Strawberry cure for gout.' [Letter in] *Nature*, **60** (1899), p.125.

'Pedigree stock records.' *British Association Report*, **69** (1899), pp.424–9.

'The median estimate.' *British Association Report*, **69** (1899), pp.638–40. Summary in *Nature*, **60** (1899), p.584.

'Finger prints of young children.' *British Association Report*, **69** (1899), pp.868–9.

'A geometric determination of the median value of a system of normal variants from two of its centiles.' *Nature*, **61** (1899), pp.102–4.

[Discussion on 'The metric system of identification of criminals as used in Great Britain and Ireland', J. G. Carson,] *Journal of the Anthropological Institute*, **30** (1900), pp.195–6.

[Introduction to] *William Cotton Oswell: The Story of His Life*, W. E. Oswell, Heinemann, London (1900).

'Souvenirs d'Egypte.' *Bulletin de la Société Khédiviale de Géographie*, Vᵉ Serie, **7** (1900), pp.375–80.

'Analytical portraiture.' [Letter in] *Nature*, **62** (1900), p.320.

'Analytical photography.' *Photographic Journal*, **25** (1900), pp.135–8.

'Identification offices in India and Egypt.' *Nineteenth Century*, **48** (1900), pp.118–26.

'Biometry.' *Biometrika*, **1** (1901), pp.7–10.

'The possible improvement of the human breed under the existing conditions of law and sentiment.' *Nature*, **64** (1901), pp.659–65. Also in *Report of the Smithsonian Institution* (1901), pp.523–38.

'On the probability that the son of a very highly-gifted father will be no less gifted.' *Nature*, **65** (1901), p.79.

'The most suitable proportion between the values of first and second prizes.' *Biometrika*, **1** (1902), pp.380–90.

[Letter in] *Truth*, **52** (1902), p.786.

'Finger print evidence.' *Nature*, **66** (1902), p.606.

'Sir Edward Fry and natural selection.' [Letter in] *Nature*, **67** (1903), p.343.

'Pedigrees, based on fraternal unities.' *Nature*, **67** (1903), pp.586–7.

'Our national physique—prospects of the British race—are we degenerating?' Article in *Daily Chronicle*, 29 July (1903).

'Nomenclature and tables of kinship.' *Nature*, **69** (1904), pp.294–5.

'African memorial.' [Letter in] *The Times*, 25 May (1904).

'Eugenics. Its definition, scope and aims.' *Nature*, **70** (1904), p.82. Also in *Sociological Papers*, **1** (1905), pp.45–50, pp.78–9.

'Distribution of successes and of natural ability among the kinsfolk of Fellows of the Royal Society.' *Nature*, **70** (1904). pp.354–6.

'Average number of kinsfolk in each degree.' *Nature*, **70** (1904), p.529, p.626, and **71** (1905), p.248.

'On the character and ancestry of Lord Northbrook.' [Letter in] *The Times*, 17 November (1904).

'A eugenics investigation: index to achievements of near kinsfolk of some of the Fellows of the Royal Society.' *Sociological Papers*, **1** (1905), pp.85–9. Also R. Clay, London (1905).

'Studies in national eugenics.' *Nature*, **71** (1905), pp.401–2.

'Number of strokes of the brush in a picture.' [Letter in] *Nature*, **72** (1905), p.198.

[Review of] *Guide to Finger Print Identification*, Henry Faulds, *Nature*, **72** (1905), Supplement iv–v.

'Nomenclature of kinship—its extension.' [Letter in] *Nature*, **73** (1905), pp.150–1.

'Eugenics: I. Restrictions in marriage; II. Studies in national eugenics.' *Sociological Papers*, **2** (1906), pp.3–13, pp.14–17, pp.49–51.

Noteworthy Families. With E. Schuster. John Murray, London (1906).

'Request for prints of photographic portraits.' [Letter in] *Nature*, **73** (1906), p.534.

'Anthropometry at schools.' *Journal of preventive Medicine*, **14** (1906), pp.93–8.

'Measurement of resemblance.' [Letter in] *Nature*, **74** (1906), pp.562–3.

'Cutting a round cake on scientific principles.' [Letter in] *Nature*, **75** (1906), p.173.

'One vote, one value.' [Letter in] *Nature*, **75** (1907), p.414.

'Vox populi.' *Nature*, **75** (1907), pp.450–1.

'The ballot box.' [Letter in] *Nature*, **75** (1907), pp.509–10.

Probability, the Foundation of Eugenics. Henry Froude, London (1907).

'Grades and deviates.' *Biometrika*, **5** (1907), pp.400–4.

'Classification of portraits', *Nature*, **76** (1907), pp.617–8.

'Suggestions for improving the literary style of scientific memoirs.' *Transactions of the Royal Society of Literature*, **28** (1908), Part II, pp.1–8.

'Address on eugenics.' *Westminster Gazette*, 26 June (1908).

Memories of My Life. Methuen, London (1908).

'Local associations for promoting eugenics.' *Nature*, **78** (1908), pp.645–7.

'Identification by finger prints.' [Letter in] *The Times*, 13 January (1909).

'Sequestrated church property.' [Letter in] *Nature*, **79** (1909), p.308.

[Foreword.] *Eugenics Review*, 1 (1909), pp.1–2.

[Preface to] *Primer of Statistics*, W. P. and Ethel M. Elderton, Black, London (1909).

'Deterioration of the British Race.' [Letter in] *The Times*, 18 June (1909).

'Segregation (of the feeble-minded)' in *The Problem of the Feeble Minded*. P. S. King, London (1909).

Essays in Eugenics. Eugenics Education Society, London (1909).

'Eugenic qualities of primary importance.' *Eugenics Review*, **1** (1910), pp. 74–6.

'Note on the effects of small and persistent influences.' *Eugenics Review*, **1** (1910), pp.148–9.

'Numeralised profiles for classification and recognition.' *Nature*, **83** (1910), pp.127–30.

'Heredity and tradition.' [Letter in] *The Times*, 31 May (1910).

'Alcoholism and offspring.' [Letter in] *The Times*, 3 June (1910).

'Eugenics and the Jew.' [Letter in] *Jewish Chronicle*, 30 July (1910).

'The Eugenics Laboratory and the Eugenics Education Society.' [Letter in] *The Times*, 3 November (1910).

Chapter notes and references

Letters that are dated in the text are not normally referenced; they are all to be found in the Galton Archives, University College Library, London.

The following abbreviations are used:

G.A.: Galton Archives.
Memories: F. Galton, *Memories of My Life*, Methuen, London (1908).
Life: K. Pearson, *The Life, Letters and Labours of Francis Galton*, 3 vols. Cambridge University Press (1914–1930).

Chapter One

1 For a recent account of Erasmus Darwin's life and work, see D. King-Hele, *Erasmus Darwin*, Macmillan, London, (1963).

2 Anna Seward, *Memoirs of the Life of Dr Darwin*, S. Johnson, London (1804), p.24.

3 *Memories*, p.10.

4 See R. R. Schofield, *History of The Lunar Society of Birmingham*, Oxford University Press, London (1964).

5 *Memories*, p.8.

6 Elizabeth Ann Wheler, *Reminiscences*, G.A.

7 S. T. Galton, *Diary*, G.A.

8 Elizabeth Ann Wheler, *Reminiscences*, G.A.

9 *Memories*, p.14.

10 *Life*, **I**, p.66.

11 Violetta Galton, *Biographical Sketch of Francis Galton by his Mother*, G.A.

12 L. M. Terman, 'The intelligence quotient of Francis Galton in childhood', *American Journal of Psychology*, **28** (1917), p.209.

13 L. M. Terman, 'The psychological approaches to the biography of genius', *Science*, **92** (1940), p.264.

14 *Memories*, p.17.

15 *Memories*, p.20.

16 F. Galton, *Art of Travel*, fifth edition John Murray, London (1872), p.2.

17 Dr Jeune to S. T. Galton, 7 December 1836, G.A.

18 S. T. Galton to F. Galton, 9 December 1837, G.A.

19 F. Galton to S. T. Galton, [1838], G.A.

20 *Memories*, p.25.

21 *Memories*, p.35.

22 F. Galton to S. T. Galton, 16 October 1839, G. A.

23 In F. Galton to S. T. Galton, 6 December 1839, G.A.

24 F. Galton to Elizabeth Galton, 14 April 1840, G.A.

25 F. Galton to Adèle Galton, 7 May 1840, G.A.

26 *Memories*, p.42.

27 F. Galton to S. T. Galton, 10 February 1840, G.A.

28 F. Galton to S. T. Galton, 6 December 1839, G.A.
29 *Memories*, p.48.
30 F. Galton to S. T. Galton, 30 July 1840, G.A.
31 F. Galton to S. T. Galton, 11 August 1840, G.A.
32 F. Galton to S. T. Galton, 22 August 1840, G.A.
33 F. Galton, *Diary*, (1840), G.A.
34 V. H. Green, *The British Universities*, Penguin, London (1969), p.301.
35 F. Galton to S. T. Galton, 25 January 1841, G.A.
36 F. Galton to S. T. Galton, 11 November 1841, G.A.
37 F. Galton to S. T. Galton, 22 March 1842, G.A.
38 F. Galton to S. T. Galton, 2 November 1842, G.A.
39 F. Galton to S. T. Galton, 28 November 1842, G.A.
40 F. Galton to Emma Galton, [March] 1841, G.A.
41 F. Galton to S. T. Galton, 19 March 1842, G.A.
42 F. Galton to S. T. Galton, [May] 1844, G.A.
43 F. Galton to S. T. Galton, 6 March 1844, G.A.
44 S. T. Galton to F. Galton, 9 March 1844, G.A.
45 F. Galton to S. T. Galton, 9 March 1844, G. A.
46 Elizabeth Galton to F. Galton, [March] 1844, G.A.

Chapter Two

1 F. Galton, *Egypt, Soudan and Syria, 1845–6*, Manuscript (1885), G.A.
2 H. F. Hallam to F. Galton, 3 October [1845], G.A.
3 *Memories*, p.86.
4 *Memories*, p.88.
5 *Memories*, p.90.
6 E. Glanville, *Personal communication*.
7 *Memories*, p.92.
8 Mansfield Parkyns is best known for his book, *Life in Abyssinia*, John Murray, London (1853), the second edition of which is available in a modern reprint, Frank Cass, London (1966).
9 *Memories*, p.93.
10 *Memories*, p.95.
11 F. Galton, *Egypt, Soudan and Syria 1845–6*, Manuscript (1885), G.A.
12 Ibid.
13 M. Boulton to F. Galton, 30 September 1846, G.A.
14 C. D. Darlington, [Introduction to] F. Galton, *Hereditary Genius*, second edition, Macmillan, London (1892) reprinted Collins (1962), p.20.
15 F. Galton, *Egypt, Soudan and Syria 1845–6*, Manuscript (1885), G.A.
16 H. F. Hallam to F. Galton, 24 June 1846, G.A.
17 *Memories*, p.111.
18 F. Galton, *Art of Travel; or, Shifts and Contrivances available in Wild Countries*, fifth edition John Murray, London (1872), reprinted David & Charles (1971), p.46.
19 *Memories*, p.119.
20 Donovan, *Manuscript*, G.A.
21 Galton's doubts about phrenology were based on the then recent work by physiologists concerning the localisation of function in the cerebral cortex. The faculties of the phrenologists were shown to have no correlation with brain tissue and phrenology's theoretical basis was undermined. But some of their observations could have been valid and have never been scientifically tested.

Galton's comment will be found in *Life*, **III** B, p.577.

Chapter Three

1 F. Galton, *Tropical South Africa*, John Murray, London (1853), p.3.
2 Ibid., p.11.
3 Ibid., p.29.
4 F. Galton to Violetta Galton, December 1850, G.A.
5 F. Galton, *Tropical South Africa*, p.37.
6 Ibid., p.39.
7 Ibid., p.40.
8 F. Galton to Jan Jonker, October 1850. Copy in *South African Notebook*, G.A.
9 F. Galton, *Tropical South Africa*, p.54.
10 Ibid., p.52.
11 H. Kleinschmidt, in H. Vedder, *South West Africa in Early Times*, Frank Cass, London (1966).
12 F. Galton, *Tropical South Africa*, p.115.
13 *Memories*, p.141.
14 F. Galton, *Tropical South Africa*, p.81.
15 Ibid., p.118.

16 Ibid., p.109.
17 J. M. White, *The Land God Made in Anger*, Allen & Unwin, London (1969). White claims that Galton did not see the unusual fish in the lake which are of the mouth-breeding genera. But Galton certainly mentions seeing them and wonders how they got there (*Tropical South Africa*, p.122).
18 *Life*, **I**. Note to Plate LVII opposite p.216.
19 F. Galton, *Tropical South Africa* p.129.
20 Ibid., p.129.
21 C. J. Andersson, *Lake Ngami*, Hurst & Blachett, London (1856), reprint of second edition, C. Struick, Cape Town (1967), p.196.
22 F. Galton, *Tropical South Africa*, p.130.
23 *Memories*, p.143.
24 C. J. Andersson, *Lake Ngami*, p.238.

Chapter Four

1 *Memories*, p.66.
2 F. Galton, *Diary 1853*, G.A.
3 *Memories*, p.150.
4 R. Murchison. Quoted in T. W. Freeman, *The Geographer's Craft*, Manchester University Press, Manchester (1967), p.26.
5 F. Galton, *Tropical South Africa*, John Murray, London (1853).
6 C. Darwin to F. Galton, 24 July 1853, in *Life*, **I**, p.240.
7 *Memories*, p.158.
8 F. Galton, *Diary 1854*, G.A.
9 F. Galton, 'List of instruments, etc.' in 'Hints to travellers', *Journal of the Royal Geographical Society*, **24** (1854).

10 C. Markham, *The R.G.S.*, Manuscript, R.G.S. Archives.
11 F. Galton to C. Andersson, 11 July 1853, G.A.
12 F. Galton to N. Shaw, May 1855, R.G.S. Archives.
13 F. Galton, *Diary 1854*, G.A.
14 F. Galton, *Art of Travel; or, Shifts and Contrivances Available in Wild Countries*, (fifth edition of 1872. With an Introduction by Dorothy Middleton. David & Charles, London (1971)).
15 *Memories*, p. 160.
16 F. Galton, *Diary, 1854*, G.A.

Chapter Five

1 Emma Galton, *Diary*, G.A.
2 *Life*, **II**, p.11.
3 H. Pearson, *Modern Men and Mummers*, Allen & Unwin, London

(1921), p.71. There are several inaccuracies in these recollections by Pearson of his great uncle.
4 *Memories*, p.171.

5 C. Markham, *The R.G.S.*, Manuscript, R.G.S. Archives.
6 C. Markham, *The R.G.S.*, Manuscript, R.G.S. Archives.
7 F. Galton to N. Shaw, 22 October 1856, R.G.S. Archives.
8 F. Galton to N. Shaw, 22 February 1858, R.G.S. Archives.
9 F. Galton to N. Shaw, 25 October 1858, R.G.S. Archives.
10 C. Markham, *The R.G.S.*, Manuscript, R.G.S. Archives.
11 *Memories*, p.185.
12 F. Galton to N. Shaw, 7 April 1862, R.G.S. Archives.
13 C. Markham, *The R.G.S.*, Manuscript, R.G.S. Archives.
14 C. Markham, *The R.G.S.*, Manuscript, R.G.S. Archives.
15 Notably in Alan Moorehead, *The White Nile*, Hamish Hamilton, London (1960) and in the recent biographies: Fawn M. Brodie, *The Devil Drives: A Life of Sir Richard Burton*, Eyre & Spottiswoode, London (1967); Alexander Maitland, *Speke*, Constable, London (1971).
16 *Memories*, p.199.
17 C. Markham, *The R.G.S.*, Manuscript, R.G.S. Archives.
18 R.G.S. Expedition Committee Minute, 21 May 1860, R.G.S. Archives.
19 R.G.S. Council Minute, 10 December 1860, R.G.S. Archives.
20 *Memories*, p.201.

21 F. Galton, R.G.S. Council, 8 April 1861, R.G.S. Archives.
22 Alexander Maitland, *Speke*, Constable, London (1971), pp.209–19.
23 Ibid., p.227
24 F. Galton, *Vacation Tourists and Notes of Travel*, Macmillan, London (1860), p.437.
25 *Life*, II, p.10.
26 F. Galton, *Vacation Tourists*, p.228.
27 Ibid., p.436.
28 A. L. Mumm, *Alpine Club Register, 1857–1863*, E. Arnold, London (1923).
29 F. Galton, *Art of Travel*, fourth edition, John Murray, London (1867).
30 E. Whymper, 'Camping out', *Alpine Journal*, 2 (1865), p.3.
31 A. L. Mumm, *Alpine Club Register, 1857–1863*, E. Arnold, London (1923).
32 F. Galton, *Vacation Tourists and Notes of Travel*, Macmillan, London (1860).
33 *Memories*, p.187.
34 Anon, *Knapsack Guide to Switzerland*, John Murray, London (1863).
35 Anon, [Review of] *Knapsack Guide to Switzerland*, *Alpine Journal*, I (1863), pp.89–90.
36 F. Galton, 'The avalanches of the Jungfrau', *Alpine Journal*, 1 (1863), pp.184–188.
37 He reviewed books by Speke, Grant and Burton in vol. 4.
38 *Memories*, p.168.
39 Ibid., p.168.

Chapter Six

1 F. Galton, 'Notes on modern geography', in *Cambridge Essays Contributed by Members of the University*, edited by J. W. Parker, Parker, London (1855), pp.79–109.
2 Ibid., p.97
3 F. Galton, 'On stereoscopic maps, taken from models of mountainous countries', *Journal of the Royal Geographical Society*, 35 (1865), pp.99–104.
4 A report in the *Sonntagspost*, 23 April (1865) correctly attributed the idea to Galton.

5 F. Galton, 'The exploration of arid countries', *Proceedings of the Royal Geographical Society*, 2 (1858), pp.60–77.
6 F. Galton, 'Recent discoveries in Australia', *The Cornhill Magazine*, 5 (1862), pp.354–64.
7 F. Galton, 'Zanzibar', *The Mission Field*, 6 (1861), p.130.
8 F. Galton, 'The climate of Lake Nyanza', *Proceedings of the Royal Geographical Society*, 7 (1863), pp.225–7.
9 F. Galton to J. A. Grant, 7 Sept. 1863, R.G.S. Archives.

10 F. Galton, 'A development of the theory of cyclones', *Proceedings of the Royal Society*, **12** (1863), pp.385–6.

11 F. Galton, *Meteorographica, or Methods of Mapping the Weather*, Macmillan, London (1863).

12 T. W. Freeman, *The Geographers Craft*, Manchester University Press, Manchester (1967), p.34.

13 F. Galton, in Louisa Galton's *Annual Record*, Entry for 1897, G.A.

14 F. Galton, 'On the conversion of wind-charts into passage charts', *Philosophical Magazine*, **32** (1866), pp.354–9.

15 F. Galton, 'On the employment of meteorological statistics in determining the best course for a ship whose sailing qualities are known', *Proceedings of the Royal Society*, **21** (1873), pp.263–74.

Chapter Seven

1 W. Hopkins to F. Galton, 3 August 1863.

2 Louisa Galton, *Annual Record*, G.A.

3 *Memories*, p.287.

4 F. Galton to C. Darwin, 24 December 1869.

5 Francis Galton, *Art of Travel*, edited with introduction by Dorothy Middleton, David & Charles, London (1971), Introduction, p.12.

6 *Memories*, p.155.

7 F. Galton, 'Hereditary talent', *Macmillan's Magazine*, **12** (1865), pp.157–66, pp.318–27.

8 F. Galton, *Hereditary Genius*, Macmillan, London (1869).

9 *Memories*, p.155.

10 Violetta Galton to F. Galton, 14 February 1866, G.A.

11 Elizabeth Ann Wheler to F. Galton, 15 February 1866, G.A.

12 *Memories*, p.215.

13 Louisa Galton, *Annual Record*, Entry for 1868, G.A.

14 F. Galton, G.A.

15 C. Markham, *The R.G.S.*, R.G.S. Archives.

16 Ibid.

17 F. Galton, *Hereditary Genius*, second edition, Macmillan, London (1892), reprinted Collins (1962), p.26. (All subsequent references are to the 1962 reprint.)

18 F. Galton, *Hereditary Genius* (1962), p.49.

19 Ibid., p.56.

20 Ibid., p.66.

21 *Life*, **II**, 90.

22 F. Galton, *Hereditary Genius* (1962) p.74.

23 Ibid., p.76.

24 Galton's error is pointed out by L. Penrose in a letter to the *Eugenics Review*, **42** (1951), p.211, in which he criticises the proposed re-issuing of *Hereditary Genius*.

25 F. Galton, *Hereditary Genius* (1962) p.76.

26 Ibid., p.77.

27 Ibid., p.84.

28 Ibid., p.111.

29 Ibid., p.108.

30 Ibid., p.123.

31 Ibid., p.126.

32 E. Darwin, *The Temple of Nature*, S. Johnson, London (1803).

33 C. D. Darlington, [Introduction to] F. Galton, *Hereditary Genius*, London (1962), p.13.

34 F. Galton, *Hereditary Genius* (1962) p.322.

35 Ibid., p.334.

36 Ibid., p.247.

37 Ibid., p.374.

38 Ibid., p.382.

39 Ibid., p.395.

40 For a recent review of much of this work, see H. J. Butcher, *Human Intelligence*, Methuen, London (1968).

41 F. Galton, *Hereditary Genius* (1962) p.397.

42 *Life*, **II**, p.107.

43 Malthus, *An Essay on the Principle of Population*, second edition, printed for

S. Johnson by T. Beudley, London (1803).
44 G. Himmelfarb, *Victorian Minds*, Weidenfeld & Nicolson, London (1968), p.103.
45 F. Galton, *Hereditary Genius* (1962) p.410.
46 Ibid., p.410.
47 Ibid., p.411.
48 Ibid., p.415.
49 A. Wallace, *Nature*, 1 (1870), p.501.
50 C. Darwin to F. Galton, 3 December 1869, in *Memories*, p.290.

Chapter Eight

1 P. M. Sheppard, *Natural Selection and Heredity*, Hutchinson, London (1958), p.33.
2 *Memories*, p.298.
3 F. Galton, 'Experiments in pangenesis', *Proceedings of the Royal Society*, 19 (1871), p.404.
4 Ibid., p.404.
5 *Life*, II, pp.157-62.
6 C. Darwin, 'Pangenesis', *Nature*, 27 April 1871.
7 F. Galton, 'Pangenesis', *Nature*, 4 May 1871.
8 Transfusion experiments were revived in Russia by Lysenko and his followers in the 1930s. See I. M. Lerner, *Heredity, Evolution and Society*, Freeman, San Francisco (1968), p.283.
9 F. Galton, 'On blood relationship', *Proceedings of the Royal Society*, 20 (1872), pp.394-402.
10 Ibid., p.394.
11 Ibid., p.400.
12 Ibid., p.402.
13 F. Galton, 'A theory of heredity', *Journal of the Anthropological Institute*, 5 (1875), pp.329-48.
14 Ibid., p.336.
15 Ibid., p.346.
16 F. Galton to C. Darwin, 19 December 1875, in *Life*, II, p.189.
17 F. Galton to C. Darwin, 28 March 1872, G.A.
18 F. Galton to C. Darwin, 19 April 1872, G.A.
19 Leonard Huxley, *Life and Letters of Thomas Henry Huxley*, 2 vols., Macmillan, London (1900), II, pp.144-9.
20 *Life*, II, p.67.
21 F. Galton, 'Statistical inquiries into the efficacy of prayer,' *Fortnightly Review*, 68 (1872), pp.125-35.
22 Galton took part in the controversy. See his letter, 'The efficacy of prayer', *Spectator*, 24 August (1872), p.1073.
23 Irwin to F. Galton [1869], G.A.
24 F. Galton, 'Statistical inquiries into the efficacy of prayer', *Fortnightly Review*, 68 (1872), p.129.
25 Ibid., p.135.

Chapter Nine

1 Tim Jeal, *Livingstone*, Heinemann, London (1973), p.315.
2 H. Rawlinson, *Proceedings of the Royal Geographical Society*, 16 (1872), p.241.
3 Byron Farwell, *The Man Who Presumed*, Longmans, Green and Co., London (1958), p.82.
4 My account of the B.A. meeting is based on Ian Anstruther's account: *I Presume. Stanley's Triumph and Disaster*, Geoffrey Bles, London (1956).
5 Byron Farwell, p.83.
6 H. M. Stanley, Letter to *Daily Telegraph*, 27 August (1872).
7 H. M. Stanley to C. Markham, 5 September 1872, G.A.
8 On this occasion Stanley was awarded the Victoria Medal. See Ian Anstruther, reference 4.
9 H. M. Stanley, Speech at the Savage Club reported in *Manchester Examiner*, 2 September (1872).

10 In W. B. Carpenter to F. Galton, 8 September 1872, G.A.

11 In W. B. Carpenter to F. Galton, 12 September 1872, G.A.

12 F. Galton to H. W. Bates, 17 January 1872, R.G.S. Archives.

13 F. Galton. [Letter to] *Daily News*, 7 September (1872).

14 'The Second Report of the Livingstone Search and Relief Committee,' in *Daily News*, 14 September (1872).

15 Messrs. Negretti and Zambra,

[Letters to] *Daily News*, 17 and 19 September (1872).

16 L. S. Dawson, [Letter to] *Daily News*, 18 September (1872).

17 H. R. Mill, *The Record of the Royal Geographical Society 1830–1930*, The R.G.S., London (1930), p.119.

18 F. Galton, 'Letters of Henry Stanley from Equatorial Africa to the *Daily Telegraph*' *Edinburgh Review*, **134** (1878), pp.166–91. (Unsigned.)

19 *Memories*, p.207.

Chapter Ten

1 A. de Candolle, *Histoire des Sciences et des Savants depuis deux Siècles*, H. Georg, Geneva (1873).

2 *Memories*, p.292.

3 C. Darwin to F. Galton, 28 May 1873, G.A.

4 F. Galton, *English Men of Science: their Nature and Nurture*, Macmillan, London (1874), second edition edited with introduction by Ruth Schwarz Cohen, Frank Cass (1970). All subsequent references are to the 1970 edition.

5 F. Galton, *English Men of Science: their Nature and Nurture* (1970) p.34. This finding still holds. Cf. S. Steward West, 'Sibling configurations of scientists', *American Journal of Sociology*, **66** (1961), pp.268–74.

6 Ibid., p.29. Recent work in this field is reviewed in R. F. Winch, *The Modern Family*, Holt, New York (1952), and in E. Berscheidt and E. H. Walster, *Interpersonal Attraction*, Addison-Wesley, London (1969).

7 Ibid., p.66.

8 Ibid., p.79.

9 Ibid., p.81.

10 Ibid., p.85.

11 Ibid., p.90.

12 Ibid., p.101.

13 Ibid., p.128.

14 Ibid., p.149.

15 Ibid., p.149.

16 Ibid., p.151.

17 Ibid., p.158.

18 Ibid., p.196.

19 Ibid., p.207.

20 Ibid., p.218.

21 Ibid., p.227.

22 Ibid., p.257.

23 For example, S. Cotgrove and S. Box, *Science, Industry and Society*, Allen & Unwin, London (1970).

24 F. Galton, *English Men of Science: their Nature and Nurture* (1970), p.39.

25 F. Galton, (i) 'Short notes on heredity etc., in twins, *Journal of the Anthropological Institute*, **5** (1875), pp.324–9, (ii) 'The history of twins, as a criterion of the relative powers of nature and nurture,' *Fraser's Magazine* (November 1875). Revised version in *Journal of the Anthropological Institute*, **5** (1876), pp.391–406, to which subsequent reference is made.

26 Ibid., p.402.

27 Ibid., p.403.

28 Ibid., p.400.

29 Ibid., p.393.

30 Ibid., p.401.

31 Ibid., p.402.

32 Ibid., p.404.

33 Ibid., p.404.

34 For a recent review, see P. Mittler, *The Study of Twins*, Penguin, London (1971).

Chapter Eleven

1 F. Galton, 'Gregariousness in cattle and in men', *Macmillan's Magazine*, **23** (1872), pp.353–7.

2 Ibid., p.356.

3 Ibid., p.357.

4 F. Galton, 'Hereditary improvement', *Fraser's Magazine*, **7** (1873), pp.116–30.

5 Ibid., p.120.

6 Ibid., p.128.

7 Ibid., p.129.

8 Ibid., p.125.

9 'Proposal to apply for anthropological statistics from schools', *Journal of the Anthropological Institute*, **3** (1874), pp.308–11.

10 F. Galton, 'Notes on the Marlborough School statistics', *Journal of the Anthropological Institute*, **4** (1874), pp.130–5.

11 F. Galton, 'On the height and weight of boys aged 14, in town and country public schools', *Journal of the Anthropological Institute*, **5** (1876), pp.174–80.

12 F. Galton, 'The opportunities of science masters at schools', *Nature*, **22** (1880), pp.9–10.

13 F. Galton, 'Address to the Department of Anthropology, Section H', *British Association Report*, (1877), pp.94–100.

14 Ibid., p.98.

15 A. L. Austin to C. Darwin, 6 November 1877 in F. Galton, *Inquiries into Human Faculty*, fourth edition, The Eugenics Society, London (1951), p.227.

16 F. Galton, 'Composite portraits', *Journal of the Anthropological Institute*, **8** (1878), p.134.

17 Ibid., p.135.

18 F. Galton, 'Generic images', *Proceedings of the Royal Institution*, **9** (1879), pp.161–70.

19 F. Galton, 'Generic images', *Nineteenth Century*, **6** (1879), p.158.

20 Ibid., p.170.

21 F. Galton and F. A. Mahomed, 'An inquiry into the physiognomy of phthisis by the method of "composite portraiture" ', *Guy's Hospital Reports*, **25** (1882), pp.1–18.

22 Ibid., p.18.

23 F. Galton, 'Conventional representation of the horse in motion', *Nature*, **26** (1882), pp.228–9.

24 Ibid., p.229.

25 F. Galton, 'Analytical portraiture' *Nature*, **62** (1900), p.320.

26 In the 1950s, David Katz made extensive use of the technique. See, for example, D. Katz, 'Le portrait composite et la typologie', *Revue internationale de Filmologie*, **2** (1952), pp.207–214.

27 A. Thomson, in *Life*, **II**, p.290.

28 P. Frazer, in *Life*, **II**, p.290.

29 W. H. Sheldon, *The Varieties of Temperament*, Harper, New York (1942).

30 *Memories*, p.276.

31 Ibid., p.276.

32 F. Galton, 'Psychometric experiments', *Brain*, **2** (1879), p.150.

33 Ibid., p.152.

34 Ibid., p.153.

35 Ibid., p.155.

36 Ibid., p.157.

37 Ibid., p.158.

38 Ibid., p.159.

39 Ibid., p.161.

40 K. Paul to F. Galton, [undated, 1877] G.A.

41 F. Galton, *Brain*, **2** (1879), p.162.

42 Ibid., p.162.

43 F. Galton, 'Psychometric facts,' *Nineteenth Century*, March (1879), pp.425–33.

44 G. Zilboorg, 'Some sidelights on free associations', Paper read at 17th International Psychoanalytical Congress, Amsterdam, August 1951.

Chapter Twelve

1 F. Galton, 'Statistics of mental imagery', *Mind*, **5** (1880), p.305.
2 Ibid., p.306.
3 C. Darwin to F. Galton, 14 November 1874, in *Life*, **II**, p.194.
4 F. Galton, 'Mental imagery', *Fortnightly Review*, **28** (1880), pp.312–24.
5 F. Galton, *Mind*, **5** (1880), p.303.
6 F. Galton, *Fortnightly Review*, p.319.
7 A. Bain, 'Mr Galton's statistics of mental imagery', *Mind*, **5** (1880), pp.564–73.
8 M. J. Horowitz, *Image Formation and Cognition*, Appleton-Century-Crofts, New York (1970).
9 U. Neisser, 'Visual imagery as process and as experience', *Bulletin of the British Psychological Society*, **23** (1970), p.65. (Abstract). More recent experiments do not, however, support this conclusion. See D. F. Marks, 'Individual differences in the vividness of visual imagery and their effect on function', Chap. 4 in P. W. Sheehan (ed.), *The Function and Nature of Imagery*, Academic Press, New York and London (1972).
10 A. Richardson, *Mental Imagery*, Routledge & Kegan Paul, London (1969).
11 F. Galton, 'Visualised numerals', *Nature*, **21** (1880), pp.252–6, 494–5.
12 F. Galton, 'Visualised numerals', *Journal of the Anthropological Institute*, **10** (1880), pp.85–102.
13 Ibid., p.95.
14 F. Galton, *Inquiries into Human Faculty and its Development*, fourth edition, The Eugenics Society, London (1951), p.104.
15 Ibid., p.109.
16 Ibid., p.111.
17 F. Galton, 'The visions of sane persons', *Proceedings of the Royal Institution*, **9** (1881), pp.644–55.
18 F. Galton, 'Hallucinations and half-hallucinations', Manuscript, G.A.
19 F. Galton, *Proceedings of the Royal Institution*, **9** (1881), p.654.
20 Ibid., p.655.
21 F. Galton, 'Free-will—observations and inferences', *Mind*, **9** (1884), pp.406–13.
22 C. Maxwell to F. Galton.
23 F. Galton, *Mind*, **9** (1884), p.407.
24 Ibid., p.407.
25 Ibid., p.407.
26 Ibid., p.407.
27 Ibid., p.408.
28 Ibid., p.409.
29 Ibid., p.410.
30 Ibid., p.412.
31 F. Galton, *Human Faculty*, p.1.
32 C. Wissler, *The Correlation of Mental and Physical Tests*, Press of the New Era Company, Lancaster, Pa., New York (1901).
33 G. Wheatstone to F. Galton, 1875, G.A.
34 F. Galton, *Human Faculty*, p.27.
35 Ibid., p.27.
36 F. Galton, 'The relative sensitivity of men and women at the nape of the neck, by Weber's test', *Nature*, **50** (1894), pp.40–2.
37 D. R. Kenshalo (ed.), *The Skin Senses*, Thomas, Illinois (1968).
38 F. Galton, *Human Faculty*, p.20.
39 Q. McNemar and L. M. Terman, 'Sex differences in variational tendency', *Genetic Psychology Monograph*, **18** (1936), pp.1–65.
40 F. Galton, *Human Faculty*, p.21.
41 Ibid., p.39.
42 Ibid., p.42.
43 Ibid., p.146.
44 Ibid., p.148.
45 Ibid., p.194.
46 F. Galton, *Human Faculty*, first edition, Macmillan, London (1883), p.210.
47 Ibid., p.212.
48 *Life*, **II**, p.259.
49 F. Galton, *Human Faculty*, first edition, p.294.
50 Ibid., p.296.
51 Ibid., p.302.
52 Ibid., p.302.
53 Ibid., p.334.

Chapter Thirteen

1 *The Guardian*, 4 July (1883).
2 *The Spectator*, 11 August (1883).
3 G. Romanes, *Nature*, **28** (1883), p.98.
4 Emma Galton to F. Galton, 2 May 1883, G.A.
5 Millicent Lethbridge to F. Galton, 25 September 1883, G.A.
6 F. Galton to Millicent Lethbridge, 27 September 1883, G.A.
7 Millicent Lethbridge to F. Galton, 30 September 1883, G.A.
8 Marianne North to Louisa Galton, 2 August 1883, G.A.
9 *Memories*, p.160.
10 F. Galton, manuscript note, G.A.
11 F. Galton, 'Medical family registers', *Fortnightly Review*, **34** (1883), pp.244–50.
12 Ibid., p.245.
13 F. Galton, *Record of Family Faculties*, Macmillan, London (1884).
14 Ibid., p.13.
15 F. Galton, *Life-History Album*, Macmillan, London (1884).
16 H. T. F. Rhodes, *Alphonse Bertillon*, Harrap, London (1956), p.191.
17 F. Galton, *Outfit for an Anthropometric Laboratory* (Privately printed, 1883).
18 F. Galton, 'On the anthropometric laboratory at the late International Health Exhibition', *Journal of the Anthropological Institute*, **14** (1885), p.206.
19 *Memories*, p.249.
20 H. Pearson, *Modern Men and Mummers*, Allen & Unwin, London (1921), p.75.
21 D. J. Cunningham and A. C.

Haddon, 'The anthropometric laboratory of Ireland', *Journal of the Anthropological Institute*, **21** (1891), pp.35–9.
22 See, for example, M. F. Ashley Montagu, *An Introduction to Physical Anthropology*, third edition, Charles C. Thomas, Illinois (1960).
23 F. Galton, 'On the principle and methods of assigning marks for bodily efficiency in the examination of candidates for the public services', *British Association Report* (1889), pp.471–3.
24 *Memories*, p.214.
25 Ibid., p.315.
26 F. Galton, 'The measure of fidget', *Nature*, **32** (1885), p.175.
27 J. Jacobs, 'Experiments in prehension', *Mind*, **12** (1887), pp.75–9.
28 F. Galton, 'Supplementary notes on "prehension" in idiots', *Mind*, **12** (1887), pp.79–82.
29 A. Binet and Th. Simon, 'Methodes nouvelles pour le diagnostic du niveau intellectuel des anormaux', *Année psychologique*, **11** (1905), pp.191–244.
30 D. Wechsler, *The Measurement and Appraisal of Adult Intelligence*, fourth edition, Williams & Wilkins, Baltimore (1958).
31 F. Galton, 'Measurement of character', *Fortnightly Review*, **36** (1884), pp.179–85.
32 F. Galton, 'Measurement of character', manuscript notebook, G.A.
33 F. Galton, *Fortnightly Review*, **36** (1884), p.185.

Chapter Fourteen

1 C. Darwin, *Cross and Self-Fertilization of Plants*, John Murray, London (1876), pp.16–18.
2 F. Galton, 'Typical laws of heredity', *Proceedings of the Royal Institute*, **8** (1877), pp.282–301.
3 Ibid., p.285.
4 F. Galton, [Presidential address,

Section H, Anthropology.] *British Association Report*, **55** (1885), p.1207.
5 F. Galton, 'Regression towards mediocrity in hereditary stature', *Journal of the Anthropological Institute*, **15** (1885), pp.246–62.
6 Ibid., p.252.
7 Ibid., p.253.

8 Ibid., p.255.

9 Ibid., p.260.

10 See P. Froggatt and N. C. Nevin, 'The "Law of Ancestral Heredity" and the Mendelian-Ancestrian Controversy in England, 1889–1906', *Journal of Medical Genetics*, **8** (1971), p.5.

11 Ibid., p.7.

12 R. G. Swinburne, 'Galton's law—formulation and development', *Annals of Science*, **21** (1965), p.19.

13 F. Galton, 'Hereditary talent and character', *Macmillan's Magazine*, **12** (1865), p.326.

14 See R. C. Olby, 'Charles Darwin's manuscript of "Pangenesis"', *British Journal of the History of Science*, **1** (1963), pp.251–63.

15 F. Galton, 'The average contribution of each several ancestor to the total heritage of the offspring', *Proceedings of the Royal Society*, **61** (1897), p.403.

16 F. Galton, 'Family likeness in eye colour', *Proceedings of the Royal Society*, **40** (1886), p.402.

17 *Life*, **IIIa**, pp.34–40.

18 F. Galton, 'Pedigree moth-breeding as a means of verifying certain important constants in the general theory of heredity', *Transactions of the Entomological Society*, Part 1 (1887), pp.19–34.

19 F. Galton, 'The average contribution of each several ancestor to the total heritage of the offspring', *Proceedings of the Royal Society*, **61** (1897), pp.401–13.

20 F. Galton, 'A diagram of heredity', *Nature*, **57** (1898), p.293.

21 *Memories*, p.300.

22 F. Galton, 'Co-relations and their measurement, chiefly from anthropometric data', *Proceedings of the Royal Society*, **45** (1888), pp.135–45.

23 Ibid., p.135.

24 *Life*, **IIIa**, p.51.

25 Ibid., p.56.

26 F. Galton, *Natural Inheritance*, Macmillan, London (1889).

27 Ibid., p.2.

28 This point is elaborated by R. G. Swinburne, (see reference 12).

29 F. Galton, *Natural Inheritance*, p.28.

30 Ibid., p.43.

31 Ibid., p.62.

32 *Life*, **IIIa**, p.24.

33 Ibid., pp.65–9.

34 F. Galton, *Natural Inheritance*, p.158.

35 *Life*, **IIIa**, p.66.

36 Ibid., p.68.

37 F. Galton, 'Good and bad temper in English families', *Fortnightly Review*, **42** (1887), pp.21–30.

38 F. Galton, *Natural Inheritance*, p.238.

39 *Life*, **IIIa**, p.70.

40 F. Galton, *Natural Inheritance*, p.175.

41 Ibid., p.197.

42 This point is made by R. G. Swinburne, (see reference 12).

Chapter Fifteen

1 T. H. Huxley to J. Hooker, 24 October 1885, in *Huxley Papers*, **III**, p.276.
An interesting account of the medal award scheme is provided by R. M. MacLeod, 'On medals and men: a reward scheme in Victorian science', *Notes and Records of the Royal Society of London*, **26** (1971), pp.81–105.

2 Louisa Galton to Emma Galton, 4 November 1886, in *Life*, **IIIb**, p.476.

3 F. Galton, manuscript note, G.A.

4 F. Galton, G.A.

5 F. Galton, 'Personal identification and description', *Proceedings of the Royal Institution*, **12** (1888), pp.346–60.

6 F. Galton, 'The identiscope', *Nature*, **30** (1884), pp.637–8.

7 H. Faulds to C. Darwin, 16 February 1880, G.A.

8 F. Galton, 'The opportunities of science masters at schools', *Nature*, **22** (1880), pp.9–10.

9 G. W. Wilton, *Fingerprints: History, Law and Romance*, W. Hodge & Co. Ltd., London (1938).

10 H. Faulds, 'On the skin furrows of the hand', *Nature*, **22** (1880), p.605.

11 W. Herschel, 'Skin furrows of the hand', *Nature*, **23** (1880), p.76.

12 F. Galton, *Finger Prints*, Macmillan, London (1892), reprinted Da Capo Press, New York, (1965) with introduction by H. Cummins, p.28.
All subsequent references are to the 1965 reprint.

13 F. Galton, [Review of Henry Faulds, *Guide to Finger Print Identification*], *Nature*, **72** (1905), p.4.

14 G. W. Wilton (see reference 9).

15 F. Galton to G. Darwin, 13 March 1910, G.A.
'Dr Faulds is a most difficult and troublesome person to deal with . . . I think you would do best to keep clear of him.' Faulds' personality is described in much the same terms in H. T. F. Rhodes, *Alphonse Bertillon*, Harrap, London (1956) p.139.

16 F. Galton, *Finger Prints*, (1965), p.48.

17 Ibid., p.63.

18 *Memories*, p.257.

19 H. Cummins and C. Midlo, *Finger Prints, Palms and Soles*, Dover Publications Inc., New York (1961).

20 F. Galton, *Finger Prints* (1965), p.97.

21 Ibid., p.197.

22 Ibid., p.209.

23 Ibid., p.211.

24 F. Galton, *Finger Print Directories*, Macmillan, London (1895), p.18. Most of the Asquith Committee's report is reprinted in this book.

25 F. Galton, 'Identification by fingerprints', [Letter to] *The Times*, 13 January (1909).

26 H. Cummins, [Preface to] F. Galton, *Finger Prints*, Da Capo Press, New York (1965), p.xiii.

27 F. Galton, 'Identification offices in India and Egypt', *Nineteenth Century*, **48** (1900), p.119.

28 *Life*, **II**, p.341.

29 E. R. Henry, *Classification and Uses of Finger Prints*, A.M.S. Press, London (1900).

30 A. Bertillon, *Signaletic Instructions, including the Theory and Practice of Anthropometrical Identification*, translated by R. W. McClaughry, Kegan Paul & Co. Ltd., London (1896).

31 H. T. F. Rhodes, *Alphonse Bertillon*, Harrap, London (1956).

32 H. Pearson, *Modern Men and Mummers*, Allen & Unwin, London (1921), p.74.

33 F. Galton to A. Bertillon, 19 May 1889, G.A.

Chapter Sixteen

1 C. Markham, *The R.G.S.*, R.G.S. Archives.

2 F. Galton, 'Promotion of scientific branches of geography', R.G.S. London (1877).

3 G. N. Curzon, [Letter to] *The Times*, in H. R. Mill, *The Record of the Royal Geographical Society, 1830–1930*, The R.G.S., London (1930).

4 *Memories*, p.210.

5 Further evidence that Galton did not feel convinced that women had a right to Fellowship is contained in a letter that he wrote to Emma, 4 May 1893, G.A.
'The President and secretary, both such excellent men in nearly every way, have got us into a thorough entanglement and quarrel with a pack of angry admirals, who are *right* in the main, but we on the Council all suffer.'

6 According to the reply written by Thorndike to Galton, 4 December 1901, G.A. That this was Galton's view is also clear in a letter from W. Bateson to Galton, 2 May 1897, G.A.

7 K. Pearson to F. Galton, 15 December 1908, in *Life*, **IIIa**, p.359.

8 F. Galton to G. Darwin, 9 April 1886, G.A.

9 H. Pearson, *Extraordinary People*, Harper-Row, London (1965), p.143.

10 F. Galton, 'The just-perceptible

difference', *Proceedings of the Royal Institution*, **14** (1893), pp.13–26.

11 Ibid., p.14.

12 Letters were exchanged with two wellknown psychologists asking their advice about the interpretation of this experiment. See J. Ward to F. Galton, 16 December 1888, G.A., and E. B. Titchener to F. Galton, 15 September 1894, G.A.

13 F. Galton, 'Classification of portraits', *Nature*, **76** (1907), pp.617–8.

14 F. Galton, 'Numeralised profiles for classification and recognition', *Nature*, **83** (1910), pp.127–30.

15 Modern attempts pay scant attention to Galton's contributions. See for example, D. R. Brothwell, M. J. R. Healy and R. G. Harvey, 'Canonical analysis of facial variation', *Journal of Biosocial Science*, **4** (1972), pp.172–85.

16 F. Galton, 'The Inaudi séance', manuscript notebook, G.A.

17 F. Galton, 'Psychology of mental arithmeticians and blindfold chessplayers', [Review of Alfred Binet, *Psychologie des Grands Calculateurs et Joueurs d'Echecs*], *Nature*, **51** (1894), pp.73–4.

18 F. Galton, 'Arithmetic by smell' *Psychological Review*, **1** (1894), pp.61–2.

19 F. Galton, 'Discontinuity in evolution', *Mind*, **3** (1894), p.368.

20 Ibid., p.369.

21 F. Galton, 'The part of religion in human evolution', *National Review*, August (1894), pp.755–65.

22 Ibid., p.756.

23 Ibid., p.758.

24 Ibid., p.759.

25 Ibid., p.761.

26 Ibid., p.761.

27 Ibid., p.763.

28 F. Galton, 'Intelligible signals between neighbouring stars', *Fortnightly Review*, **59** (1896), pp.657–64.

29 Ibid., p.664.

30 W. Sullivan, *We Are Not Alone*, London (1965).

31 F. Galton, manuscript notebook (1896), G.A.

32 F. Galton to Emma Galton, 13 August 1897, G.A.

33 F. Galton to Emma Galton, 15 August 1897, G.A.

34 Note in Galton's handwriting, G.A.

35 According to H. Pearson, *Extraordinary People*, Harper-Row, London (1965), p.148.

36 Dorothy Middleton, *personal communication*.

37 For example, see J. J. Sylvester to Louisa Galton, 12 January 1885, G.A.

38 F. Galton, 'Number of strokes of the brush in a picture', *Nature*, **72** (1905), p. 198.

39 F. Galton to Eva Biggs, 30 July 1907, in *Life*, **IIIa** p. 271.

Chapter Seventeen

1 F. Galton to Emma Galton, 14 April 1899, G.A.

2 F. Galton to Emma Galton, 26 April 1899, G.A.

3 Emma Galton to F. Galton, 29 April 1899, G.A.

4 F. Galton to Emma Galton, 13 May 1899, G.A.

5 F. Galton, 'The median estimate', *British Association Report*, (1899), pp. 638–40.

6 F. Galton, *Anthropometric Laboratory, Notes and Memoirs, No. 1*, in *Life*, **II**, p.385.

7 F. Galton, 'Terms of imprisonment, *Nature*, **52** (1895), pp.174–6.

8 F. Galton, 'Corporal punishment', [Letter to] *The Times*, 4 October (1898).

9 F. Galton, 'The late Dr Haughton', *Nature*, **57** (1897), p.79.

10 F. Galton to Emma Galton, 15 December 1899, G.A.

11 F. Galton to Emma and Elizabeth Galton, 14 January 1900, G.A.

12 F. Galton to Emma and Elizabeth Galton, 22 January 1900, G.A.

13 F. Galton to Emma and Elizabeth Galton, 4 March 1900, G.A.

14 F. Galton to Eva Biggs, 29 October 1900, G.A.

15 C. Booth, in F. Galton, 'The possible improvement of the human breed under the existing conditions of law and sentiment,' in *Essays in Eugenics*, London (1909), p.10.

16 F. Galton, op. cit., p.20.

17 Ibid., p.24.

18 Ibid., p.34.

19 F. Galton, *Nature*, **64** (1901), pp.659–65.

20 K. Pearson to F. Galton, 13 December 1900, in *Life*, **IIIa**, p.241. The controversy over Pearson's paper is well documented in P. Froggatt and N. C. Nevin, *Journal of Medical Genetics*, **8** (1971), pp.1–36.

21 F. Galton to K. Pearson, 23 April 1901, in *Life*, **IIIa**, p.244.

22 F. Galton, 'Biometry', *Biometrika*, **1** (1901), pp.7–10.

23 Ibid., p.10.

24 K. Pearson, 'Note on Francis Galton's problem', *Biometrika*, **1** (1901), pp.390–9.

25 F. Galton to Emma Galton, 14 November 1902, G.A.

26 M. Butler to F. Galton, 14 November 1902, in *Life*, **IIIa**, p.236.

27 F. Galton to Emma Galton, 16 November 1902, G.A.

28 F. Galton to Millicent Lethbridge, 8 January 1903, in *Life*, **IIIa**, p.521.

29 *The Warwick and Warwickshire*, 10 January 1903.

30 F. Galton, 'Our national physique: prospects of the British race. Are we degenerating?' *Daily Chronicle*, 29 July (1903).

31 F. Galton to W. F. R. Weldon, 12 March 1904, in *Life*, **IIIa**, p.525.

32 Emma Galton to F. Galton, 17 December 1903, G.A.

33 F. Galton, 'Eugenics, its definition, scope and aims', in *Essays in Eugenics*, The Eugenics Society, London (1909), p.35.

34 Ibid., p.36.

35 F. Darwin, 'Francis Galton, 1822–1911', *Eugenics Review*, **6** (1914), pp.1–17.

36 F. Galton, *Essays in Eugenics*, p.42.

37 B. Shaw, [Comments on] F. Galton, 'Eugenics, its definition, scope and aims,' in *Sociological Papers*, **1**, Macmillan, London (1905).

38 F. Galton to Emma Galton, 5 July 1904, G.A.

39 Millicent Lethbridge, 'Recollections of Francis Galton', in *Life*, **IIIb**, pp. 446–9.

40 *Memories*, p.175. A sketch of the flower appears as a vignette at the end of Galton's autobiography.

41 F. Galton, 'Distribution of successes and of natural ability among the kinsfolk of Fellows of the Royal Society', *Nature*, **70** (1904), pp.354–6.

42 *Life*, **IIIa**, p.222.

43 A. Rücker to F. Galton, 1904, G.A.

44 *Life*, **IIIa**, p.223.

45 F. Galton, 'Restrictions in marriage', in *Essays in Eugenics*, The Eugenics Society, London (1909), pp.44–59.

46 Ibid., p.58.

47 Ibid., p.58.

48 H. Ellis, 'Eugenics and St Valentine', *Nineteenth Century*, **59** (1906), pp.779–87.

49 F. Galton, 'Studies in national eugenics', in *Essays in Eugenics*, The Eugenics Society, London (1909), p.62.

50 Ibid., p.67.

51 Ibid., p.66.

52 F. Galton to G. Darwin, 9 May 1905, in *Life*, **IIIa**, p.276.

53 *Life*, **IIIa**, p.278.

54 F. Galton to Millicent Lethbridge, 27 September 1905, G.A.

55 F. Galton to Millicent Lethbridge, 28 October 1905, G.A.

56 F. Galton to C. W. Saleeby, 21 November 1905, G.A.

Chapter Eighteen

1 Elizabeth Wheler to F. Galton, 1 April 1899, G.A.

2 Elizabeth Wheler to F. Galton, 11 August 1905, G.A.

3 Elizabeth Wheler to F. Galton, 13 April 1905, G.A.

4 Elizabeth Wheler to F. Galton, 15 July 1905, G.A.

5 Elizabeth Wheler to F. Galton, 13 October 1905, G.A.

6 F. Galton to Millicent Lethbridge, 7 January 1906, G.A.

7 F. Galton to Millicent Lethbridge, 13 May 1905, G.A.

8 F. Galton to Millicent Lethbridge, 10 December 1905, G.A.

9 F. Galton to Millicent Lethbridge, 20 August 1905, G.A.

10 F. Galton to Millicent Lethbridge, 17 December 1905, G.A.

11 F. Galton to K. Pearson, 1 February 1906, in *Life*, **IIIa**, p.279.

12 F. Galton to Millicent Lethbridge, 16 February 1906, G.A.

13 F. Galton, 'Measurement of resemblance', *Nature*, **74** (1906), pp.562–3.

14 F. Galton to Millicent Lethbridge, 12 August 1906, G.A. Millicent Lethbridge, 'Recollections of Francis Galton', in *Life*, **IIIb**, pp.446–9.

15 K. Pearson to F. Galton, 13 May 1906, in *Life*, **IIIa**, p.282.

16 F. Galton to K. Pearson, 14 May 1906, in *Life*, **IIIa**, p.283.

17 *Life*, **IIIa**, pp.284–91.

18 F. Galton to Eva Biggs, 30 July 1907, in *Life*, **IIIa**, p.271.

19 F. Galton to Millicent Lethbridge, 12 April 1910, in *Life*, **IIIb**, p.604.

20 J. Murray to F. Galton, 30 June 1906, G.A.

21 E. Schuster to F. Galton, 17 May 1906, G.A.

22 F. Galton to K. Pearson, 24 October 1906, in *Life*, **IIIa**, p.297.

23 K. Pearson to F. Galton, 25 October 1906, in *Life*, **IIIa**, p.297.

24 F. Galton to K. Pearson, 25 October 1906, in *Life*, **IIIa**, p.300.

25 F. Galton, 'Cutting a round cake on scientific principles', *Nature*, **75** (1906), p.173.

26 F. Galton, 'Tea making', manuscript, G.A.

27 F. Galton to Millicent Lethbridge, 30 March 1907, in *Life*, **IIIb**, p.581.

28 F. Galton, Diary 1904–6, G.A.

29 F. Galton to Millicent Lethbridge, 25 March 1906, G.A.

30 F. Galton to Millicent Lethbridge, 29 May 1907, G.A.

31 F. Galton, 'Probability, the foundation of eugenics', in *Essays in Eugenics*, The Eugenics Society, London (1909), pp.73–99.

32 W. P. and Ethel M. Elderton, *Primer of Statistics*, Black, London (1909).

33 F. Galton, *Essays in Eugenics*, p.93.

34 Ibid., p.99.

35 The lecture was delivered by Arthur Galton.

36 F. Galton to Millicent Lethbridge, 25 November 1907, G.A.

37 F. Galton to Millicent Lethbridge, 10 October 1908, G.A.

38 *Memories*, p.277.

39 The correspondence between Galton and Florence Nightingale in 1891 concerned her advocacy of a professorship of applied statistics to be established at Oxford University. Galton politely poured cold water on her enthusiasm and the scheme died a premature death. The correspondence is quoted by K. Pearson in *Life*, **II**, pp.414–24.

40 F. Galton, 'The average flush of excitement', *Nature*, **20** (1879), p.121.

41 *Memories*, p.276.

42 F. Darwin, 'Francis Galton, 1822–1911,' *Eugenics Review*, **6** (1914), pp.1–17.

43 A concise history of the Eugenics Society will be found in: Faith Schenk and A. S. Parkes, 'The activities of the Eugenics Society', *Eugenics Review*, **60** (1968), pp.142–58.

44 F. Galton to K. Pearson, 18 May 1908, in *Life*, **IIIa**, p.339.

45 F. Galton, *Westminster Gazette*, 26 June (1908).

46 *Life*, **IIIa**, p.340.

47 F. Galton to Millicent Lethbridge, 27 September 1908, G.A.

48 F. Galton to Millicent Lethbridge, 14 September 1908, G.A.

49 F. Galton to K. Pearson, 1 January 1908, in *Life*, **IIIa**, p.332.

50 F. Galton to K. Pearson, 8 March 1908, in *Life*, **IIIa**, p.334.

51 F. Galton, 'Suggestions for improving the literary style of scientific memoirs', *Transactions of the Royal Society of Literature*, **28** (1908), pp.1–8.
52 Ibid., p.5.
53 F. Galton to Millicent Lethbridge, 10 October 1908, G.A.
54 F. Galton, 'Local associations for promoting eugenics', *Essays in Eugenics*, The Eugenics Society, London (1909), pp.100–9.
55 Ibid., p.105.
56 Ibid., p.106.
57 F. Galton to Millicent Lethbridge, 14 December 1908, G.A.
58 F. Galton to Millicent Lethbridge, 19 December 1908, G.A.
59 F. Galton, 'Sequestrated church property', *Nature*, **79** (1909), p.308.
60 F. Galton to Millicent Lethbridge, 31 January 1909, G.A.
61 F. Galton to Millicent Lethbridge, 3 May 1909, G.A.
62 F. Galton to Millicent Lethbridge, 16 May 1909, G.A.
63 F. Galton, 'Foreword', *Eugenics Review*, **1** (1909), pp.1–2.
64 K. Pearson to F. Galton, 22 April 1909, in *Life*, **IIIa**, p.380.
65 F. Galton to K. Pearson, 29 June 1909, in *Life*, **IIIa**, p.387.
66 F. Galton to Eva Biggs, 15 June 1909, in *Life*, **IIIb**, p.597.
67 F. Galton to K. Pearson, 16 June 1909, in *Life*, **IIIa**, p.385.
68 F. Galton to Millicent Lethbridge, 22 May 1909, G.A.
69 K. Pearson to F. Galton, 31 October 1909, in *Life*, **IIIa**, p.397.
70 F. Galton to K. Pearson, 2 November 1909, in *Life*, **IIIa**, p.397.

71 K. Pearson to F. Galton, 11 November 1909, in *Life*, **IIIa**, p.399.
72 Ethel M. Elderton and K. Pearson, 'The influence of parental alcoholism on the physique and intelligence of the offspring', *Eugenics Laboratory Memoir*, **10** (1910).
73 K. Pearson, vols. I and III, *Questions of the Day and of the Fray* (1910).
74 F. Galton, 'Alcoholism and offspring', [Letter to] *The Times*, 3 June (1910).
'The Eugenics Laboratory and the Eugenics Education Society', [Letter to] *The Times*, 3 November (1910).
75 F. Galton to K. Pearson, 27 October 1910, in *Life*, **IIIa**, p.408.
76 Eva Biggs to K. Pearson, 31 December 1910, in *Life*, **IIIa**, p.433.
77 F. Galton, 'Note on the effects of small and persistent influences', *Eugenics Review*, **1** (1910), pp.148–9.
78 F. Galton, 'Eugenic qualities of primary importance', *Eugenics Review*, **1** (1910), p.74.
79 F. Galton to Millicent Lethbridge, 28 December 1910, in *Life*, **IIIb**, p.616.
80 *Life*, **IIIa**, pp.411–24.
81 F. Galton to Millicent Lethbridge, 8 October 1910, in *Life*, **IIIb**, p.611.
82 F. Galton to Millicent Lethbridge, 3 October 1910, in *Life*, **IIIb**, p.610.
83 F. Galton to Millicent Lethbridge, 5 October 1910, in *Life*, **II**, p.61.
84 F. Galton to Millicent Lethbridge, 28 September 1910, in *Life*, **IIIb**, p.610.
85 According to H. Pearson, *Extraordinary People*, Harper-Row, London (1965), p.155.
86 Eva Biggs to K. Pearson, 15 January 1911, in *Life*, **IIIa**, p.433.

Appendix I

1 F. Galton to S. T. Galton, 26 January 1841, G.A.
2 F. Galton to S. T. Galton, 31 January 1841, G.A.
3 F. Galton to S. T. Galton.
4 F. Galton to S. T. Galton, 3 February 1841, G.A.

5 W. G. S. Scaife, *Personal Communication*.
6 F. Galton, *Wave Engine*, unpublished ms., G.A.
7 F. Galton, *Measurement of Height of Wave*, unpublished ms., 22 July 1876, G.A.
8 F. Galton, *The Telotype; a Printing*

Electric Telegraph, J. Weale, London (1850).

9 *Memories*, p.119.

10 Ibid., p.165.

11 F. Galton, 'A hand heliostat for the purpose of flashing sun signals, from on board ship or on land, in sunny climates', *British Association Report*, (1858), pp.15–17.

12 For example, F. Galton, 'Description of the process of verifying thermometers at the Kew Observatory', *Proceedings of the Royal Society*, 26 (1877), pp.84–9.

13 F. Galton, 'Description of the pantagraph designed by Mr Galton', *Minutes of the Meteorological Committee* (1869), p.9.

14 F. Galton, 'Mechanical computer of vapour tension', *Report of the Meteorological Committee* (1871), p.30.

15 F. Galton, 'On spectacles for divers, and on the vision of amphibious animals', *British Association Report*, 35 (1865), pp.10–12.

16 *Memories*, p.186.

17 F. Galton, 'On spectacles for divers . . .', p.11.

18 Evelyn Biggs to K. Pearson, 25 January 1911, in *Life*, IIIb, p.618.

19 F. Galton, 'On the Anthropometric Laboratory of the late International Health Exhibition', *Journal of the Anthropological Institute*, 14 (1885), p.214.

20 *Life*, II, p.224.

21 F. Galton, 'On recent designs for anthropometric instruments', *Journal of the Anthropological Institute*, 16 (1886), p.6.

22 *Life*, II, p.227.

23 F. Galton, 'Exhibition of instruments (1) for testing the perception of differences of tint'. *Journal of the Anthropological Institute*, 19 (1889), pp.27–8.

24 F. Galton, 'Whistles for determining the upper limits of audible sound in different persons', in *South Kensington Museum Conference: Physics and Mechanics Volume*, Chapman and Hall, London (1876).

25 F. Galton, 'Hydrogen whistles', *Nature*, 27 (1883), pp.491–2.

26 F. Galton, 'On apparatus for testing the delicacy of the muscular and other senses in different persons,' *Journal of the Anthropological Institute*, 12 (1882), pp.469–75.

27 F. Galton, 'Exhibition of instruments (2) for determining reaction time', *Journal of the Anthropological Institute*, 19 (1889), pp.28–9.

28 F. Galton, 'A new instrument for measuring the rate of movement of the various limbs,' *Journal of the Anthropological Institute*, 20 (1890), pp.200–4.

29 F. Galton, 'On a pocket registrator for anthropological purposes', *British Association Report*, 50 (1880), p.625.

30 F. Galton, 'On a new principle for the protection of riflemen', *Journal of the Royal United Services Institute*, 4 (1861), pp.393–6.

31 F. Galton, 'Personal identification and description,' *Nature*, 38 (1888), pp.201–2.

32 F. Galton, 'A rapid view instrument for momentary attitudes', *Nature*, 26 (1882), pp.249–51.

33 Ibid., p.250.

Index